THE SECRET LIFE
OF
WILLIAM
SHAKESPEARE

Jude Morgan

WINDSOR
PARAGON

First published 2012
by Headline Review
This Large Print edition published 2012
by AudioGO Ltd
by arrangement with
Headline Publishing Group

Hardcover   ISBN: 978 1 445 82709 4
Softcover   ISBN: 978 1 445 82710 0

British Library Cataloguing in Publication Data available

Printed and bound in Great Britain by
MPG Books Group Limited

To my friends in Peterborough Writers' Circle

A King and No King (1582)

The storm woke him, but it was something else that made him dress and go downstairs.

A feeling.

'Father?'

He opened the workshop door. Shadows fled.

'You couldn't sleep either, hey, Will? Just so, just so. Well, step in.'

Five or six candles were burning in there. Will winced at the thought of the expense. But his father needed the light, he knew: as much light as possible. Above the house, thunder boomed again, loud and close. The whites of his father's eyes flashed, like a panicked horse's, and sweat glistened on his brow.

'Aye, there's no air tonight,' Will said, feigning a yawn. 'Shall I bring you a cup of ale?'

His father shook his head. 'Stay though, boy, stay. I was just . . .' Shirt-sleeved, hairy, he roamed about, restlessly touching cutting-block, knives, dolly-pin, then took up a glove from the workbench. 'Just looking over your stitching. Round seam? I would have thought prix seam sufficient for this quality. But it's tidy enough. The sword-hanger too. These welts, mark you, should be stronger, if—' He jumped at the crack of thunder, but Will pretended not to see that, or the trembling of the big hands that nearly dropped the glove. 'Damp air these nights, makes the hides dry slow. But one should be ready tomorrow. Have your tablets? Set down a dozen eggs for the treating, no, say two dozen—'

His voice broke into a whimper as the thunder turned vast and mad and shook the shutters, and Will began talking, anything, to cover up what he was seeing and what he was feeling.

'Lord, if we have more rain the south road will be a slough again, and another poor market. And I hear Lord Howard's Men are on their way from Banbury. Mind, players always get through. Once they loosed the horse and lugged the cart on their backs. Then there's Richard due up from London, he'll have a dirty ride of it. Still, it may clear. I thought I smelt a wind in the west this even . . .'

'I never heard that. About the players' cart.' Through the fear and shame, a new sharpness in his father's glance.

Will shrugged. 'Someone told me.'

'I think *they* told you.' Thunder sounded more faintly. His father allowed himself a small inward smile. 'The players. I know, Will. Last summer, when they came. You slipped out and spent the whole evening with them at the Swan.'

For a crushing moment Will was a child again, and his father's square forefinger was tapping at his breast: *I see all through there, my boy.* 'Yes,' he managed, 'so I did. I meant no ill by it—'

'But you didn't tell me. So you must have known I would not approve it. Oh, though I don't go about, I hear things, Will, I have my intelligencers. A man so ill-used as I have been cannot do without them.' The thunder was silent; the smell of rain filled the air like an unborn sound. 'Players are well in their way. But still theirs is a loose, low, scrambling sort of life, even with some great noble's name clapped to them. And they sow idleness and fruitless dreaming. Now consider, is that fitting for

John Shakespeare's son?' He spoke gently. He had a musical, even beautiful voice: that at least had not changed.

'You used to go to the play. When they first started coming—'

'That was before,' his father rapped. 'I was bailiff then. I was the one who granted them their licence. It was my duty to see the play, to make sure there was no foulness in it. Those were different times. I stood high—highest. Those times are stolen away.' He glanced around for his stick. It was for authority, not to lean on: bodily he was hale enough. But Will realised, as he took up the stick, that now he could probably wrest it from him or break it over his knee, because he was eighteen and fresh, and his father was a beaten, lurking man . . . if he wanted to.

'The storm's dying,' Will said. As he passed his father the stick he felt, at its other end, a frustrated strength, and saw the snake. Hugh the maltster's son had found it after school, that last term before Will was plucked away, and caught it in a sack. You could feel the desperate muscle through the cloth. He met his father's eyes, and love and hate clove him in two like an apple.

'Well, leave go, then, sir.'

One more moment: Will let go. Thunder mumbled away northward, over Shottery. His father wiped his brow.

'Cooler,' Will said. 'I'll go sleep, I think, Father.'

'Wait. When the players come this summer, Will, I want you to consider. Consider who we are.' He touched the carved head of his stick to his lips. 'Our name.'

And it crowded into Will's head what he could

3

not say: our name, no one gives a hang what we do any more—the town will as soon talk of a missing nail in the church door . . . But that was one of those things to be ignored and pretended away, like a fear of thunderstorms.

'I hope I'm always mindful of it.'

'I hope so too. And that you will show it. No more skulking in tap-rooms with a set of beggarly players, hm? You are my son, my heir, and these things matter. You must learn what it is to be a man. I want your promise, now—and freely given. Naught of threat. You know your portion has never been aught but love.'

You can beat with love, Will thought. Nothing cuts more deep. 'You have my promise, Father,' he said. But he lied; and Will wondered if he were a wicked person or, rather, just how wicked he was.

He didn't sleep. Come the wet dawn he was watching at his bedroom window, as his father crossed the yard below to inspect the hanging hides. Heavy, measured, yet noticeably upright tread: at first glance one might suppose a drunk man trying to control himself. But no: Alderman Shakespeare, Burgess of Stratford, had walked thus in procession to the Guildhall, wearing his robes of office, preceded by constables with staves, followed by an adoring boy.

Will saw his own shadow around him on the floorboards, its limits, and thought: These shall be my borders, ever and ever.

*   *   *

The storm didn't wake her. She was already awake. Since the great change had come, she did much of

4

her living in the night. And she paid little heed to the thunder. It was the tree, and the terrible mourning noise that began after it.

The night was her indulgence. In the night there was time and room to think and feel. Even to breathe.

'It's happened, and there's nothing to be done,' Bartholomew would say, during the day. 'When are you going to start living? God, that face.' A twitch of his great shoulders. 'Oh, that face of yours.' She would stiffen, going on with her spinning or kneading, and trying not to have a face.

Night properly began about midnight. She usually went to bed straight after supper—about the time Bartholomew picked up the jug and trudged down to the brew-house—and for a couple of exhausting hours would move through fantastically detailed dreams in which the great mistake, by all manner of splendid contrivances, was put right. Then she woke, dressed, and inhabited the sleeping house.

Sometimes she lit a taper, but usually touch led her surely. Her feet learned the wisdom of the floorboards, her hands skimmed the creaking panelling alert as a healer's. She didn't fear disturbing her stepbrothers or -sisters, but she had often afflicted herself with the image of Bartholomew looming from the darkness tousled and column-necked and blinking. He would want to know what the devil she was doing, creeping about the house in the middle of the night. He would want it explained. Her brother believed, perhaps rightly, that everything could be explained, and when that was done you folded it and laid it away in the chest.

'He doesn't hear us,' he had said when their father was near his end. 'So it's no manner of good talking to him.' Sighing, he had gone away, and she had resumed. She told her father about the bold fox that had come right up to the buttery door and grinned at her, about the summer visit of the players to Stratford, about Catherine's sprained ankle. Her father lay bony, drawing in fierce exacting breaths, his mouth stretching in odd shapes. Yes, he probably couldn't hear, but she was trying to make something of dying. Birth, she had concluded from observing family and neighbours, made a satisfying progress: from the first shadowy signs, to the undeniable greatness of the belly, to the solemn peril of the lying-in and then, with luck, the wonder of a new presence in the world. Dying was different. It went on like the desultory carrying away of lumber from an untenanted house. Eventually the thing was finished, but there was only an absence to show for it.

In the night, drifting from room to room, saluted here and there by the smell of beeswax or the ghost-shine of a copper vessel, she could cut through the bonds of time. Because all this would have been the same a year, two years ago: her father would simply have been asleep in his bed. But the illusion wavered whenever she approached the door at the end of the west passage.

That had been her father's bedchamber. Now Bartholomew and his wife slept there. Right and fitting: before the illness had twisted and blinded him her father had made his will and purposed the future, Bartholomew to be master of Hewlands Farm and head of the family. But there the change burned her. Only with delicate care had she found a spot far enough from the door for Bartholomew's snores to be unheard, near enough to awaken the sense of her father. She could stand there for long, sweet minutes. And it didn't matter that that was also the room where he had died.

'You keep holding fast to him,' Bartholomew had told her lately. 'You even want to hold fast to his death.' Yes, he understood her. Bartholomew didn't lack understanding. And she felt he was probably kinder than her. She had wanted to keep her father even when he was nothing but a staring gasp, propped up. 'In God's name, his life's naught but pain now. It's surely time to pull the bolster,' Bartholomew had said, raw and reasonable. And at last he had done it, too. With the farmer's brisk despatch he had tugged away the pillows, and their father's head had fallen back in a final tumble.

And then you went on. But it seemed to her afterwards that life was like a plank bridge with very few planks. Some of those steps looked impossible.

The night was her necessary shame. She knew it was a lie; and everywhere else she was particular about truth. When Bartholomew had found her dipping rushes the other day, and said, 'Margaret could very well do that, you know,' she should have made excuses. Should have said, 'Ah, but she isn't so handy as me—she doesn't let the fat cool long enough. These things need my attention for the house to be run fitly.' Instead she said: 'Yes, I know.' The truth of the situation bulked too large; she couldn't edge round it. Their stepmother was properly mistress of the farm, and her stepsisters could do the other womanly tasks—after all, she had trained them up herself—so in truth there was no role for her here. That was what Bartholomew

7

was saying.

And here he didn't understand her. Yes, she was nearly twenty-six, and it was an age when most women were married or hurrying to marry: that was truth. But he supposed therefore that she must be desperate to find a husband. He had her wrong. Truthfully she said so, but his mind could not accommodate it.

'You mustn't think, you know, that because George Godden is a widower he's running to take the first wife he can get. Not he. He's a sober proper man, and when he does take a bride there will be all the esteem and respect she should desire.' Bartholomew went on probing, looking for the twinge of pride or doubt that would explain her refusal to consider his friend as her suitor. By the end he was floundering. 'And be assured, Anne, he likes your looks. He likes your looks extremely.'

At that she wanted to hide her head. She seldom saw her own face. Her stepmother had a looking-glass, but kept it close. Whenever she had seen herself reflected, she had wanted to avert her eyes as if from a glimpse of nakedness. There was Bartholomew's gold-and-ice fairness, but instead of that great thrust he made in the world, this face seemed ready for nothing. She knew she blushed easily, but it was alarming to see how the blood surged, and the way her features seemed made for the registering of small pains and gnawing questions.

'You have a burden,' her father had once said. 'Beauty.' But he was her father, and always kind. He would even have understood—she was sure of it—her secret marriage to the night.

But on this night, with storm rolling on the

western hills, his presence was weak with her. She made a mistake and got too close to the bedchamber door, and heard not snores but urgent grunts and squeakings. She recovered from that by going to the kitchen and taking down her father's favourite cup and setting it by a dish and just for a moment creating him, sitting there, taking his modest supper . . . But it was only a moment. The thought got in, before she could stop it, that soon he would be gone altogether. And quickly came another: that that was right, that was how it should be, and this was wrong.

The storm rescued her. As if it had made a giant stride it was suddenly here, the thunder cracking overhead, lightning making cold blue sketches of the room. Quietly she unbarred the back door and stood on the footworn threshold looking out across the yard to the meadows beyond. No rain yet, but it would sizzle when it came. Luckily the hay had been cut. She could just make out a blot in the top meadow—the sheep huddling together at the far end. When lightning struck the oak tree beyond the barn it took her a few moments to comprehend what had happened. There was something almost stealthy in what she saw, the downward flick of the assassin's knife, and then her eyeballs were aching with a hot scribble and her ears ringing at the noise, not so much a noise as an axe chopped into her hearing. She blinked and rubbed. Groaning and rending, the oak seemed to be giving monstrous birth. The riven part was breaking away in smoke and din.

The other noise reached her fitfully. It, too, seemed to make no sense: a deep moaning, long and loud beyond the possibility of human lungs.

Yet it sounded so human that her heart clutched.

'God. Look at that.' Bartholomew was beside her.

'Yes, isn't it fearful? That's what woke me,' she said quickly. The moan rose again, beseeching. Bartholomew sighed. He had flung on breeches and stuffed his white bare feet into shoes, but he did not look ridiculous: he never could.

'I fear me that's the young brindle. The one that's with calf. Damn.' His jaw was tight. Plump drops of rain descended singly, each choosing a cobble. 'Go fetch the lantern, will you?' He went ducking towards the byre.

In the kitchen, while she fumbled with tinder and flint, her stepbrother John came yawning and wanting to know what went on. She gave him, perpetual eater, a gooseberry tart and sent him back to bed. Part of her still fretted simply at this invasion of the night. Yet she knew something had changed, and the screeching of the tree seemed to echo inside her.

In the byre Bartholomew was performing a soft, circling dance of caution round the brindled cow. She was standing oddly, head lowered, occasionally making a staggering half-turn, like a drunk man on a slope; and all the time she let out the terrible noise that was almost a wild voice. Blood dripped from her left forequarter.

'Hurt herself against the wall,' Bartholomew said softly. 'Ever a skittish beast. So, so . . . Bring that nearer. Set it down there. Buggery.' He dodged as the cow flung her great sad head about. Rain pelted the roof. Cool air blew in, and the cow's snorting breath made steam-dragons in the lamplight. 'Ah, damn it. See her tail, see. She's going to miscarry.

10

Shit on it.'

Anne said: 'The farrier. Perhaps—'

'Perhaps not. Who'll stir in a night like this? Besides . . .' The brindle made a new, unthinkable noise, her neck swinging lithe and wrong, like an adder. Bartholomew scrambled backwards. 'Besides, I doubt his skill will avail. It's too soon, we'll get no live calf. Only hope she'll drop easy and it won't kill her.'

There were convulsions all along the cow's side, and under her tail a red gape shrank and grew. Anne stepped nearer. 'Brother, she suffers so—'

'Keep back, she's maddened. Oh, buggery. Never cared for this notion of a herd. Father's invention. Sheep for me, hardy, no troubles.' Lightning shuddered again, illustrating a few crisp moments of the cow's agony. The sound she was making suddenly changed. It became dry and dark and plain, not protest but accompaniment. From her palpating rear came a soft slither, and then it was on the ground.

Bartholomew delicately danced again. 'There, draw back, Anne, let her lick it. See. She'll tire. Phoo, stinks. Well, look, it couldn't live.'

Anne was on her knees. The folded, soft-limbed shape did not stir. She tried not to weep. Thunder sullenly slammed doors and stamped about overhead.

'So, so . . . She's bleeding a little—only a little. She'll heal, God willing. I'll send to the farrier in the morning. Damn you, beast, be quiet now, you've dropped and it's done.' Bartholomew squatted on his haunches beside Anne: a glance. 'Ever the lady. I'll be sworn, no one would suppose you'd been bred up on a farm.'

11

'It ought to be horrible.' She fought with her voice. 'But look. It's beautiful.'

Her brother shook his head. 'Beautiful. Well, I never do understand it when you say that. Look now, she's standing away. They don't lack all sense. Never fear, beast, we shall bring the bull to you and you shall have another. Now, I want a piece of sacking—the thing will be slippery.'

'What will you do with it?'

'Get what I can for it. Nothing like the value of a grown calf, but the skin is something worth. Morts, they call them, fine gloves made out of unborn skins. I've known them come out of Ireland.' He examined her a moment. 'Why, is it worse than a skin from slaughter?'

'No. No, to be sure. Only—Bartholomew, don't hang it up by its heels.'

He hesitated, then shrugged. 'Aye, I dare say it's a thought grim. Besides, the crows might get at it.'

Rain pounded and puddled as they crossed the yard, Bartholomew carrying the wrapped burden, Anne the lantern. She set it down in the kitchen and lit another rushlight from it, then another. She smothered a strange wish to make the whole house ablaze with light.

'I've laid it in the buttery. Cooler.' Bartholomew came in, shaking the rain from his hair. 'Lord, what a night. Clove the old oak like an axe. Well, we must send to the fellmonger tomorrow as well as the farrier. Curse on cattle, they're all trouble.'

'Surely not the fellmonger. Father used to sell his hides to Master Shakespeare at Stratford. The glover—'

'Oh, him.' Bartholomew made a face. 'No, they say he's a queer, awkward fellow to deal with

12

nowadays. There was all that ticklish matter of him trading in wool, and going before the court for it. And now I hear he never stirs abroad. Half mad, or popish. Cut me a slice of the brawn, will you?'

Anne wielded the knife. The meat sighed and flopped. 'He was Father's friend.'

'Yes, but Father isn't here any more.' Bartholomew reached for the platter she offered him. Then his eye fell on the table, their father's cup and dish set out. He looked at them for a long time.

'Brawn,' Anne said, holding out the platter stiffly.

'Dear God.' Bartholomew sat, tipping his head back, looking at her as if he had caught her stealing from him and was earnestly trying to work out why. 'Dear God, Anne. Anyone would think *you* are his widow.'

Instead of her stepmother, half blind and sickly in her chamber. Once mighty-fleshed, she had been stricken, suddenly, like the lightning tree, two years since. Just as if everything Anne had wished on her, when first her father brought her falsely blushing home, had finally come true. As it happened, Anne need not have feared. She had lost no love. She was still first, until—

'No. It's only that I have to do the remembering for both of us.' The anger, tainted with guilt, came on her foul and shocking, as if she had croaked blasphemy or soiled herself.

Bartholomew stabbed a knife into the brawn, chewed noisily. His cheeks were a little red. 'What sad work you make of life. You should have married George Godden. There'll not be many such chances. The years, Anne, the years. Well, after all, you're not contented here, are you? What is it? Is it Bella? I'd hoped you might rub along well enough.'

Anne thought of Bartholomew's wife, her mild, smiling plumpness, the way she could talk comfortably on damsons, on the ailments of children, on the water boiling in the pan: on and on. She didn't dislike her. She rather envied her. And sometimes she wanted to flee from her to the furthest horizon.

'I am contented. Bartholomew, I'm sorry for what I just said.'

That seemed to irritate him. He pushed the platter away. 'Oh, we'll send to Master Shakespeare if you will, Anne. Doubtless you see it as carrying out Father's wishes. But you can make that mean anything, you know, because he's in the grave and can't answer for himself. I remember him right enough. He was a good man in the main, an honest man: too indulgent and soft sometimes, and I fear both his wives led him a dance, but there, he was mortal like the rest of us.' He rose and stretched. 'I'm going back to bed. You'd best do the same. I don't know why you must creep about of a night.' He picked up their father's cup and put it on the shelf. 'Not all men are like Father, Anne, and that's the way of it.'

I know that, she thought, but it went down into the great vault of the unsaid.

When he was gone she stood at the door, watching the rain, breathing its freshness. Then she walked out in it. She wanted to see the lightning tree. She wanted to give that calf life. The rain drenched her: her hair straggled round her face, her clothes clung to her body, their touch heavy and

14

insistent. For a moment she longed to be a witch, to work a spell and see the calf stir. She stood beneath the stricken oak. It looked crippled yet everlasting. She remembered climbing it once, as a girl—just the once. It was simply not the sort of thing she did. She saw her father smiling anxiously as she struggled down. 'Ah, you were not meant for a hoyden,' he said. He was right. But, oh, just for once, that exhilarating terror of being stranded up there, far from earth, and thinking: I did this, and it is wrong and perilous, but I am living.

*   *   *

When the message came, Will was at work paring a skin in the yard. He noticed that when the knife caught and snagged, he winced just as if he were shaving himself. Was it time to go bearded or moustached, like some of his old schoolfellows? Too often, though, the whisker was a poor ill-nourished thing, like a rafter cobweb twirled on a maid's broom.

You must learn what it is to be a man.

The message was from a farm at Shottery. A stillbirth hide, rare, delicate. 'There's little call for such fine goods hereabouts,' his father said, looking over Will's shoulder. His beard was the same shape as the paring-knife. 'Still, go see. Say sixpence or nothing.' This meant he could go up to ninepence. 'Present my compliments to Master Hathaway. I loved his father well. Ah, Richard Hathaway, now, *there* was a good man, weigh it how you will.' Often now he had this dogged, injured tone, as if someone were contradicting him.

At the stable door Will was caught by Edmund, the youngest of his brothers. Two years old, strong,

15

loudly undeniable, Edmund clung to his leg and howled. 'Hush, I'm coming back,' Will soothed. As it grew less likely that the child would die, Will was allowing himself to grow fond of him. But on his side, Edmund was passionate and exclusive. 'Coming back, coming back.' The boy's skirts were dabbled with dung.

Joan came bustling and sighing. 'Now see that muck. Mother will scold. You shouldn't let him.'

'Coming back, hush . . . I tried to slip away.'

'Here, monkey.' Joan prised Edmund away, hoisted him. 'Such tears! Now you're all besnotted. Look, look at the pretty chicks a-running . . .' She frowned at Will over the bristly tumultuous head. 'Lord, I swear, whenever you go out it's as if he thinks he'll never see you more.'

'And yet I always come back,' Will said, touching Edmund's wet hot cheek, 'don't I?'

As he set his foot to the mounting-block, he thought he heard Edmund, borne back into the house, say with an odd adult resignation, 'No.'

The mare twitched and tossed and sidestepped out of the yard, hating Will on her back. When Gilbert rode her she was peaceable. The wisdom of animals and infants. Will, no rider, managed her as he managed life. Things he loathed and had no aptitude for, he had learned to deal with in this way: he had learned to be good at them.

Last night's storm had swelled the gutters to overflowing, and the top of Rother Street was six inches under water. Three yelling boys were playing football with a bloated toad.

'Will! Good news!'

Master Field, the tanner, leading his laden donkey. Their faces were of a length. Will reined in.

16

'Richard's home. God be praised. Late last night, when we'd given him up. Five nights on fearful roads.'

'God be praised.' For once Will meant it.

'He's sleeping yet. Later you must come see him. His mother's in a pother over his looks. Says London's turned him yellow as parchment. But he prospers. Through labour he prospers. Idleness,' Master Field said, aiming his switch at one of the shrieking boys, 'see what it begets. The council should do something. They're too lax. Prentices running around after curfew, shouting and fighting. When's your father going to come back to meetings? Backbone, that's what's wanting.'

Accustomed to thinking two questions ahead, Will dodged this one easily. 'Father will be glad to hear Richard's safe arrived. He often speaks of him. Have you come by the Shottery road? Is it fair?'

Richard back. Riding on, Will cautiously allowed the thought to shine on him. Last winter he had come across a hedgehog sleeping in a briar tangle behind the midden. The midden was warm with the liveliness of rot and the hedgehog was warm too: he had managed to touch it, using his open palm. He knew about soft prickles. He knew about choosing his times to stir and live.

Now summer, and the players would soon be here. Mud from the storm splashed up to his calves but the sky was all high blue contrition, temper-fit gone; the meadows brimmed with light and the trees were heavy, nodding drunken with leaf, and everything he saw and smelt said the players, time for the players to rattle their tinker's cart of seduction over Stratford Bridge. Time to wake.

But his father wanted that promise from him,

17

and a promise of deeds not just words. And the handiwork of stitching his two selves together was getting beyond his dexterity. He could feel tugging and tearing.

He passed Two Elms, the mare splashing disdainfully between muckhill floaters, and struck the Shottery road.

This is Will, as you might see him if you were one of Stratford's two thousand citizens, chandler or seamstress, glancing from panel-dark interior through grid of window to bright summer outside. Master Shakespeare's eldest, mounted—the horse a poor nag but lucky to keep it after those money troubles. William, Will to most, brother of Gilbert, Joan, Richard and Edmund; eighteen years old, bony, back as long as a stoat's. Some of his father's good looks, but not so square and strong: a longish face, clear-cut nose, and chin that makes the lips look a little indrawn. A good manner—indeed a gracious youth, as all will agree: it is not only the Puritans in the town, like Master Field, who lament the ways of the swearing, boozing, disrespectful young. The odd lapse, but a credit to his father, all in all; hasn't bound himself prentice to him, but works hard in the trade. No *trouble* about him.

And then, probably, you look away.

*   *   *

'What? Oh, that. You're prompt.' Master Hathaway gave Will a distracted attention. In the big kitchen of Hewlands Farm it was like a fair-day: a dozen people there, or going in and out. Big voices. Master Hathaway big too, fair, hair growing out of his ears as if he were stuffed with straw. A big girl was plucking

18

at his sleeve. '*What*, Margaret? I've things to see to—'

'John took the pie. The last piece—'

'Damn you, boy, I've told you about stealing food. You want, you ask.' With easy violence, in passing, Master Hathaway slapped the ducking head of a boy who began an outrageous howling, and turned to two farmhands. 'Now *where* did the rain come in? And *how* many sacks spoiled? Well, show me, show me, then. God knows why it needed two of you to come tell me.' He thrust the men towards the door with a big hand at each back, so they tittuped like dancers, then aimed a kick at a hen that had slipped in to peck at breakfast crumbs. There was something dispassionate about all this. The smooth fair face did not suggest a man of general ill-temper. Will caught a whiff of his sour breath and saw a night drinker for whom morning was a horrible rebirth. 'Bella, when you find that wench, will you ask her why she has not been up to Stepmother's room when the poor woman has been calling out this past hour?' He turned back to Will in sudden frowning memory. 'Sir, your pardon. A man would have to be twenty men . . . Anne! Anne will show you the carcass, by your leave. The notion was hers.'

A woman came away from the fireplace. Will had been here before, a few years ago with his father, buying a hide, in the old farmer's time. He knew young Master Hathaway to nod to at market. But the womenfolk of the large household he could not identify, and this one he had not noticed at all; perhaps because she was the only stillness there.

Will bowed. 'Mistress Hathaway.'

'I am no mistress,' she said.

19

He hesitated on the edge of apology. But she had spoken informatively, with a touch of a smile, as if correcting a child's mistake. She turned and led him to the buttery.

While he examined the carcass she stood at a distance, looking out. He sensed a coldness about her, though not turned on him, not quite. While even the stone buttery was summer-warm, she seemed to inhabit winter, as if her gaze fell on frozen snow and a sky that would not lighten for long months.

'The cow lived?' he asked, replacing the sacking. He had seen animals dead, skinned, butchered since he was small: feeling was not absent, but it was mild.

'Yes. That's all we have for you.' She made him seem greedy for more. 'The storm last night maddened her and she dropped early. Did you hear the storm?'

'I watched it all.'

She turned then, with a dubious look, as if he were hiding something behind his back. Her beauty came to him piecemeal. He was too shy to dwell on it, for she was a woman, and beyond him. With girls you exchanged frank rolling eyes, all the while aware that, like you, they knew nothing. With her he stood at the foot of a vast flight of steps. But his mind dared to put some elements of her by: the shape of that face, its strength one with its fineness and fragility; the translucent soft skin at the nape of her neck, and the way all the skin he could see was like that.

'What will you give for the—for the calf?'

I am no mistress. But empowered to make the bargain, it seemed. He said, 'Ninepence.'

She inclined her head and, when he had put the money into her hand, left him. Her tread was quite silent. Passing through the place where she had stood he found faintly a scented stir: the air felt impressed, like a pillow from which a head has lately risen.

In the yard he fastened the bundle to the mare's saddle. The mare, sensing something about her burden, twitched and tugged as he led her out through the gate.

Halfway down the farm track he heard a cry.

'Wait. Please.' She was flushed from running: from something else. Will found his hand seized, the coins pressed hard into it. 'Here. I've changed my mind. Don't take it.'

For a moment he thought this some odd refinement of haggling. 'Truly, you'll get no better price, if—'

'I don't care for that.' She put up a trembling hand to brush back loose gold strands from her temples. 'It's the fitness of it, and somehow this—this is not fit. When my brother last killed the pig I caught the blood in a pail. I cured the meat and dressed it and I ate of it. It was in the course of things. But that calf—it's something that never was. It's wrong and wry to make something of it.' A sob caught her: she turned from him, sagged, looked as if she would fall. 'I wish it undone, that's all. Everything. It's so hot, it's the heat, no more. Pray you, don't look at me.'

'It's fearful hot, and you'll take sick. Come. Step into the shade.' Pity made him bold. He took her arm and led her under a tree and tethered the mare to a low branch.

'This isn't the one,' she said, as if to herself, back

21

against the bole, looking up. Green tinged her wet, distracted face. 'Dear God, but if I bring it back my brother will think I'm a fool. As I am, a great fool. I don't know what to do.'

It was not so much the tears. It was the knowledge that she must hate his seeing them, hate it like death, that spurred him to speech. Words could do and undo. 'The beast was stillborn, yes, before its time,' he said quickly. 'And so, certainly, a thing that never was. But everything that never was is also a thing that might have been—and such a thing has more existence than you or I, for it has a thousand potential existences, and we have only the one we were born to. And of all those possibilities, what could be more fantastical a transformation? Not mere gloves. The gloves from such a skin are so fine, they say, you can fold them into a nutshell. Who could suppose from poor sad dead flesh a creation so airy? A fairy's dream of gloves. You wouldn't—you couldn't wear them to warm your hands. No, no, you would slip them on in the dog-days, to make your hands feel cooler.'

He held her gaze—a test for him, because he could never look anyone in the eye for long: it always overwhelmed him.

After a moment she shook her head. 'Your pardon,' she said distantly. 'I never thought . . . I know nothing of these matters.' But her eyes were dry.

'Take the money. It's a fair purchase,' he said, and offered her the coins on his open palm. Now words took him by surprise. 'Why did you say you are no mistress?'

She looked up at him. He was half a head taller but she seemed to be looking down, and his youth

22

shivered over him, as if he found himself standing ribbed and shirtless.

'I spoke without thinking,' she said. She picked the coins from his hands without touching his skin. 'Do you never do that?'

'Let me think about that question.'

She did not smile; but he saw the smile as, at least, one of those thousand possibilities of unborn things. 'I'm not the mistress of Hewlands Farm. That's my stepmother. Or my brother's wife, while she's sick. That's all I meant. I am—how does it go?—a woman at my own government.' She shook out her skirts, looked blinking and shrewd around her, like someone arrived from a long journey. Sister, then, not wife to the strawy farmer. That fairness. It changed nothing, of course. She was still a woman, and he felt her using it against him, like a carter bunching his muscles at the reins. 'I've been a great fool over the calf. Please forget all about it.'

'I needn't take it home,' he said, loud and urgent, as if she were already far off. 'If you wish, I could—I could bury it somewhere.'

'What would you tell Master Shakespeare?'

'Say I looked over the carcass, and it was fit for nothing.'

'And then what of the money you have given over?' She shook her head. 'Besides, I wouldn't force you to lie to your father.'

He nearly said: 'My father is made of lies.' But in fact he could say nothing. Words had flown out from him and done their work, like the hawk flying to the kill from the falconer's wrist. Now the hood was back on. Now Mistress Hathaway was restored and queenly, and Will was reduced again to the unsatisfactory flesh and bowing low as she left him.

23

She said softly: 'Thank you.'

He imagined her thinking: No one saw it, no one saw me. Only a youth. No one saw.

*   *   *

Benjamin. The name often given to the son of an older father. Child of my age.

But why, Ben sometimes asked of his dead father's shade, just why did you leave it so long? Why did your loins not stir with the making of me when you were young? Then you might have seen me grow—seen me born at least—instead of going to your grave when I had yet a month in the womb.

And, above all, I might not have had a stepfather.

It was on an evening of hot storm over Westminster, in his eighth year, that he first learned about the business of loins stirring, and what came of it. At that time he went whenever he could to the little parish school in St Martin's Lane. On this particular day, with his stepfather in the beating mood, Ben decided when the clerk clanged the bell that he would not go home. One of his schoolfellows, seeing him loitering, said Ben could come home with him. So instead of darting across the spattering Strand, between cattle and cartwheels, he followed his friend into a warren of courts and alleys behind St Martin's. The boy said his parents wouldn't be there—his father was a barber, his mother a cow-keeper—but his sister, he added with a special look, would be home. Ben could see his sister.

In an upstairs room above a stable, Ben saw. The girl was about fifteen, swart, big-breasted, simple. She giggled over the shoulder of the man who, Ben thought at first, was trying somehow to kill her by smothering her while half naked. The man didn't seem to mind the boys watching. He winked and commented on the progress of the work. When he was done he fastened his breeches, saw Ben's bewilderment, and gave him a brief explanation.

Ah. So when, Ben asked, would the baby come? The man laughed. Never, with any luck: he believed the mother knew her business and dosed the girl. Before he left, the man threw a farthing on the floor. It rolled. Giggling, the girl chased it down.

It was grim, but it was knowledge, therefore precious. And it even helped him understand the mystery of his stepfather. To whom, of course, he still had to go home that night, and who beat him all the harder for being late.

When the man had gone to the tavern, Ben came out with it: why?

'Why do I have to have a stepfather at all?'

His mother looked at him, considering. Her eyes were large and mild but the rest of her features sharp: sometimes she looked like two people at once. She seemed to decide that Ben was a child who could be told hard things. 'Because of money, Benjamin. When your father died, he left us with no money.'

'Why? Did he spend it all?'

'None to spend. A minister's living dies with him, and he had no estate. Oh, once he did, but it was lost in Queen Mary's time. She brought back the Romish rites, but the Jonsons would not conform to them. For a time your father even lay in prison.'

'Good,' Ben said. 'To go to prison for what you believe.'

'So say I,' his mother said, after a silent, still

25

moment. 'But that was why we needed money when he died. More than I could earn with my needle. A woman cannot shift for herself in this world, Benjamin, save she be bred up to it. Even then, it's hard to make your way unprotected. For my sake and yours, I had to marry again. Not because I longed for linen sheets instead of hempen. No. To keep us safe.'

And Ben understood. So far, and no further. Marrying again, very well. Marrying *him*—marrying Robert ham-fist brick-dust dull-wit Brett, not so well.

Once when his stepfather tired himself out plying the strap and sat down to yawn and rub his arm muscles, Ben said: 'As soon as I'm big enough, I shall hit you back, you know.'

His stepfather grinned. 'That day's not yet.'

'It will come, though.'

His stepfather shrugged. He was a heavy, full-lipped man with colourless eyes. 'It will come, aye. The same with our death, boy. Same with our death.'

Not mine, Ben thought. He intended living for ever, and could not imagine anyone living with any other aim.

What he saw in the room above the stables gave him firmer ideas about many things. His mother was a stronger woman than that poor idiot creature: still, she was a woman. Ben watched when his stepfather was in loving vein and she turned small in his embrace, offering him little kissing troubles. 'Poor chick, how dost?' he cooed. 'Thou hast a world of grief on thy pretty brow tonight. Wilt let me love it away, hey?' The back of his neck formed two precise rolls of flesh, like some pastry-cook's

26

confection. Ben watched his mother's fingers caress them.

Hempen sheets or linen, it didn't matter.

So he turned to the next page of the Bible. He was not devout—except about reading, and this was the only book in the house. Books were precious and expensive. The parish clerk kept his locked up in a trunk in the schoolroom. Ben might have had one to borrow—but you had to get the clerk's favour, usually extended to delicate, sweet boys, and Ben was plain. One day, he assured himself, he would have books. He would live among them night and day. It was all his desire. And though the clerk did not like his looks, he admitted that Ben was the best scholar he had ever taught.

And there Ben hungered for his future, beyond this dense drab slice of Westminster, where brew-houses smoked and fishmongers kept their heads down over the bloody slab. Hereabouts, his stepfather stood pretty high, being a master bricklayer. Beyond Charing Cross, where blaring London rose, lords and rich citizens alike were putting up houses in new, luxurious brick, and Robert Brett was busy in their service. He had an apprentice. The last had turned out bad, run off, become a handler of stolen goods, and ended up hanged; but the new one promised well, took his beatings, and would surely become a master himself when his seven years were out.

And after that, of course, there was a natural successor in the family.

Never—please, God, never. Ben had to make good his escape. Learning, learning, learning. He urged himself on. And the winter after he saw the empty giggling girl, grace descended. The clerk came home with him to see his mother, when his stepfather was at work.

'Westminster School?'

'Madam, you must have thought of it. To speak truth, he knows everything I do. And there is nowhere superior in the kingdom. My lord Burghley oversees it; the Queen has a special care for it. You cannot do better by him.'

Ben sat quiet. Neither looked at him: the clerk because he found him unattractive, his mother because she was not thinking of him but of someone else.

'The cost,' she said.

'Being so near, you have an advantage. He can live at home instead of boarding. Yes, you will have to find him in writing-gear and books and candles. It is an expense, but surely a worthy one. And after a year, he's eligible for a scholarship.' The clerk sniffed. 'It would make a vast difference to his prospects, madam. Even the universities might lie at the end of it.'

His mother sat and thought. Ben slipped away, to be sick in a corner of the yard, sick with wanting.

He was not quite sure how his mother did it. When she first told him he was to go to Westminster School, she said that a clerical connection of his dead father's had provided the funds, in his memory. Certainly his stepfather would not have spared the money. He shook his head over the scheme; could not see the use in it. But, then, he could not see the use in Ben at all— until he was of prentice age.

As for his mother, Ben thought: I can forgive her anything, for this.

Now the world begins. Such was the solemnity

28

with which Ben first entered the long schoolroom. It was crowded and noisy and stank to the rafters, and he was down among the lowliest, the Oppidans, local-dwelling day boys, conscious of his rough shoes and frayed bands; and the headmaster lashed and thrashed. But he knew he was going to enjoy everything. Latin he already loved: now came stranger Greek to baffle and beguile.

'Many boys find Greek difficult at first.' Master Camden smiled. 'But I've never known any find the difficulty gratifying before.'

With William Camden, the undermaster, perfect understanding and even intimacy. Nothing of the parish clerk: he was a long-nosed, abstracted young man, whose brown eyes were untreacherous and without desire. Patiently he supervised forty Queen's Scholars in their noisome dormitory before retiring to his chamber above and studying until dawn put out his taper.

'The history of ourselves.' That was his passion. 'Britain, land and legend and truth. The Romans walked here, Benjamin, and many a farmer turns up their coins with his plough; and there are in our western shires giant circles of stones put up by human hands of which we know nothing. The ancients took pride in their history, and we still learn from them. Perhaps we in turn may be a pattern to future ages. So my studies. I'm not so vain as to think they matter now. But if I can lay a small stone in the path of posterity—'

'I want to do the same,' Ben burst out.

Master Camden smiled again. 'Well, now, leave me my scholar's field, at least.'

'Not the same. I don't mean that. What I want—' Could he say it? Yes, to this man he could; this man obliterated all thought of the whistling strap and the fat neck. 'I want to be the most learned man in the kingdom.'

And Master Camden paused only a moment, eyebrows up, before nodding. 'A commendable aim. But what is it you would seek to do with your learning?'

Ben ran his eyes over his schoolfellows: the stupid talking loudly, the ugly mocking themselves to make the handsome laugh. Alliances and need. He heard a farthing rolling on floorboards.

'Make people better,' he said.

2

The Malcontent (1582)

'Now I'm alive again,' Will says, turning the pages. He does not want to laugh or to cry, not exactly: he feels on the edge of some third expression, surpassing either of them.

They are in the bare, swept, godly parlour of the Field house, a little drunk but not as drunk as they mean to be. Will has supped here and now godly, black-clad Master and Mistress Field have gone, climbing the stairs to their unthinkable bed, cautioning about candles, leaving them to it. Allowing that Will and Richard still have much to talk of.

Schoolfriends, they have been separated these three years since Richard went to London as a printer's apprentice. His master is taking a cure in the country and has given Richard a fortnight's indulgence. At supper they drank small beer, but Richard has a secreted bottle of something fine from London, on the table now alongside his very different treasure.

'I would have brought more.' Richard is smallish and dark and compact, little different from when they were at school. As if he has made a decision about growing. Will's knees graze on church pews, and nothing fits him. 'But I could only carry so much in my pack. Now, that one's faint, the whole batch of ink turned villainous—we thought of selling it but there's reputation, you know. That one hung on our hands. It's pretty but no one bought. *That* one, I don't know what happened. There was a sort of ripple when it was pressed, and so you have to fill in the words in the middle of every line. It's—'

'That's what I'm doing,' says Will, greedy, abstracted: rude as a child. A princely gift, these loose sheets from the printer's workshop, spoiled or unsold. *A Jest for Prentices*. Rough, deckle-edged paper, as communicative to the touch as skin. Will has read everything in Stratford: all the books borrowed of the schoolmaster, ballads and broadsides bought on fair-days. *The Mirror of True Repentance*. The paper smells, he fancies, of London, dense and hot. *The Play of the Pardoner*. He looks up, dizzy. 'Your master prints plays?'

'Some few. He esteems them trash for the most part. Now try this wine. Madame Vautrollier made me a present of it.'

'Oho.'

'Not oho. No oho about it.' Richard pours: the liquid pearls bobble. 'Mind, she is a magnificent creature. Your Frenchwoman, Will, is a different

31

breed altogether—the way she carries herself . . . Savour it, man, don't swallow it down.'

'Latin.' Will is still turning pages, wading in and out of the stream of words. 'Damn, I'm rusty. What case is that?'

'Ablative.' Richard coughs 'Well, look, I've kept it up because we print a deal of Latin. Also you're soused. Master Vautrollier has just got a patent to print Ovid. The *Metamorphoses*. Do you remember? Beautiful.'

'I remember.' The words on the page fade, and instead Will sees his last day at Stratford grammar-school: jokes, hand-shakings, little orations. The schoolmaster on his dais grave and saying nothing. *My father needs me at home, sir*. No one saying, indeed, that something has gone wrong—that Will who always outpaced everyone should be leaving now, when he might surely . . . 'How old is she? Your Madame Vautrollier?'

'She's not my Madame Vautrollier. I don't know. Older. A woman.' Richard sips his wine, then reaches out and puts his arm round Will's neck. 'Pardon, Will. About school. Cess and piss on that, what happened, shame on it.'

They would often touch like this, back then—lie while reading propped against each other, in long grass. Now the gesture seems to fall short. Will pats Richard's narrow back. 'No matter. I do very well.' Smiling painfully they disengage—Richard sitting back into London, Will into Stratford. 'What became of your lute?'

Startled, Richard shakes his head. 'Upstairs somewhere. I didn't take it to London. No place for that in a day's business, Will: at the press cockcrow to curfew, three hundred sheets a day else Master

Vautrollier swears the devil out of hell. And then I take a taper and study till midnight. Is your heart bleeding?'

'A drop. Go fetch it.'

'We'll wake the old ones.'

'Then we'll go out. There's a moon. Down by the bridge—remember?'

So, with lute and bottle and flagon, they bundle out a little breathless and hilarious—though a last sobriety plucks Richard: 'It will mean leaving the door unbarred—'

'You forget you're in Stratford now, not the great wicked city,' Will says. 'We don't have thieves and murderers here. Only hypocrites.'

Exhilaration of being abroad in soft night, of slithering down the turfy slope by the last buttress of Clopton Bridge. Life in the dark: frogs creak like hinges, a moth blunders against his hand. Setting his back against the cool stone, Will is content for a moment just to cradle the lute: to feel its speaking shape. It came from Richard's great-uncle, once steward in a lord's household; he had taught Richard, who had taught Will, so that between them they could manage a dozen songs, all full of tears and cruel mistresses. His fingers search the strings for memory. He thinks suddenly of the woman at Hewlands Farm, of the upright set of her head on the slender neck: of swans and silver goblets and things perfectly made.

'Tune it, for God's sake, tune it.' Richard groans. 'The second course is all out. And the chanterelle. Sounds like a sow in farrow. Better.'

'"If pity do not move your heart,
These tears of mine behold . . ."'

33

'How does it go on?'

'"That ever thus do burn and smart."'

'"In fire I waste, whiles you are cold . . ."' Damn. I sound like ten sows. I used to know this song backwards.'

'You're out of practice. And I told you, man, you're piss-eyed.'

Will stills the strings. 'So is it like that, Richard? The sighing and burning and wanting to die at her feet?'

'Why ask me?' A laugh, but moonlight finds a flash of alarm in his eyes.

'You're a Londoner now. It must be different. There must be—there must be women, many women—'

'A great many women, of every condition, aye. And one sees, and often admires. But I'm a prentice, and I mean to do well. I must live cleanly. And I may not marry till my time is out. So.'

'To be sure . . . but how if the killing dart strikes you—if a glance smites you with a wound there is no healing.'

'That only belongs in songs and sonnets.' Richard grunts. 'Besides, in London the wound there's no healing is likelier to strike you in your cods.' A laugh, but Will realises he has touched the Puritan in him. Here comes the return. 'Will, have you not bound yourself prentice to your father?'

'No. But I live, God knows, cleanly as any prentice.'

'I didn't mean that. People—people wonder about him. Father says he still doesn't come to council meetings. Some say he fears arrest for debt. They even excused him the poor-rate last session.

34

Yet he can't have lost so much, surely? He still trades—'

'Well, you know as much as me, it seems. Do you suppose he takes me into his confidence?' Will lays the lute down on the grass, with a momentary picture of himself lifting it on high and smashing it. Not a good thing to do: but clear-cut, at least. 'Two years since, he sold off the last of my mother's property. No doubt the shades of her old Arden kinsfolk wailed at it, but I think most of his creditors were satisfied. What happened? I don't know.' And that would be the worst shame of all for my father, Will thinks, if I were to know. 'I believe he overreached. He had risen so high and it was all so golden—he even made application to the College of Heralds for a coat of arms. John Shakespeare, gentleman. Then suddenly he stopped talking of it. I know he burned his fingers trading wool. Perhaps there were other misadventures . . . Richard, do you think it possible that a man may be doomed to ill-fortune? Nature and circumstance meeting in him, so potently, with such black perfection, that there is no escape?' Another moth comes and alights on his sleeve: he cups it in his hand. 'He may do what he will. There is no escape.'

'A pagan notion. Will, there are whispers that your father cleaves to the old religion.'

'Only whispers? Come, this is Stratford, where we bawl our innuendoes over the fish-slab.' Will lets the moth go.

'Will—is he papist? Aye, I know, I shouldn't ask. And I honour him still, whatever the truth, and so does my father, though we're so differently affected. Only I fear for you.'

Will breaks into such a shout of laughter that

Richard jumps. 'Sorry. Oh, you needn't fear that. Trust me.' The old religion? Perhaps. His mother sometimes swears by Our Lady, and occasionally she and his father pray privately together. And this suspicion is much in the air lately: Will has heard of these shadowy men landing from Rome with their pockets full of Catholic writings, moving about the country, moving from house to house. Not difficult to imagine his father warming to it. In the days of his glory he was a public man, doing for the Queen public and Protestant things. Now, an outsider, he may well seek to wrap himself in all the outsider's bitter comforts. Every man's hand is against me— and, if not, I shall make it so.

'I'm thankful for that. Because it is a question just now, Will, a great question.'

'Too great for an answer. Somewhere behind it is this God for whom one burns people, or for whom one is willing to be burned, and damn me if I can conceive him. I'm drunk, pay no heed.'

'There are men coming out of the universities talking like that.' Richard's voice is pained and precise. 'Atheist, or near it. You must be careful.'

'I'm never anything else.' Will laughs. But the truth remains: he cannot imagine living for God or dying for God. Being able to imagine almost everything else, he feels it as a failure, confirming his suspicion of himself as a person of light weight. Place him in the mortal scales, and they would scarcely quiver. 'As for going prentice to my father, he wants it, I don't, and so we rub along.' A sort of truth. In very truth, thinks Will, he wants me to be him. To live him over again, only this time . . . 'We shall see. Look, you. When you are made Lord Mayor of London—'

36

'As I will be.' Richard sits up, taut and solemn. 'I aim at nothing less. You may think me a vain fool—'

'No, no, I don't. If you can see it, then you can reach it. If you can't . . . if it's not to be seen, then . . .'

'What?'

'Invent it, perhaps.' He shakes his head, turning from Richard's too-enquiring gaze. 'Do it, Richard. Lord Mayor. For Stratford. Bring glory to us left behind here. God knows the old hole needs it.'

'Is that what you truly think, Will?'

'I thought it just then. In an hour's time, who knows?' Will is trying, at least, to be truthful. 'And tomorrow, who knows?' And then he plays and sings loud again, to erase that look from Richard's face, to drown that note he heard. The note of pity.

*   *   *

It could never be the same again. Still, Will and Richard were much together during his stay. They walked in the fields and talked, and Richard lost his city pallor. And when Richard spoke of London, Will listened and was careful not to listen devouringly, not to ask too many questions: not to let the pictures become too vivid. He treated himself like a fever patient. The goldsmiths' shops, one glittering after another, a goblin's dream-hoard; and then the spiked heads of the executed on London Bridge, the bull-baiting yards, Smithfield Market all bludgeoning and blood; and then the young gallants practising archery in the Moorfields in the dewy morning . . . Yes, the pulse a little fast but not so bad. And then the booksellers lining St Paul's churchyard—step in

37

beneath the signs of the White Greyhound and the Red Bull and the Green Dragon, encounter quires and reams, and then the dubious lanes of Shoreditch, mentioned by Richard with a grimace, for here had lately risen the theatres, and cutpurses and queans flocked with the crowds to the flag and trumpet . . . Now the pulse was hectic and the patient in danger. Will turned the talk to the state of the crops.

Just once, Richard supped with Will's family. In the days of his glory John Shakespeare had been a notable host: always room at his board, no need to bring your own knife, send in the dressed pork and manchet bread. Now a guest was a rarity. Will's father was for a time easy, expansive, talking to Richard of London trade and London ways, until he fell into a low silence and stared at the candle-flame. His mother was tenderly anxious over plague, and thieves lurking in alleys. Joan, at first, gazed and swallowed and turned scarlet, reminding Will of how much his friend had changed: always seemly and civil, he now seemed rooted in assurance, calmly listening, breaking bread in thin, elegant fingers. But by the time the apple tansey was brought in her look had changed. Joan was thirteen, learning scorn, and Will saw her touching her upper lip in imitation of Richard petting his infant moustache.

'He's a pretty figure of a man,' she yawned afterwards, 'but he needn't give himself such airs. Just because he had some fiddle-faced Puritan godfather who could put him in the way of a London prenticeship. They *always* look after each other.' Her upturned chin and glinting eye invited Will to be scurrilous with her: they often did it. But Will responded with temperate loyalty, declining

38

to hear a word against Richard. Because if he did, he might reveal how much he envied him. The envy would hurtle out, snarling and dripping foam from its jaws.

Will read twice over all the books Richard had brought him, and when he was not reading them he had the words inside him and drew on them—the way, he supposed, the Puritans drew on the spirit and the papists drew on the faith. Once he made the mistake of reading at the workbench. He didn't hear his father approach.

It was not so much the throwing of the books on the floor, as the way his father threw them: with a grunt and heft, like a roadmender heaving stones. A reminder. They didn't need to say anything.

It would have been easier, of course, not to love him. Will's love for his mother was simple; it merely claimed you, as thirst made you drink. His love for his father was like an illness, or a wound. You could not rest with it; it must come to some issue.

Will was there to see Richard off, early on a hot July morning. Richard was making the journey with the Stratford carrier, young Will Greenaway, who was taking the job on from his father. Ah, just as it should be. A merchant from Leamington was travelling with them too: safety in numbers. The saddlebagged horses flicked their ears at the teasing flies and looked mournful. They did not want to be striking the road to London. They wanted to graze in the paddock for ever. Will and Richard clasped hands, then stood shuffling while Greenaway tightened pack-threads and the Fields intoned godly advice. The young, Will thought, are not good at greetings and farewells. They feel their hollowness.

'I didn't think me,' Richard said at the last. 'You could have had my lute. Father—let Will take my lute.'

'No, no, I can't,' Will said urgently. He had no idea why.

'Will, if ever you—' Richard said, and broke off with a rueful, surprised look, like a sleeper who wakes himself up talking. 'God be with you.'

Soon after the riders were out of sight Will found himself walking down Wood Street for no reason. A window banged open and an ill rainbow of slops hit the cobbles. An open yard-gate showed him a brawny maid plucking a live goose, its legs tied over its back. She was not doing it well: blood spotted the white drift at her feet. She was a moon-faced creature but pretty dimples appeared as she set her little pearly teeth against the shrieking goose's struggles. Some man would see her beauty; or else lunge and fumble, thinking she would do. Perhaps, Will thought, he could carry on like this for ever: circumambulate, loiter, watch. Perhaps it would do, as a fumble at life.

But at last he turned his steps for home, as if he were making a choice. On Henley Street the Shakespeare house stood roomy and solid and unassailable. A few rents in the roof tiles could not gainsay it: here dwells a man of substance. Cloud-flashing sunlight passed across the upper windows, like sly eyes rolling.

Indoors, dark wood panels after summer dazzle made him grope blindfolded for a moment. His mother was finishing the baking. 'You'll miss Richard, I should think,' she said. There was flour on her nose and cheek, and as she kissed him she placed a little on him, like a token of her understanding, or a mark. Someone was in the workshop with his father, talking of the price of dyes: elder, indigo, madder. 'Oh, but as to madder . . .' his father rumbled. Joan popped her head in: when did they last change the rushes? Thursday fortnight. No, stay, not so long. Madder. Feeling of a day beginning: turn over the rushes, they'll serve. Turn over the new-old day. He thought of the hour-glass in the church, always the same grains running through. The thought gave him a curious panic. His head and stomach seemed to change places as if the hour-glass of his being had been turned over.

As if drawn by instinct, Edmund blocked his way at the bright door.

'Where going?'

Will vaulted right over him, landed running. He ran as, it seemed to him, he had never run before: not when running races with his schoolfriends, not when they had filched fruit from mad Dame Harris's orchard and she had set her mastiffs after them—never running like this, knees almost up to his chest, lungs tearing at the air. Faces mouthed as they flashed by, but he heard only the pump and snatch of his own breath. At Clopton Bridge, still running, he clawed his doublet over his head and flung it, pounded on in sweat-wet shirt, grinning hard and grim against the sun, twitching the salt drops from his eyebrows and eyelashes. The stone-dry ruts of the country road seized at his ankles, trying to twist and break. Tawny fields, harvest-ripe, ringed his reddening vision. Stratford was lost behind him and somewhere ahead, soon, over the next heat-wavering rise, the horses and riders and wagging packs, bound for London . . .

41

Only a wide empty shimmer, though. Only the extinction of his breath, the aching slap of his slowing feet: truth, stern kind parent, cuffing him as he staggered in heat and his throat bubbled. No good. He could not reach the horses. Already, far out of his parish and with no destination, he was in law a vagabond. If he caught up with them it would be no different: there was only freakish folly in this. He could not reach so far. Will heard little contemptible groans coming from himself as he made a mazy stumble, and the hard green ground, springing up as if on a hinge, slammed against his cheek.

For a time he could only lie with his heart thundering in his chest and his stupidity raging in his mind. It seemed at least probable that one or the other would kill him there, by the side of the road: it certainly did not seem unjust.

Faintly his roaring ears picked up the sound of hoofs and rumbling wheels.

'Sleep it off, that's the way.'

'God-a-mercy, what hour must a man begin drinking to be soused flat before noon?'

'The night before, of course.'

'Hold, look, he's half stripped. Think you he was robbed?'

Will sat up and coughed. When he saw the painted cart he was swept with a feeling of unworthy relief. The players' troupe, arrived at last. Of all the people in the world, he thought, they were the least likely to find him ridiculous.

One approached. His face was nut-brown, his worn clothes dust-white from travel: a scorched scarecrow. Yet that something in his walk, in his voice. 'Are you hurt, friend?'

42

Will shook his head. 'A rest,' he gasped. 'A little rest on God's good earth, sir.'

'We thought you ready to be buried in it. Are you faint? Set your head low a moment. It's a trying heat.'

'Let's get on.' A fractious voice behind him. 'Are we turned village constables now? Let him . . . God's blood. Don't I know you?'

Will looked up into the blue-grey eyes, and memory at once filled in the tall, slender figure. Towne. Jack Towne. He had been the principal woman-player with the troupe who visited Stratford last summer. Will had talked long with him at the Swan after the play, buying him drinks, hardly able to believe that this dazzling world-changer was his own age.

'Master Towne. Your servant, sir.'

The fair youth's eyes narrowed. 'I do know you. Will Something. God, yes. We have an admirer here, friends. When I was with Lord Strange's Men, this pretty fellow stood us a good hogshead of ale, I swear, and then recited our speeches back at us.' Towne grasped Will's hand and hauled him to his feet. 'Still in Stratford, hey, Will? I thought you hankering after a better place. You're in a muck of a sweat, what have you been about? I suppose it's harvest and whatnaught.' Towne gestured disdainfully. He was a Londoner, Will remembered. He remembered him, too, playing a robber's stolen bride, spirited and sorrowful: you wanted to jump on the stage and fall before her. 'Come, up and ride on our chariot; the beasts will bear.'

'No, no, there's no need—'

'To please me, then. I've a whim for being the dispenser of benevolence. Naturally it'll pass.'

Will sat on the cart-tail. Above his head pans and tankards swung alongside stage properties: helmets, crowns, banners, a bearskin. A human skull grinned at him through a lady's veil. Jack Towne walked alongside, grumbling about his feet.

'A plague on your country roads. I feel bastinadoed. So how goes it in Stratford, hey, Will? Are your citizens plump in the purse and begging for a play? In truth we've had a wretched season—and to speak frankly, my friend—' Towne raised his voice slightly—'this is a sorry sort of company compared with my last. We have the most lamentable clown. Mind, there's still Knell, mighty shouting William Knell, do you remember him?'

Oak voice, leonine, just warding off fat. 'He played the Lydian King.'

'Aye, and he never ceases to play the king, trust me. But when it comes to kinging it over me . . . He should remember I only *play* the woman.' Towne suddenly, coldly, smiled: it was like something one should not see, a dagger in a drawer. 'Aye, he can act. But his temper's another matter. You can't play and live in the same place. Partitions, Will, nail 'em up secure. God, you look like a man racked.' He reached out and brushed the sweat-sticky hair from Will's brow. 'What *have* you been doing? Not making the beast by the wayside, I hope, and pushing poor Moll in the ditch when you saw us coming.'

'No, chasing a fay,' said Will. He didn't know he could speak so sharply, cutting off the moment like a fowl's head on the stump. 'But I couldn't reach it. Such are our country follies.'

Towne drew back his hand. 'You need a drink. Another way of saying I need a drink. Remind

44

me, what's the best here—ale, cider? I'll share the reckoning.'

'Ale, but I can't. I have work to do.'

'Hang your work. Hang everything, because we are here now, Will, and we bring a little beauty. The one thing there is no living without.' Towne leaped up beside Will and twisted round to prod the heap of blankets in the bed of the cart. 'Isn't that so, shit-pan? Rouse yourself, you lazy bastard, the rest of us have walked all night.' Finding a groan, he added a quick fist. 'There, alive now?'

A great pink tiny-eyed poxed face, like a ham studded with cloves, blubbered up to blink at them.

'Our clown. You'd suppose he'd only to step on the stage to set them laughing, but he counteracts nature, this one. Beauty, sweetling, that's what we bring, eh?'

'Go fuck your mother.' The clown yawned, sitting up and scratching.

'For him, that's wit exceptional,' said Towne, tapping Will's knee. Will refused himself the sight of that long-boned and expressive hand. Rations only, remember, short commons: shrink the appetite. 'I'm right, though, am I not? Oh, to be sure, you can live without beauty—live like a pig in a sty, that is. Life as a long, heavy, drunken sleep with no dreams.'

'Sounds perfection,' the clown said, belching long and musically. 'Who's this?'

'This,' Towne said, clapping Will's shoulder, 'is my excellent friend Will, of Stratford. Will . . . No, don't prompt me, damn it, I have a memory. Will Shakespeare, the glover's son.' He turned on Will a slightly anxious smile of triumph. 'Yes? Or is it the shoemaker?'

45

'No, you have it right,' Will said, firm and dry: the words in his mouth like the heel of a loaf. He prepared to jump down from the cart. 'That's who I am.'

* * *

He slipped out that evening, while his father nodded by the fire. When he chose, Will could wipe himself from the room like chalk from a slate.

Not that this was choice. He couldn't help himself.

* * *

'I can't believe you remember so much of the piece. *Devil's Brother*, the mouldiest thing, full of ranting.' Jack Towne stretched his rangy arms and looked appraisingly at the tankard Will set before him. 'Rots the guts, your rustic brew. Heady, though, agreeable heady.'

'Not the piece so much as what you made of it,' Will said. 'It held so tight. I remember I could hardly believe it was over. Two hours gone in an instant. I had to stamp and pinch myself.' Two hours, like a minute full of everything. All along his body and mind there had been a fine humming, as if the play had plucked him like a bowstring.

'Well, it suited the crowd well enough. Mind, your country John-a-Noakes hardly knows what he claps his great paws for. Not you, though, not you.' Suddenly he ruffled Will's hair from brow to nape. It felt curiously as if all his clothes had been taken off. 'You feed on it, don't you? Feed, gorge,

46

devour.'

'It eats me,' Will said.

'So. Confide.' Towne stretched out his leg to the hearth: it seemed to go on for ever. He was very fair, fine-boned, full-lipped; when he gazed into the fire the robber's bride flickered into life—yet a shift, and you saw the line of stubble under his jaw. It was dazzling and queasy. 'What are you, Will? What do you do between our visitations? I notice you don't stand toes in and chuckle like most of them. Belong to some noble's house hereabouts? Say yes, I pray, you might put me in his favour.'

'Nothing of that. I live with my father. Lately burgess and alderman of Stratford—also bailiff.' Curious that he should now be making much of his father's lost eminence.

'Pretty. And are you eldest? Ah, there must be a tidy property waiting for you.'

Will stared into his untouched ale. A worm of candlelight wriggled in it. 'My father is—still a man of some substance. But his fortunes are decayed of late.'

He struggled with something unsaid, but Jack Towne had flung his long legs out with a sharp laugh. 'Not so bad. *My* father left me naught but whipping-scars. See.' He faced his narrow back to Will and clawed the shirt off his shoulder. Dull pink strokes sulked across the luminous fair skin. Will seemed to feel heat on his face. 'Well, I call him my father. Only God and my mother know who he truly was—but he had the run of my hide every night for five years. How I wept at his plague-bed. I couldn't believe such access of joy possible.'

Towne shrugged his shirt back, and Will thought of his own father: thought of him dying. Or, rather, sprang away scalded from the thought.

'They say it's wrong to be a player,' he burst out, lunging at his drink.

'Aye, they do that, and what, I wish to know, can they mean? We only game and booze, and have no settled place or station, and die in want when we're cast off.' Drunk—yet not as Will was used to seeing men drunk—Towne seized Will's hand, an urgent reinforcement to the scrambling words. 'You know this ranting godly fellow fastened on me at Banbury—Sudbury—some pisshole—and consigned me to his hell because I was an invitation to sodomy. I could only answer that it was not an invitation I would ever extend to him.' He laughed loudly, but the sound was anger diverted. 'Well, *you* surely don't think it wrong, or you wouldn't be keeping company with us.'

'I don't know,' Will said. 'I don't know what I think.' He meant it as a general statement. He spent most of his time thinking, but thought was a current on which he drifted: he didn't steer.

'You're scared of your honest alderman father, no doubt,' Towne said, yawning. 'God's blood, Will, only look at those great baboons.' Across the tap-room two of the players, Knell the king-player and a red-haired gangler, who was drinking sack by the pint, had drawn their swords and were lumbering at each other. 'It's play, good sir, only play,' he called out to the innkeeper, who came sweating and muttering. 'They're running over the last scene of *Alphonsus of Lincoln*. Every stroke planned, sir, like the steps of a galliard. Or should be,' he added to Will. 'Knell is so very apt to forget himself.'

'A most desirable thing,' Will said, feeling the

48

drink quicken and sorrow him all at once.

'But there you have it,' Towne said excitedly, 'exactly what your virtuous, godly citizens do not see. Oh, it's wrong to be a player, they declare. But what do they do when they wake up in the morning? Straight be themselves? No: they remind themselves who they are. They have to. Ah, yes, let me see, I am Goodman Bollockchops, esteemed burgher of Hole-in-the-Road, and yonder lies my wife, whom I choose not to see is faithless, and though I have just dreamed of running naked in the fields with a set of wild lads and lasses, I would see all whores and gypsies and players whipped at the cart-tail and I am grave, deep . . . They have to, because otherwise they're walking on ice and it's cracking. Ever been to London? Well, to be sure, no.' The pitying look was meant, no doubt, to be kind. 'Some winters the Thames freezes clean over. River turns to road. Everyone goes on it—they set up a fair on it and roast chestnuts and tell fortunes, all pretending they're not walking on water—'

'Dear God, don't.'

'Ah, there, you've broken my image. It was about to be mighty profound, I think. I'm drunk, though.' He emptied his tankard, then leaned on Will's shoulder. His breath was unnervingly sweet, like a child's. 'Got a yearning for London, hey? Well, I can understand it. I'll tell you what it is, Will, it's the worst place to starve in. Hereabouts you can lay your bones down by a stream and drink the clear water and, I don't know, perhaps catch a coney, or the old goodwife who's known you since you were a tacker will help you. London, no such matter.' He touched Will's cheek with a gentle, even timid finger. 'What are you looking for, then? It helps if

49

you know where it's to be found first of all.'

'I—I don't know if it's been made yet.'

Behind him a dropped sword skittered on the flagstones. Knell heaped curses on his weak wrist. Towne sat up and raised his tankard to him, catching Knell's eye with a smile that seemed prepared: unpacked from a box.

'Now watch him bluster,' he said, between his teeth.

Knell stalked over. 'Well, now, Master Will, what tales has this stripling been telling you? All lies, whatever they are.'

'We're players,' Towne said, wagging his empty tankard. 'Lies are our business.'

'Another pint? That means he'll be singing "Willow, willow" next. Then declaring his love for all the world. Then challenging all the world to a fight. Then he weeps and sleeps together. All pat without a prompt, for once.'

'Chatter on, old man, while you've still got the teeth for it,' Towne said amiably. 'Will's in love, you know. But the object of his love doesn't exist. What is he to do?'

Will said:

'"You do me wrong to take my guileless words
And free them to the world, like caged birds
That ne'er have op'd their wings beneath the
   sun
Nor learnt the eagle and the hawk to shun."'

'God. I remember that,' Knell said. 'What is it, *Fountain of Ardena?*'

'*Devil's Brother.*' Towne watched Will. 'How does it go on?'

'"For when my heart misgives me, straight my tongue
Must give it ease, as we the—something stone
That galls the tender sole, unthinking shake
From forth our shoe, though—something . . ."'

'No, it's gone.'

'Villainous stuff.' Knell groaned. 'A beautiful maiden hopping about with a stone in her shoe.'

'Errant stone,' Towne said. 'Yes, a feeble figure. Still . . .' He gazed at Will, half drowsy, half penetrating. 'Where do you keep it, Will?'

'Why, man, here,' Knell said, rapping on Will's head. 'You can tell he's no country dull-wit. He admires us for one thing. I only wish you had such a memory.'

'I keep it here,' Will said, after a moment, and touched the space beside him, gently, as if another Will sat there, preferring not to be disturbed.

*   *   *

He was hurrying home, a piece of the night.

Above the roofs the stars swooped with him, and no dogs barked because his feet only skimmed the ground here and there. In his mind a wonderful handiwork was going on. Yes, he had promised his father he would have no more to do with the players, but his father need not know, and even if he did, perhaps he could be brought to understand what was so remarkable about them, the way they conjured something new out of nothing, through craft and wit: that they were makers.

Perhaps that was the true lesson of the day: everything was possible. He had felt it so in the

White Hart tonight, as the talk grew wilder, exciting him even more when understanding ceased. The world was a vast and wonderful thing, and it was also an apple just within reach, heavy for the tug and pluck.

He slipped in through the door of the back kitchen, where the serving-girl slept on a pallet and the old hound on the floor. When the dog stirred he rubbed its jowls and hushed it back down: the beast never realised how much he loathed it.

He got to the foot of the stairs, and there was his father. Will was never sure if he had come out of the parlour, or had simply been standing there all the time, taper in hand.

What he could be sure of, alas, was his own face: how, taken by surprise, he had been unable to hide his expression. His father must have seen it—how weary Will was of him, and how he wished he was not his father.

It was there, in his distant, hurt eyes.

'You needn't lie,' his father said. 'I know where you were. I sent a lad to look.'

'Father . . . I know you don't approve it, but still it can't be so very bad—'

'It's how you make me feel.' Spoken strong and plain, as if to emphasise that Will would not evade this with a great flourish of words. 'It is not the matter itself. When you go against me, it is how you make me feel.'

A quiver on the last word; and Will wanted to cry out, *Do you suppose I don't understand that?*

Understanding was easy. He had understood it when Master Ridley's great grown half-witted boy had laughed at the little child that got mangled under the wheels of the soil-cart: it had been a

52

blaze in that dun, damp mind. Will didn't like or dislike this capacity for picking up feelings; it was like being able to read, you simply couldn't undo it.

And I know how you feel, Father: how life is a barbed sharpness in you like the hook in a fish's mouth. They talk of you behind the hand, pityingly; and Mother is so loyal she will never permit herself the merest whisper of reproach, and so your ears strain and strain in terror of hearing it. And if your own son should turn against you, what deeps of failure are left?

'I'm sorry, Father.'

A shrug. 'I dare say you are, for this moment.' That was acute. He glanced about as if for somewhere to sit down, or to lie: lay himself down for ever. 'And then you go your own way. It's hard, Will. Not merely that you won't be my prentice: that's only the surface. The poison's beneath.'

He turned and groped for the banister, and Will saw that he still bore his stick; and his knuckles as he gripped it were white as the bone beneath.

*   *   *

His mother, soft-spoken and gentle and steely as a cat's paw, came to his room, somehow knowing he was still awake. She sat on his bed.

'I can't bear discord. I know it's wrong of me, because it will always come in life. And I know what the quarrel was about, and I shan't speak on that, Will. Only I hate to see you so . . . so bitter.' She spoke judiciously. His mother handled words like needles and knives.

He sat up. 'What makes you suppose that?'

'I'm wife and mother, I have a hundred eyes

53

and ears. Your father is not always an easy man,
I know that well.' She took his hand. Her fingers
explored as if to discover a palmed coin. 'But try
to understand him. He made his fortune—aye, it
didn't come from what I brought him when we wed,
though there were folk aplenty saying I stooped
to marry him and my portion would soon be lost.'
Mary Arden she had been, kin and heiress to the
highest folk of the district. 'He made himself, and
I was proud. I was proud when he stood highest in
the town. I was proud still when his troubles came
on him. And when my property was lost, then too.
It is the germ and kernel of a man that matters, and
there my love is fixed, and my pride, and I would
have yours too.'

'Yes,' Will said, restive, 'I see it, but we are what
we do, surely.'

His mother's silences were not like his father's.
They made room for you on the soft couch of
second thoughts.

'Let's not talk of this,' he said. 'It's as you say, we
want no more discord.'

'You look weary. I'm keeping you from rest . . .
But do you know what your father said when he
took me to wife? "I feel myself a king." I hope I had
more sense than to let my head be turned by it. But
he is proud as any king, Will. And a king must have
a prince.'

She had got hold of his hand in both of hers now.
Her grip was tight.

'What would you have me do?'

'Nothing: nothing you don't want. I know you
don't wish to be bound prentice to him. But there
are other bonds, natural bonds, and to go against
nature . . . Oh, Will, sometimes you are a little

54

frightening. I don't mean there is anything to fear from you. Only that sometimes—I see you go so far away.'

He shook his head, trying to smile. He thought that no one could be more frightening than her, when it came to it.

'I've mended matters with Father, or I mean to. And—'

'Oh, Will, it's what I wish to hear. Thank you.' She got up. 'Make a proper peace. Don't defy him any more.' Her smile was bright and cool as she looked down and it chilled him. 'Make up your mind to it, Will.'

* * *

It was Joan who took the question out of their hands: Joan who was not yet fourteen in years but twenty in her buxom, bustling figure and twenty more, any age, all woman in her worldly-wise equality to anything. Lately, when the maid had had toothache and fought shy of the barber-surgeon, Joan had borrowed a pair of pliers from the blacksmith and efficiently pulled the tooth herself, drowning the cries with lusty singing.

Will adored her. He sometimes suspected that his father was a little afraid of her. Joan loved light and was a great thrower-open of shutters, and when her guts were disordered she would say so and warn everyone against the privy. Contrast their mother, whose characteristic, muffling phrase was *Let's not speak of it*—especially when John Shakespeare gazed into ale-cup or memory and saw grievance at the bottom. Suspicion, indeed, that Joan was quite capable of saying, *No, let's speak of it, let's open the*

55

shutters on it.

'Father, the players are here and I have never seen them yet. Can I go?'

'Hm. A year or two older, Joan, and then we may speak of it.'

Joan would have none of that judicious rumbling. 'Bess Quiney goes. She's younger than me, and the Quineys lose no reputation by it. And Mistress Sturley was *married* at fourteen. She was telling me of it.'

Will caught a glance from his father that said, *Your doing?* But since dawn he had been making a full, dull, dutiful inventory of the Henley Street premises. And, besides, Joan would not be evaded.

'I don't often ask a boon, Father. Many a girl is forever pestering for trinkets and baubles. But you always find me plain and sober, I hope. Do I disgrace you with trumpery ribbons and bracelets? Lord, I pray not.'

'That is a different question.'

But the question was already lost. Joan was not to be refused what was granted to Alderman Quiney's daughter. She could not, of course, go alone.

So it fell out. Will looked at it as if it were a coin found in the street. Keep it, spend it: still it was not really yours, just a tainted chance. And only a fool would live the rest of his life looking for money on the ground.

*   *   *

Impossible, of course, not to feel it as they shuffled into the Guildhall and the warm wave of babbling sweaty expectancy broke over them. But Will tried

56

to take his cue from Gilbert, who had come along because, as he said, it was better than swatting flies: Gilbert who, at sixteen, had suddenly become a lank, long yawner, wholly phlegmatic in humour, seemingly preparing himself for a lifetime of being unimpressed.

Still Will's senses roared, and at a twitch of the tiring-house curtain his mind went furiously questing like an unmuzzled dog—would there be rhymes and how would they use them? Stamp on them flat-footed or touch them in flight, like a squirrel leaping from branch to branch? Beware. Muzzle, muzzle. Will brought back the picture of himself running frantically towards an unreal horizon, in all its self-pitying absurdity. That did it.

'What a crush,' Joan was saying cheerfully. 'Have a care for your purse: I see low, knavish faces. Brummagem faces, I'd venture. Day to you, day to you. Lord, *she*'s aged. Shouldn't we push forward? However will we hear?'

'The players' voices carry,' Will said.

'You mean they shout? I shan't care for two hours' shouting.'

'No. Or only the worst. It's different . . .'

As he turned, the face turned, like a page in a book trying to bring the next with it.

She was ten feet away. For some stilled, carved moments they looked at each other. Nothing of greeting or recognition. It was as if the look came in the middle of a deep discourse, at the posing of an unanswerable question.

Joan prodded him. 'What are you staring at?' She followed Will's gaze. 'Oh, her.'

'Mistress Hathaway. From Shottery,' he heard himself say.

'Aye, I know her. Well, we've often passed the time of day at the butter market. Her name is Anne,' Joan said loftily. 'Let's give her good day, then. Lord, I wonder men ever come to know anyone.'

True enough, thought Will, as Joan accosted Mistress Hathaway with easy nothings, joining the parties together. Such heat! Aye, but then the season—aye, so . . . The big boy was with her, round-eyed and damp-fringed. 'My stepbrother,' he heard her say—just: her voice was the very opposite of carrying, a leaf swept away by the swollen stream of noise.

'Sweet chick. Never been at a play before, heart? No more have I. We shall look to each other.' Joan took Will and Gilbert by the arm. 'Now, these great burdens are *my* brothers. Was ever woman attended by two such loobies? Like overgrowing beans, and me the stick.'

Anne smiled. Her name—'Mistress Hathaway, I pray you well'—her name is Anne. She acknowledged his bow. That smile. It touched like the waking from a nightmare—the realisation of the beauty of reality, which never lasted as long as it should. Anne.

On the stage the clown burst out, cutting a flaccid caper: Jack Towne was right. But the audience rippled and quieted and gathered its attention. Anne among them: her long, tight-sleeved arm gathered the boy in front of her as they faced the stage. Two hand breadth of white neck between collar and coif-netted hair—like caged honey— presented itself to Will's fidgeting eye. But what then? This: everything about her was beautiful. It made that lazy, spoiled word do its work at last,

58

and he had known that when he had stood boyish before her at Hewlands Farm, but what then? It was nothing to do with him. Will glanced around. Townsfolk standing at ease, country folk craning, still smutted with the dust of their journey. Children perching on shoulders, clapping uncertainly. The clown, teetering on the edge of the stage, was yelling back at a fist-shaking woman. 'You want to cuff me, did you say, sweetling? Cuff me? Spell it backwards, that's what you truly want.' He mimed it with fat thrustings, feeling himself through his parti-coloured breeches.

That smile. It didn't last as long as it should. It seemed to Will that to coax and tend that smile, to bring it into the world, would be something worth.

The clown waddled off, the play began. 'The Right Tragical History of Darius King of Persia, as it has been acted before Her Majesty the Queen . . .' The King hurried to the edge of the stage to tell them urgently of the fate that hung over him. It was William Knell yet not so: all king now, no player.

The rafters of the Guildhall became the arches of Babylon. A shift, a change. You couldn't be aware of it any more than you could pinpoint the moment when you fell asleep. Joan threw herself into it, Will saw with pleasure, gasping at every cruelty, hands flying to her cheeks in pity: as if everything were really happening in a room that she happened to be in. As it should be.

But for the first time Will's attention was split. He kept watching Anne's face, almost as if it were part of the play. Judging the tragedy by the lights and shades it drew on that face. It seemed to him that other faces were like blank leaves compared to hers, where a whole busy page of text invited the eye to read.

Meanwhile two vast young women at her side, sharing a cider-jug that they passed to each other like an infant to be nursed, grew larger with drink and self-love and began crowding her out. They wanted to be reproved, so they could enjoy a quarrel or shouting-match. But Anne simply coiled her stepbrother closer and took up less room. He saw not shyness, not absence of will, but a pure refusal of contention: so pure it stretched out for ever, an infinite quiet denial of the stupid and ugly. He moved.

'Mistress, come this side of me, there's more room.'

He made the space, and preserved it with taut back and stiff elbows. Her lips moved, perhaps thanks. He preferred none. As the play neared its catastrophe, he observed her—as Joan was— shifting her weight from one foot to the other: the boy was sitting on the ground at her feet. A play was a long time standing unless you were, like him, insane about it.

'Will! What are you doing?'

'Offering comfort,' he said to Joan, on his knees. He had sometimes seen men do this for their womenfolk at the play, as two hours turned into three. Young men often propped each other up back to back. 'Lean on me. Do it, please.' He did not quite turn his head. 'Mistress Hathaway—if you will.'

Joan, giggling, leaned her weight on his shoulder at once. In Anne's short hesitation he found time for a surmise that he had mortally, everlastingly, offended her; and to wonder what that meant to him. When she laid her hand on his shoulder everything else, thought, emotion, gave way to sensation. The breathing weight and warmth of her astonished him. It was as if he had never touched a human being before. Eighteen years old: eighteen years' worth of living, and now it seemed a long, fusty drowse before a proper waking.

He never wanted a play to end. But this was different. Of course he could not kneel for ever; but it was enough to imagine doing it, to see himself lit by the new blaze of possibility.

* * *

Outside the Guildhall Joan, stretching, yawning, chattering all at once, was still in command. 'Lord, how bright it is—I feel like a mole. That clown was monstrous, was he not? He tried to fix *my* eye when he did that shocking jig, but I would have none of him. Still, I had to laugh. Pooh, don't look, mistress, the beasts, they might wait until they get home.' Along an alleyway beside the Guildhall a file of groaning men were emptying their bladders against the wall. 'A pity the play brings out the low sort, for it's a pleasant, pretty diversion after all. Does no one fetch you, Anne? Then you must have Will attend you home. No, I insist, I have only Henley Street to go to and Gilbert with me, but I can't think of you and your chick plying the Shottery road alone, not when I've seen such Brummagem faces about.'

It should have been me proposing that, Will thought. He was glad to be doing it but faintly sick, queasy with doubt. Why? Perhaps because, although they took the Shottery field path at a slow enough pace, in his mind he felt himself running again full pelt, running beyond his reach.

'Looks like a poorish harvest,' he said, then wondered if these were her brother's fields.

'Does it?' Her look was surprised, then awkward. 'I'm never good at judging these things.'

He had an empty-handed feeling, as if he were trying to make a purchase with no money. Then he remembered the unborn calf, and thought that perhaps she could never forgive him for seeing her in extremity, and wondered if they could walk all the way to Hewlands Farm in silence. They might have, if it had not been for the boy, John. Freed from physical constriction, he was a wild thing, climbing, leaping, tumbling, rolling in mud.

'John, come down from there—you'll hurt yourself.'

'I never hurt myself.' He landed at their feet clutching a broken branch, thwacked himself across the head with it. 'See?' He squinted up at Will. 'Did you like that play?'

'Aye, did you?'

'It went on too long.' The boy flung the stick and hared off, flapping his arms and shrieking.

'I can remember being like that,' Will said, then stilled his tongue disgustedly. The remark exposed his youth; besides, it was sheer cant. He could not recall ever feeling that degree of abandon even as a child. Yielding to the moment—no, it meant losing sight of the moment before and the moment after. He needed to see all round.

'Did you really like the play?' she asked.

'I like all plays. I like them better than life.' A crude statement, but it was a relief to find himself saying something true. 'Did you not care for it?'

'I wonder they can remember all those speeches. It is very clever.'

'But no more?'

Even so gentle a pressure seemed to make her withdraw, her lips biting back the words. Hers was no token blush: you were reminded that it was made of blood. He thought: Shyness? But how could you be shy, fortified by that beauty and grace? How not cry defiance from the battlements?

'I felt it was not real,' she said at last. 'But perhaps I take after my brother. He says the play is idle feigning and breeds vain dreams.'

Will had not supposed Master Hathaway a Puritan; though, of course, there were many shades beside the hard crow-black piety of the Fields. 'But he didn't mind your going?'

She shook her head. 'I may do as I like,' she said. Somehow it sounded like the wretchedest of confessions.

John came back to them, leaping and stamping. 'There, Anne. I treaded on your shadow, that means you're dead.'

'Trod, not treaded.'

'Treaded and deaded. Treaded and deaded . . .'

'All that rhyming has got into his wits,' she murmured, without approval. The boy sang it over and over, wildly stamping.

'You're dead, you're dead, and that's good . . .' He rasped his tongue, dancing backwards. Suddenly there was fury in her face and she was after him.

'For shame—shame on you, to say that . . .'

Will wanted to call her back, to say it was only childish silliness. But there was, after all, something grim about it. And when she caught up with the squealing boy she did not collar him or hit him. Her blue, crackling-blue, eyes were all she needed to hold him still. Hitching her skirts she jumped neatly

63

on his shadow.

'Now you're dead,' she said. 'Is that good?'

The boy pouted, big face half stricken, half mutinous. Will saw the resemblance to the farmer. He seemed to see other things, in vanishing glimpses.

'Come now, let's kiss,' she said, on a plain tender note. The boy clung to her passionately for a moment, then pulled away, pointing at Will.

'Make him dead now.'

She straightened, glancing at Will's shadow on the grass, then at his face.

'No need,' he said. 'You've already killed me.'

'No, she hasn't.' The boy groaned impatiently. 'Here, I'll do it.' That gave a little space, in which what Will had said could reverberate. He wondered at himself for having said it: not with regret—though that might come—but with a giant amaze, for suddenly it seemed possible that he could say anything.

Anne shook her head slightly; a slight smile likewise. He felt she would always temper the sharpness of the negative. 'No, I think you are living yet.'

She turned to walk on. To her mind he had said, perhaps, one of those things that were not real.

He followed. It was not far to Hewlands Farm now, but it didn't matter: now, with his heart clanging rough music to break an age of silence, it didn't matter how far he had to go.

64

3

The Triumph of Beauty (1582)

A gift of gloves.

Is this, Anne wonders, the moment?

When he presents them to her they are outside, naturally. Outside is their indoors, the wood their closed chamber. (*Not the house*, she told him, when they first began to meet.) Summer holds fast. Woodbine and dog-rose grow in tangles, in aromatic and sticky tunnels. Butterflies stumble along winding lanes of hot air. Too warm for gloves, but these are a gift, made by him.

A silent signal. She extends her right hand. With infinite care he draws the glove on to it, though his own hands are slightly trembling. Perhaps that is the moment: observing that tremble, and how it elevates her, so that the fallen trunk she sits on sheds its moss and fungus, and turns throne.

The limp kid fingers fill and stiffen. He inches the cuff up her wrist, past a million thrilling pinpoints.

And surely this should be the moment—if she is certain of her throne, certain of him at her feet. She doesn't shrink from anything in him: looking on the dark waving crown of hair, broad brow, long-lashed salt-grey eyes, she is invited and beguiled. His youth, of which he is so conscious, seems to her a zenith, not a falling short; hard to imagine him burning any brighter than this.

'It's beautiful making,' she says, flexing her hand, as a wand of sunlight conjures the intricate tracery of beads.

He shrugs. 'An attempt. I wanted to put myself into every stitch.' He laughs nervously. 'And then I wanted to take myself out. To make the making better . . . No matter. Next your skin it can only be a snarl and a cobble.'

Anne accepts the gift of gloves. But beyond that lies another acceptance, and there she still shrinks. Because now she knows something terrifying about herself: that her *yes* is not a word but a shout; that you can set the world before her and she, for the right thing, for the right love, will tip it all over like a drunkard with an inn-table, devoted to that dreaming fire in the head.

But before the gift there was Lammas-feast: perhaps it began then. Bartholomew invited Will to it, after he had escorted her home from the play. 'My thanks, Master Shakespeare. We hold Lammas-feast tomorrow, come join us.' It was thrown out in absently genial mood. Later, across the tumult of the supper-table, she intercepted a speculative look from him. 'So, Anne,' he said. But soon he was diverted by Bella: pregnant, and not eating hugely enough for his liking. Though she hardly shows, he is always touching and caressing her belly lately: as if he wants to hatch it. He is convinced it will be a son. For Bartholomew the past is of no interest at all, and the present an impatience: he lives in the future, of which he is amazingly unafraid.

And lately he has also been making some changes, like the disposing of the last of their father's clothes as gifts to the farm servants. Good and right. She is bored by her own grief, its slow circularity, the windmill creak of it.

Lammas-feast, then. Bartholomew is one of the few farmers to keep it up: some call it popish. 'If they work hard, let them have a little play,' is how Bartholomew sees it. Trestles in the barn, a hogshead of ale, flitches of bacon; the farmhands at ease with him as he trades jokes and matches them pint for pint. When Will comes in she realises she has been waiting for this: not simply his arrival but how he will look against this background.

Bartholomew beckons him to the seat by his side, sets before him a heaped trencher. Her brother's white teeth crunch away at onions and crackling as if noise is half the pleasure of eating.

Will—he eats too, converses, he doesn't look out of place. But again Anne notices this about him: while many people sprawl in the world as if it is their own fireside, to see him is to think of a traveller at an inn, making a temporary separate comfort with wrapped cloak, the corner of a settle, his thoughts.

Evening squeezes its juicy light through the high slit windows, an incredible gold: the pewter dish in front of her glitters like a precious artefact. Resentfully she seeks and avoids Will's eye. *Why*, she thinks, *do you come to destroy my peace?*

Bartholomew is on his feet and seizing Nathaniel, the shepherd's lad, by the shoulder. Hauling him up.

'Now hark ye, good people, I heard a tale about friend Nathaniel here, as you have likewise perhaps. A tale of a man and a maid, or shall we say a maid unmade?' Bartholomew's arm grips Nathaniel's neck, not letting go. 'How old are you, my buck? Eighteen? We'll say a man, then. Certain you've played a man's part with little Alice Barr, and now she's not so little neither. Where is she? Come, Alice, now's not the time to be shy . . .'

Everyone is laughing as Bartholomew marches the lad over to staring blushing Alice.

'Come, clasp hands. There's a picture. Tell me, now, if I'm mistook, for it's no small matter. Eh, Alice? Not small, was it?' Bartholomew's grin is broad and hard. 'What I surmise is, you were both thinking so much of your marrying day that your thoughts ran clean away with you. Well, as long as you fix the day now, my friends, I've naught to say against it. I'll even give you a bridal present. To the church in the morning, Nathaniel, to pray the banns, hey? Yes or no?'

It is admirable how he sets these things straight. Loud claps and cheers as he pushes the pair into a kiss. No bastards on the parish. On the way back to his seat he slips his arms around Bella and again caresses her belly. Teeming wombs and proper households. Anne rises to her feet, feeling sere and light, as if a breeze would bowl the husk of her across the threshing-floor.

She has to get away from this, but conscience will allow only an escape to duty. Her stepmother's chamber. Before her apoplexy, Stepmother would have been on highest form at Lammas-feast: the overflowing hostess, dancing, joking, ladling, rapping knuckles. A little better today, she completes a turn of the room on Anne's arm; her speech is clearer. One day soon, she mews, as Anne settles her, she wants to come downstairs.

'You will.' Anne has no doubt of that. She's strong, determined: she'll take her place as chatelaine again. 'I want . . .' She tucks the pillow behind her stepmother's neck. 'I want a world where nothing is cheap.'

At the foot of the staircase Anne finds him waiting for her.

'I wondered—I thought you unwell, perhaps.'

'No. I wanted to be, just for a little, without company.'

That comes out harsher than she intends it—but, no, she is angry. Angry at herself, for the vertical spider-ascent of her heart when she saw his face. Angry at him, for the fear he prompts in her—the fear that he does not mean it. If he does not mean it, then—

'I'm not company,' he says. 'I can be, if you like. Otherwise I can be nothing.'

'No one can be nothing,' she says, thinking: Oh, yes, yes, they can.

'Just the creak of the board under your foot, then. The fly on that window-pane. That feeling in the air, when there's feasting, of something unsatisfactory that makes you want to smash through it all. You feel it, I know.'

His smile, his eyes are bright and fierce: a glitter from the bottom of a deep well of unhappiness. But, then, perhaps Bartholomew has been plying him with too much drink.

'Really, you know nothing of me,' she says, ready to pass him.

'Certain, for I know nothing of myself, and I have lived with myself these eighteen years. But what's knowing? You know what clouds look like. Lie on your back and gaze at a cloud until you feel yourself turning into it. Still you wouldn't know its twin next day.' From the barn comes the squeaking of a rebec. 'They're dancing.'

'Then go dance.'

'I don't know whether to say how afraid of you I am. It might make you pity me, which would be something.'

Oh, drunk, nonsensical. 'You make a game of me.'

He only touches her arm to detain her, but when she shakes off his hand he seems still to be holding her. 'Never,' he says. 'Never, that's all.'

'I've heard about men and their *never*, sir. Never will I forsake and never will I this and that—'

'I am not *men*. Nor Stratford man nor Englishman nor young man, I hate that, damnation on all flocks and herds,' he says, breathing hard. 'Am I allowed to fall in love with you, yes or no?'

'No,' she says, all fear now: because now it is as if a fay sits in the corner of your chamber, and says, yes, all the tales were true, we're real, and so let us bargain.

'Not even hopelessly?'

He has drawn a smile from her before she knows it; but with everything he says she has a sense of trying feverishly to catch him up.

She says: 'You're very young.'

'I shave, I'm breeched. And you, are you a grandam disguised? If my youth is the only fence I must climb, then tell me. There's hope in that.' The music rises. 'That's a bransle. Dance it with me. Then I'll ask nothing more.'

'Until the next time.' She realises that this is a kind of yes. Was this the moment? 'You can't—you can't truly be afraid of me.'

He thinks. Then answers, reasonably: 'What else is love?'

*　　　*　　　*

70

A gift of gloves.

When he was stitching them, he tried to think beyond the deadness of kid and thread to the living hand, all the things it did, gesturing, touching, lying curled and defenceless in sleep. The beauty beyond.

Sometimes he asked himself what he was doing. And he had no answer. With Anne, with this beauty, he had been shown something: something for which there were no available responses. As if an old friend had taken you to his stable and there shown you, with a shrug and a smile, a unicorn quietly feeding.

Sometimes he took out Richard's bundle of print and read over again the set of love-verses, as if they might help him. But often the poet seemed in love with love, which made him uncomfortable. And the hopelessness was excessive. The poet didn't even aim to win the fair mistress. And Will, though he might doubt his reach, was certain of his aim.

*   *   *

A Queen's Scholarship: Ben aimed at it with every dram of will.

The Queen's Scholars had their whole education paid for by the Crown: no more niggling guilt about the cost of his schooling. Then, once a Queen's Scholar, you could compete for a further scholarship to Oxford or Cambridge. Ben had never been further than Tottenham Fields, but he knew those universities as places of the mind, and mightily beautiful places they were. He dreamed of them often as he grew out of the first form, out of three pairs of shoes, out of all intimidation—

his large hands, he found, made superb fists. The dreams were all the more exquisite compared with the reality of his stepfather spitting into the fire and grumbling about the dearness of the times. Oh, Ben was on the right road, and grateful—a hundred times grateful. He had to assure himself of that when he first met disappointment, the stinking hairy beast.

'They don't judge only on your abilities as a scholar,' Master Camden said afterwards. 'If it were simply that, then . . . Look here, I'll say this and trust you never to repeat it. If it were only learning and aptness, Benjamin, you would have no competition, anywhere.'

'Thank you,' Ben said whitely.

'I'm not looking for thanks. I'm trying to explain. They must take into account other things. There may be boys of promise—perhaps not promise like yours—who have no friends at all to help them. No mothers, fathers, perhaps. Whereas you—'

'Whereas I have a stepfather in a respectable line of trade,' Ben said dully.

They were walking in the old cloister, and Master Camden seemed in two minds about whether or not to put his hand on Ben's shoulder. It suggested, of course, commiseration, and he was trying to avoid admitting there was anything for which to commiserate. Ben was mentally engaged in going over it again: his examination before the seven reverend gentlemen, the gowned scholars of Oxford and Cambridge, close caps tight on their skulls, as if bandaging their throbbing minds. He had been conscious of nothing but exhilaration at being asked questions; and a certain whooping surprise at how easy those questions were. Really they might have thought of something more original. Asked to decline *amicus*, he did it backwards, to liven it up.

'It's a pity, but you will still be here, and I will still be here,' Master Camden said. 'Whatever I can do for you, I will, trust me. The scholarship is not all.'

Alas, untrue.

Well: here it was. Failure. Ben shed some tears—so privately, in such violent solitude, that he reckoned God himself could hardly see their blotted sparkle—but, after studying himself, did not anticipate more. For one thing, he knew he was the best, whether it was recognised or not. For another—well, what sort of person did he wish to be? Looking about him in Westminster's tight, toiling streets, he seemed to see so many people who were resigned to life. Not him. The best way to wake up in the morning, he felt, was with the thought: Right—today I get my revenge.

The scholarship vanished, but Master Camden remained, and he devoted as much time as he could to Ben. 'If I can leave one classical scholar behind me,' he said, 'it will more than make up for my poor broken-backed history.' He spoke of it always in these terms; but in his lodging Ben saw the pages of manuscript growing, and letters came to him from scholars all over Europe. In Latin, language of the civilised man from Scotland to Sicily. 'English will do for a bill of lading, a ballad or tale perhaps,' Master Camden said, 'but it is still not a fit instrument for higher literature.'

'Yet you're writing our history.'

'In Latin. Our tongue is loose and profuse, perhaps because so many tongues have gone into the making of it. And still do. English is capacious, a great full warm cloak—but lacking shape and order. No one can agree even on a simple spelling.'

'I prefer order,' Ben said. It was true. But he knew its riotous opposite—looked, sometimes, flinching and fascinated, into its mirror-face. There came the time when his stepfather's longing for a child of his own bore fruit. His mother quickened: what had seemed impossible, after so long, was here at last. His stepfather went around whistling. At night Ben heard his hammer in the attic room: making a cradle. Robert even invited Ben to look at it.

'Well? What do you think?'

Ben wasn't touched, exactly, but it was possible to imagine being so. The cradle was a little lopsided: his stepfather was oddly unhandy about everything except bricklaying, which was perplexing—Ben liked people to be consistent, even in their failings. His stepfather flushed at Ben's silence.

'What, jealous already? The poor babe's not born yet.'

He spat and went away. The next evening when Ben came home from school he found his stepfather sitting grey with his great hands loose between his knees, and the parish midwife there, though with nothing to do.

'She's abed, resting up. Miscarried.' From upstairs he heard his mother weeping, a restrained, limited sound like a cat's mew. 'Naught to be done. She'll mend, and that's a blessing, but I doubt you'll see a live child from her womb, not this late. As for that poor little thing, good master, I've heard the priest say when it's so early there's no sin in just putting it on the fire.'

And later Ben was a spectator of his stepfather's rage. The man took an axe to the cradle, made a fire in the yard with the pieces, then, snorting, got hold of the tiles with which he had been meaning to mend the outhouse roof and tossed and flung them. The smashing noise brought his neighbour out complaining, and a part of Ben said eagerly: *Now* we shall see something. But the fury and violence seemed to Ben half-hearted, in the circumstances: his stepfather broke the neighbour's head and kicked his dog bloody, but then tailed off into oaths, and finished with tears. So great a grief needed killing, Ben thought, and, hearing his stepfather's footsteps outside his room that night, wondered if the true blows would fall on him. But the man staggered on to bed, and snored.

All he said to Ben the next day was: 'Neither of you wanted it. So between you it didn't stand a chance.'

His mother never spoke of it. Sometimes afterwards Ben would see her gaze at her husband when his back was turned, as you might gaze at someone in a crowd, trying to remember where you had seen them before.

'Begin with prose,' Master Camden told him, pen hovering over Ben's Latin verses. 'These lines are running away with you, and taking the thought with them. First see the thought clear, next set it out straight in prose. Only then turn it into verses. Otherwise you are writing into the dark.'

Ben obeyed, because in Master Camden he saw a mind superior to his own. But writing into the dark—he knew about that, reading likewise, eking out the taper with a wedge of moonlight. In fact, it was a fair image of how he lived. For now, there was the certain daylight of the school; beyond, all was dubiety. He had heard of the grand grammatical combats when the Queen's Scholars competed for the university scholarships, parsing and construing with the speed of fencers; tried not to imagine himself among them, and failed. He was too young and vigorous for despair. Still, he took to walking home a different way, because outside the pastry-cook's there was a blind bird in a cage, and somehow he could no longer bear to look at it.

*　　　*　　　*

It is a kind of double courtship—allowing her, perhaps, to think of it as no courtship at all.

There is Will as the acceptable presence in the house, on the loose rope of acquaintance, genially tugged by Bartholomew: 'How, Master Shakespeare, what cheer? Come see the nag I've bought.' (But since Lammas-feast, since they danced the bransle, there is a new crisp look of assessment in her brother's eye even as he shoulder-claps.) Bella, all vast breasts and placid ankles, urges Will to sit here, take another bite of this, come eat up. As if men are like geese, only good when fattened. This Will is, for Anne, miserably reduced. Just Master Shakespeare the glover's son, who goes often to Hewlands Farm, they say: aye, I wonder. It is like that—like nothing, in other words.

Outside is different.

Outside the gift of gloves is possible. Outside he is not diminished but multiplied. Along the bare field path he conjures a company; he peoples the wood. Daphne runs from Apollo towards the

76

Evesham road.

'It's a heathen tale, surely . . . But which part of her turned tree first?'

'However you like. I always see leaves fluttering at the ends of her hair.'

'Pretty. But, oh, fie, heathen. These gods, falling in love with people.'

'The more gods they.'

Or when the mimic mood is on him, he brings all Stratford before her. The Goodwins, tailors, father and son. You suppose Master Goodwin the oldest man in the world until Old Master Goodwin totters after him. Will gives their high, hissing voices and blinds himself with their rheumy chuckle-tears. 'Small beer only for the younker—he's boisterous.' The invisible tankard weaves an incredible trembling journey to his lips, only to be dashed by the entrance of Master Hobb, now Puritan, once a drunkard. 'Do you know how it feels to have a spear thrust in your side, friend?' Poor Master Goodwin ashamed that he does not. 'And then the laying-on of whips, and scorpions—'

'What have scorpions to do with anything?' cries Dame Summers.

'I can hardly give you a notion of her carriage,' Will says, 'except that she smiles with her breasts.'

'Fie, Will, for shame.'

'Aye, but she does. A woman of courtesy, though.'

'Leave go your preaching, Master Hobb. It's lucky I'm a lady, else I'd say you're a shitten hypocrite. And not to speak ill of the dead, but your wife was a double-dyed strumpet. Lord, I only mention common knowledge!'

And now who is this treading gravely on to the

scene, with Will leaning back a little at the hips to suggest a belly, his slowly twiddling fingers evoking heavy rings? 'Enough of this frippery. We must speak of matters of true import. After the late fire in Sheep Street, which consumed, item, one signboard, item, one sack, it is our decision that henceforth every alderman shall supply at his own charge two leather buckets, and every burgess one leather bucket, against the possibilities of future conflagrations. Alderman Quiney asks whether he may not supply one and a half buckets, given the dearness of the times, but the council is not empowered to consider the question of half buckets—'

'Who is *that*?' Anne cries, laughing as she pulls him, breathless, to the ground.

'Nobody.' For a moment he looks as frightened and furtive as if he has found a dripping dagger in his hand.

She wonders, touches his face. 'Are you afraid you'll lose yourself altogether when you do that?'

'That's the last thing I fear.'

'I do want this, you know.'

He brightens. 'I know.'

'Oh, conceited man. Give me that kiss, then.'

'Which?'

'The one from yesterday—that went so. So . . .'

And outside this is possible too. This, the urgent collapse, sun a straw-stabbing halo round their heads, which push and fight for the angle of kiss that will surpass the last.

She does want it, this overthrow of sense and senses, though it is a jewel without a setting and she cannot imagine it stitched on to any part of her plain-stuff life. At last the freeing of lips and hands leads them to a new licence, where the forbidden is hardly distinguishable from the unknown.

'I'll stop. We should stop.'

'No.'

This is surely the moment, because of what it is not. Oh, she knows what the voice from the well of dullness would call it: *a roll in the hay*. But that comprehends nothing of this green bower they have made and the terrible intensity they bring to it. It comprehends nothing of the vast inquisition in Anne, expanding mind, heart, flesh; how she sees every part of her life funnelling towards this moment—the dutiful child, the young woman who wished for the child's certainties, the woman hiding in the night. As she holds him to her, gasping not so much in pain as at her own body's opened strangeness, she realises how long she has been waiting for something she can give herself to.

*   *   *

'And this maiden was so gentle,' Will went on, 'that wild birds would take food from her hand.'

Edmund, who would not sleep without a tale from Will, lay slowly blinking at the taper. There was a special, final blink, before sleep, that seemed almost audible, like the click of a latch. Not yet.

'More.'

'She put the breadcrumbs in her hand, and whistled to them . . .' Not the way it really was, but that belonged only to him. They had taken a loaf and cheese out to the fields. Anne threw bread to some sparrows and starlings, drawing them nearer. At last she had put breadcrumbs on her palm and laid it flat on the grass. The sparrows would have none of it. One starling strutted in a circle, eyeing her from every angle.

'They won't,' Will said. 'Not wild birds. Or only in a starveling winter.'

But in a laughing way she was determined. 'I look too big, I think,' she said, and dropped down, hand extended. The starling fluttered, retreated, circled.

'You're still human.'

'It's because I'm looking. Dumb creatures can never meet our eyes.' She had rolled slowly over on to her back, till she was staring at the sky, arm outstretched, bread still on her palm.

'Now it fancies you mad,' he said. But he realised that Anne could never look ridiculous: nature would not allow it. He was often confronted by these sudden revelations lately, as if he were starting from sleep even while he was awake. The starling had waddled forward: then scurried, snatched the bread, was gone all in a second.

'I never felt it,' Anne said, sitting up, laughing at herself, but pleased. 'So light and quick—I never felt a thing . . .' Will had trapped her laugh with his open lips.

'More,' murmured Edmund.

'This maiden was so tender-hearted,' Will went on, 'that she could not bear to see an egg broke in the pan.' Or rather, he thought, her tender-heartedness was how she apprehended the world: she carried it delicately before her, like the tapping stick of a blind man. 'She lived in a high castle far beyond the clouds.' He wrested the tale towards fantasy as fierce surges of memory shook him. All that schoolboy talk of rutting and rooting—how wrong it had been, with its robust purposefulness,

80

when the act was really so indeterminate, a ticklish tightrope of almost-pain and held-in sneeze, an insane wanting of what you already had, as if you were sated and hungry all at once. Afterwards, that first time, he had been divided between wanting to sob helplessly in her arms and wanting to become immediately a greatly good, strong, sober, wise person, whom she could trust for ever more.

He found himself saying: 'We should not do this again.'

'No,' she said. She covered herself neatly, modestly: not with haste. He knew they would.

Once, in the house. He knew her feeling about the place, but that day Bartholomew had taken everyone to the churching of a cousin at Temple Grafton, and Anne had stayed home to see to her stepmother, and somehow it fell out. He wondered afterwards if it had been a test— whether of him, or of herself, was another question. He liked the amplitude of the house, the stored hen-belly warmth under the thatch, the feeling that another room would always open out beyond the next footworn step. But Anne moved about it stiff-necked, always just beyond arm's-length, as if leaving space for a third person between them.

So Will asked about him: what he was like.

'Oh, Bartholomew thinks I'm a great fool about him. You will hear nothing but nonsense from me on that matter, believe me.' Her eyes roamed painfully behind a tight smile.

'I don't much care what Bartholomew thinks.'

'But you should.' She began trimming the apple boughs that hung from the kitchen beams, and she, too, was sharp and dry and splintery. 'He is a good deal better than me. He's healthful. I'm sick. No, I

81

am, Will: you should see this about me, you should see clear and true.'

'There isn't any seeing true,' he said. 'There's only seeing.'

She crushed the withered twigs in her hand. 'No. You're sick too, if you think so.'

'Good, I want to be. Look there, you've made dust. Turn this way, look at it in the beam of light. See how it dances.'

She eluded his grasp. 'Dust, dead dust.'

'Living. Why all this of health and sickness? Do you miss your father too much, is that it?'

'Aye, there's my brother's true note, well struck, Will, only have a care. You personate so well that some might say you never speak for yourself at all, never sincere, never from the heart.' She twisted away from him, looked him up and down as if to assess the wound of that. 'Is this to say I loved him too much? What has love to do with *too much*?'

'I don't know. You see, I still don't know what he was like. Was he always dead? I only wonder, because I can't see the purpose of a man's living on this earth and striving and laughing—aye, did he laugh, Anne, plump from the belly or high through the nose?—and loving and being loved, only to be thought of as someone who died. Naught else to him. A pinch of dust. A sigh. And this by the one who loved him best of all—'

'I didn't love him best. Bartholomew loved him best—straight and honest, according to his bond, not changing his feeling when Father took the stick to him. If Father had taken it to me, do you know what I would have done? I would have withheld my love from him. I would have made him suffer, made him pay. That was my love, Will. All conditions. As

82

long as he let me be wrong, and never tried to make me right . . .'

'Don't weep. Come, hush, don't.'

'And now you indulge me as he did.'

'So I shall always. I'm yours, you see.'

'He did laugh. It was low and soft, half hidden somehow—like a man feeding scraps to a dog under the table. Oh, I'm yours too, Will. But isn't it frightening? Love isn't like anything else. It's saying, "Here is the secret vein, here is where I bleed."'

Later they went into her bedchamber. It was full of dancing dust as he undressed her. Some of her tension had eased—or passed to him, perhaps. How complex these garments—the sleeves laced to the gown, the kirtle tied to the bodice, bodice pinned over shift: clothes as a maze. She smiled, white above gartered hose. 'Believe me, easier to undo than to do.' Even as her nakedness blinded him, felled him like a stick across the back of the knees, he felt the presence of the house. He was almost inhibited. Light melted from the window, died along the floorboards; cooling timbers gave sudden creaks, loud as slamming doors. They clung and whispered, made love like conspiracy, planting gunpowder.

'More,' Edmund croaked.

Will blinked and shuddered.

'There is no more,' he said. 'That's the end of the story.'

*   *   *

It's the butter and eggs that set it off. The smell of the butter especially, but also its yellowness and

83

greasiness and the soft weight of it in the cloth. She sells hers quickly, going below fourpence a pound just to be rid, but it seems to cling to her fingers and she has to swallow hard, again and again, trying to fix her eyes on something still and astringent. But everything in the market looks in sweet, greasy motion. Women's necks and breasts ripple like buttermilk; and the noise of their voices swirls round the fragile basin of her head.

'There, Mistress Hathaway, I'm glad there's someone feels as I do. It *is* unseasonable warm, is it not? There ought to be that sharp apple-bite in the air by now. Instead I feel, phew, quite smothered.'

Joan Shakespeare clasps her hand. Joan's presence is tart and refreshing—good: Anne swallows successfully. But then Joan draws her attention to the eggs.

'A pretty basket there, but they aren't selling, are they? I think folk mistrust eggs in this weather. An egg may look fair, after all, but what's inside?'

That does it: thinking of what's inside. Anne runs retching.

Come, butter, come. The rhyme goes through her head as she finds an alley-corner and leans in, spattering helpless shame. *Peter stands at the gate, Waiting for a buttered cake.* Recited over the churn to make it turn. Churn, churn. She has never been so sick, unless you count yesterday. Joan waits at a tactful distance.

'I'm sorry. This is dreadful—' Impossible, but there's more.

'Dreadful for you,' says Joan, drawing back her skirts. 'But at least we know what it is now.'

Bent double, Anne gasps and stares and blinks up at the sagely nodding girl.

'Bless you, don't try to talk yet. Why, it was when I mentioned eggs, wasn't it? I'll lay odds you've eaten a bad egg this day. It's curious how someone has only to say the word, and up it comes. Oh, I beg pardon, I shouldn't say that.'

'No, no. Better now . . .' Better, but not good, and soon kind, bracing Joan has taken her arm and her weight and is insisting she come to Henley Street and rest. It's but a step, and she surely cannot go back to Shottery like that; indeed, Joan won't hear of it . . .

So now—of all times—she is to see Will's home, meet his family: to cross over. Oh, it has hung there as a thought, like a bunch of herbs drying in the still-room, eventually to be attended to. But not like this, with her new knowledge. (Thinking of what's inside.) How *does* she know? It's not just the missed courses and the sickness. Somehow an inner voice has said, *Yes*, a voice she hardly recognises as her own: womanly wisdom, it must be, though Anne has never believed herself liable to such a thing. She can imagine herself old, very easily, but not wise.

And here it is, the house where he was born: her lover. Is that how she should call him? Nothing named, that has been part of the beauty of it. But the time for names is coming. She swallows hard again, crossing the threshold, conscious as a smuggler. Darkly dignified, the house, if a little subdued—likewise the man bowing to her.

'. . . so, Father, I said she must come and rest herself here.'

'Quite right. Mistress Hathaway, you are very welcome.' Low, deep voice: Will's eyes, stranded in a grey face. 'It's a sickly season, I fear. Pray, take your ease.'

85

And Anne does feel very welcome: here is the curious thing. Such deliberateness and gravity ought to make you feel awkward. Will's mother has it too, noiselessly appearing, softly enfolding Anne's hand in her own, eyes busy. 'My dear, will you try a cordial?' When Anne refuses with thanks, there's no pressing: they let her be. Such a difference from the hospitable racket of Hewlands Farm, where it would be *Come, speak out, what's amiss? Drink it down.* Here, she suspects, you can hide your feelings around the edges: none of that hauling into the open space of frankness. Yet she shouldn't relax: she brings poison to this sober air. They wouldn't be so kind if they knew, she thinks. She talks of prices at the market, wondering where in God's name is Will, wondering also whether she really wants to see him just now. Of course she will have to see him soon, now she knows, but that's different. Everything is different.

Suddenly Will is there. She realises she never hears him enter a room. He is shirt-sleeved, sweat-damp from work.

'Lord, Will, clothe yourself, for here's Mistress Hathaway come to us for once, instead of you going forever to Shottery,' cries Joan.

Ah, so it is spoken of. Their eyes meet: for a moment they are together in the wood.

Then: 'Mistress Hathaway, your pardon, a moment,' and he slips away to put on a doublet. And slips away to put on something else, it seems; when he returns, though he is still Will, he is a different version, armoured for pleasantries, with the far pale gaze of a sentry. He maintains it even as he listens to Joan's unstinting account of Anne's sickness. The truth seems to Anne like

86

a bird trapped in the room, flapping shrill and unignorable about their heads. But grave, mild, the elder Shakespeares smile on her: gently they protest when her own tension twangs her upright and she says she is well, perfectly well to walk home . . .

Not to be thought of. She is to ride the mare, and Will is to lead it. Master Shakespeare looks as if a refusal will pain him in some profound rarefied way; she finds herself thinking of defeated royalties, quietly glowing in the shadows of exile. And then of Bartholomew remarking, *If a man loses money he should make sure it's his own.*

When they are outside the town Will helps her dismount. She stays in his arms for a moment, then draws away. Speech without touch is necessary, now: another innovation.

She looks down at a tuft of grass. Wonders if she will remember this little wickerwork of green, the dry strand of chickweed, the late five-spot ladybird crawling. 'Will, I'm going to have a child.' Of all the ways to put it: as if it is some peaceable decision, like keeping geese.

'What shall we do?' he says, after perhaps three breaths, with something of the same neutrality: you might suppose they are going to stroll and have a chat about it.

'Oh, God,' she moans, bleats it out, 'don't forsake me.'

'Forsake you, how so? I love you, and I am your servant—'

'Yes, I think that's true, but you see you are saying it, and you're very good at saying things, and there—there's my fear.' Having revealed her great naked weakness, she is bold: no sense in trying to cover yourself with shreds. 'I don't mind you inventing, Will. I know you can't help it. As long as it's not now, not about this.' At some point they have moved together, her hands are gently pounding his chest, there is an intention of lips. But no, look at him, fix his eyes.

'Our child,' he says. 'Our life together. This we shall have. What could we desire more?' He makes a sweeping gesture, as if the question has stirred a little swarm of stinging answers; sweeps them away. 'Anne, you are the great gain of my life.'

'And you . . . that is you . . .' The great gain: yes, trust him to find the right words. She holds him, and doesn't need to say, no one needs to say, that something also has been lost: choice.

*   *   *

Stabling the mare, Will looked up to see his mother.

'Mistress Hathaway was better, I hope?'

'Much better. She sends her kindest thanks and remembrances.'

His mother stroked the mare's nose. 'Getting blind, I fancy, poor old creature, though her step is still sure . . . That sickness goes off, Will, after the first few months.'

Will had the bridle in his hands. He stared at the rosette as if he had never seen anything like it. He should have known.

'We have spoken of it, Mother.'

'Who? You mean you and Mistress Hathaway? For you certainly have not spoken of it with us.'

Not harsh, but a new firmness about her. He thought of school, of leaving behind the usher with his gnawed nails and yawning half-attention to their exercises, and moving up to the master. Impressive—but you knew now the questions would be harder: there would be no hiding.

'I mean to. I'm going to do what's right, Mother. But I am not being driven there. Neither of us is. We go freely to it.'

'Your father should hear this, not me alone,' she said, taking the bridle from him: he saw that he had been twisting, throttling it. 'You must have his permission, for one thing. It must all be talked of properly, openly. Discussed.'

For a moment he heard that word wrongly: perhaps because of what he saw in her face. Moving away from him, she hung up the bridle. Not quite her son any more, Will said: 'Never mind Father for the moment, what do *you* think?'

'I think as he does, always.' She shook her head: as if the pupil were not proving promising with these new lessons. At any rate, thought Will, as she left him, soon I shall be new-clothed: I can wrap myself in the cheap grandeur of the parent.

*   *   *

No, Anne told him when he wanted to come into the farmhouse and speak out now, no and no. 'Because that would make it seem something *you*'ve done. Instead of both of us. Go, sweet. I'll do the first speaking. There, see, I'm playing the shrew-wife already.' They laughed at that, high and nervously.

Now, indoors, she half repents; wonders, watching Bella at her spinning, whether to tell her first. For Bella is not an unkind woman— unkindness requiring a certain imagination, after all, the ability to picture what will hurt; and most

89

importantly, she is a woman. Yet still it seems unnatural. She and Bartholomew have the rich closeness of rancour.

After supper she follows him to the brew-house, stands watching him as he taps a new keg.

'What, Anne, turning toper?'

'Brother, I want to be married.'

'Hm. Is this a mere general wish, or have you someone in mind?' He frowns at the ale seething to the jug's rim; then with a shrug drinks straight from it. 'You never like my jests.'

'I thought you'd be pleased.'

'I am. I think. It's just the way you land it on a man, as if you want it to slap him down. Is it Will Shakespeare?' A glance, though their eyes skim away from each other. 'Dear Lord. Curious business. You know, of course you know, he's very young. And while he may talk of betrothal and marriage and all, remember a young man's tongue will run away with him. I can see, I can well see, that you might be flattered. But consider. Consider George Godden, who's still much taken with you, you know. Think on it, is all I say.'

Now she wishes she had spoken first to Bella, to anybody, rather than say what she has to say to her brother. 'I don't—we don't need to consider, Bartholomew. The match is made up.'

'Aye, so, but you can still change your mind, Anne—'

'No, I don't want to. Also I can't.' She finds her voice rising sharply: a mouse scuffles. Bartholomew, setting the jug down, nearly drops it. Ale slops and stinks and Anne tries not to gag, not to put her hand to her belly, not to look at him. 'I can't.'

'Oh, dear God.' After a moment he bursts out laughing, in a terrible wheezy way, as if someone has punched him in the stomach while telling him a joke. 'Lord, I'll be hanged. I'm a blind buzzard. Oh, Father, do you hear this? You're buried at last, old man, you can rest . . .'

She turns. 'It's true, I never do like your jests.'

'Wait. Anne. Tell me this—there was naught against your will?'

'No.' She feels various kinds of disgust. 'Hark to this too, Father: this is Bartholomew being the good brother.'

'I always am. So I thought.' His face now is cold and stripped. 'Well, then, there's not a great deal more to say, is there? It's not as if you need permission. Not at your age.'

He leaves her to clean up the spilled ale, as if the mess is hers. She fetches the mop.

*　　　*　　　*

Church-time: the best moment for his son and heir to seek audience with John Shakespeare, who—papist, debtor, or just himself—still risks the fines and does not go.

'Father.' I seek, I ask, I beg . . . 'I want your permission to marry.'

In the churchyard boys, looking like Will ten years ago, clamber about the graves, resisting imprisonment to the last minute. Inside, autumn rheums make ragged the psalm that rises up to the whitewashed walls. A beggar squats in the porch and delicately unwraps his sores, like relics, for inspection; and at home in Henley Street Will bends to stir the fire and tells his father that his

91

chosen bride is pregnant.

His father leaves Will skewered on his sharp-tipped silence for a while—not too long. 'How old is she? Mistress Hathaway?'

'Twenty-six. Does it signify?'

'There. At once you suppose I speak against her. I do not. Richard Hathaway was a good man, an excellent worthy man, and I hear no ill of his heir, nor any of the family—'

'I don't intend marrying the family, Father.'

'No man ever does,' he says, with a crusty laugh, in which fury may lurk: no telling yet.

'I'm thinking only of Anne. I love her truly and—'

'So I should hope. She is fair and gracious. If you were not to do right by such a woman, I should think you deserved whipping for it . . . Ah, now you've spoiled the fire with poking.' For a moment Will thinks this is some bawdy proverb—but that has never been John Shakespeare's way. He goes frowning over to the hearth, rubbing his hands. 'Look. Let the ash lie atop. No, Will, if you had not forced the matter, I would still have thought well of Mistress Hathaway, trust me. But it's not a matter of her years. It's yours.'

'Men have married at eighteen before.'

His father gives the slightest of shrugs. 'To be sure. Often when folly has pushed them to it and they have no choice.'

'Often, yes, which means not always, not in every case, and now what else would you have of me, Father? Am I to have your permission or not? After all, if you stand against it, I'm not the one who will suffer.'

'How you fire up.' His father smiles aridly. 'You

love the maid and wish to wed her. Who doubts you, Will? Who?'

Will sits down heavily. He meets his father's look. Knowing that someone sees the worst of you gives a kind of ease. Yes, somehow his father has glimpsed them—those bat-flutterings in the dusk of his thoughts. The idea that he has not designed his future, as a pair of gloves is designed from hide to finish, but has put it ramshackle together from odds and ends.

One day, Will swears inwardly, he will see the best of me; and wonder.

'Naturally you must marry,' his father says. 'But that's only the beginning. Does she know what to expect, your condition, estate?'

'I have created no illusions about myself, Father. That would never do, in this house.'

'Must you put such hate into it? Perhaps you must . . .' Like clandestine love, the enmity issues urgent and passionate while it can. Quite still, gaze level, they pant like wrestlers. 'Once married, besides, you can never be my apprentice. You'll have thought of that.'

'Oh, faith, that was my chief reason for falling in love, what else?'

'Still you must settle, Will, settle. Hast thought on it? For I won't say yea if I suspicion you are not in earnest, and will want to skip away once the wedding-clothes are old. Settle and be a husband and father, work hard, plan for the morrow, *know* the morrow, its very shape and colour. And if you find you don't care for it, who shall you blame?' He does not smile, but parts of a smile appear on his face. 'Not me, not this time, my boy. That's a luxury you must forswear.'

Will says: 'I intend that there will be no regrets on either side, Father. Above all, that my wife will never blush for her choice.' The slightest emphasis on that *my*. He knows how to distribute the stresses, to produce the most telling effect. The parts of his father's smile disintegrate.

A brutal bout—but still only a Brummagem dog-fight, the beasts hauled back at last on their chains to have their wounds dressed; not the baited badger Will saw last month, his black and white turned spiky red, undefeated, yet clubbed to death at the dull end.

And while the shape of a new generation is hacked out in Henley Street, in the church the congregation cough and shuffle and submit themselves to the sermon. The question of sin is posed in the vicar's odd, high, niggling voice; to some there it sounds like a wife or a master complaining from the kitchen, urging that something drearily necessary must be done. Others, perhaps, hear it hardly at all, are busy missing the wall-paintings, the crucifix where the royal coat of arms hangs, wishing the jawing priest could float above them in a swirl of vestments. Perhaps: a lot of faith is habit, and even the deepest thoughts are easily scattered, by a twinge of sciatica, by the cry of a crow from the churchyard, incredibly loud, full of sulphur.

'You'll want to marry before she starts to show. We'd best apply for a bond,' Will's father says. 'Hm, a poor turn-out it will be. Your mother went to the altar slender as her bride-lace.'

Will has a vision of Anne's naked whiteness blazing against the dark bed; and likening that moment and this, it seems to him that there is no

94

principle of connection in life at all, only jolts, blind alleys, severance.

'A great belly, a hurry, and no prenticeship, aye, very well,' says Will, 'but are we not allowed to rejoice a little, somewhere along the way? This is love, not death.'

'Did I not say I wish you happy? I do, for both your sakes. I wish you happier than I fear is likely, Will. You are not a villain or a wastrel, no, but you excel at small disappointments.'

* * *

This could have been worse, Anne thinks, as she serves the spiced ale to Master Shakespeare. And it is he who makes it so surprisingly tolerable—her future father-in-law, who has most unusually stirred from Henley Street and ridden out to Hewlands Farm for this, the meeting.

'Thank you, my dear.' His eyes meet hers, smiling a little, above the nutmeg steam. Yes, the business is solemn, and trouble and shame are in it, but when he looks at her she has the feeling of an exception being made: like a blanket being gently tugged over you as you fall asleep. 'Aye, sir,' he goes on, 'I recall in your father's time that was never accounted good barley land. Too strong . . .' There is this refusal also to be hurried to the subject: first we prepare the ground, we converse. Bartholomew's foot taps and fidgets at it; nevertheless he has put on clean bands, he has put forth the solid, sober, goodman side of him. Lately he has been informing himself of the Shakespeare fortunes, the losses and court summonses, the property remaining. It is all out in the light of day now—of market-day—this love that belonged to green dusks roofed over with birdsong. But Master Shakespeare's gravity makes the occasion bearable.

And Will, of course—though there is something skewed now about their time together, which is neither snatched nor granted. Papers lie on the table, ready to be attended to when Master Shakespeare has concluded his civilities: when the talk must turn to dowry and jointure and bond. Though her father once began teaching her to read with Bartholomew's hornbook, she never got much further than the criss-cross row, and she cannot think her presence will be of much use when they fall to conning those inky thorns and loops. Will that be a fit time to say, 'Come, Will, let us walk a little in the herb garden'? Is it seemly—or where if anywhere does seemly lie, when she is pregnant and their families are arranging their marriage in haste?

In the end it is the men (as she thinks of Will's father and her brother) who leave them alone for a space, Master Shakespeare wanting to look over the farm, which he has not seen since old Master Hathaway's time. She hopes he will not harp on that string too much, knowing Bartholomew's intolerance of the past—but, still, they tramp off pretty cordially together. Cordiality, indeed, is the note of the whole business so far; and if you take out the sickness and tender breasts and the fact, soon to be loud and undeniable, that she is no maid and a baggage without a shred of regard for her family's name, it might almost be a normal marriage that is being arranged.

She wants to say something of this to Will, to make him smile; above all to break the tightness that his father's presence seems to set on his brow.

Instead they find themselves sitting together on the settle by the fire, holding hands. Courtship backwards, she thinks but does not say. Somewhere a voice both familiar and strange nags, *Hot love soon cools.*

'Well,' Will says, 'at least they trust us not to get up to anything we shouldn't.'

Though his tone falls so desperately wide of the mark, they laugh together: the laugh a kind of promise, or—in the spirit, perhaps, of those papers on the table—a down-payment. There will be more laughter to come, in their life to come: surely.

* * *

At a wedding, a gift of gloves is sometimes made to the guests. Not this one.

For the marriage that John Shakespeare would in due time have hoped to solemnise between his heir—once out of his apprenticeship—and the daughter of, say, a fellow alderman with a tidy property, there would have been a gift of gloves for every guest; there would have been everything befitting. But that is the life that did not happen.

See in a wood or on a heath how a path forms. When does it begin? Someone habitually walks that way, perhaps, and then another, and another; and then someone walks that way simply because it's a little flattened, a little easier. Eventually the path becomes broad, smooth and permanent: like a thing that has always been there. But look carefully among the trees or the gorse, and you may faintly see the lost beginnings of other paths, paths that through an accumulation of little chances and choices were never made.

So with the life that did not happen for John Shakespeare. And, perhaps, his son.

No time, besides, for the gift of gloves, with a wedding by licence: skip the banns, hurry it through. Two friends of Bartholomew's put up money as a surety—meaning, if the groom isn't serious, he'll be held to account for it, oh, yes. Stratford is, intermittently, diverted by it all. No end to Master Shakespeare's troubles, they say. Some moralise, or in other words gloat—remembering his remarkable marriage to an Arden, his dizzy rise, and then the wool-dealing and rumours and murkiness and fall: so, here's the Shakespeare name stumbling a little more, probably to fall at last from the ranks of the foremost, from the possibility of a coat of arms, of a Sir somewhere along the next generation or two. It has happened before. Across Warwickshire men hack at ditches on land their great-grandfather might have owned. Altogether, it is not a great matter for anyone who talks about it, set against this quarter's rent that must be paid, the little sickly son whose vast eyes say he won't live, the chimney-fire that has disrupted the workshop.

Master Field stops Will in the street the day before the wedding, shakes his hand. 'Marriage,' he pronounces, somewhere between congratulation and condolence, 'is a blessed and solemn state for the Christian man and woman.' Rumour murmurs that lately the respectable house in Middle Row resounds with nocturnal fighting, and that once Mistress Field locked him out of doors. Will thinks of Richard in London: pictures him setting up type in a dark print-shop ringed by roof upon roof. Setting up, character by careful character, the text of his future. But love, surely, can be an opportunity too.

We must be everything to one another. We will be. We must be. We must be, and we will. So it goes in his mind, until it's like the game of hands he played as a child with Joan, one hand atop hers then hers atop his and faster and faster until you could hardly tell which was which. And now his hand covers Anne's, as they stand together in the church at Temple Grafton to which no procession of musicians has accompanied them. Anne wears her hair loose for the last time, before marriage binds and conceals, and it seems to Will that he has never truly seen its magnificence before, its beautiful unlikelihood. Each tress round her face has a precise hang and spring, like peel descending from an apple. They stand in the sight of God and a dozen mortals, breathing cold, damp November in their responses. A single shaft of light falls slantwise from the narrow window, looking both solid and temporary, like something propped there for now, soon to be taken away, sawn up. And between two calls of a crow from the churchyard, they are made man and wife.

Now the path through the wood takes shape. Anne will return with Will to live as his wife beneath his father's roof, and there the child will be born and the new generation raised among the leather and the account-rolls, and that path takes such a definite direction and the ground is so clear it's difficult to see how any other way could ever be taken. There would have to be, surely, hacking and burning.

And Anne: she experiences a happiness that is at once startling, pure and complex, as if an icicle should form into a love-knot. *Forsaking all other keep thee only unto her.* That is what Will is going to do—she believes and trusts it, which is the exactness of her love—and it is so wonderfully definitive that the unsatisfactory falls away, the haste and the bond, the roundness of her belly and the emptiness of the church.

This spirit even seems to infect Bartholomew, who has been dour and hunched all day, swinging the purse containing her dowry like a weapon, frowning at the wedding-ring, which he considers a popish trinket. Service over, wine uncorked and handed round the church, he brightens and broadens, shaking hands and slapping shoulders. And so perhaps when it happens he doesn't mean it, and it is just ill luck the way it comes out.

'Well, Anne,' he says, embracing her, 'you caught him in time.' And says it just as Will turns, and hears.

4

Love's Metamorphosis (1587)

Entering his fourteenth year, Ben grabbed the strap from his stepfather's hand one humid midsummer eve and did as he had long ago promised.

Ben hit him informatively, as it were, rather than vengefully—just clearing things up; and the man took it pretty well. He even invited Ben to the alehouse with him the next evening. 'Now we are men together,' he said. Ben went, just the once. It was interesting to see the fuss the man liked to make around himself, with his own fireside chair and polished tankard, and everyone treating him as an oracle. He confided to Ben, after the fourth pot, that he aimed to be nothing less than Master of the Worshipful Company of Tilers and Bricklayers.

Ben nodded thoughtfully: not so much at that, for he found his stepfather's bristling stupidity no more attractive with its soft belly turned up, as at the experience of drinking. He greatly liked what the ale did to him, and wondered if he might come to like it too much. But he still rose at five the next morning, doused his head under the street pump, and read Horace as he walked to school, feeling none the worse. He suspected that drink might indeed be an ally and resource against what he could see was coming to him.

'If there were any other way,' his mother said. She had turned notably bony now, brisk, to the point: always like someone measuring out emotional rations. 'But there isn't enough money for the university. So, you must have a trade. And it makes no sense paying a prentice premium to another master, when you can stay at home and learn a trade for nothing.'

'No,' he agreed, 'it makes no sense.'

Master Camden's great history was published. *Britannia*. Tremblingly Ben turned over the great folio leaves in the master's study. Not appropriate for him, a non-Queen's Scholar, to be here, but it didn't much matter now, as he was leaving Westminster School.

'But this is magnificent. It must make your fame.'

Master Camden frowned in modesty. 'It has attracted favourable notice. My lord Burghley has been especially kind. All I can see now are its imperfections.'

Ben shook his head. 'There has never been anything writ like it. Yet you're staying here.'

'Schoolmastering, yes. Does that surprise you?'

'No, because you are the best of teachers. Yes, because—well . . .' He was going to say *if it was me.* If it was me presenting my great work to the public, I would not carry on quietly teaching grammar in an old monk's cell, I would shout to the skies. 'There's a world out there.'

'Which I may visit a little during the vacations, and which may very well soon tire of me. Meanwhile I will hope to teach other such pupils as you.'

'Ah, but to what end?' Ben closed the volume and rested his hands on the panelled calf cover. Books, he had noticed, were warmer than any other inanimate objects. 'Never fear, that's the last of my self-pity.'

'You need never stop learning, Benjamin. As long as you can read, as long as you can lay your hand on a book. Which reminds me. These are for you.'

Half a dozen volumes, ready bound in a satchel. The names shimmered and danced for him: Virgil, Plautus. 'I can't take those.'

'No? It would please me. Call them borrowed, if you prefer. As I said, I am staying at Westminster, and your apprenticeship will doubtless keep you hereabout. We shall still, I hope, be friends.'

'So I hope,' Ben said, and smiled, and accepted the books. And thought: The kingdom's finest historical scholar, and Ben Jonson the bricklayer, friends. Very pretty. Very unlikely. He saw Master Camden's eye stray to the fresh heap of correspondence on his desk, sealing-wax clustering and drooping, erudite fruit. He did not exactly want Ben to go, but once he did go there would be much to occupy him, he would turn brightly to it, necessarily forgetting. And somehow it was this that made Ben say: 'I don't regret it, you know. The way I faced the examiners. They looked haughty on me, yet I knew almost as much Latin as they did. I wouldn't bend. And I never will bend, you see, when I know I'm in the right.'

Master Camden seemed about to say something, then shook his head, and smiled sadly. Probably the sad smile meant: *You will change.* But Master Camden, though Ben esteemed him more than anyone in the world, did not really know him. No one did, which Ben found acceptable enough: he knew himself. And that was the first principle, after all, behind all the greatest thinking of the ancients: know thyself. Strange, he thought, that so few people could manage it.

'Spare me all that stuff about teaching me the art and mystery of thy trade,' Ben said to his stepfather, on the first day. 'Just show me what I have to do.' He looked up at the long ladders, the scaffolding, and realised he had no fear of falling.

*   *   *

Consider the events of a single day—no, much less. About as much time as it takes to roast a fowl on a spit.

Time enough to change a man—and, perhaps, the world.

The place: well, two places, fifty miles apart, linked by consequence. One is the Oxfordshire market town of Thame, amply straddling the

103

London road, a wool-rich burgher town, prepared to lay out good money if it gets good value—as it did earlier this day with a performance by the most estimable of touring theatre troupes, the Queen's Men.

They pitched up in White Hound Close, and to a large, appreciative crowd played *The Famous Victories of Henry the Fifth*, and now at the Spread Eagle they feed, drink and tally. They have bespoken the whole supper-room for themselves: no rowsy ragged rabblement these, they are the Queen's Men, put together from the choicest players of several companies to bear Her Majesty's name about the country and to play before her at the Court. The Queen, when cares of state are laid aside, dearly loves a play, and is proud to own it: a blow, then, to the Puritan haters of the stage, though not a silencing one.

'Sweet sound.' The Dutton brothers, red-bearded and foxy, tip the jingling contents of the box on to the table. William Knell, tall and florid, masterful player of kings, watches. Not happy. Snatches up a coin. Bites, bends.

'Bastards. Bloody cheating bumpkins.'

'Hush, man, you're not on stage now,' says Jack Towne. His fair, long-limbed handsomeness is still notable: a groove between the brows, though, as if it can only be maintained with effort. 'Mine host will hear you.'

'Pox on him. And on thieving Thame. The men are clods. The women all ugly.'

'Naturally they are. You're not drunk enough.' Tarlton, the snub-nosed clown, pours. 'Wine, the transformer. A glass, and you'll be commending the men's wit and the women's beauty. Another glass, and you'll be commending t'other way round.'

Jack Towne's eyes narrow at that. Not perhaps in mirth. But Knell rounds on him. 'Don't you smirk. Never mind mine host hearing, Towne, look to your damned audience. Your voice failed. By the end, nothing but croaking.' He rasps in scornful imitation. '"Why then belike, all that I have here is yours." Pitiful. Not piteous.' The bumper of wine goes down, gulp. 'Give me more.'

Tarlton pours. 'When you play the flatterer you quite turn my head. Water with it?'

'Save your jester turn for the Court.'

'What in God's name is wrong with you?' John Dutton stacks coins. 'They liked us. Takings twice what we got in Beaconsfield. Why so foul?'

'I need some air.' Knell gets up from the table, goes to open the single window. It yields reluctantly, squeaking and grinding. The room sucks in a little scented summer. 'Bloody town. Did you mark it? Church here. Grammar-school next. Dunghill there. And so with every dreary hole we have to drag ourselves to 'twixt now and September.' He throws a backward glance. Bloodshot eye falls on Towne. 'Well, why do you stare? You're always the first to mourn when we leave London gates.'

'That's why I stare. I am usurped. Take away a man's cherished miseries, and what do you leave him?'

'Come, come, friends, at least we have a proper equipage. When I was first with Leicester's men, we made the tour with a villainous old cart and worse mule.' This is Robert Wilson, wit and scholar of the company: elegant, watering his wine, acute grey eyes taking in everybody, everything. 'Laid bets on which would founder first. Singer, you were with

105

Leicester's then, weren't you?'

Anecdote springs up all round the table. Towne slips away from it to join Knell at the window.

'Come, Knell, what cheer?' Tentatively he pats the big shoulder turned to him. 'You can tell me. All the years betwixt us, now companions, now not. Storms and havens. Hast heart-pain? Share. Trust me, I can deal wisdom to beat any gammer winking over her turf fire.'

'Go your ways, Towne,' he growls.

Towne shrugs, walks back to the table, pours a drink. Tarlton calls for another bottle, Wilson for pasties; the Duttons scoop the money into pouches; a moth as big as a fieldmouse blunders in and flirts dangerously with the candles, and in less than an hour there will be a dead man.

And fifty miles away, over the Oxfordshire border into Warwickshire, in another town of church and grammar-school and dunghills, another moth flutters around the weak smoky flame of a rushlight, until a pair of white hands closes about it.

'Why will they destroy themselves?' Anne says, carrying the little dusty pulse to the parlour window. 'No other creature does it.'

'Except for man,' says her father-in-law, smiling from the shadowed chimney-corner. Though the midsummer evening breathes as warm here as at Thame, a small fire burns: John Shakespeare has a fire every night. It is one of his things.

'Tut, none of your gloomy thoughts,' Anne says, freeing the moth, clapping the window to. 'Will you take something hot for supper?'

'Not for me alone. Where's Will?'

'Down to Sadlers', to see if they can change that crown. He'll not eat late, you know that.'

'I will,' yawns Gilbert, lifting propped tousled head. 'What's for cooking?'

'He ought to eat more. He's all bones,' John Shakespeare grumbles.

'You were the same at his age,' says his wife, holding her needlework up to the light, squinting. 'Lean and spare, it's in the blood. Who gave the crown?'

'I forget. Lord'—rising, Anne listens—'never say that's the twins waking?'

'Cats fighting,' chuckles Gilbert. 'An easy mistake.'

'Master Steels, at Snitterfield, for the belts and purses,' John Shakespeare says. 'No fear for the goodness of the coin. I knew his father well.'

'Cats. Dear heaven, daughter, you should know your children's cry,' her mother-in-law says, wetting thread in scarcely smiling lips. 'We want no hot eating at this late hour, I think. The kitchen fire will be out, besides.'

'Not so late, surely. Is Joan not back from the Quineys' yet?' her father-in-law cries, stirring.

'Those field mushrooms.' Gilbert sighs reminiscently. 'Broiled with leeks. I shall wake brother Richard before cockcrow, go find some more. That black juice.'

'Never mind Joan, she will do very well.' Wetted thread into needle: now stab, and yank and tug, as if administering just deserts. 'My daughter knows right from wrong. I thank heaven.'

'Aye, those mushrooms are good eating. And yet Will won't even touch them.' John Shakespeare looks across at his daughter-in-law. 'Was there ever such a curiosity, my dear, as your husband?'

She smiles back at him. 'We shall win him over,

one day.'

Anne's favourite time, the supper-hour. In summer the shadows seem to roll across to your feet like mild purple waves. With every trundle and creak, bolts and shutters create a soft castle about you. The Henley Street house is not like Hewlands Farm, where she was only alive at night. Here she moves round the household day as comfortably and steadily as the hour hand of a clock.

In the kitchen Anne cuts bread and, after a glance at the hanging flitch and a mental calculation, a wedge of cheese. It is not that they are poor here, but money always matters: you feel it pressing and rubbing like a tight shoe. She has tried to help with innovations, like saving the old floor-rushes to light the fires. Her mother-in-law goes along with them, while seeming to find them faintly distasteful.

But with her father-in-law, she is a favourite, has been since the first morning she woke up here as a bride, five years ago. She can see where he gets his reputation for being difficult; yet to her he is seldom less than tenderly chivalrous. A kind of alliance, even, has formed between them: an alliance about Will; slight yet strong, knitted together from frayed ends of suspicion, jealousy, fear. Sometimes Anne allows the thought: Will's father likes me because I pin Will down, to this house, this trade, this town. And sometimes she looks at the thought properly, all round, its shape and shadows. Then Bartholomew's jest on the day of their wedding shouts through the muffling of the years: *Well, Anne, you caught him in time.*

But not for long, she does not allow it for long, because of what she has. Look, feel, so real and tangible: the husband, the children, the intense life she lives with them. Children beautiful and infinitely surprising; husband who is, still, husband, revealing no vice or foulness, unestranged . . . Well, go no further. She remembers her father teaching her, when a small girl, the rudiments of arithmetic. He counted fat plums into her stretching hands. And three more: 'Now how many have you?'

All she could say, in greedy surprise: 'Oh, I've got lots.'

No, she can see nothing to regret in her sole act of rebellion—giving herself to young Will Shakespeare: not when it has led to this. Perhaps in fact that rebellion was a necessary part of her. Whereas Will seems to have laid his by, like a trifling pastime once taken up. The Will she lives and works and lies beside is more phlegmatic than she could have imagined: pliable, measured, the least noticeable person in the brimming household. A swift maturity, perhaps, from marrying so young, fathering three children. Making him different from most men of—of what? Twenty-three? Yes. Somehow she always has difficulty naming his exact age. There is something elusive about it.

And about him? No, no, her hands are filled with fruit, she has abundance, and she need not consider the question of whether she knows him less now than she did five years ago. Nor why, when Joan or Gilbert casually asks, 'Where's Will?' she has an impulse to say he might be underground or in the roof or in the air all around them or anywhere, anywhere, for all they know.

*   *   *

'Knell was drinking before the performance,' says Robert Wilson, in a low voice.

'Well, don't we all?' shrugs John Singer: spindle-shanked, easy comedian, faintly mad eyes.

'Ale, ale, to moisten. This was strong liquor. Missed a couple of cues.'

'Towne thinks it's all come about since he married that young piece in London,' says Lawrence Dutton—too loudly: quickly they burble of new subjects, while Knell, solitary chair drawn up to the cold hearth, neatly stabs mutton slices with his knife.

'He won't even take a jest now,' Tarlton sighs at last.

'Not even funny ones? To be sure, you wouldn't know about that,' says Singer.

'He's absolutely indispensable, you know,' says Jack Towne, at the table-end, drawing in spilled drink with his finger. 'The *sine qua non* of our enterprise, Knell. Can't do without him, as he is good enough to remind us. That's why he carries it so high.'

Glances pass and bounce round them. Tarlton waves the swooping moth away, frowning. He is the most acclaimed clown of the day, he has property in London, and, as long as he doesn't go too far, is the favoured fool of the Queen herself; but he started out as a troupe player and still believes in it, the group, the way they hold together. 'Nobody can claim that,' he says. 'Not in the Queen's Men, nor in the poorest hedgerow company.'

'But none of us are going to say that to him, are we?' This is the youngest of them, Lionel Cooke, principal woman-player, usually bashful as any maiden, now bold with the wine. 'Because we're afraid to.'

'Afraid of Knell?' Towne, feet against the table edge, thrusts his chair back with a squeal. 'Great God, I should hope not.' He looks at the cup in his hand as if someone has just pissed in it. 'Knell has many qualities, but beshrew me if ever I begin to fear him.'

'Oh, you know what I mean, everyone's afraid of the *noise*,' Cooke says. 'It's less tiring just to let him be.'

'As for doing without him,' Robert Wilson says carefully, 'to be sure, we wouldn't want to. But when he was laid low with a quinsy last season, John Dutton took his parts to admiration—and no, man, I'm not just saying that because you're here. The company must come first.'

'Oh, Jesus,' bursts out Towne, cradling his own face. 'I know what it is now. I know what it's all about.'

* * *

Stale and broken loaves, like days you lived and can't remember living. Hamnet Sadler, charitable and prosperous enough to be so, gives the last of them away to an old poor woman. Will, change in his purse, lingers with the midsummer light, helping Sadler put up the hinged shop-front, talking. Since his marriage he has grown close to Sadler, who stood godfather to his son. The baker is a big, curly-haired man who carries his flesh gracefully, like a dancer. Tender-hearted, he will weep at a sad tale or a song, and is known for it. Tearful Sadler, they say: 'Oh, go stuff yourself,' he will reply amiably. He blinks at the world in perplexity, but always with profound interest.

'Master Eames, over to Clopton, you know him? They say he's taken to wearing a hair-shirt and scourging himself night and morn. Can you understand that, now?'

'The same impulse that makes you drink strong ale,' Will says.

'Ah, but that I enjoy.'

'Has the ale never given thee a thick head as penance?'

'Well, I'll grant thee that. It's a wonder, though, what wild things men will do.'

'And never lack a reason for them.' Guilt, Will thinks, is the real garment underneath that hair-shirt.

'Little ones thriving? Judith suspicioned another for us, but it was just the full moon putting her out of order. Women are curious made, aren't they? I never cease to wonder.' Like Will he had married young. His wife is a pretty, high-coloured woman with a taste for finery and a formidable temper. Occasionally Sadler seems on the brink of saying something to Will about—well, about marriage, but though they are close enough friends to use *thee*, that step is never taken. Will wonders if there is something about himself that discourages it.

Sadler sniffs the air as the light dies of its own redness. 'A sweet summer. Pray God it stays.'

'We're owed a good harvest.' Yes, he can do this; he can keep this part of himself working for a long time. 'Well, best go.'

'Aye, they'll be sending after you, lest you've been stole away.'

Will laughs at that. The laugh sounds a little wrong in the empty street.

'I know what it is,' Towne says, snapping his fingers. 'Damn, it was my fault. It was when we were running over *Famous Victories* this morning. John Cobbler saying farewell to his wife to go to the wars, and Dericke says—'

' "Fie, what a kissing and crying is here," ' says Tarlton, softly. ' "Zounds, do you think he will never come again?" '

'Damn. And I made a jest to Knell about it. Just one of those things you throw out.' Towne glances over at Knell, going out on slightly unsteady legs to the close-stool. 'I said something about leaving a young wife at home, and how she would never lack consolation.'

'Ah.' Tarlton grimaces, nodding. 'And what did he say?'

'Nothing.'

'That is ominous.'

'Will someone please tell me what you're talking about?' young Cooke cries, looking as if he might soon be sick.

Wilson says: 'Knell's new wife, sweetling. Only— what is she? Sixteen?'

'Fifteen,' Towne says. 'And now left behind in a fine house in London to sew and sing psalms.'

'She might,' Tarlton says. 'She might be doing exactly that.'

'Not what one hears, though,' Wilson says.

'Oh, you've heard it too?' says Towne. 'Shit. I didn't entirely mean it—it was just one of those jests you make.'

'One of those jests *you* make, certainly,' says

Wilson. 'Look you, we must put him in a good humour somehow. He mustn't think we're ever talking of him.'

'As we are,' Singer says.

Knell is back, with a slight dull smile, and a stare, and a thirst.

'Knell, we were talking of digging up old *Roister Doister* for Oxford,' Wilson says. 'What think you?'

'You weren't talking of it,' Knell says, pouring, his glance skimming Towne, 'but let us pretend you were.'

*　　　*　　　*

Crossing the High Street, Will finds himself imagining a hair-shirt: the feel of it riding roughly against your skin beneath your clothes. Eventually, surely, you would get used to it—which would defeat the purpose. Perhaps then you had to leave it off to feel the required discomfort. Until you got used to that. Ahead he spies and catches up with Joan, returning from the Quineys'.

'Didn't they send a manservant with you?'

'I made him go back. He vexed me. He has a wen and I can't stop looking at it.' Joan takes his arm.

'Not wise, after dark.'

'Why, I trusted to my luck, and here you are.'

'Hm. And how goes it in the kingdom of Quiney?'

'A dull spot just now. Too much occupied with marrying people off.'

'Dull indeed.' With a sideways glance he measures her expression. 'You've too much sense to be in a hurry for that, I think.' To him she is bright and pleasing as a robin; but smallpox has

114

marked her, and there's scant chance of a dowry.

'A deal too much sense,' she says sharply. And for a few moments they allow something to walk silently beside them. They have this ease. Both a little out of sorts, neither has to account for it, as you have to with lover, husband, wife: that constant diagnosis of intimacy.

But, then, they were children together and, in a way, have never stopped being so. He reads it in Joan's bemused look sometimes, when he hoists one of his own children on to his shoulders: Will a father, Will doing these great grown things? Surely not: surely this is a game of dressing-up. He thinks it himself sometimes.

'Where is his wen?'

'On his neck, and as big as a strawberry.' Joan shudders. 'And yet *he* is new-married.'

Will smiles in the darkness. Hair-shirts, wens: perhaps, indeed, you can get used to anything. Suppose you committed a murder, but were so careful or lucky that not the slightest suspicion fell on you, and no evidence pointed your way. For a long time you would hardly be able to believe it: you would be on your guard every moment, suspecting every glance, never easy in your skin. But eventually, at last, you would *have* to relax: normality would force itself on you, and no longer would you wake every morning to the thought: *I haven't been found out yet.* As Will still does, sometimes, blinking at the folds of the bed-curtains, next to soft breathing, a tumble of hair, a white still hand like a plaster-cast.

As soon as he steps inside his mother's face appears round the parlour door. 'Will, you're home.' She seems to draw comfort from statements.

'Anne's seeing to supper. I said you'd want none.' Another statement, heavier. He doubts his mother and his wife will ever be good friends. Not exactly that they are too alike, but they have the wrong similarities.

His father calls him in. 'Any word from Ditchley?' He half mouths it, mindful of dozing Gilbert. Secrets and stratagems. Even Will—shaking his head—doesn't know all of it. Only that Ditchley is something to do with wool, and that his father is on the edge of unlicensed dealing again. He remembers the stored wool in the barn last time, his father urging him to dig his hands into the greasy, muttony coarseness of it, then seeming to repent of showing him. *Say nothing.*

Oh, needless instruction. Saying nothing is a rare luxury in this house of two generations and thirteen people. Will relishes release into silence, cultivates the art of effacement, of being ignored, for once there, the selfish mind is like a rich fabric kept folded away from the sun. Open it out, and your eyes dazzle at the brilliant complexity of the pattern.

'Not for me,' he says in the kitchen, at Anne's look, knife over bread. 'Just a cup of ale. Phoo, there's no air tonight.'

'I know. The twins won't rest, I heard them again. *Not* cats.'

'I'll go up. Maybe open the window a little.'

She nods. 'Do it quietly.'

Because his mother might hear, and she believes the night air dangerous, full of poisonous humours. So they balance it.

'I do everything quietly,' he says. They move about the kitchen without touching, but there

116

is something not quite empty about the spaces between them. 'You know that.'

'Aye, you are a very cat yourself. Save when you wake to use the pot.' She glances at him, shakes her head. 'No, not true.' She picks up the tray. 'You were long with Hamnet Sadler. What do you men find to talk of?'

'Same as women. Babes and ailments. And then the state of the crops, and the crops of the state, and the price of the north wind and whether the goose-down will fall from the sky before the Dutchmen catch the end of last year in a net with no holes.' He adds a smile: she is watching him with that look, faintly anxious, as if he is going out of sight. 'Let me take that.'

'No, no. He likes it from me.'

'You spoil him.' And yet he is happy for her to do so, isn't he? Anne pleases his father: does that one job he has never been able to do.

And he does so many things. Works leather, still, though at thirteen his quiet brother Richard— stocky, painstaking, father-adoring—is more adept in the shop and yard than he could ever be. Reckons accounts, chases customers for payment. Then the other work. Once a week he goes to his old grammar-school to teach handwriting, which the present master doesn't trouble himself with. And when wanted, he earns a little more copying documents for a lawyer of Warwick, who is wealthy and rising and—so Will guesses from the things he copies and which the lawyer's clerk is not to see— thoroughly corrupt. These are the things Will does: likewise being a husband, being a father. And he seems to belong to each of them, like a portrait that suits any frame.

Upstairs, in the room adjoining theirs, he finds three small quiet mounds. The two-year-old twins, Hamnet and Judith, have settled to awkward sleep again, arms outflung, blond fringes soaked as if after furious exercise. Four-year-old Susannah sleeps decorously as ever, dark brows lifted as if her dreams amuse and surprise. Susannah: fruit of the wild courtship, born six months into wedlock, and never giving the slightest trouble from that moment: as if her work is done. (Will and Anne created her, but just as surely she created Will and Anne—what they are together, and must be, for always.) He decides against possibly waking kisses, and inches the window open. The clattering pail and tuneless song of the maidservant emptying ashes on the midden comes in suddenly strange and distant, the note of a foreign bird in a magic wood. Violently he jumps at the little hand touching the small of his back.

'I hushed 'em. He woke up and then that made her wake up. So I came and hushed 'em.'

Edmund, nightshirted, wriggling from one bare foot to the other, peers up through the mists of a yawn at Will's clifftop face.

'Thanks, 'twas well done.' Will ruffles his brother's head, urges and turns him with hand between the butterfly shoulder-blades. 'Now haste, thine own bed, else thou'lt not be astir tomorrow.' The boy goes, drowsing, unerring, with flat slapping feet. Edmund the late child is only seven years old, and thus closer to Will and Anne's children than to the rest of his siblings—but something more than that besides: he frequents their two rooms, their company, as if choosing a family within a family. Here he chatters; around his father he is dumb.

Before going down to check bars and shutters, Will glances again at his children; seeking assurance that they are real. From birth, they continually astonished: the fact that they did all the things they were meant to do, cutting teeth, speaking first words, seemed in itself the most brazen unlikelihood. And so his conclusion: every ordinary thing is a miracle.

Which carries its inverse: every miracle is ordinary. You can live on one, the other is killing. How to place himself between them is the question that he addresses in those rare moments when the mind-cloth is unrolled. Times when he allows himself to ask, what's wrong, what's right, what would I have. Unholy times, they can be: showing him horrible pictures of himself. Here are some. First married, Susannah new-born: wakened at midnight by her cry, he took the opportunity to light a taper downstairs, open his book-bundle. And then Anne appearing at the door, creamy-white, sleep-ripe: *Whatever are you doing?* Mild bewilderment: as if she had found him counting peas, or playing with a toy drum. Or worse: when little Hamnet, inquisitive, destructive, found the book-bundle, and Will came upon him in the midst of merry tearing. How terrifying he was, to the boy, to himself: the red haze, the voice he did not recognise booming curses. (Never again: absolute certainty, never that part of himself again.) And some time after, another picture, salutary: tiptoeing Will lighting another midnight taper and taking up the unbound books and finding them, simply, coming apart in his hands. Dry leaves falling.

And then that bumpy passage, that muddy little side-road to nowhere: Anne wanting to know just

119

what this fascination was.

'I know you are much addicted to plays and verses. Such verses you used to recite to me . . .' (He thought: Did I?) 'But I had no idea you were such a scholar.' Pronounced with faint, dubious dismay.

'Reading . . .' he breathed back his impatience '. . . reading isn't a matter of being a scholar. It makes—it makes a new world.'

'Is this one not enough?' Tart and suppressive. Not like her—Anne who loved to dream. Or did she? If he had her wrong, then the floor fell away: he stood on nothingness. No: she was simply frightened—this new thing she couldn't understand. And that could be changed, if she so wished.

Yes, she did wish. 'I should dearly love to read that tale of Melibeus for myself.' It seemed so good, so right, as perhaps only the most disastrously wrong things could: he would teach Anne to read; it would be a delight to both of them, bring them even closer together.

Perhaps if she had been a child, not grown; perhaps if she had been a stranger; if he had been more patient, perhaps, perhaps. For several weeks they struggled, seated late at night at the dinner-table, askew, untouching; they had never been so physically awkward with one another. Susannah's waking cry would come as a relief. Melibeus was a long way off, when even the word *this* reared like a dread obstacle.

'Same as *the*. Same sound, *th*, look . . .'

'I see it,' she said, 'but I don't see it.' She looked at his face, then blindly down at the hornbook: Edmund's. There was hatred somewhere in the room; a bastard emotion; neither of them would own it. 'I should have learned when I was young.'

'No, no, you shouldn't.' Uncontrollably, slamming his hand down. 'Trust me. Better not to . . .' Terribly close to revelation at that moment: the bitter beast almost snapping its chain. Did she see it? He squeezed a smile. 'It's late. Let's try tomorrow.'

'Late. Yes. Too late, I think.'

Try tomorrow . . . but they didn't. In some dark version of the mutual impulse that moved them together in bed, they stopped. And have never spoken of it since. He read, and reads, alone. Oh, he presents an ill picture, this other Will who dwells apart and, in between the summer visits of the players, strings his soul along posts of dream and fantasy and invention and imitation. He looks guilty in it: everything screams that his innocence is a lie, the murdered ghost walks abroad. Please, God, let her never see it. Will descends the stairs at a run and puts up the shutters and slides the bolts on the doors, hard, slamming and panting: as if there is something out there.

*   *   *

Glass smashing has a dual sound, a deep and explosive bass-note beneath the bright tinkling. Exciting. So Knell seems to find it, as he hurls another bottle into the grate, his laugh like the belling of hounds.

'No more, for God's sake, the landlord will turn us out,' says John Dutton.

'Turn us out, will he?' Knell is wreathed in shining, sweating, dangerous hilarity. 'What strange manner of landlord is this, who wants a quiet house and no money?'

121

He looks around for something else to smash. This element remains among the players: yes, there are the Wilsons and Tarltons, socially aspiring, anxious of reputation, but always this dark flame licks beneath. Jack Towne watches, expression divided. He has exerted himself greatly to chivvy Knell out of his dumps, and it seems he has succeeded. And yet that sound of smashing glass hangs in the air, and there is jaggedness in Knell's desperate eyes too.

'Where are you going?' Knell calls out.

'To see if there's more meat in the kitchen,' Towne says. 'You need food.'

'I *need*,' says Knell, holding his arm, 'one, more drink; two, less of your coddling.'

'Hello, what's this?' cries Singer. A young girl has slipped into the room and is eyeing the company with—what? Speculation? Fear? 'Has mine host sent you to complain of the noise, poor chick? Let him come himself.'

'No, no, I don't belong to the house, sirs. I only saw your play earlier and thought it was a rare thing—and then when I heard merrymaking I wondered if I might step in . . .'

Ah: a local punk or doll or doxy, trying her luck. Very, very young this one—in small towns they're usually either green or overripe—and awkward: her paint clumsy, her stiff stomacher making her breasts not so much peep as squint. But Singer hails and hauls her in and soon he and Tarlton are passing her from knee to knee, inviting her to a drop of this, a nibble of that. An unfortunate addition to the company, Towne thinks, at least as far as Knell is concerned. His liverish eye falls on her without pleasure; he stops breaking things, sits and sips and is silent. And then Lawrence Dutton plays his lute and sings and the girl, both bolder and clumsier for liquor, skips and twirls about, bumping legs, landing in laps. No more than fifteen, Towne breathes. Oh, God, there she goes. For a gurgling moment she drapes herself across William Knell, who, after a glaring, blazing moment, sends her flying.

'For God's sake, man,' Towne hisses at him, 'she don't come a-purpose to try your temper. Consider for a moment that the attention of the whole world is *not* fixed on you and your private affairs—'

'Consider for a moment that I don't want to hear the shite that comes out of your mouth, now or ever,' rasps Knell, and his arm goes up as if he would send Towne spinning across the room likewise.

Towne looks at him. 'Touch me and you'll not find me like a wench of fifteen.'

'Now, you two, the girl's well padded fore and aft and takes no harm, and you've been like a pair of cats on a roof all night,' says Tarlton, interposing himself between them, 'so pad paws now, pad paws.'

Knell turns on him. 'What the devil do you mean by that? Cats, cats, what?'

'Oh, sweet Jesu, man, he's trying to sweeten you with a jest, and I urge him to give it over,' says Towne, turning, 'give it over as lost.'

'Why do you turn your back on me, Towne?'

'God knows. Why did I ever? I want some air—it's rank with self in here.'

Stumbling a little on the step, Towne gets out through the tap-room. Slow faces turn to watch him, and then the man following him. Another

123

moth flits in as they pass out to the summer dark.

*   *   *

'You're right, there's no air tonight,' Anne says, unpinning her sleeves. Helping her, Will leans in for a kiss. 'Have a care, I ate a little onion with the cheese.'

'Feeding so late, you'll be troubled with dreams.'

'My dreams never trouble me.' She wishes now she had not eaten the onion, or that she had thought to wash her mouth with vinegar. Not that his kisses are so infrequent but . . . 'Oh, there's another.' A moth aims for the single tallow candle on the clothes-press, unerring: Anne is too late. It falls from the flame with the faintest of clicks. 'Shall I put it out? It's rather a foul one, I fear.'

'Aye, there's a moon now.' The extinguished candle gives off a last whiff of butcher's grease. Will's shirted slenderness takes form from the entering moonlight, still, thoughtful. 'Do you ever wish we could afford wax candles? Straight and tall and sweet-smelling and white as lilies?'

'A pretty thought. I don't set my heart on it.' She speaks easily, but this whole matter of *wishing* for something is no light one for Anne. It involves her relation to the world, what she expects from it, and hopes and fears from it. She lives with the world and its power like a deer in a wood: her walks, her sweet grazing are deep within, and the sun warms her hide. But all the while she can see through the beautiful trees the movements of hunters.

*   *   *

'Leave me be, will you? I came out to be free of you and your damned humours.'

'Oh, no, it doesn't work like that, Towne. You planted the seed. You started the hare.'

'You're mixing your figures. Like a bad poet.' Towne tries to shrug off Knell's hand. They are almost beyond the lights of the inn, and the moon that shines on Stratford is touched here with cloud: they are a few facial angles, a flash of eyes. 'Aye, I know what it is, I made a jest about young wives straying. Just that. And you have been brooding and chafing over the whoreson thing all day and I tell you, man, I'm fair sick of it—'

'What didst mean? What hast heard?' Knell sprays as he speaks: his fingers dig and claw into Towne's arm. 'What tales—what lies about her?'

'None, damn you, or none that I would have hearkened to before. But, in God's name, you go a fair way to convincing everyone she's a whore when you carry on like this.'

Knell hits him: an unmeasured punch in the semi-dark, it lands on Towne's left ear, sends him staggering but not sprawling.

'Very well, there, it's done, what you've been wanting.' There is a drag in Towne's voice as he puts a hand to his face, walks away. 'Be content now. Be content with it, Knell. Or is that not possible? Can't get it up for your little piece, is that it? Hm?' Towne turns, walks backward on the turf, the town close where they played earlier. A smear of light in the sky, enough to show the smears on his cheeks. 'Miss my sweet *culo*, do you? Ah, we're getting there, I think. Pity we had to come this way, but we're there at last.'

'Enough!'

'No, Knell, that's for me to say. You were the one who dropped me, remember? *It's not meet any more, sweeting*. Remember? *Our day is done for these frolics*. Never mind what I felt. So what has your little town bride taught you, then, hey? Which way the compass needle truly points? What do you want, Knell, what would you have?' And during this there are two sounds: a distant shout, and a slithery whistle. That last is Knell drawing his sword.

*   *   *

From the bed Will watches drowsily as Anne tiptoes into the next room to look at the children. He knows what she will be doing: stroking back hair, making small noises of love in her throat. Too indulgent, both of them, his mother thinks. And he thinks: Perhaps, but that attachment to her children is one of the beautiful things about Anne, Anne who first showed him beauty. And now?

Anne lies down beside him. He sees his love for Anne and it is there, so clearly shaped, like a bird's nest in a tree revealed by winter bareness; and it was there all the time, but you only see it when it is empty, and nothing more can come of it.

*   *   *

'You're mad,' cries Towne. Moonlight runs its finger along the lifted blade. 'I'll not fight you, Knell, you're a madman . . .' But just now it seems this is true, for Knell, advancing on him, grunting, unspeaking, slashes with wild intent and there are only two things to do: run or draw. (Towne wears

126

a sword, they all wear swords, and the shouts are from Tarlton and Wilson, coming after them with an instinct for danger and knowing what happens when men wear swords and lose reason.) Stumbling, swearing, half weeping, Towne tries both to draw and run. Knell's sword whips and whistles and Towne flings his up, desperate and clumsy, parrying somehow, anyhow; they have fenced a hundred times on stage, never like this. Backwards Towne goes, up rising ground, blocking and warding. 'Stop.' The swords have a dull, clattery, kitcheny sound in the soft night. 'For God's sake.' Knell bears down, bunched and big—he has never seemed so big, even striding the boards in swirling kingly cloak. 'Please.' Tarlton and Wilson are almost upon them, Towne can see them over Knell's shoulder, but too late, surely too late. A mound of earth rears behind him: nearly, so nearly falling, he scrambles up it, begs again. Strikes out as Knell looms. There is a short, tight, meaty sound as the iron point of Towne's sword goes three inches into Knell's neck between ear and larynx.

*   *   *

'What was that?' Anne gasps, lurching up in the bed, hand at her throat.

'What? I heard nothing.'

She blinks several times in the moonlight, in the silence. 'I don't know.' She lies back.

'Perhaps it was—perhaps I was just falling asleep. That jolt.'

'Oh, yes, I know.' He always understands.

*   *   *

127

Knell pitches forward like a butchered bull. The spouting blood looks black in the moonlight. It is still spattering and pooling when Tarlton and Wilson get there: oh, God, oh, Jesus. Knell lies mountainous. It takes two of them to heave him twitching over. Jack Towne, sword at his feet, weeps, grinding his eye boylike with the heel of his hand. Wilson tries to bind and stanch, Tarlton shouts to wake the town. A surgeon, a surgeon.

Too late, too late.

5

The Faithful Shepherdess (1587–8)

Events of a summer night: 13 June 1587. Though what they have created can't be unmade, it doesn't yet show. Like conception, it is invisible and silent and unknowable, until a month or so turns it into pregnancy, and we make way for a change in the world.

A month after William Knell died of a sword wound on the grass at Thame, the depleted company of Queen's Men arrived in Stratford.

'Players. Now we shall see nothing of him,' sighed Joan to Anne, when the news came. An exaggeration, of course. Will was husband and father, and his duties must always call him home. But, contrariwise, he was a man at his own government; and if he chose to walk up to the Swan to talk to the players after his work was done, there was nothing to stop him.

Events of a London apprenticeship, 1587. Ben hated it, he concluded after his first year, with his mind rather than his body. The heavy labour did not tire him, because he did not tire. Even the science of making a wall, the laying of the courses, the pattern of headers and stretchers, made a certain impression on his senses.

But as far as all this touched *him*, the essence of him, he hated it. He became reasonably adept with his tools, brick-axe and brush, trowel and hammer, and took good care of them, cleaning them every evening before storing them away—and never saw them without wanting—physically, literally—to be sick. Because of how they claimed his mind: ravished and despoiled it, over and again, took it grunting and thrusting up against the brick wall.

His hatred of his stepfather persisted, but when they were so much together it was inevitably cooler: you couldn't keep your hackles raised all the time. Ignoring him worked best. Ben carried a book in his pocket, and it came out whenever there was a pause for a drink or a consultation with the builder. Once he lifted his eyes from the page to see his stepfather, stone jar in hand, regarding him across the half-made floor with a sort of wonder; wonder, perhaps, at the sheer immeasurability of the distance between them, sitting six feet apart.

But Ben found other places to go, beyond the pages of a book, and they were what kept him braced and alive, ready to believe that the world, if properly managed, was a glory. They were plays, and women.

One led to another.

Though his stepfather had been once or twice to a play, like many he preferred the Bear-garden, over the river at Southwark, for when he had leisure and spare pennies. Ben found the spectacle of bear-baiting repetitive at best, but while the blood spurted and the white guts uncoiled there was time for a little philosophy: to study and reflect on the much more instructive spectacle of the audience, their merry cheeks and nightmare eyes. Going to the play was a different matter. He started with the White Hart at Southwark, where they were still putting on plays in the galleried inn-yard. The piece he saw made no sense: the verse was lumpily ill-writ, and the players gabbled their lines and bounced off one another at every entrance and exit. But he stayed till the end. He had to find out what became of these pretend people, tissue-thin though they were: they lived, they mattered.

Soon he was regularly attending the new purpose-built playhouses, tramping north to the Theatre at Shoreditch, south to Newington Butts among the archery-meadows. He found it piquant that they bore such a strong resemblance to bear-pits with their circular structure, rings of galleries, open space in the centre; piquant, too, that the godly citizens banished them beyond the city walls. Even his mother shook her head a little over the morality of these brash new places.

But by fifteen Ben was his own man. His stepfather might growl when he packed up his tools at the sound of the theatre-trumpet, but he was not going to risk another hiding. As for his mother's fears, they were right, in a way. It was at the play that he encountered his first lover—or made his first conquest, perhaps, though he wasn't sure who conquered whom.

She was a citizen's wife, her husband perhaps one of those Puritan worthies who would have these sin-palaces levelled. But he was surely in his Cheapside counting-house and she was here in the gallery, no more than thirty, prettily dressed, showing a great deal of creamy neck, and somehow failing to catch the eye of the principal player. Ben knew that restless ladies often invited their favourite players to supper and a private performance afterwards. Perhaps this one was already promised, or else his tastes ran in the other direction. Whichever, it was Ben's gain. When he first realised her eye had wandered to his, he was startled, then violently curious, then thought, Why not?

'What say you to the piece, madam?'

'Do you address me, sirrah?'

Was this part of the game? He guessed it was, and didn't mind it. He was in the yard, she at the front of the lower gallery; he was tall enough to be on a level with her notable breasts.

'Aye, madam, I do. You seem something distracted. It's a mouldy sort of piece, is it not?'

'And you are a judge, are you?'

'Of plays, I hope. I am no more than an honest prentice,' he glanced down at himself, plain stuff suit, bands without lace, 'but even I can tell they have taken an old piece of Terence, lopped and cropped it, and added some jig-jog rhymes for the lovers, which set my teeth on edge. Yes, I am a judge, as I am of beauty: that's why I look your way.'

Being a matter of words, this was so easy, and

he was fascinated by the blush that started at her cheeks and spread downwards. 'Faith,' she said, looking away, 'I really care nothing for the play, or for what you think on it. I'm only parched with heat.'

The usual hawkers were going round the crowd. Ben bought a half-pint of perry.

'It's over-sweet,' she said, sipping; but she drank it all, watching him, while he watched the movement in her throat. When she had done she handed him the mug; he did not move. 'Well? What do you wait for? Oh, to be sure—you are a poor prentice, you will want paying.'

He said: 'It's not a matter of money.' Why not say it? At the very worst, she would snatch the mug and hit him round the head with it, which was nothing. But she did not.

She took him to her bed late that afternoon—not in Cheapside, but neighbouring Poultry. She made a great deal of the favour she was doing him, so he let her believe it. He found, from this and the subsequent encounters with her and numerous others, that he had an eager, undiscriminating appetite; that, though he was not at all handsome, it didn't matter as long as he didn't think about it; that the titanic gloom and disgust which overwhelmed him as he rolled aside lasted only a minute; that he enjoyed lust very much, without being misled into finding it interesting in itself. The women were variously beguiling, but he did not much revise the opinion he had formed in that sweaty room above the stable.

Usually there was a husband somewhere. Oh, a brute, my sweetling, a mere stock; a silent clod, a chattering monkey; negligent, impotent, overbearing, weak. It was hard to imagine how women with such charms as they were all convinced they possessed could have ended up marrying these monstrous men. Strange misfortune. Often meeting them at the play, watching comedies of disguise and concealment, Ben would find himself later acting the piece in reality, hiding in closets or bundling out of windows in his shirt.

This was an education of sorts, he supposed. The many faces of folly. But what he really liked about the act of lust was the way it was at once so compelling and so meaningless. The theatre was a different matter—though to what degree he could not decide. He spent hours standing in the pit in exacting attention; seldom was he stirred, as Nicol was.

'The players must make the best of the lines writ for them. And likewise the finest lines ever writ must take their chance with the players. It's an image of imperfection to place, look you, beside mankind's fallen state. We can aspire to heaven, but our mortal frailty pulls us back as we reach up to it. So with our almost-great stage.'

That was Nicol: like Ben an apprentice, a haunter of the theatres, a scholar, and—though neither of them said as much—an expert in disappointment. He was apprenticed to a vintner, but the Church had been his desire before his father had run into debt and hanged himself for it. Now at nineteen he was the self-appointed high priest of the London theatre.

'Where, then, is the remedy? Who will learn the players not to rant, and the poets not to write fustian?' Ben said, or rather shouted. Nicol was half deaf, as a result of going to sleep in a snowdrift last winter, for a dare. The sin of pride, he said proudly. Now his ears forever ached and bubbled, and he could hear his beloved plays only if he pushed to the front of the pit.

'Perhaps, to pursue the analogy, the drama will be redeemed when a saviour comes along,' Nicol said, spitting nutshell. 'So, what was it in *The Tragedy of Elidure* that displeased?'

Emptying his pint-pot, Ben said: 'The tragedy was no tragedy. Aye, tragic things happened, but they tumbled out like an ill-tied bundle.'

'Why, man, the trouble is you don't *give* yourself to it. Besides, you've not heard *Hieronimo* yet. When you have, then you'll confess what work a mere play can wreak on a man's mind and soul. See yon long fellow in the green? I swear he's with the Admiral's Men. I'll go ask if he knows when it comes on again.'

This Shoreditch tavern where they met was often frequented by players. Also bullies and their whores, fences, card-sharpers, rogues various; the Puritan citizenry, much as Ben despised them, did have a point. So, he admitted at last, did Nicol, when he attended a performance of *Hieronimo*, as people called it. *The Spanish Tragedy*, as the playbills posted about the city properly proclaimed it.

'A tear, a tear, I saw a whole tear trickle,' exulted Nicol, dancing round him. 'Now say if it is not sublime.'

'It is full of faults and absurdities, and sublime,' Ben said, wiping his eyes. 'Say, then, who is this Master Kyd, where does he come from, how does he do it? I suspect his learning. Showing off those great stretches of Latin.'

'I'll tell thee what, thou art heart-sick with jealousy. Where the man comes from I don't know, but I know he is young, well favoured, with all the wit and learning you'd expect. See how the piece held that crowd, made 'em stare, even kept the fool groundlings quiet. And then deny, thou whoreson, that here is art incomparable.'

Ben did not; and the grieving madness of Hieronimo, finding his beloved son hanged, kept interposing itself between him and his work. More surprisingly, it fretted him when he was with a lover. He tried to speak to her of it, but she shrugged: she assumed he was losing interest in her, which happened to be true, so he could not deny it. He went home, having wiped the spit from his face, and found his stepfather snoring before the fire, one hand down his breeches. He thought still of Hieronimo weeping for his murdered boy: he wondered what it was like to have a father to weep for you. Then he wondered if his own father's spirit watched over him, and suddenly doubt put its brute shoulder against the door of belief and charged it down, shouting that there was no spirit, that his father was dust and nothingness. He called up swift arguments and got the beast out, but the echo of it lingered. He decided then it was dangerous, morbid, to investigate one's feelings.

As for discussing the theatre with women, beware of that too—though he fell into it once more, over *Tamburlaine*.

That was during the summer of the Armada, when fear and death were in the hot air, and London was madder than usual. Along with hundreds of other apprentices, Ben drilled twice a week on the green at Mile End, preparing to meet

135

the Spanish tercios if they landed. Privately he suspected it would be a brief meeting. He at least had a pike and knew how to use it, but Nicol had been given a bow and arrows, though he had never shot one in his life; and some of the captains still wore their aprons from smithy and shop. Still, when the hilltop beacons flared to say the ships were coming, Ben felt more uplifted than fearful. This was grand, this was vivid.

'And is it not all empty vaunting?'

She was a goldsmith's wife; she could read and write; she liked to climb aboard Ben but could push him off to drift once the booty was taken; and they had seen *Tamburlaine* together.

'All of it, empty,' she said. 'Men and their soldiery, Spanish or English. Drums and trumpets and vainglory. And Tamburlaine making his fine prodigious speeches.'

'You said they excited you. In fact, I saw the evidence of it.'

'Aye, aye, the first time,' she said, moving his hand away. 'Then afterwards, you know, one falls a-thinking. And in truth all that splendid noise hurts the ear. They say we women are loose with our tongues, but men are the noisy sex.'

'Hm. Will you call it empty vaunting, when we stand between you and the Spanish ravishers?'

'I thought they were coming to make us popish, not ravish us.'

He had to smile, but he was needled. She seemed intent on making the world smaller, when *Tamburlaine* had made it so much greater. Everyone who went to the play was on fire for *Tamburlaine* that season. The Scythian shepherd, rising through sheer will to become conqueror of half the world, made furious conquests of audiences likewise; they gasped and swooned and fell before him. Ben bowed with the rest. The hero was barbarously cruel and you knew that in reality he would have mown you down and slaughtered everyone you loved. But you followed it all with ticking blood, followed him on his sky-striding course, because the words would not be denied. Just words. A gunpowder discovery, a pregnant secret. A man called Marlowe was behind it.

'What's best, then?' he asked the goldsmith's wife. 'Welcome Sir Spaniard when he lands? Melt down every sword? Put an end to all that's heroical? Live prosy, live long and tamely?'

'Well, at least that means staying alive.'

'"And with our sun-bright armour, as we march,
We'll chase the stars from heaven, and dim their
   eyes
That stand and muse at our admired arms."'

'You men,' she said, absently opening her legs.

It lasted a little longer—not much. Her violet eyes, faint lisp, habit of undressed thinking all fell away from his esteem, though they were later the occasion of reminiscent cock-stands.

The Armada loomed menacingly on the horizon of the mind. Rumour darted about the town, like harrying English ships. Nicol, deaf and impatient, sought only for news of the true conqueror, Marlowe: was he writing a new piece, when would it come on? In the Shoreditch tavern a group of players, well in their cups, humoured him a while.

'Who are we to know? Master Marlowe gives out the lines, my friend, as you'd throw bones to a dog,' said one, fire-faced and baleful with liquor. 'You wouldn't get down on the floor and mumble 'em with him, now would you?'

'Oh, for shame, you're unfair on the man,' said another, palely lounging. 'Kit Marlowe's a very pretty fellow, and if he carries it a little high, who's to blame him? He comes down from Cambridge the complete scholar *and* with a play under his arm that sets the whole town by the ears. All this prodigy— and no older than Will here.' He touched the ear of a lean young man in unadorned black who gave a moment's smile and returned to rolling a broken spill between his fingers, absorbedly, as if it might mend, as if something might happen. Ben hadn't even noticed him there.

'New piece or old piece, just let us be allowed to play something,' groaned a fourth, head in hands. 'With the Spaniard on the waves we can't go about. Let him land or sink, so long as we can get a crowd.'

'Jesting, mere jesting and poor,' the lounging player said, with a quick glance at Nicol and Ben, 'for we are loyal subjects, naturally, and no one should think otherwise.'

'What?' snapped Nicol. 'Oh, for God's sake, we're prentices, not Walsingham's spies. As for that, I hear the Queen has a ship ready to fly if they land, and is going to throw herself on the King of France's mercy.'

'A wild libel,' said Fire-face. 'The one thing you can rely on, if the Spanish land every papist in the kingdom will rise to aid them. We're all like to be murdered in our beds.'

'Well, there are worse things,' said the young man named Will. 'At least you'd be comfortably asleep when it happened.' He spoke with a certain

138

hesitating thoughtfulness, as if scrutinising the joke on its way out, wondering if it were serious after all. His eyes met Ben's for a moment, with a peculiar awkward intimacy, as when feet accidentally touch under the table. They seemed to read reason in one another, before the page of recognition was whisked over, Fire-face furiously banging his beer-mug down.

'And where do you stand, Will? Since you scoff at our peril, I would know just where you stand.' Ready to fight over the disposition of a hair—Ben recognised it from his stepfather.

'I stand nowhere,' the young man said. 'I hate the Spanish. I hope they burn and plunge to Hell and that our Englishmen consign them there. And I stand nowhere.' He kept still, his face angular in repose, but his fingers turned the spill faster. 'Once you stand anywhere, you turn to stone.'

'The Admiral's Men,' Nicol persisted, conning faces, 'they had *Tamburlaine* for themselves—pray you, are any of you with them, know them? They must have first refusal of Master Marlowe's next work, surely . . .'

Nicol's hearing, as he admitted to Ben a while after, was growing worse. Hence his anxiety to hear *Tamburlaine* again, or anything of spell-binder Marlowe's, because soon he would be stone deaf. When that came, he said thoughtfully, he might kill himself, like his father, and make a proper job of it.

But the players in the Shoreditch tavern could not enlighten him; and when Ben and Nicol left, Fire-face and Pale-face were furiously quarrelling over the bill. The young player called Will watched them with a peculiar intensity: like a fair-juggler, Ben thought, watching his sticks turning in the air.

Follow the dark young player called Will when he leaves the Shoreditch tavern a little later.

Follow his rapid progress through the baffling noonday London streets, where breath is always on your face and human life is collision. Follow him precisely—the trail of his body-shape through the crowds—and you find that you touch no one; that somehow, without slackening pace, he ripples and sidles and at every moment presents a slender fencer's breathed-in profile and reaches his destination as free of contact as if he had walked there across a gleaned field.

Off Cheapside he slips into an eating-house where even the front door seems like a back door. Across the way great timbered frontages, inns of note and renown, hold out their heavy signs like back-braced heralds. There is a Star: there are Three Cups; and on a corner plot there is a Mermaid, slowly grinding her wriggly painted half-self against the wind. But this most ordinary of ordinaries suits him well: the food is cheap and filling, and you can call for writing materials and find the ink usable, where in many inns it comes clogged or overwatered.

Ink and quill, and an order for a roasted fowl. He has brought his own paper—a string-bound manuscript written in various hands, some neatly marching, others staggering across the downhill page. He uses the blank versos to write on, in fidgety bursts. In between he gazes towards the great hearth where his meal is cooking and sometimes his left hand moves oddly on the table-top, like a dancing caterpillar. The verse, the pulse, you must make sure it counts.

What he is doing: patching and cobbling a thing already patched and cobbled, a play written in collaboration by three men and altered by three others before he got to it. Make the thing work. Not greatly different from other men of business you can see repairing to city tables, bum-shifting round the steaming joint, consulting their tablets. A worldly task.

Except that through the cracks of his busy fierce dissatisfaction shines something else: something that belongs to another life, another world, distant and present as the workings of gods.

This Will: and Will the glover's son who walked up the Stratford street to the Swan to pass the time of day with the travelling players.

How could one become the other?

*   *   *

'Dear God.'

'Aye, Will, so you keep saying. What, are you training to be a priest?' Jack Towne drew a scarlet jerkin from his pack and irritably shook it out. 'Look at that! Crushed to buggery and I laid it up so fair . . . Look, it was self-defence, the coroner saw that from the first. Ask Tarlton, ask Wilson—'

'No, no, I don't doubt you. I only wonder at—at what a man can do. When life suddenly takes such a turn.'

'Suddenly is the word.' Towne looked icy and pared: as if he expected every surface and shadow to draw a sword on him. 'He would have killed me, you know. I was looking at my own death—there, just there.'

141

'Dear God. How did it feel?' Will asked, with passionate interest.

'Which? That, or killing a man?' Towne dragged out a pair of round hose. 'Torn, look. Disgrace. A Queen's Man tricked out in shreds and patches.'

'Show.' Will reached out. 'Only the seam. I could mend that for you, neat, not a stitch to be seen. Both, both, I mean: mortality.' He glanced up. 'Naturally you're sick of talking of it.'

'Could you mend?' yawned Towne. 'How so? Art seamstress?'

'No, hand-craftsman, as thou know'st.' Will tossed the garment back, cold now. He had a suspicion of how cold he could be: the vast potential of it. 'And if I pry or offend, just say it.'

'Oh . . .' Something seemed to shiver through Towne, sorrowful. 'I'm not sick of talking of it, Will, because I don't. We don't. It's there always. But we've had to go on. You must go on, you see? Even after . . .' Momentarily Towne was imploring; and he looked at his own beautiful hands as if contemplating a deformity. 'I'm not safe yet, man. Yes, the coroner found for me, but I'm on, whatsname, recognisances, awaiting Her Majesty's word. I would have given everything I have for this—this thing not to have happened. But he wouldn't stop. He wouldn't stop, Will.'

Will touched Towne's shoulder. Towne looked at him with complete, stranded surprise, as if he had just woken up. 'Let me stitch up your clothes, I can't stitch up your mind.'

'I don't know. If anyone could . . . You're a strange one, Will. Here you are, an old wedded man with six children—'

'Three, for pity's sake.'

'Three may as well be six. Here you are, and you seem no different from the youth who used to come dog-foot after the cart as soon as we crossed the bridge. Still no flesh on you. Don't good townsmen start to plump the moment they turn twenty-one?'

'You suppose me a good townsman?'

'Oh, surely. You do have this odd look, mind: a sort of guilty look, which I can't account for. How do you transgress hereabouts? Poach a deer?'

Will laughed. 'Why would I want to do that? No, I'm something far worse than your common thief and despoiler.'

'What?'

'I'll leave you to guess. So who takes Knell's parts? How do you go on?'

'We go on as we go on,' Towne groaned, 'which is to say, like a three-wheeled wagon. Knell's parts we divide, and we contrive. But with everyone moving up a step, so to speak, there's a hole left at bottom. Consider. *True Tragedy of Richard III* has sixty-eight speaking parts. Even at full strength four of us have to take seven parts each, and then we have to doff costumes like lightning. Take one man away, and you can picture: there's only so much doubling you can do. Makes a poor spectacle for the Queen's Men. We have a name for laying on the grand shows, look you, where the whole history goes in majestical procession before their eyes. And then I swear we shall all be jaded to a shadow before we— What's the matter?'

'Nothing.'

'Why look so, then? As if you'd reprove me. Yes it's my doing, but not my choosing.'

'I don't reprove you.'

'Are you ill? Hold off if you are, we want no

sickness fewing us further. Is there any ale in this house?'

'I'm not ill. Did you say *fewing*?'

'Did I? Yes. Fewing, making few, it sounds right. Damn words, man, they're ours to do with as we will. If not ale, cider. I'll not touch wine any more. No, it's all a wry pickle: at the least we want a hired-man from London to make up the company, but how to send for one suitable? One of us would have to go, which would only compound the problem. But we surely can't give over the tour.' Towne looked Will up and down. 'What *is* the matter? Are you drunk? If so, at least let me catch up.'

'Nothing. No, I—' The cloak he was inspecting slid from Will's fingers. The room listed and swung like a pieman's tray. He put out a foot to steady himself and heard his voice say from somewhere: 'I can't stay, nor—nor anything. Good luck to you.'

He got out to the yard without falling. There was a horse-trough, so he dunked his head in it to rid himself of strange raptures and rash possibilities. And when they would not go he stayed thus, upside down and breath-stopped in floating hair: thinking, There is always this instead, always.

*　　　*　　　*

As the twins burst in John Shakespeare was working leather on a staple, arm muscles corded, shadowed face grim.

Anne hurried after them. 'I'm sorry. But they won't think of bed without Grandfather . . .'

Instant transformation: she had known it would come, but still she relished it. He dropped his work,

144

flung out his arms, and tossed them up laughing and biting.

'And I can't think of bed without my tasty supper, and here it is. Which first? Mm, thou art both sweet. Peace, peace, wilt wet your clouts a-laughing. Now where's thy father?'

He raised his tousled head from their squealing, the question alighting on Anne.

'Home soon,' she said.

*   *   *

He came up with the biggest breath he had ever drawn, and he was still snarling air into his lungs and shaking gouts of water from his hair as he pounded back into the inn and slammed the door open, and Jack Towne, jumping, said, 'My God, what? Are you mad, what?' and Will, dripping, heaving, glaring, said: 'Take *me*. Try me. Try me, take me.'

*   *   *

' "The richest ransom that the kingdom yields
Shall be thy portion; and if my jesting cousin
Sets his cruel wits to darker mischief—" '

'Not the text,' John Dutton put in. '*Wicked* wits, *further* mischief. I thought you said you knew this piece by heart. You'd better have the playbook.'

'I do know it,' Will said. 'But my text is better.' They were in the Swan tap-room, with the benches pushed back. His audience, six Queen's Men, stood or squatted, chewed lip, plucked beard. Unimpressed, or unimpressible. This country

145

hind? Jack Towne had persuaded them to give him a hearing. Will fixed his eyes on Towne's, moving downstage. Trying to be easy and graceful and not hobbled by a dozen years' longing.

'"His proper toils I shall upon him turn.
For though the snake its venom tastes
   unharmed,
'Tis otherwise with e'en the supplest villain
Kindred to the serpent kind."'

'Why do you say your alteration is better?' Robert Wilson, the quietest.

Will knew about quiet ones. '*Wicked wits* trips too merrily. We don't feel it. *Cruel* catches like thorn or nettle.'

Wilson inclined his head. 'And *further*?'

Will shrugged: he wanted to be performing. 'Oh, *further* says only one thing. *Darker* says several things at once.'

'Which *can* lead to confusion.' Wilson smiled.

'Have a care, my friend,' Tarlton said, uncorking a cider-jug. 'Master Wilson had a hand in the composition of this, did you not?'

'It's your work?' Will swallowed. 'I'm sorry— sorry a thousand times.'

'I had a hand in it, as Tarlton says, along with half a dozen others,' Wilson says gently, 'and we all wrought as best we could. The thousand apologies are rather too many.'

'Oh, but still, I wouldn't have spoken. Anyone who writes—who makes these things—'

'Can we get on?' John Dutton said, shuffling through the playbooks. 'That wasn't perhaps a good choice. Peristratus is a chief part, after all. And if

146

we *were* to think of taking on a hired-man outside London—which I for one am far from sure about—then you must understand what would be required of you.'

'Mere drudging factotum,' Tarlton said, beaming at Will and drinking to him, 'with your choicest part the Second Squire, who says, "Yes my lord", twice.'

'Care of the wardrobe besides,' said John Singer. 'Scribe the parts, and shoe the horses if put to it.'

'This isn't scaring me,' Will said.

'Try *King Leir*. It's new, you won't know this.' Dutton passed him a playbook: manuscript, and the hand not at all clear. 'Proud old dolt of a king divides his kingdom between his daughters. Two of them are bitches. This is one, Gonorill. You're Skalliger, her toad-eater. Oh, damn it, we need Cooke for her. Where is he?'

'Gone to stool again,' Towne said. 'He will eat of the green fruit. Here, I'll take the part, I can still outwoman the best of 'em.' Will saw an eye roll, a cheek distend at that. 'Come, Will, we must look over the same book. Where, now . . . "I prithee, Skalliger, tell me, if thou know, By any means to rid me of this woe."'

Towne did not so much raise the pitch of his voice as lower it, finding helpless softness deep down. His hand rested lightly on Will's arm: inviting, urging.

'"Your many favours still bestowed on me, Bind me in duty to advise Your Grace . . ."' Throw the voice forward without shouting: how was it done? These last few years he had recited only in a whisper, alone in dead of night or on the open road, like his father pattering prayers. '"The large allowance which he hath from you, Is that which

147

makes him so forget himself . . ."' Resurrect the Will who used to declaim to the fields, putting all his love into it. Towne's eyes searched his, challenging. You have to put all your love into it. None left over. This, this, I want this. The crabbed script wavered before his eyes; he blinked sweat.

'"For why, abundance maketh us forget
That ever frugal pinch and dearth existed.'"

'That's not the line,' John Dutton grumbled. 'It's *The fountains*—'

'"As when the fountains fail, and men bemoan
Who yesterday full cups threw in the dust—"'

'Text, text. You're making it up.'
'Making it better,' Wilson said narrowly. Tarlton's jug was suspended. Stratford faces peered at the smeared window: what's afoot? 'Go on.'
Towne touched his fingers.

'"Well, Skalliger, for thy kind advice herein,
I will not be ungrateful, if I live . . ."'

Will made out the word *Exit* on the shaking page. Shaking because he was shaking, because from nowhere had come this chance, mad and unmissable, as if old and dozing stiff-jointed by the ashes you found a fairy before you saying, *Be young*. He blinked the slouching words upright. Short soliloquy, make it count.

'"Go, viperous woman, shame to all thy sex:
The heavens, no doubt, will punish thee for this:

148

And me a villain, that to curry favour . . ."'

What? *Have given the daughter counsel 'gainst the father.* God, writ with a ham fist. '"Have blown her daughter's hate, unnatural kindled—"'
'Text—'
'Bugger the text, listen.'
'Constrain, Will, don't saw the air,' Towne whispered. Will put the book down, drew closer to his audience. He was not Will, he was Skalliger, counsellor to an ancient princess: he was someone else; never had he been so entirely, freely himself. He turned out his palms, levelled his voice. For this to happen, a man had had to die, and so he must be glad of that. A lesson.

'"But us the world doth this experience give,
     That he that cannot flatter, cannot live."'

Towne glanced at Tarlton. 'Pitched well, hey?'
A man had died; what else must happen? Frightening, this huge acceptance. Write your name with the proffered pen of fire, knowing that once done, something far off in place or years was being prepared for you; hear, perhaps, the faint chunk and clink of it. The Queen's Men were whispering, heads down. The craning heads at the window blotted the everyday sun.
'And this experience shows, there's nothing made, Without some other thing is sore betrayed,' Will said.
'What?' Dutton tossed down the playbook. 'You invent too much.'
'How is that possible?' he enquired politely; then thought, No, don't. Step back. 'Your pardon. I—
149

gentle sirs, you know I will do, I will be, anything. I will . . .' And suddenly you find you have said it: the real last line.

*   *   *

He told his father first, in the workshop: it seemed natural.

John Shakespeare roamed back and forth, stared at Will's face and then at the door. He had nowhere to go but outrage, and even there he found precious little room. He could only repeat himself: 'They are players.'

'They are the Queen's Men. They act under royal patent. They are everywhere assured success. If I were offered a place in any other trade that prospered so—'

'It is not a trade.' His father's voice was dull with shock. 'They are players.'

'Call it a profession, then, or what you will. No, call it this: a living. They have need, and I have ability, I have readiness, I have—inclination, a very great inclination. Father, here is opportunity. Their travels end in London, where there are theatres, permanent theatres, being new-built all the time, and a man following the player's trade will never lack employment. It's a prosperous chance, just like Richard Field going to London to be a printer.'

'Richard went as prentice, bound by seven years' articles to a guild trade. There's no Worshipful Company of Players, I think?'

No: thank God. Will tried to keep the thought from showing on his face.

'And you say they will take you only as a hired-man. Not a company member—such as it

150

is. Will . . .' His father gestured helplessly: his capable hands couldn't hold or shape this. 'This is speculation, of the wildest sort.'

Again Will thought behind the screen of his face: not like speculation in wool, with the courts watching you. 'Father, to this profession—to these people, I am worth something. What am I worth here? Aye, I turn my hand to your business, but there's Gilbert working for you too, and Richard likely to be handier than either of us. In the fattest year, this shop couldn't support three grown sons. And, besides, I have—'

'You have a wife and three children,' his father said, with a faint smile, like someone answering a riddle.

'All the more reason to make something of myself. On my own account.'

The screen must have shifted, for his father said, with sudden violence: 'It would have been better, more honest, simply to run away one night, surely. If escape is all you want.'

Will turned away from him and breathed deep while thinking: I could kill you, Father, for saying that. I truly find it possible and palatable in the imagining . . . But, then, he had never had any trouble imagining anything. It was the living part that was problematic.

'I don't want to escape,' he said at last. 'Though escape is at least an action, and so has a little of bold spirit about it, hey?' He glanced around the shop, as if estimating its dimensions. 'Unlike hiding, hiding for the rest of your days.'

'You'll come back. You'll crawl back in patches with nothing.' His father's face was suffused with blood, livid like a hanged man's. 'That's what I

151

dread to see, Will. Your humiliation. If I say I forbid it, it's because of that—'

'Forbid? How? For God's sake, I'm a man grown, husband and father myself. You're in no place to forbid.'

'Aye, so.' All at once his father was calmer: soft, almost playful. Almost. 'You are husband and father, as you say, and there lies your responsibility. And if your wife should say nay, it's a different matter. Yes?'

Yes: Will didn't have to say it.

*   *   *

'I don't understand,' said Anne. 'These players want you to go with them? They asked you?'

'I asked them. They have need . . . I have need.'

'How long would you be gone? What do you— Will, what does it mean?'

She listened to him explaining, while she picked up after the twins. Never Susannah, always neat. *The north of the country, then the east coast . . . Lodging and eating together.* Hamnet's old teething-ring: needed throwing out, but he was perversely attached to it. An emotional child, quick to trouble. *Then London. Anne, you know I have always loved the play, and it seems I have aptitude enough . . .* I ought to be more surprised. Oh, I'm shocked and sick and wondering and angry and terrified, but there's this at the centre: call it unsurprise. It was never—it was never *likely*, was it, this happiness? *Once in London, if I can establish myself . . . then when I return . . .* She picked up the wooden toys he had carved, the doll, the horse. He had put so much detail into them it was almost

152

excessive: the children had been frightened of them at first. *With luck—with good fortune—I should be able to send home money—*

'And our marriage?' she said. How flat her own voice sounded, as if she were reminding him to bring firewood. But the fire was in her.

'Anne, it's sudden, I know.' He reached for her hand: she got hold of his and tossed it aside, like something slimy crawling.

'No, Will. Nothing of that, I thank you. I just want to know—which marriage is this? The one I thought I had, against all the odds, the sweet one top-full of worth and truth? Or the one the gossips rubbed their hands over—the one you were forced into, the bitter one, the one folk said you'd *rue?*'

He stood hollow-eyed and handsome, holding out weakly beseeching hands to her, and he was every man craving indulgence of his folly before every woman fuming with hands on hips, and nothing was unique or valuable any more, and she ran from him. Out of the house.

The Shottery field path. Well, whatever hidden part of her heart impelled her here, it wasn't that she was seeking the old home. No, she had only one home, ever: it was with him, alas. Across the gold day, across the fields moved one of those summer rain-showers that you can see whole, like a net trawling the land. She was wetted, then dry in moments, except her face.

Will caught up with her. 'I love you. It isn't about love.' He panted, holding the stitch in his side. 'And when I come back—'

'What for?' She wanted to lash and sting, though any weapon she took up would only rip and lacerate her own hands. 'Come back, what for?'

'This is where I began and this is where I begin and end, with you. Give me a pin.'

'What?'

Pale, deft, he took one from her waist. The touch was still familiar and beautiful and therefore a screaming insult to her pain. He waded through long grass into tree-shade, knelt down, and plucked up a little bare patch of soil.

'What are you doing?'

'Blood. Call it heart's blood.' He had driven the pin deep into his thumb and left it there, obscenely protruding, while he squeezed the rich dribbling redness on to the earth. 'Wherever I go, I will still be here.' He began scraping together stones over the spot, heaping them up into a little cairn. Soon his hands were red.

She said weakly: 'Don't.'

He shrugged as he worked, his face long and white. 'It's blood. Not words, or not just words. I know you don't trust those. When I come back, I'll find this.'

'It's a show. It doesn't mean anything.'

He rose. Tugged the pin from his thumb, looked at it, dropped it on the ground. 'Perhaps not.'

'I always thought—' She struggled with her voice, which seemed about to go wildly out of control—to shrill like a gale or growl deep as a bear. 'I was sure, always I was sure that if you were unhappy, I would be able to tell.'

His glance was briefly puzzled, as if she had posed him a quick sum. 'Oh! Unhappiness. That would be different. There's a cure for that.'

Blood beaded and dripped from his hand. Anne reached into the neck of her smock and tore off a length of lace. 'Give me.' They looked at each other

154

while she tightly bound his thumb. 'Money, you say. Is that what you want? Money, fame?'

'You've spoiled your lace . . . I dare say I would like them. If I can get them, I will. For us. For our—well, our name.'

She shook her head. 'No. It's not that.' She felt herself scowling. A little shudder of warm raindrops fell from the leaves above, and for a moment she imagined it blood. 'And you could never speak to me of this. This wanting. Because I can't read, perhaps, because I can't understand? God knows. It must have been so strong, all the time, and I never felt it. I wonder what else I missed.'

'Thou hast only to speak the word, Anne.' Suddenly his voice and look came from somewhere different, from a place of high, resounding challenge, like the wedding-altar. 'Dost know? Only speak it.'

'And thou'lt stay?'

'And I'll stay.'

They walked back in step, in two different kinds of silence.

*   *   *

The Queen's Men performed *The Famous Victories of Henry the Fifth* at Stratford Guildhall that day. It was only a moderate success. Even with a cut text, the shortage of an actor left them straining. Once Robert Wilson rushed off and rushed on again with such an obvious hasty change of wig that the audience laughed when they should have been thrilled; and it was hard to win them back after that.

'Aye, aye, let's say you're right, then.' Lawrence Dutton: who had held out to the last against recruiting Will Shakespeare, and been grumblingly outvoted. 'But, look you, it's an expedient only, so the tour don't disgrace us. Once in London, he goes his own way.'

*   *   *

'You can forbid it, you know.'

Her father-in-law had sought her out in the kitchen. The quietest place in the house just now: since finding out last night that Will was going away Edmund had been unmanageable, which in turn had affected the children. Anne stirred the broth. 'How?' she said.

'He won't stand against both of us. Alone I can't move him.' He took her elbow and turned her to him. 'But you, Anne, you have the power.'

She studied his eyes, so like Will's eyes, except for those lines around them, rays of irritable weariness. 'To change him?'

'Damn it, to bring him back to his senses. He's always been a dreamer. But this is the worst.'

A dreamer—yes, Anne thought, and he had the true hardness of the dreamer. And on this matter of joining the players he was diamond-hard, glittering, resolved. Yet her father-in-law was right. She was the one who could tie up all her anger and grief and bewilderment and place it neatly before him as: no. As my husband, as father to our children, you do wrong. No. She did indeed have the power—such power. It was like being a giant, hesitating where to set down your great killing foot. How horrible, to be a giant.

'Did he invite you to meet them? These players?' her father-in-law went on, as she turned away.

'Yes. The Queen's Men. I said no—though I don't doubt, as the Queen's own company, they are of a decent seemly sort.'

'Now thou art the dreamer, daughter,' he said gently. 'Why dost think they need another man, hm?'

'Will told me. One died while they travelled.'

'Died how, I wonder. Shriven, peacefully settling to last sleep? Dost think?'

'I don't know.' She put her hands to her temples. 'It's not that I fear.'

'Ah.'

'I don't want to change him. I don't want to bend him and turn him against his will. There's no loving in that.'

He snorted. 'Oh, yes, there is.'

'But there is more,' she said carefully, 'in a wife's loyalty to a man, no matter what befalls.' Daring: his flush showed he took the point. Daring, for could she rely on John Shakespeare's goodwill any more? After all, she had failed to tie Will down as he had hoped.

'My dear,' her father-in-law sighed, sitting heavily on a stool, 'don't you see that if he pursues this folly, it will change him? Change him beyond all your power?'

She thought of that. And, yes, there was terror in it. Again she pictured him a player, walking beside the painted cart, stepping on a distant stage, speaking and acting as though he were someone else and not her Will at all. It was dreadfully easy to picture, she found.

And yet was this a diversion from the journey that had begun with green passion in the wood, or the journey continued? *You made me*, he had said

157

once. *Your love, it made me*. Last night or, rather, on the brink of dawn, they had talked, kissed, fought, wept. And he said again, *You made me. This me*.

So, stop him going? Unmake him?

Part of her wanted to, yes. She was realistic about love: she knew love was inimical to freedom. Love was a dungeon-keeper and would rather see its object chained and miserable than not see it at all. And yet: *Bring him back to his senses*, John Shakespeare said—relying on her. And, God, how doleful a fate that was, she thought, to be someone who brought people back to their senses! Is that me? Once, not so long ago, I could rob Will of his senses with a glance, a finger-touch. Now, yes, I am mother and helpmeet and my waist is thickened, but I am still that same Anne who could make him weak with love. I would still be his witch, not his corrector. In the end, I am on the side of madness and enchantment, and so I must let him go.

'He might do great things,' she said. 'None of us has thought of that.'

She spoke temperately, but her father-in-law flinched as if she had screeched in his face. 'The right thing,' he said, after a moment. 'That's all I want him to do.'

He had not moved from the stool, but his presence seemed to reach out and fill the room. She made a feint of tasting the broth again. 'Needs salt,' she said. 'And our box is empty. I'll go borrow some of Judith Sadler.'

She went out cloaked and hooded. Not to the Sadlers'.

She slipped over to the Swan, and asked the ostler to show her into the presence of the players.

158

They were gathered round a table heaped with papers. Ah, papers, pens, writing—her gentle enemies. But listening, and observing one of them counting with a frown on his fingers, she realised this was a matter of numbers not words: a reckoning of accounts. She hesitated, studying faces, postures, dress. They were different, certainly. Everything about them seemed a little more quick, a little more defined. One—the clown?—had a rich pink laugh that made you smile just to hear it, though she wondered what it would be like to have that laugh directed at you. All were rather older than Will, except a youth who must be a woman-player, and a tall fair young man with beautiful arching eyebrows: a beauty that somehow made her uncomfortable, like the sight of money or jewels left nakedly open to the thief.

Rogues and vagabonds, not at all, and when the players saw her, they were mannerly and sober, bowing: Mistress, your pardon, what do you seek, may we serve . . . ? But she drew down her hood, said she was mistook, and went away. She was not sure what she had wanted to see, but she was satisfied: some gaps had been filled in. Master Smart the draper used an abacus for his counting— you could see him through his window, flicking and tapping—and that was Anne at this juncture of her life; that was Anne hurrying home in warm street-shade, flicking the beads of love, loyalty, fear, in search of a reckoning.

One figure would not alter. 'Anne, Anne, I can hardly believe it,' as Bartholomew had said on his last visit—Anne, turned thirty, who would believe it? Hard to tell whether he was being malicious or not. He might simply be observing the fact: the blowsy fact that could only grow bigger and more blatant.

You are older than Will, Anne—and with each year it will matter more.

A reason not to let Will out of her sight, then, not to let him roam the great world and behold a thousand objects of comparison. A powerful reason—but an ugly one. Beauty was where they had begun.

She found him in the yard, splitting firewood. He was shirt-sleeved, sweaty, homely; but as he raised his eyes she could perfectly imagine him taking his place with those players at the inn, oh, yes. Just then it even seemed a wonder that he was here at all.

'Will. Listen.' She put out a hand—to touch him or ward him off, who could tell? It stayed between them, wavering. 'You must never belong to anyone else.'

And he took her seriously, she thought: he breathed as she had seen a mouse breathe, trapped in the corner before the shovel came down.

'I won't,' he said. 'My life on it.'

She laughed a little. She felt so tired, as if she could sleep a year away. She felt she could smash the world. 'Very good, very apt. Because if you do, I will curse you. And by that I mean lay a curse on you. I will do it, somehow.'

He fell to his knees. His brow convulsed, his eyes half closed, he groped at her hand. 'It's fair,' he said. Fingers clenched fingers for a moment, jolted away as if burned. Though his head was lowered, his voice was strong and clear: 'Yes, it's fair.'

*   *   *

160

Before Will left Stratford, with his trunk stowed in the Queen's Men's cart, his father came to him to say something. Not trying to undo what was already done: Will credited him with that. If anything, it was like the lost old days when they could bear to look into each other's face. Advice, given from kindness.

'A man cannot split himself in two, Will.' He paused. 'One half will die, sooner or later.'

It was simpler with his mother. Always calm, she had in the last year or two restricted her range of expression even further: against the unpleasantness of the world she pitted her folded hands and patient, frowning smile. She warned him against the barbarity of the north and the corruption of London. She gave him her blessing. He thought it probable she would never forgive him.

*   *   *

Some responses of Stratford citizens, on Will Shakespeare's leaving the town to travel with a company of players.

He had gone mad.

He was taking a poor sort of risk, and would rue.

He had always been strange.

He had never been strange.

He had married and saddled himself with a family much too young, so he was bound to break out like this in the end.

He was always inclined that way.

He would never make a fortune under his father's roof, for times were hard and there wasn't enough trade to go round, so it made sense to strike out on his own.

He hated his old wife.

* * *

At Two Elms Gilbert, panting, caught up with the cart. Will experienced a blinding, sweating memory.

'Oh, no, no, not another one,' Tarlton said. 'We are not a charitable foundation.'

'Will. In London—find me something,' Gilbert gasped. 'A trade. Prenticeship. Like Richard Field. Anything. Out of here.'

Will grasped his hand. 'I'll try.'

They waved.

'*He*'s not married, is he?' said Lawrence Dutton. He swept his cloak back pettishly. 'Well. I merely ask.'

* * *

Ben: he trained and drilled and readied himself for the fight, but no Spaniards came to try the question.

God blew, and they were scattered, declared the Queen's Medal, after the Armada broke in bits and the beacon-fires were damped or used to roast the celebratory ox. Ben stood among the gazers at Ludgate as the procession of the great wound into St Paul's for the service of thanksgiving. Relief, he observed, was somehow less exciting than fear. He glimpsed the Queen's coach, yawing and bouncing behind four skittish greys, and wondered if she thought the same.

A week later, at the foot of King's Street he ran into William Camden.

For the first time ever, from the way Master Camden looked at him—up and down—Ben wanted to run and consult a mirror. But then his old master stopped that, and put a friendly hand on his shoulder: they walked and talked as if they were equals.

Tamburlaine—yes, Master Camden had seen it. And it had conquered him too, or conquered his aversion to what he had previously regarded as the triviality of the theatre.

'The abandoning of rhyme, jigging rhyme, as the poet calls it, has given the verse a new strength and grandeur, without doubt,' he said approvingly. 'Now, can it be flexible also? Is it capable of sweetness? Here are new seas for our bold English tongue to sail. To be sure, the perfection of the ancient languages is still far to seek . . .'

Keeping pace with Master Camden, hearing him discourse and sift and discriminate, Ben realised he had not been thinking of these things at the theatre. Even when admiring, he had been half thinking of Madam's jostling breasts seen from the corner of his eye.

'Our measure, granted, is of accent not quantity, so the effects of Latin verse can never truly be reproduced . . .' Master Camden stopped at the corner, the parting of their ways. He studied Ben genially, as if trying to undo that earlier look. 'So, when will you be out of your time?'

'Five years,' Ben said.

'It will go quickly.'

Ben grinned. 'You've never lied to me before.'

For a year he gave up plays and women. He took the decision like leaping into cold water. He read and, exhausting his books, saved to buy more. Prowling the booksellers around St Paul's Churchyard, he bumped into a dark young man, recognising him without knowing him. That narrowing broad-browed face, the disquieting eyes tender as bruises. The young man gave him the wall.

'Sir.'

'Y'r servant.'

Ben never gave the wall. The young man went on, nimbly picking his way through the kennel-shit, and then Ben remembered him. The Shoreditch tavern: the player, Will. Suddenly he found himself wondering why he never gave the wall. The question followed him nagging into the next shop, where the bookseller hung anxiously over him, watching his bricklayer's hands turning the precious leaves. Catullus: poems of love, thousands of kisses. He laid it down. Martial: wit crackling like a pot of fire, better. Horribly, he found that he did not want to buy either. He could think of nothing in the world that satisfied him. Head spinning, he got out of the shop. He wandered. He tried giving the wall, but he hated it—not the splashing muck, but the way people stared past, taking him for granted. His breath came short. There must be *something* in the world, cried his mind, but it was like trying to remember a dream too late in the morning.

Temperance: he snatched at the thought. Aye, too much temperance of late, that was his trouble: a thorough drunk, a good sweat, and oft you woke restored to life. He found himself at the foot of Paul's Wharf Hill: entered the first alehouse, dingy, full of watermen trying to outswear each other. The first two pots took him about as many minutes to drink; time enough to peel back and inspect the nasty festered truth that neither Catullus nor Martial, neither lust nor learning, could alter the fact of his stepfather—or put off the day when Ben would turn into him.

Neither could drinking, but he persisted anyway. He passed through various states—hating all, knowing all, sorry bliss—and emerged in deep conversation with a big, keen-eyed, russet-coated man, who kept the settle by the fire. He must have had a long purse, for he had a manservant who waited by the door and brought over fresh drinks whenever he raised a finger. The man liked only to question and listen, and soon learned everything there was to know about Ben. In turn he took out clay-pipe and lily-pot and taught Ben the fashionable new art of drinking smoke. An agreeable companion; and even when it dawned on Ben what he was, as the man exchanged a wink with the landlord and the servant drew the bar across the door, he did not much alter his opinion.

'You've said nothing of yourself,' Ben said. 'But I fancy yon fellow is not really your servant.'

The keen eyes twinkled through the smoke. 'Not exactly. Company clerk.'

'Ah. Then you must be a captain.' The man bowed. 'Prettily played. And we . . .' He glanced around: the other drinkers, half stupefied, seemed to have noticed nothing, yet. 'We are fish for your net.'

'Such as I choose not to throw back. Some may have the strength to wriggle free likewise. The Queen still has need of soldiers, Master Benjamin, to fight Spain alongside the Dutchmen. I came Thursday sennight from Flushing, resolved to find some bold fresh spirits to take back to Holland with me. Good Sir Philip Sidney was not the last gallant Englishman, that I'll swear.'

'Nor the last dead one,' Ben said, finishing his ale: he had lost count, but he could still see nearly straight.

The eyes twinkled still. 'A half-gallon of beer a day. Taking ship to a new land. The glory and fame attaching to a man at arms. Women, you'll find, take powerful notice. Then there are always spoils, for those with a sharp eye to 'em: a soldier's cloak is soon lined. What say you? The clerk has the roll with him, and in a moment we can have your name on it.'

'You speak as if there were a choice. Aren't we being pressed?' A vast pure curiosity, untainted by fear, buoyed him.

'Well, it's ticklish.' The captain dabbed up some shreds of tobacco. 'No doubt some of these men are masterless and easily swept up. But you, you've a place, prentice to your father.'

'Stepfather. I didn't say father, never, the man is my stepfather only.'

'Soft, soft, I mistook. Your master, whatever else: guild member, a man with a little say in the world, a little substance, hey? Look, I'm telling you this because I like you, and because I am a poor captain, as all the damned captains are over there. Some go on drawing their men's pay after they're dead, and so are not sorry at all to see them killed, and I'm not one of those, but still I must live. Apply to your stepfather, and you can surely slip this net, Master Benjamin. We can come to terms.'

Ben stared at him, then at the tobacco-smoke curling and drifting, transforming itself from pleasure into nothingness. The image of his stepfather moved through it, fantastically detailed: he could number every pore and bristle. Amazing, the mind. *Sir, I have a boon to ask.* Yes, his stepfather would pay up: it would disoblige him to lose his prentice, and he would think of Ben's mother; yes, ask. And in those few smoky moments Ben knew that he would not ask.

Simply because, if it came from *him*, he did not want it.

'When would we sail?'

'Soon enough.' The bright eyes narrowed in reappraisal, as if a shutter had been thrown open, thrusting in hard light. 'A march to the port with the baggage train, and then await the weather. But—'

'My name on the roll, then. I'd like to see something of the world. And I'm not averse to a fight, if the cause be just.'

'Oh, every cause is just,' the captain said, with a lazy chuckle. 'Are you sure you won't change your mind? You are drunk.'

'I tend to think the same, drunk or sober.'

The captain motioned to the company clerk. 'You'll have time to say your goodbyes, naturally.'

So, his greatest leap of decision: the cold water so far below he could hardly see its glitter. Behind him, on the cliff edge, figures: his mother; Master Camden; Nicol; no one, really. What was it the young player, Will, had said? *Once you stand anywhere, you turn to stone.* It occurred to him that joining the army he might get killed; or, worse, slowly die, like gallant Sir Philip Sidney, gnawed away by a month's gangrene. But, then, there was more than one way of slowly dying. He looked at his rough hands, as Master Camden had. I want to be the most learned man in the kingdom. Tamburlaine leaped up on his chariot. I am a lord,

167

for so my deeds shall prove. Ben became strangely aware of his own blood in his veins, as if the fluid were transformed along with his future, liquid fire, seed and ink and tears, who knew? Come on, then. The company clerk's hand was vile: Ben brushed him aside, took up pen and inscribed his own name on the roll. He loved to write his name: if only he could write it across the world. Come. Leap.

6

When You See Me, You Know Me
(1588–9)

Will's leap. First: it was a horror.

He missed Anne. Everything, everything about her, from the clean curve of her calf, to her soft fluty *by Christ*, to her indecisiveness, which was really a refusal to rule anything out of life. He ached for his children's arms round his neck. He had never been further than ten miles from Stratford, and now he was confronted with difference upon difference, air and landscape and building and faces and dialect, and sometimes he felt he might have been in Muscovy or Virginia—that far, that lost.

And he was ever in the company of a small group of men, all of whom knew each other much better than they knew him, who were an over-sensitive quarrelsome set generally, and who were even more on edge because one of their number had died on the sword of another, and several of whom didn't approve of him. And instead of dreaming plays and whittling lines for pastime in his head he was having to learn parts overnight, small parts but multiple, and make the voice carry (Jack Towne's hand pressing on his upper belly, there, and fill your lungs as if to yawn) and learn how to walk the boards and express with gesture (too little, too much) and do a hundred other menial jobs besides—sewing costumes, sorting dog-eared play-parts, baiting the horses.

And they might be the Queen's Men, but that did not alter the tramping along dusty or boggy roads in every weather, the comfortless halts between towns with hose dripping from tree-branches and a pan of grey pottage belching over a sulky fire, the indifferent lodgings with flea-ridden mattresses and stinking privies and swindling landlords. Or sometimes the hostility, the bullfrog stare of nay-saying aldermen—even the refusal to give them a roof.

'God damn you, we're the Queen's Men!' John Singer yelled, one rainy evening at the barred door of a second-rate inn on the Chester road. 'Never heard of the Queen? Never heard the name of Walsingham, hey? You'll recall it quick enough when you're stretched on the rack! Thieving Welsh bastards!'

'We're not in Wales.' John Dutton sighed, tugging him away.

They put up at last in a barn. The farmer charged them outrageously and took his lantern away. Will knelt in something rank, fumbling with the tinderbox. All around him was vivid, fierce and heartfelt swearing.

'A rat,' Singer wailed, dancing, 'a rat just ran over my foot! Shit, shit . . .'

At last Will managed to make a light.

Singer glared at him in it. 'What the devil are you smiling about?'

'Pardon,' Will said, busying himself. 'I didn't know I was.'

And it was true. Because the horrible loneliness and homesickness and discomfort and doubt were all so very real, and yet they took up such a little room inside him. And all the rest, amazingly, was boundless hunger and joy. He had great Americas within.

Later, wrapped in blankets and cloaks, drunk, most slept. Will lay blinking, thinking of a little heap of stones. Close by he saw Jack Towne sit up, shivering, rubbing his hands across his face. In the bleary moonlight Towne's fair hair was the colour of ashes.

'Can't sleep?' Will said softly. 'Or don't want to?'

Towne showed his teeth. 'A little of both.' He threw off his blanket and hitched himself closer to Will. 'Sometimes the night's like a blindfold and a gag. Smothering. And then the dreams . . .'

'Do you go through it again? Or is it different?'

'Oh, every time it's different.' Towne laughed, a sound like the fluttering of wings. 'He gets up and laughs—or he gets up and kills *me*—or the swords turn to butter and everything, everything is well . . . Sometimes she's there too. The little miss he married. I feel for her, though I know she won't weep long, and naturally he should never have married her at all.'

'Naturally?'

'Players and the domestic hearth don't go together. Is there any more drink there? Never mind. What about you? Can't sleep for wondering

170

how you ended up in this shitten pot?'

'If I felt that, I would be on my way home.'

'Would you? Because, after all, there's pride, you know. You might not want to admit you've made a mistake.'

Will felt as if he had swallowed ice. 'Is that what they're saying? Am I not good enough? Tell me—'

'Peace, peace.' Towne's hand searched his shoulder. 'Aye, they doubted, some of 'em. Not that you had a gift for it—but you've been bred up so different, you see. You were so much the honest burgher.'

Now it was Will's turn to laugh, in the same feathery way. (Often this happened, he took on the tone of whoever he was with, had even offended a stutterer once by seeming to mimic, but no help for it.) 'I see.'

'So they wondered, some of 'em, how you'd take to it. Not me, though. This is what you've wanted, isn't it? To be sure, you've much to learn. Instance, it's no good looking fear with your eyes, for that don't reach across the inn-yard—let alone when you get to London and stand on the stage of a proper theatre. You must throw it into your posture.'

'What—gibber at the mouth, and saw the air?'

'No, coxcomb, imp.' Towne grinned, gripping Will's neck. 'Look, wouldst learn from me or no?' Suddenly his other hand was in Will's shirt, lightly caressing his chest from nipples to breastbone; his voice sank low: 'Naught amiss with this, heart, if thou hast a mind. Sometimes a man wants comfort, not conquest, hey?'

Will laid his hand on Towne's wrist. How prominent the bones and veins, yet not without

171

softness. He was stirred, partly through memory of first thinking on these hands and their touch, a long-buried fancy of youth. But also, yes, he was stirred.

'I offend,' Towne said, in a small, squeezed voice, as Will pushed him gently away.

'Dost not, Jack. Thee, never. It's only—'

'Because I killed?'

He had thought of that, as the hands touched him: of what they had done. But that, shockingly perhaps, made no difference. He shook his head. 'It's only the time.'

Towne sat back. His eyes were smudges of light. 'Late, you mean.'

'Too late.'

The eye-shines dwelled on him for some moments, and Will had a strange sensation of small unworthiness: as if he had told a needy friend he had no money while his purse chinked.

'Alone, then, Will, eh?' Towne said at last, lying down and wrapping himself in his blanket. 'That's how you think to do it? Well, we'll see.'

Alone, then. Will lay on his back on the cold barn floor, miserably tingling, and remembered— how long ago? Lying on his back either in cot or first truckle-bed: very young indeed, and with a definite sense in him of being new in the world. Bed-time. The rays of the setting sun through the half-shuttered window were sharp. They clustered at you like a handful of dry straws. You could grasp them if you weren't so tired. His mother bade him good-night. He heard her skirts swish away. And then it was just him, and the rays. At last they softened and spun before his closing eyes—and there would be morning again, his mother returning to him, and restoration; but still, when it came to it, you went alone into the darkness.

By the time of the first few yellow leaves, the Queen's Men were within a day's trudge of London, and Will was different. Not one of them, not quite, but he was a player now, an actor, instead of the faintly embarrassing but useful country tyro who had got them out of a difficulty. He had taken a few larger roles when John Dutton went down with an ague in the poisonous Cambridge fens; and he had learned to fetch his voice from somewhere below the base of his spine, to move and speak as a giant must in a world of giants; to see a woman in front of him and not a youth wigged and painted; to be ready with invention for lapses and forgetful fish-mouths and leaps ahead of ten lines; to not mind it that Robert Wilson, the quiet, scholarly one, did not like him and tried to undo him; to spot when a child was trying to climb on stage, to hurry the piece when the light was fading, to respond, always respond, to what went on beyond the little circle of the play.

'You'll be a goodish actor,' Richard Tarlton had said to him, the day before London, 'but bear in mind that you've been rather protected from competition, touring with us, and now you are a little fish in a teeming pond and the crumbs are few. Luckily you're adaptable. Some men, as soon as they walk on, you think: kingly. Knell was like that. I put my ugly snout round the curtain, and people laugh. You—you don't suggest anything. A valuable quality. Yes, young Will, I've been watching you,' he said, at Will's surprised look, 'and thinking how you'll get on. I came from the country too. Lord, I was green when I began. Knew naught.' He patted

Will's arm. 'Have a care in London, sweet, and don't drink and whore too much. Come see me if you *entirely* starve, though I shall expect to see ribs before I'll open my purse.'

Now, as the road broadened and flattened and the rumbling cart became one of many and a great city began to occupy the horizon, like troops moving into position, Will struggled for a response. He had seen so many places, grovelling hamlets and fine towns, he had seen high peaks and glittering seas: now London demanded something of him, and he almost felt he did not have enough left to give. Especially as he felt, obscurely, that this place would not be satisfied with a little. As if he had made it some deep blood-promise, long ago.

Jack Towne slapped his shoulder. It hurt a little. After the barn he had been distant, then at last friendly again, especially since a messenger had ridden out to them in Essex to report that the Queen had graciously granted a full pardon to her loyal servant John Towne for his part in the affray at Thame. Now he was all Towne, all high flamboyance, becoming more himself as London walls took shape in the smoky dusk, and becoming, somehow, a man Will would know less and less.

'There she lies, Will, the great strumpet of the kingdom. And, by God, I love her still, and will catch my dose of her any day o' the week. What dost think, hey? Want to turn tail and run home to Stratford?'

'You were the first person who told me of London,' Will said. 'You said it was the worst place to starve in.'

'Did I? When?' Towne shook his head, quickening his pace. 'God's blood, Will, that

174

memory of yours.' Ahead the world was swathed in a great dark shawl embroidered with lights. The Queen's Men broke out chattering and shouting, transformed. Will was quiet. 'Ah, Shoreditch,' he heard, as scrubby streets closed in, 'grimy as ever, aye, but our place, by the mass.' There were still fields, cows being led, but the very air was different: hundreds, thousands of voices swarmed in it. Towne hung back to nudge him and point. The Theatre. And, look you, the Curtain. They were smaller than Will had imagined, yet still he marvelled at the way the playhouses rose up among the sober proper dwellings, so impudent, so defiantly unlike other buildings: were they allowed—were they really allowed?

A wall, a gate. The city admitted them indifferently. Bishopsgate. Now it felt to Will as if they were driven along the packed street like sheep in a pen. Houses rose five, six storeys— palaces, he would have said once, but worldliness was coming on apace, and he saw them for the rich merchants' houses they were. But what merchants, he thought, and his father passed sadly before his mind's eye, worn with the effort of pride. He saw a water-carrier bearing on his back an iron-bound jug as big as himself. He saw a dancing-bear led through the crowd, like a helpless waddling man. He tried to analyse the stink of this place. Just an ordinary town stink, he thought at first, but it was more than that: nurtured here in such concentration, it had become strange, like the fantastically shaped fungus luxuriating under a fallen tree.

Keep faith, he told himself, keep faith. Blood and stones: he pictured them. For this was Will's bargain and how he proposed to distribute himself. Everything I want of living may be here—but everything I want of love is back there. So let it be, or the curse, yes, the merited curse. Was that a sensation of tearing he felt? But so many sensations, excitement, sickness, exhaustion, and the hard tugging of a beggar at his sleeve, a beggar who seemed to have no nose or mouth, only the imploring eyes.

'Drive him off,' Robert Wilson said at his side, cuffing, 'else you'll have them all round you. Well! Yonder's the Bull. Journey's end. I'm not sorry.' He yawned. 'You'll be wanting a lodging, Will.' It was not an offer of help, or even a statement. It was a notification that Will was, yes, alone.

*   *   *

'Sing another song, Mamma,' said Hamnet. At his side Judith was asleep, but his giant, tireless eyes seemed scarcely to blink. He resented sleep, like a dose or a smacking.

'That's all there is,' Anne said, coming back to herself. 'I don't know many songs.'

Somehow she must have sounded pathetic about it, for Susannah, who had her head in Anne's lap, looked up indignantly. 'But the ones you know are beautiful,' she said. 'That's what matters.'

'Is it?' Anne hadn't meant to say it. She stroked Susannah's hair. Hamnet reached out for her, wanting caresses too. They all wanted so much of her, but she didn't mind that at all: there was more than enough of her to go round. In the window-seat Edmund settled himself more comfortably, looking out at the dusk. She could have told him there was no use looking out. She bade herself be content, and began to sing again: an old song.

*   *   *

Jacqueline Vautrollier.

The name first struck Will in all its head-spinning beauty when he heard her speak it. Before that, as Madame Vautrollier, she had impressed him enough: charmed too. Calling for the first time at the Vautrollier shop in Blackfriars, Will had found himself feeling awkwardly deferential. He was coming to see Richard Field, and Richard he remembered as the dutiful apprentice, and he half expected the pair of them to be consigned to the kitchen to talk quietly with small beer. He had forgotten the years—or, perhaps, had fallen back into his Stratford habit of mistaking adulthood for lack of expectancy.

Richard was no longer the apprentice. He was out of his time. He was a Member of the Worshipful Company of Stationers, and he looked it. Will surreptitiously fingered his own face after they shook hands: was he growing jowls too? Or was it just Richard's expression that created that fullness, that repletion?

'I should never have supposed it,' Richard said. 'Lord, Lord. A player, eh? Well, well. It's a bold undertaking, Will. Let's hope it will answer. Mind, you were always one for the play, and sometimes I suspicioned . . .' An older, younger Richard flashed through, admiring. Then, jowly again: 'A pity it's so uncertain as a profession. A bad bout of plague, and the theatres are closed, and then what? You'll have thought of that, naturally, with a family to feed—aye, I heard, Greenaway always brings me a budget of news from Stratford. They thrive?'

No small beer in the kitchen, then. Richard was easy, like a man in possession, rapping the knuckles of the prentice-boy dawdling at the press as he took Will through to the living-quarters behind. Will sniffed appreciatively—ink, hot paper—and tucked away, like a tattered shirt-tail, the longing to investigate those shelves of books he had seen in the shop. The Queen's Men had paid him off, and after finding a lodging and having his ravaged shoes mended and his beard barbered, he had one shilling and sixpence left in the world.

'Madame Vautrollier. Here's my good friend from Stratford, William Shakespeare, lately come to London . . .'

Richard was very much at home in this close parlour where, though the day was mild, an oddly scented fire burned and reproduced itself in Venetian glasses, polished marquetry, a round mirror. Will began to understand, as the woman in black looked up, pen in hand, from the velvet-covered table. He made his bow, his London bow, as he already thought of it. To his surprise he saw she wore no shoes.

'Madam, your servant.'

'Sir. You are very welcome. Please be easy, and pardon me one minute . . .'

The tour of England had made him a connoisseur of accents, but he had heard nothing as fascinating as this. French, of course. The Vautrolliers were Huguenots—numerous in London now. 'Too numerous,' grumbled the fat cat-faced landlady of his Shoreditch lodging as she supped her almond-milk, 'naught but foreigners

178

coming in and taking up all the trade, and no doubt papists to boot . . .'

'They're Protestant,' he said, 'that's why they seek refuge with us.'

But he had had nothing to do with them yet. Madame Vautrollier was the first, and she was all unplaceable difference, like that resinous fire: very dark, yet with something waxen about her skin; about thirty, he guessed, wide-hipped, round-armed, yet not at all matronly, her mouth a sad bow as she held up a paper to the tactful light.

'I have written it again,' she said to Richard, 'to end so: "As for the debt, I have had much ado to recover it, and trust in your patience. Yours in Christ, Jacqueline Vautrollier."'

And that was when Will first heard her pronounce it: that exquisite mixture of liquid and guttural. It came not from France, he felt, but from somewhere he had dreamed or fancied in a broken midnight.

Richard took the paper, glancing over it. Madame Vautrollier watched him, and Will watched them both.

'Yes.' The jowls were back. 'Yes, this will do very well. Brief is best. If you say too much, you look unsure of your position.'

'I know my position well, Richard.' She sighed. 'I am a poor widow, and so they all try to take advantage of me.'

Poor widow—well, the widow he had guessed, and *poor* could not be taken literally, not in this room, and with those jewels in her hair.

The wry smile she turned on Will seemed to acknowledge it. 'You must forgive us talking business, sir. It's three months since my husband

179

died. There is so much to do. All this now belongs to me. But I don't belong to it. I know that is not good English, but it is good truth. Thank God for Richard.' Returning her pen to the inkstand, she grimaced and showed her inky fingers. Richard brought ewer and finger-bowl. The spout of the ewer was shaped like a lion's mouth. Will watched in fascination as Richard washed Madame Vautrollier's fingers and patted them dry. Something of the humble servant, but intimate too; and something of the officious parent besides. How people lived. The infinite detail of it sometimes made him reel a little to think of, especially here in London, with another world behind each and every door. Fascination, but unease too: an intensified version of a curious feeling often lurking in Will that he shouldn't be here. Here meaning anywhere; that he really ought to make his excuses and go, and the world was waiting, fidgeting for him to do so.

'So, Richard, how long is it since you and Master Shakespeare met? Faith, so long? And yet you stand there as if it's a usual day. Wine, fetch wine. Drink to such a friendship, mark it. Lord, you men.' But the sidelong look she gave seemed to mean not *men* but *Richard*.

They drank, and Madame Vautrollier asked about their schooldays together; but even to Will that felt stale and artificial stuff, here amid the invoices and money-pouches with the creak and boom of the press coming from the shop. Soon enough they were talking of business again, in tones that Will knew already, from a few weeks in London: everything depended hugely, everything stood at a moment of crisis, and there had never been such times. Meanwhile Madame Vautrollier

180

stretched out her slender stockinged feet towards the fire, flexing them, seeming to look critically on the shape of her ankles. She caught Will looking too, and he wondered if he was supposed to: Richard, deep in the threat of Spain and the price of paper, did not seem to notice. Will wondered what one would do if the news came that the Spanish had landed and all was lost. Run indulgent riot? (Those books. Those ankles.) Or finish one's wine and sigh at the inevitability of things? He wondered when Richard and Madame Vautrollier would marry.

'Come any time,' Richard said, at the street-door, when Will left. He winced at the openness of that, as if he had walked into a bad bargain, then relented and shook Will's hand. 'Any time. Ask young Maarten to place you a chair in the shop if I'm not about. I know you'll love the books. I look to expand, go beyond Monsieur Vautrollier's limits. His list was strongly devotional—oh, all honour to him for it—but I want to bring in more poetry, languages, grammars.' He lowered his voice. 'It's understood, you see, though we haven't spoken of it publicly yet. Madame Vautrollier can't manage the business alone. Indeed she doesn't want to. I fancy even Monsieur Vautrollier, in his last illness, had it in mind . . .' Really? thought Will. *Really?* But, then, who was he to question the power of wanting to believe? It moved worlds. 'We think to marry when six months' mourning is up, perhaps. Though there are plenty who'll do it after three months . . .' Richard wagged his head in a generalised way, indicating a moral question he had no time to go into. 'Madame Vautrollier is an excellent creature, Will, as you have seen. And

181

I believe the matrimonial state is the best, the most natural for a man in this world, if he wants to apply himself. Well, you must know that.'

Later, in his cold lodging, Will sat and watched his taper dwindle and listened to the mice pattering behind the panels. He thought he was very stupid, or bad, and could not decide which was worse. When his taper was gone he thought he might go and seek Jack Towne, who had said he was lodging at the sign of the Dolphin in Bishopsgate, though when Will had gone there last, they had never heard of him, and he had wondered if he had the right Dolphin. Every street had so many of these damned signs: how would you ever know? How . . . ?

He sat on after the taper went out. At some point, in the darkness, he put his face in his hands.

*   *   *

A starveling winter set in. If I can survive this, Will told himself, I can survive anything; but that did not mean he could survive this. Money, money. The Queen's Men, reorganising from top to bottom, no longer needed him. Well, there were other troupes, there were the Admiral's and Leicester's and Lord Strange's, and there were the theatres—look, another one was growing up on the south bank of the Thames, its timbers putting on flesh even as Will's ribs began to protrude, Master Henslowe's splendid new Rose. All this, and he could not get enough work. His talents, such as they were, did not stand out here. He was a goodish player with not much experience and a turn for improvising. So *nearly* handsome, as one veteran player remarked, waving him away. Persistence got him hired here and there, usually when a player was sick. For a fortnight with Leicester's Men he stood in as book-holder, giving the prompts, a job he excelled at, for he quickly had virtually the whole play memorised and did not have to leaf and search. Then the regular got out of debtors' prison, and that was an end. The excitement of appearing on the stage of a true theatre turned fitful at best: aye, a brave sight, an astonishing sight, when he slipped on to mouth his few dull lines, and all round and up and down except for a topmost slice of sky was people, a great roaring ring of them; yet they were as indifferent as they were many—you couldn't thrill or tickle them as you could the willing gazers in the country inn-yard. They were impatient for novelty; and in the tiring-house he was brushed aside because the hero's entrance was due, and the groundlings were hissing, and tomorrow was another harsh, brash new day, in which he might or might not exist.

Once he sat down and began to write a letter to Stratford for money. But if to Anne, someone would have to read it to her; and if to his father . . . To finish the letter, besides, would be to finish this. If he had been acting, he might have crumpled the paper with a fierce motion. But paper was expensive, and he used it for writing something else.

Forty yards down the street from Will's lodging, a man sleeping on the bulks froze to death one night just before Christmas. The shopkeeper, opening his shutters in the morning, saw him there and gave him a shove with a stick, and he thumped to the ground like a rolled log. Someone added that his fingers snapped off like twigs, but Will doubted

183

that part.

'Within a week there'll be twenty people ready to swear they saw it with their own eyes,' as Richard Tarlton said. He was the one who helped Will avoid a similar fate. A boy came running after Will in Shoreditch that iron-hard afternoon, said that Master Tarlton wanted to speak to him, and escorted him back to a roomy house hard by St Leonard's, where the clown was sitting in the window-seat, smoking tobacco and drinking sherris-sack. He had seen Will go by. 'Or half of you. What happened? Are you ill?'

'No. Just—under-employed.'

'Jesus. Philip, run down to the kitchen, chick, have the girl bring up bread, meat, whatever's there. Bless thee. My son,' he said, as the boy scurried off. 'The best thing, the only truly good thing I ever did. His mother was a trull, so I must take all the credit. Is that your best cloak?'

'Only cloak.'

'God save us. You have to dress well, man. It's how they judge you first, the looks, the port. Ever thought of an earring? To be sure, it's money. Sit, sit. Why didn't you come to see me? Didn't I say come and see me?'

'Yes.' The heat of the fire was making him feel pleasantly faint and distant: not a bad way to go, if it must be . . . 'I thought it one of those things a man says . . .'

'And doesn't mean. Lord, you must have learned a sad, worldly sort of lesson from us. Mind, I'm a changing man. I'm ill.' Tarlton said it with a certain pride, as of some subtle accomplishment. 'That's why I've retired. I drink, but I can't eat. And sometimes I piss blood. Oh, yes, I've consulted a

184

physician. He mumbles of sol and sulphur, and Saturn in the house of life, and looks forward to a good long fee—for I seem hale enough, don't I?' He lifted his shrewd round snub face to the window-light, eyes sliding to Will's. Hard to say what was different, except that the skin looked curiously soft, like a bathed child's. 'Well, I can let you have some money. I've been careful. You should be too, Will, once you're fairly set up. Put money in your purse. Not for its own sake, but to make a fence.' A maid brought in a tray. 'Eat, eat it all. Keep it over there, though, the smell turns me up. Within that fence, ah, you can be yourself, safe from the wolves and the creeping woods. Have you tried Sussex's Men? They always seem to be on the tramp now, mind.'

Tarlton fed him, lent him enough money to buy a new cloak and to prevent his landlady throwing him out, and helped equip him for the London players' world. He dropped an influential word here and there. He passed on hints about who to flatter and who to ignore, who was on his way up and who was drinking himself to death; likewise on the tortuous relationship between the owners and managers of the theatres and the leaders of the companies. You had to be part subtle and rarefied, part brutally assertive: spiderish. Little by little Will found himself learning to move on the great quivering web. He was grateful to Tarlton, who shrugged it off: as he did indeed seem to be dying, good works were in order.

'I don't know what it is. Who knows what goes on inside our bodies? For fifty years I've been a human ox. I drank and ate all I wanted and never broke a sweat; I whored and never caught a dose.

185

Now this.' It was not so much that he was going thin: his bones seemed to be thrusting their way to the surface of him. Looking into Tarlton's face, Will saw his clean-picked skull at the same time. 'I've left off the physic. Now I'm doctoring my soul. See, I've always been a tolerable good Christian, for all my little profanities. And I've always thought that when the time came I would properly set my wits to these great matters.' Ensconced with high-backed chair, footstool, pillows and furs—he refused bed—Tarlton gestured to the books on the table. 'See there. Works of devotion. Oh, I've tried. But you can't stop a book and say, "Hold there, let me pursue that." So I have divines come talk to me. Last week a good solid Queen's Protestant who said all will be well. Yesterday a hungry Puritan who was not so sure. I think to smoke out one of those secret papists next and have him put his side of the question. You have only to send to Yorkshire or somewhere, rap on the walls of your gentleman's manor-house—the priests are rattling about in there like old rats' nests. What d'you think?'

'I think we shouldn't speak so.'

'Oh, fuck it, man, I'm dying. If you're popish I couldn't give a damn, and if you're t'other way and thinking of reporting me for a good stretching on the rack I couldn't give a damn likewise.' Tarlton reached shakily for his wine-cup. Will put it in his hand. The fingers felt like the blades of a fan. 'Sorry. Years of being jovial, you know, take their toll. Besides, you . . . I can't fit you in either way, Will. Tell, now. Do you fear for what may become of your soul?'

'Fear?' Will tried to think. The word itself gave him a fearful feeling, but that was words, more

186

prompt and powerful than the sluggishness of things. He shrugged. 'No. Not as long as it's mine.'

'Tut tut, it belongs to God,' Tarlton intoned, in a preacher's reproachful voice. Mock, but not quite. He closed his eyes for a moment. 'I'm from the country too, did you know? Shropshire. People have odd ways in the country. When I was very young I saw a shepherd's lad put his prick up a sheep. The beast just carried on grazing while he pounded away. Not a bad preparation for married life, in truth.' His eyes sprang open, but their gaze was distant. 'In the village over the hill the churchyard was flooded. The ground fell apart like cake and there, in a fantastic tumble and tangle, were these bones. The sexton heaped them up, skulls atop and smiling. It became a favourite of young lovers courting thereabouts, to go see the bones: she would get the shivers and he would lay a comforting arm about her. When I saw the bones like that, I thought: Very well, sir, very well, I have you.' Tarlton lifted the cup to his lips, using both hands, in sudden sardonic communion. 'Now you want some pat conclusion like, "And so I became a clown." Naught so neat. Though I'm sure I did think that making a jest is, at least, making something.'

Will grinned, then felt his face fall. 'And so is making an enemy.'

'Ah, hast been foiled again? I've told thee, it's like fencing, parry, forte to foible, you'll come back the stronger.'

'No, no, nothing so bad. Pembroke's have paid me for another fortnight. Only I heard that Robert Wilson had spoke against me to them, and I puzzle me why. He sits high and secure with the Queen's, wherefore do I threat him?'

'Why, man, he's jealous. Look you, he's an excellent pretty actor, but he would be more. He's fitted up several broken-backed old plays, and writ two more of his own devising. Lord, how he laboured over every line! I remember him soaking linen in cold water to press on his poor bursting head as he wrote. Then *you* come along, and you can swell out the blank verse extempore when your memory's out, or patch in a few comic lines to please the locals, and you don't even seem to think. It just comes. That's why.'

'A strange thing to hate a man for.' So Will thought: but he thought more on it.

*   *   *

Until his fortunes turned with the year, Will did not go often to the printing-house in prosperous Blackfriars. Too shabby, too conscious of his growling stomach.

And it wasn't because of Richard, or not chiefly. It was Madame Vautrollier. Perfectly pleasant, hospitable, even kind. Yet somehow not a person you cared to see you at a disadvantage.

'We never see you, William.' It was nearly *Guillaume* as she pronounced it: not quite. Betwixt and between, like her eyes, almost blue, almost violet. And who she was: sombre widow yet young, mother of the black-clad little boy, who occasionally appeared in the scented parlour to make an obedient bow, yet how narrow the waist she liked to smooth with hands that seemed appreciative, or reminiscent, or something else. 'You ought to sup with us. Richard would like it. I would too.'

'Thanks. In the evenings I often have to study parts, and so—'

'You could do that here—no? We could help you. It would be diverting.' She sighed. 'We are often dull, these winter evenings.'

And yet they were to marry. It was made public now: in six weeks Richard Field was to marry his old master's widow—the apprentice's ultimate dream—and take possession of her fair body and business. *We are dull in the evenings.* Revealing—too revealing. Will told himself not to go, but he did it, once: took his newest part along to supper and ran through it with them. Richard was interested, though godly disapproval kept crossing his face like dyspepsia.

'This isn't the full playbook, surely.'

'No, just my lines, and the cues. It looks difficult to get a sense of, I know. But there are plots pegged up in the tiring-house—story outlines, so you know where you are.'

'And do you?' Richard said. 'I should have thought you would half forget what's real and what's fancy, sometimes.'

No: never. Will had a highly developed sense of the real; he was alert to its hovering like a chicken with a kite. Madame Vautrollier took charge of the paper. Will tried to recite rather than act, for some reason. The part was an old fond foolish lord. He was good at old, apparently. Madame Vautrollier's hand beat time as he spoke, following the blank verse rhythm, which surprised him, since he understood the rhythms of French were entirely different.

'Well,' she said, when he had finished, 'you are perfect.'

The food was excellent and almost made him dizzy with its richness; or the wine, perhaps, or something else. She wrapped some cheese and cold stuffed mutton for him to take home with him. 'A gift,' she said, in a faintly warning tone. Walking back to his lodging—absurd to say 'home'—he was nudged by the aroma of cloves, nutmeg, verjuice. He had a curious sensation, as he lit a taper to reveal his room in all its worm-eaten nullity, of having been followed.

*   *   *

'Soon I shall be Mistress Field. A strange thing, William, to be a woman. We change our names and become someone else. As a man you can hardly think of this. You simply stay who you are, all the time.'

'Do I? Most mornings when I wake I'm not sure who I am. And seldom does the day reveal it.'

They were in the tiny courtyard behind the house where Madame Vautrollier grew herbs and other plants. In summer, she said, he should see it in summer, but even now greenery quivered in the numberless pots and trays. Looking up at the hatch of sky, Will wondered how she did it.

'Oh, you mean because you are a player,' she said, plying the water-jug, pressing down loam. A cloth always at her waist, prompt to mop spills, dab sullied fingers: she would never, he felt, be taken unawares. The indeterminate eyes saw far.

'Something like that.' It wasn't what he meant.

'Well, after all, you wake alone,' she said, looping back a strand of black hair. It seemed heavy as a string of pearls. 'That's never good for anyone.'

Will knew who Jacqueline Vautrollier was,

though. Temptation. She was temptation personified, in the way of the older plays that still pleased the inn-yard sort, with a Vice who stalked on winking at the audience and demonically chuckling over his villainy. Useful, he thought, if everyone you came across in life located themselves in this way, so you knew just where you were.

That was what he believed when he was not at Blackfriars, at any rate; when he dwelled on blood and stones and renewed the terms of the pact with himself. Fidelity, absolute fidelity to Anne, was the price of his being allowed to leave her and pursue this dream, otherlife, firstlife, coin it how you will. Whatever he was seeking in London—and he glimpsed it here and there, through the brakes and thickets of the everyday—it must be untouched by anything of flesh and heart. That was elsewhere, under seal and promise.

When he was with her it was not quite so easy. She was not a Vice or one of the Seven Deadly Sins: she was too interesting for that. Her Frenchness: some quality beyond complexion and accent that he could not define, and fascinated him, though she was not forthcoming about the country of her birth. 'France is dead to me now,' she said. 'And to all the godly. A land of ghosts. Here we can live.' Conversation with her sparked and kindled him. And Richard was so very busy, and it was pleasant and agreeable to everyone for Will to pass a little time with her in the courtyard among the tender shoots and fronds. And when she spoke out to him one afternoon, bare and honest, he thought that at least she was not playing the coquette, and so . . .

'Richard is from home. Business at Gravesend. He lies there tonight.' She laid her hand on Will's.

191

She made it seem a very natural action, almost as if he had asked her to do it. 'Now you're surely not going to run away because of that, are you?'

'You are to marry Richard very soon,' Will said, after a moment. 'Isn't that so?'

'Yes, so I am. And you are Richard's old friend, yes. All this is very easy to get over, very smooth, but the English go along so heavily. Like carthorses.' A twitch of a smile: more nervous, perhaps, than she appeared.

'Carthorses,' he said, gently disengaging his hand, laughing a little. 'Madame, such flattery.' He had a brief hope that it could end thus, dissipate in froth. But she stepped forward and kissed him on the mouth, and then stepped back: formal, as a dance or duel.

'Call it running away, if you like,' he said, 'but I must go.' His voice was strangely thick; and though he meant to move, nothing happened.

'Who are you afraid to hurt? I ask because I am truly curious. Richard? He won't know. Richard has the measure of his bargain. He esteems me pretty well and he esteems the business very well, and he knows that I need someone to manage it and maintain my household as I am used to it. Marriage means looking at the same face every day, you know: it's best if it's an ordinary one, not exciting; it's more restful. Are you afraid to hurt me? That won't happen. Once married, I shall be faithful. William, I mean only a little fair-day together, a little indulgence, and then back to work, with some sweet honey memories for the savouring.'

'Marriage. There, you've said the word, and that's all that was needed. You can't have forgotten that I am married—'

'Indeed no, and how is your wife?'

He jerked his head back: he had not thought her capable of this. 'Madame, your servant—'

'William.' She held his arm, forcing him to turn. 'I mean no insult to your wife. I wish her well. I wish her all happiness and you with her, when you return to the country one day. But I ask how she is because you don't know—do you? You suppose this and that. It's all supposes. You're miles and miles away. Distance, time, they change things. When something is very, very far away, it appears small. God made it so. Otherwise the stars would blind us and the birds in the sky would look like dragons.'

It would have been so easy to kiss her. He could hardly think of an easier thing. But he remembered where they stood: their roles. The essence of temptation was that it appeared harmless. 'Sweet honey memories may spoil,' he said. 'And I don't think God is pertaining to this, you know.'

She smiled. He supposed pride would let her do nothing else. But, no, she was at ease, picking up her basket and jug, glancing over her plants. 'Come spring, I mean to have tulips. Have you ever seen tulips? They come from the gardens of the Turks, they say. Too beautiful for the infidel. Are you in love, William?'

'With my wife, yes.'

She stared as if he had made a crude joke, then laughed lightly. 'Very well. I'll say no more—except that life isn't like a book, you know: you can never turn back to a page. Never mind. You will still come to see us, won't you? I mean it. Because it really doesn't matter.' Her eyes were large and candid. 'That above all is what I wanted you to understand.'

Will attended the wedding of Richard Field and Jacqueline Vautrollier; and come spring, he was there, in the little courtyard, to see the tulips blooming. Rich upward-sucking mouths without faces. They seemed to him, like most things in life, fearfully unlikely. He had in him a sense of conquest or defeat, as elusive as the colour of the bride's eyes.

*   *   *

In Stratford, spring was becoming summer and summer the first without him. But Greenaway the carrier arrives from London one bright warm afternoon, when all the talk is of the Spaniards landing and Gilbert and Richard are doing pike-drill with the local muster, and puts a packet in Anne's hand. It contains two crowns, one gold, one silver, and a letter from her husband.

John Shakespeare is hovering beside her in the doorway. He snatches up the letter and reads it to himself, lips moving, breathing the words. Will is the only person she has known who can read silently.

'Bravely, I thank you . . . And how does Mistress Greenaway now? We were sore grieved for your little one. He rests with God . . . Bonfires built all along? Nay, if they come they'll have such a fight shall make them wish their bread dough . . . And Will was in good looks, say you? So, so . . .'

She has to do all of this, while her father-in-law broods blindly at her side. He grows more and more awkward in company, she thinks. But then this, this moment is exceptional, as Will enters their lives again, if only remotely. And though she cannot

194

read the words, it does not feel remote, really—his presence: when it was his hand that made those rippling ink-marks, and his hand, too, touched these coins. They feel warm to her: an illusion she is quite happy with, for she judges illusions by their quality. Torn between missing him, hating him, and imagining him deserting her for London for ever, she has not expected hearing from him to produce this: simple happiness. Complexity will follow, no doubt, but for now she is content to clutch the warm coins, and wait to hear the letter.

Bidding farewell to the carrier, Anne goes in to find John Shakespeare sitting by his unseasonal fire. The letter—the letter is on the floor.

Edmund's feet pattering.

'Oh, is that from Will?'

'Hie down to the cellar, Edmund. Fetch me ale.'

Anne draws close, puts a hand on his shoulder. The fire in the warm day seems to her scarcely bearable, but perhaps that is the point: a refusal of the real.

'What does he say?' Suddenly fear possesses her. 'For God's sake, what does my husband say? Is anything wrong? Will Greenaway said he was hale when he saw him—'

'Peace, peace, he's well.' He twitches away from her. 'How much did he send you?'

Anne opens her hand. The coins do not glitter, London coins dull with use, but they have their brilliance.

'Well. A man in a proper way of trade would do well to earn such in a fortnight.' He looks away from them. 'Are you happy with it? A husband in London, far away, naught of him but this?'

'A husband still.' Her voice surprises her with its

sharpness. 'A son still.'

Edmund appears, solemnly balancing the ale-jug. His father watches him as if expecting him to drop it. This is his look with his children now: a steady expectation of disappointment. Anne takes the jug from him and pours. But drink never alters John Shakespeare, not in the way of making him softer or harder. It only makes him more stubbornly himself. In the end it is Gilbert, coming in sweat-soaked and sunburned from drilling, who reads the letter out.

It is short. Recommends himself to the favour of his father and mother, presents his truest fondest love to his dear wife Anne, earnestly prays that this finds all at home well. Reports that he finds himself, after some small travails, in good case, and regularly employed in the London theatres as a player by my lord Sussex's Men, on such terms as enable him to send by his good friend Greenaway the enclosed sum, with the firm hope of more anon. Reports that there is but little sign of summer plague in London this year, praise be to God. Reports that he will soon be undertaking a summer tour of the southern and midland parts of the kingdom with his company, and hopes to be among them for a short time when they come by Wycombe and Oxford. To Anne his wife again much love, and for the babes kisses . . .

Her father-in-law drains his tankard. 'So, you see. He will try just to include us on his way about the country with his players. A few days, perhaps, think you? And after, gone again. That's all there is, daughter, and all there will be.'

Anne makes a subtle face at Edmund to wipe his nose. 'Well, we'll see. He's new in the profession, so he has to work hard. In time—'

'You delude yourself, Anne.'

'Do I? I try only to hold fast to my belief, and not change it. After all, you told me he'd come slinking home like a beaten dog. Now he's a coxcomb who won't come at all. He can't be both, Father John.'

He stares. Anne feels the enormity of it too, and tries not to flush. This is new: she has never quarrelled with him before, never found the grounds. She sees it in his eyes also—if we fall out, where will the power shift to next, and who will be the winner or loser?

'As long as you are happy with this—this life that he forces on you,' he says at last, 'who am I to speak? You do well to reproach me, daughter.'

He goes out. There is still ale in the jug. Gilbert, after a moment, scoops it up and drinks from it. Over the foaming rim his eyes salute Anne's with a crackle of rebellion. Another shift.

But Anne fears it as she fears all change. She is summoned to the yard by a roar from Hamnet, who has been shoved over on to the cobbles by Judith. She wipes his tear-mashed face, soothing, wondering whence the easy sentiment about twins: sometimes these two resemble overgrown birds in a small nest, each trying to push the other out. Then she goes in search of her father-in-law.

She finds him at the front of the house. He has borrowed the neighbour's ladder and propped it up so that it reaches the roof on the west gable and he is climbing. A few spectators have gathered, as they will for anything, a dog-fight, a drunk spewing.

Anne grips the wobbling ladder. 'What are you doing?'

'Attending,' comes his voice. 'Attending to matters.'

197

The holes in the roof. Reaching the top, he begins poking at them ineffectually. Nonsense: the tiler's job. He lunges and sways and Anne tastes metal. Strong, yes, but he has put on weight lately, grown splay-legged and stiff, like the spinster's overfed cat.

'Come down, Father John.' Try to keep the voice level, no pulse of panic in it. Like when Susannah cut open her knee: don't let her tell from your face how bad it is. 'That's no work for you, and it can't be patched. The rain doesn't come in. Leave it.' The ladder wobbles again. She feels his stubbornness, stabbing down with the sun: recognises it. 'You'll hurt yourself.'

'Aye, what then?'

Then, of course, it will be Will's fault. She understands the reasoning. Susannah has it when she throws one of her rare tantrums; she herself had it when her father was dying, and she preferred him to suffer rather than leave her. 'If you won't come down,' she says, 'I'll come up.' Anne hates heights, but grimly starts the climb. A fine pair of monkeys on a stick . . . The overburdened ladder creaks. He looks down, white-faced. 'Climb as high as you like,' she says, 'but he still can't see you.' Nor will he pity you, come home, and change. She does not say that part, but her father-in-law feels it, perhaps, as an emanation, for he makes a growling sigh and begins to descend.

On the ground they face each other.

'You may not direct me, Anne,' he says breathing hard. 'I am not yours to direct.'

'Love doesn't seek to direct.'

'Then love is oft the loser.' He shakes his head. She sees him at a point of perplexity, about to ask,

198

Whose side are you on?

Which is a good question. My side, Father John: my side alone. It occurs to her that you have only one life. All the time as you walk on, the ground falls away behind your heels.

That evening her father-in-law loses his temper with Edmund over something and nothing, and raises his arm to beat him. Her mother-in-law intervenes. No more trouble, she mourns. Her sad, bitter look is inclusive: she wishes they could all be better. Follow her example. Anne mixes his favourite drinks and stirs his fire, and secretly promises Edmund a tale later. Gilbert's expression is habitually cool and dry, but she sees more in it now when his eye falls on his father: sees the contempt. Would it have been better if Will had reached that point? The point of looking at his father and thinking, you sad old fool. And then the break, without mess. But she shivers, imagining a Will so single-minded, so terrifyingly capable.

She tells Edmund a tale separately, after her own children are asleep, the way he likes it. Only three years older than Susannah, he keeps adult hours, has an adolescent's eager pallor.

'Edmund,' she says, 'bring your hornbook.'

'Oh,' he groans, 'study now?'

'Not you, me. Will you teach me a little, Edmund? I barely have my letters. I want to read swift and clear. Let's learn together, hey? But a secret betwixt us.'

'Oh, yes.' Nothing he likes better: he already belongs to her and Will, bought and sold. Then a little grin of calculation. 'And after study, we can dance?'

They danced at Christmas, at Hewlands Farm,

on one of her rare visits. (Bartholomew on Will's defection to London: dear God, a hundred carefully withheld remarks, a thousand wry faces.) Since then, whenever there is music in Stratford, a wedding, a street-fiddler, Edmund hankers for it. Sometimes Anne foots it with him, just humming the tune, to please him. But here is a fair bargain. 'Yes. After, we shall dance.'

They do, trying not to make the floorboards creak, while vowel sounds skip round her head. She ignores the voice that says, *You'll never learn*. Edmund looks so much like Will she could almost weep—but Anne is setting a course away from those rocks, where the wrecks of tears lie wasting.

*   *   *

Will reaches Stratford a day before his company by walking all night. Anne, coming down early to light the fire, finds him in the kitchen drinking in great blind gulps. For a moment she thinks she has actually imagined him into being. Even the curious whiteness of the image seems to confirm it, as if her longing sorcery could not quite manage the colours.

Then she sees: he is covered with road-dust.

'Your boots,' she says.

He looks down at the floor, then pats his doublet so the dust puffs out. 'My everything,' he says. And then: 'My everything.'

*   *   *

Here, coiled in the crook of his arm, all is well and it is hard to see how all can be otherwise. And it is only a night, but nights can stretch themselves out and in

200

them you can do and say and think and feel much, much that won't fit in the squeeze of day.

'He's not always like this,' she says. They have talked of many things: the beautiful progresses and infinitely varied impossibilities of the children; his life in London, his lodging and living, the struggle up the slope; crowds and coaches, processional court ladies with white barn-owl faces above great icy ruffs, Bridewell prisoners clearing dung from the streets with a cart they pull themselves like horses; the sweaty agitation of the theatre tiring-houses where the mutter has changed from a hostile *Who's this?* to an indifferent *It's Will Shakespeare*. (And she is glad of this knowledge, but gladder, a hundred times, of her own secret conclusion: on his lips she has tasted him only, the hands that devour her body have been long empty, thank God. And, of course, that's not real knowledge, that's mere mind-magic too, but what else does she have?) Still their talk comes back to this: John Shakespeare, the peg to which they are chained.

'Not always, meaning very often?'

'No. This is—exceptional.'

His laugh gently shakes the bed. Yes, here they can even laugh, recalling how he was today: the giant silences, the sickly flicker of a smile when Joan or Gilbert shouted aloud at some anecdote of Will's, the way he would say *nothing* in response but would turn, like a slow sunning lizard, to Anne. Well, Anne? Well, daughter? Throwing it all on her. For who was he . . . ?

'I've come back,' Will says. 'And I shall come back whenever I am able, Lent, summer, whenever I have space and money to ride home, and if I can rise higher as a player then I will be freer to do so

. . . Isn't this enough for him?'

'Let me see. No.'

He sighs, though she can tell in the darkness that the sigh is shaped by a smile. She can still create those, here.

'We need a home of our own,' he says. And she doesn't ask, even in her mind, how that is going to happen. He sets it up as a star to steer by and that is good. For now, everything is for now.

*   *   *

In the morning they walk in the fields, and Will tries to find the little cairn of stones where he bled. But somehow, as he remarks, even the disposition of the trees looks different; and he has to give it up. She could tell him, but doesn't, that she came looking for it very soon after he left, with a very clear memory of the spot, and that it was absolutely gone as if it had never been.

*   *   *

His troupe arrives in Stratford, and Will joins them to take part in the performance at the Guildhall. Anne doesn't go. The price of peace, exacted by her father-in-law, whose brooding has become unreal, outrageous, as if a headache should not go but get worse for ever. Will has already promised him not to advertise his presence in Stratford; and he is wigged and hooded in both his parts in the play, so perhaps he will go altogether unnoticed by his fellow citizens.

But besides that, Anne doesn't want to go. Last night he was telling Gilbert of counterfeiters in London, of their subtle skill, such that you can

202

hardly tell if the money you hold in your hand is something or nothing worth. Counterfeit: even the word sounds like a hollow whisper. No, she won't watch Will acting, for fear that she will see him gesture, smile, vow as she knows him; for fear that on that stage she will see not a posturing stranger, but the Will she thought was hers alone.

7

A New Way to Pay Old Debts (1589–91)

London: Will returns to it not so much torn apart as in flittering tatters, as if a sharp gust of wind could scatter him for ever.

Over there, the husband, loving but absent and therefore failing: over there, the father who thought his children looked huge and alien; over here, the man of the theatre lusting for new lines and loud, quick-witted citizen-crowds, and over here, too, someone grim and purposeful, thinking: Put money in your purse, aim, make right, win—win over your father else nothing won will ever count.

Is his father right after all? That a man can't split himself in two? Well, here he is in Shoreditch trying painfully to scrape himself together from a hundred ragged shreds. The curious thing is, Will doesn't feel any less himself because of it.

Also here, newly arrived, is Gilbert. Will had done as his brother had asked on first going to London, looked around for some opening in trade. Richard Field knew a haberdasher in nearby St Bride's whose apprentice would soon be out of his time. 'If I say the word, you know, I can secure his interest,' Richard said, laying a finger to his nose. Will wondered then if he could ever do that—be *weighty*, in life and not on the stage—and he wonders it again now, as he accompanies or delivers his brother to St Bride's. He ought to say some weighty wise things, as the elder, as the one already established in London. But who is he to give advice?

Fortunately Gilbert doesn't seek it. As soon as Will mentioned the haberdasher, back in Stratford, Gilbert said, 'Yes.' As soon as Will meets him at the Bell, hard by St Paul's, Gilbert looks fresh, ready, in need of nothing. 'Whenever, if ever you need me,' Will says, giving the address of his new lodging— still Shoreditch, a little more salubrious. Gilbert is twisting his neck and noting signboards, landmarks: at home, or soon will be.

But here's something unexpected: their father cautiously approves of Gilbert's move. It was the only moment the sullenness lifted: when Will said, 'Haberdasher in St Bride's, in a good way of trade,' a spark had come into his father's eyes. 'Indeed, indeed, how long a master? How many prentices? So, so . . .' A spark of poetry, in fact.

Perhaps, Will thinks, as he unpacks his trunk, perhaps that is my way to him. Become an alderman of the stage, a merchant of mummery: licensed to deal in plays.

Certainly he needs money, for it was not much of a tour, and London is testy. Comedy doesn't play well just now. They want blood and grandeur. They want, above all, Marlowe. *He* wants Marlowe: that is, from the moment he heard *Tamburlaine* he has wanted to hear it again, read and memorise, live it in his dreams. Act in it also—but the Admiral's Men have made Marlowe their own, and somehow he has made no headway with them.

Jack Towne, whom he runs into in a Bishopsgate tavern, shakes his head knowingly. 'Your acting don't suit a piece like that,' he says. As for Towne, he is still with the Queen's Men, but they are not the force they were: the word is that they are falling apart without Tarlton, and will turn into a tumblers' troupe. Towne has a young doxy with him and is making much of her. He laughs too much. His fairness seems faded to a sparrow brown. He doesn't notice Will go.

Forsake thy king, and do but join with me,
And we will triumph over all the world:
I hold the Fates bound fast in iron chains,
And with my hand turn Fortune's wheel about.

He beats the lines out with his mind and with his striding legs as he makes his way to Tarlton's house. But the shutters are up, and evergreens wreathe the door. So, Tarlton was right.

Will goes to see his burial. Even actors must have their obsequies, and St Leonard's Church, Shoreditch, marks their mortality among the pullulating alehouses and brothels and skittle-alleys. Will Sommers, King Henry VIII's fool, is buried here too, Will notes; and thinks of Tarlton's story of the Shropshire bone-heap. Perhaps in time the jester skulls will grin at each other. But, then, all skulls grin. A bad thought to take home with you to an empty lodging. You wake alone, Jacqueline Vautrollier (Field now) told him. A driven pig squeals across his path, bloodied from the boy's

205

lashing stick. The boy grins. Will fills his mind with Marlowe again.

> *And sooner shall the sun fall from his sphere*
> *Than Tamburlaine be slain or overcome.*
> *Draw forth thy sword, thou mighty man-at-arms,*
> *Intending but to raze my charmed skin,*
> *And Jove himself will stretch his hand from heaven*
> *To ward the blow, and shield me safe from harm.*

The brazen words blaze, though still he doubts he could say them well, or say them as if he meant them.

Pregnant, luminous, Jacqueline Field welcomes him to the Blackfriars house in her usual way. 'Here's Will: here you are.' Having revealed herself that day in the courtyard, she might justly have hated him for ever more, with the special hate reserved for those who have seen us weak. Instead, this: nothing more than a mild, benign surprise at his continued existence. Here's Will, yes: but he loses himself gratefully in the shop. Daily now he enters the field of shelves and stacks, where print springs up and showers him from the pages like a volley of sweet-thinking arrows. And like Blackfriars itself, like Southwark and Smithfield, the shop is a babble of tongues. The shipborne Spaniards may sink to hell, but here we are in a world where English twines with other languages, like tails of snakes in illuminated letters: where the curlicued French of Mistress Field meets the plain bold type of broad-faced Dutchmen in street-market and church: where the chequered splendours of Italian, of tender myth and triumphing murder, are set out in dictionaries and primers and stories: such stories.

Will is not alone. They stare at each other, in Field's shop and elsewhere, above the turning page. They jog bony elbows around the bookstalls of St Paul's Churchyard. Young men on the rise, walled with suspicion, wanting to break it down.

'Put your hand on your heart. Now feel it, pa-pum, pa-pum—'

'I can't. I can't feel my own,' says Will.

'I know, nor mine, what the devil is that about? You might work it up, you know, into a reflection on how we mortal men can't apprehend our own selves, the glass of the bosom ever murky, very profound, that. Now, feel and hark, pa-pum, pa-pum, see? It's where your heroic verse measure comes from.'

' "Forsake thy king and do but join with me—" '

'You see? Though in this case a little too—if I dare say it of Kit, my fine and puissant friend—too regular, too pa-pum.'

'God, yes, how can you? Marlowe's verse—it's magnificent and perfect and fine.'

'It can't be *all* of those.' Tom Nashe sighs at his own pedantry, like someone with an habitually embarrassing companion. Younger than Will, not long come down from Cambridge to throw his siege-ladder of learning and wit against the ramparts of London. They strike up a friendship among the books. Nashe writes; Will, shame-faced, confesses he writes too, and is cheered and braced when Nashe quizzes him about it.

'Oh, I'm unsure of what I do, because I lack learning.'

'Because you haven't been to university? But not all learning is there—though assuredly there are those who come from those penned precincts scribillarious, and *think* they know all, and know all too little.'

'Scribillarious . . .'

'Do you like? The root is in a good soil, *scribillare*, Latin if not Cicero's.'

'From *scribere*, and better.'

'There, you see, you have Latin, yes?'

'Small Latin,' Will says, 'and less Greek.'

'A pretty phrase, you should remember it. And then, look here, has learning a beginning and end? Hunt among those groves of books, William, and there the quest is ever. And, besides, here's another university lying all about.'

They are passing through St Paul's, along the great aisle, along the great stinking trading-crowded roofed-over first-place of the kingdom, where nobody properly should be except in worship, and where the noise and thunder of voices and walking feet expresses a hundred markets and guildhalls. God and his angels are up there somewhere, above the scriveners with bundled scrolls under their arms, bare-breasted whores, gallants and tailors and quacks.

'There's Goodman Applecheek from the country, chasing a lawsuit, and, oh, handsome Deborah, her father is a cit and a very mint of a man and seeks to husband her well. Will it please him look over here?' Tom Nashe is not so much tall as long: a loose, lean, asymmetrical fellow with a half-handsome, drowsing spoon-face and a slow, burred voice. 'And is she really innocent? I would like to set it to the proof or demonstration . . .' A sort of fanciful, mildly romantic lechery characterises Nashe, who is always talking of the ladies, disguised as Clorindas and Chloës, who have wounded his heart. Some of them seem to belong to the highest circles, which makes Will wonder a bit; Nashe's father is a Norfolk minister, and there is no fortune, unless he earns it by his pen. Which means winning himself a powerful patron.

'Unless you write for the stage,' Will says. 'There's money there.'

They are drinking in a Cheapside tavern called the Mermaid, a proper prodigious inn straddling two streets and shelving up three storeys: rather expensive, but getting up a reputation for choice witty company.

'Ah, the stage now, William, this mighty fat infant theatre we're raising. I'm in two minds about it. Oh, in the seclusion of my closet I have turned my own pen to it, a speech here and there, you know—only I wish it had all begun in a different way. Wasn't it good Master Burbage who put up the first theatre, and decided in his carpenter's wisdom to let the lowest sort in for a penny?'

'So it was, and every player thanks him for it, trust me. That's how the box fills, that's how we thrive.'

'Ah, but thrive in the right way? As an art? Are you serving delicate sweetmeats to the dainty palate, or ladling out hog-broth for blind, greedy appetites? Tell me, William, when you act on the stage, they are mighty close, aren't they, the crowd?'

'Oh, you can feel their breath. And when they laugh, the great wind of it smacks your chops.'

Nashe pales. 'I admire—and shudder.'

'Come, sweetmeats and broth together, is that not palpable? And what of your friend Marlowe?'

A little giddy dip of jealousy as he says this, as if the world has gone over a pothole. For Nashe knows Marlowe well: he moves in that little gilded circle linked by Oxford and Cambridge, who touch the theatre at pen's length only. Wits they are accounted; shits they are sometimes called, in the world of the working player. 'He pleases, he sets those crowds gasping, what would he say?'

Nashe laughs. 'He would beat me like the blind bear for asking, and then dizen my wits with a subtle answer. Where did you get your earring put in?'

'Jeweller in Wood Street. You like?'

'It's a curious fashion, but I've heard sweet Lucilla say it beguiles her, to see it on a man . . . Does it hurt, the piercing?'

'A mere tickling. With the ale you've drunk, you wouldn't even know when it was done.'

So they go forthwith; and Nashe howls and blubbers.

'You said it wouldn't hurt. You swore by the Holy Name it would not hurt, that it would be soft and sweet as a buttercup under the chin.'

'I swore no such oath. Lord, I'd never have urged it if I'd known you were such a craven.'

'Ah, there's the crux of it. You don't know me well enough yet, William, else you'd know that my essence is pure poltroon.' Nashe comforts himself with more drink, handkerchief clapped to his ear. 'Do you know I fear thunder too? Poor thunder that never harmed a finical, filamentary hair of the most luckless man's head. Ow, it hurts like buggery. I use the phrase only as a rhetorical figure, I should add, not from experience.'

Will has heard the name of Marlowe in that

connection too, but he keeps quiet.

'What do you fear, William? Come, tell, tell. The drink isn't working, man, medicine me with speech, narrate me a narcotic. What?'

'Oh, nothing. Or only the afternoon. A dull grey afternoon in tardy spring, perhaps, or mild autumn, and no matter where, country or city street, it's the same. Feeling of leaning numb shoulder against the dead wall of life. But never mind because evening's going to come, night's going to come, with lights leaping in windows, brilliance, a new crisp air. Now, what if evening never comes? Afternoon is eternal and perpetual and the thing you await never is, was, nor will be.' He blinks at what he has made. 'That's my fear.'

* * *

What he wants: he wants to write a play.

A natural progression, in one sense, as he has always loved them. And from the Queen's Men on, he has improvised speeches, patched and polished the individual parts. He is acknowledged to have a talent for this, and for players every extra talent is useful—a good singing voice, an ability to fence, a well-shaped leg.

But he wants to write a whole play of his own—or, if need be, write in collaboration. The wanting is a gathering of many things. Understanding, first. As an actor he knows what works. He knows what makes the audience gasp or freeze, chuckle or fidget. He knows what speeches exhaust the player's lungs, when a quick change of role in the tiring-house is too quick for adjustment, how an exit-speech must be timed so there's no standing

211

and staring while you get yourself off the stage.

And he knows plays. A good dozen he has entirely by heart, several dozen more he can fill in the speeches from cues. Any day, as a player, you may be presented with a new one. Plays are everyday things, baked like pies, sewn like gloves. The companies buy them as the miller buys flour or the tailor cloth: necessary stock. Usually the leading players will assess a play in tavern conclave, candles and beef-juice and beer spotting the pages as they leaf through the manuscript, sounding out a phrase here and there, questioning the writer, is it grand, merry, how many boys needed? (Lately with Pembroke's Men, though he is still only a hired-man and not a sharer in the company, he has been called in to a couple of these conferences because of his reputation as verse-cobbler.)

Sometimes, if the writer is proven and trusted, the money will be handed across the table on the strength of a jotted outline. Rare, but it does happen. And how the writer tries not to snatch at the purse of coins. Its pouchy weight: he remembers Tarlton making great obscene play of the suggestiveness of that, dangling it on his palm— oh, ladies, is there aught belonging to a man that feels better in the hand?

Then the play belongs to them. If it works, they'll place it in their repertoire: a really popular piece, a *Spanish Tragedy* or *Tamburlaine*, will come round half a dozen times a month. Don't overdo it, though. Nothing pleases like a new play. New plays are wanted, and he wants to write one.

And he knows plays, their sorts and styles. Comedies boiled up from the dry bones of the old Latin comedies he recited at grammar-school:

212

high, stiff-necked tragedies of emperors and blood: rumbling pageants of kings of England interspersed with hinds and horseplay. He knows the language they're couched in, from the donkey-jog verse and sedative rhymes of the older plays to the new surge and splendour of Marlowe. And what those words must do: from the moment the play begins, they must make everything; they create the earth and sky and the people who move there. A soldier's breastplate, a painted throne—these tawdry bits and pieces are the only aid the words can call on. First, words. First and last, words.

He wants to make, with words. He wants to try it. He doesn't think it's his destiny—it's necessary to be clear about that. But still, there is a gathering: droplets must gather to make a storm.

Drunk with Nashe another night, he speaks of it: the wanting.

'Make something bigger than ourselves, you see,' he says, 'but make it from ourselves.'

'Excellent, more.'

'Make my father proud of me.' Will is very drunk.

'With words?'

'With what words will make. Make my wife forgive me.'

'For what, things done?' Gulp and grin. 'Tell.'

'For what I might yet do.'

Very drunk. A warning. Will shivers at his own exposure. Careful of the drink now. Remember to make the most of your assets. There are some players (better actors than him) who drink themselves out of work: they can't memorise their parts, or they spoil their voices, or they're sleeping in gaol when they should be trying-out. With care I

213

can beat them.

For this is part of the gathering too—wanting to be a success. Selfishly. Not to flounder here, and be fished back, half drowned and pitiable, to Stratford. Prove himself. Push his way up alongside the wits and the shits. Emulation is there, too—or call it by its proper name, envy. Will envies Marlowe so much he could be sick.

Dipping his pen, he tries to think of everything but Marlowe. And it all keeps coming out like Marlowe. But he carries on. He writes on, adding, not subtracting. He does not like to still the pen. He even prefers not to cross out. Superstitiously, perhaps: unmaking what is made. The inscription of regret. No, write on.

And in that suggestive soft pouch pushed clinking across the table there can, he knows, be as much as ten pounds. If I can get richer I can make things better. (See, my love, what I lay at your feet.) Practical motives, again—but, then, what makes a human being if not the practical? First of all a little lust in a bed; and after that, water and bread for the flesh, sleep, toilsome dullness, all go into the making. If there is anything else—some spark not of earth—well, that lies in the proving. He can't say: he would be the last to say.

*   *   *

Christopher Marlowe: called Kit Marlowe by some, and not inappropriately, since there is something feline about him, a prowl, a purr. But, then, some have pronounced his surname Marley, and he hasn't corrected them. So best be chary of hasty conclusions about Marlowe—since, above all, he seems to invite

214

them.

Marlowe has so many affectations, for instance, that in the end they cancel each other out. He challenges you to find the real self among them, like a sharper at the fair with the three cups and the elusive pea. At first sight you may think: How dazzling, I am not equal to him.

This is how it happens with Will. Pembroke's Men are rehearsing at the Curtain—not a Marlowe piece—when he appears. 'Go on, go on,' he bids them, but they don't, not with him there; somehow they all feel like candles beside the sun. He has come to see the principal player—settlement of some sort of wager. They chuckle over it aside. Marlowe is dressed like a gallant: every inch of him slashed and panelled and jewelled, a short smudge of a cloak over one shoulder. No older than Will, but a remarkable fresh boy's complexion that makes Will feel sallow, overused. His teeth when he laughs have a pointed look. He has a fox's beauty.

When his eyes briefly meet Will's they seem to see and know everything about him—especially the low, grubby things—and find none of it very surprising.

They do come to know each other, even before Tom Nashe introduces them. Inevitable, perhaps, when the theatre world is not large. But Marlowe, though he has written so magnificently for the stage, doesn't have a great deal to do with it. Steps in occasionally at the Rose to lend an ear to his own work transfixing the general—but certainly has never acted himself. A player? Good God. (Or not, as the case may be, for it is mouthed rather than spoken that he *does not believe*—there's another side to Marlowe, another facet of the diamond or

slash in the silk, flashing into view and then gone.)
No, he is here to ravish the theatre, not make love
to it. No more jigging rhymes of mother wits, as he
says. This homespun drama needs a hero. Here I
come.

The first time Marlowe and Will are together
in company at a tavern—in a group of players and
scribblers—he yawns in Will's face. Yes: Marlowe
does that as you're talking, and shuts his mouth
with a catlike snap and an unashamed blinking of
his heavy-lidded eyes at how dull you're being.

Such arrogance: Will hardly knows what to do
with it except laugh—but, then, Marlowe has a
reputation for a quarrelsome temper, and it isn't
funny enough to bleed for. But now Marlowe
laughs, high and nervously.

'Do you hate me? Good, for now we're on a level
footing and we can talk.'

'I don't hate you.'

'What, then?'

Will shrugs. 'Find you unmannerly.'

Marlowe laughs again, gravelly this time. Which
is his real laugh? Impossible to say. He has a
peculiar husky, thickened, up-all-night voice that is
almost like two voices laid one on the other, drone
and descant. 'Don't I tell you I hate myself, good
Master William? And don't you believe me?'

Will considers him. 'I think a man who truly
hated himself would not be so ready to say so.'

All at once Marlowe is dark and remote.
Slowly he pronounces: 'Well, let me tell you I
hate myself far more than you can ever imagine,
Master William.' He makes the impotency of Will's
imagination sound pathetic, a boy's knock-kneed
inadequacy. (And Will thinks: Damn it, I have

a wife, I have children who call me father, I have laboured in the world. Yet his tongue sticks.) Soon Marlowe is talking animatedly and sunnily to someone else, though not for long. Marlowe is never around for long, wherever he may be. You feel that for him to linger would be an admission of terrible dreariness—nowhere to be but here.

Where *does* he go? At some point, presumably, he retires to his lodging to read, study, write—the one thing that certainly isn't put on for show is the genius. But otherwise, he is almost professionally elusive. Rumour has him all over the place. Cambridge, that was real, but even there he had these peculiar absences, which the university forgave him after a word from on high—from *very* high, rumour says. Services for Her Majesty, rumour adds, trips abroad, dealings with papists and anti-papists. Rumour states more firmly that Marlowe knows the Walsingham clan well, and that is enough to put you in the inner circle of circles.

Personally Will finds Marlowe quite probable as a spy, simply because he seems so unlikely. If he were looking out for a spy, he would look out for someone neutral and self-effacing, whereas Marlowe cannot enter a room without turning it into a procession.

Will admires his work extravagantly, he longs to know more about him—yet that encounter seems to set the tone for those that follow, bumpy exchanges of *non sequiturs*, smiles that don't match. It's especially galling for Will because rubbing along well with people is another of those minor talents he hopes will help him get by, in this tight world where men blow little damp quarrels into destructive flame.

And Marlowe seems to spot that, too. 'You like to please, don't you?' he says, from nowhere and about nothing, one day when they meet and pass the time of day in the street.

Will stops. 'I thought we were talking about the sweating-sickness at Westminster?' Confrontation, of a sort.

'Do you have to do it? Is it a compulsion, this desire to please?' *Please*—Marlowe has a way of drawing out the vowel that makes the word vaguely obscene. And sometimes, for a moment, the whites of his eyes entirely circle his pupils so he looks flashingly mad; yet of course you don't know if he's worked that up in the mirror. There's more than one kind of actor. 'You were going quite the other way. But I put a hand on your shoulder and steered you my way as we talked and you simply went along with it. Why? I'm not *so* masterful.' Marlowe is, in fact, as the steering and walking reveal, not very tall. 'If I resisted, you'd take me up on that, too, wouldn't you? Why, Master William, will you never *please*?'

Will actually feels ready to hit him: feels keen for it, as if it were the answer to some niggling problem that has just occurred to him. But Marlowe laughs—warmly, appreciatively—and puts his arm through Will's. 'Come with me. I need a companion.'

'And naturally I have nothing else to do.'

'Ah, Master William, you are too good to be true.'

'I certainly won't come,' Will says, stopping dead, 'if you persist in calling me that.'

'But I want you to come,' Marlowe says, suddenly childlike, simply imploring.

'You don't listen, do you?'

'No, never.' Marlowe smiles as if a little misunderstanding has been cleared up.

'How, then . . .' Will wants to say: How do you make words do such enchanted things, if you never listen to them? Instead he says: 'Where are we going?'

'A dinner or banquet or debauch laid on by Henslowe. At the sign of the Anchor, Bishopsgate—do you know it? It's one of his properties, I think, or he has a share in it, so the profit goes back to him. God bless him for a usurious grasping old sinner.'

'I'm not invited.'

'But I am. Besides, you're a player. I've seen you in a dozen things in London, so you must know good Master Henslowe. Even if you only owe him money. Which is the strongest bond the old pawnbroker knows.'

'I know him. I doubt he'll remember me.' Will has done a few jobs for Philip Henslowe, proprietor of the Rose theatre—correcting old play-scripts, putting some comedy into a tragedy. A consummate man of business: you felt he didn't see your face any more than you saw the Queen's head on a coin. 'Every player knows him: half are in debt to him.'

'But not you?'

'I have a horror of belonging to anyone.'

Marlowe hugs his arm. 'Oh, Master William, man o' my heart, we may after all be friends. What? For Jesu's sake it's a name. Adam's privilege, you know, giving names to the creatures of the earth. D'you not recall the joy of it when you were a lad, bestowing a name on your favourite pup? Made

219

him yours.'

'I'm not yours.'

'Made him real, then. Imagine a human creature without a name. Would he not seem less than human? Why else do we clap a name to a babe as soon as it's born? We confer humanity on it. Give it a soul. I jest, of course: that belongs to almighty God and let none suggest otherwise. Master William suits you.'

'You mean it suits you.'

Marlowe pouts. 'If you like. You see, you are rather older than me, and I feel the seniority should be honoured—'

'Older, how? I'm not quite five-and-twenty.'

'We're the same, then. Here we are. Looks cleanly enough, but no telling. Henslowe is landlord to more than one brothel, and we were best have a care the waiting-maids aren't queans o' the stews, looking to your codpiece for vails.' Marlowe's expression of disgust is as elaborate as a painted vizard. But a mask is a real thing too.

'Why did you think me older?'

'My dear Will, if we are to be friends, you must understand something,' Marlowe says, turning on the threshold and taking Will's hand. His is surprisingly rough, as if from hot scrubbing. 'I never answer questions.'

But we are not going to be friends, thinks Will, as they go in. Not that he doesn't think it possible, but something in him resists it. For some reason he thinks of his father, stockpiling wool, waiting for the price to go up, barring the barn door, moistening lips: the drug of it.

Besides, Marlowe drops him as soon as they enter the supper-room where food in bushels

and dripping meat-sides deck the long tables—
the table-legs, Will sees, actually splay under the
weight, like a poor man's dream of a feast. Plentiful
drink, too, though few of the two dozen men here
seem drunk yet. 'What are you?' Marlowe shouts,
attacking the best Rhenish. 'A funeral procession
stalled?' No, theatre people, most of them known
to Will, many beholden to Philip Henslowe, who
disdains the host's chair and comes genially among
them. Everyone wants his favour: some hope for his
mercy, to keep them out of debtors' prison. He is
a large, square-cut man with a loud, flat, frequent
laugh that he uses on you like a father holding
his little punching son at arm's length. What the
occasion is for this largesse no one seems to know,
which is perhaps the idea: let everyone furiously
speculate. Apparently on his way past Will,
Henslowe shakes his hand sideways.

'Master Shakespeare. You thrive, I hope. I have
a play you might mend for me. We'll talk.'

Will feels himself rise a little in the estimation
of watching eyes. He gets a nod from Ned Alleyn,
who is standing around looking beautiful and
pained with the burden of being the greatest actor
in the world. Ned Alleyn created Tamburlaine,
has a voice to fill a honeycomb or smite an anvil,
and is responsible for Will's firm conviction that
he himself will never be anything more as an
actor than goodish, fair, solid. Yes, good Master
Shakespeare, my good sir, that's how he's coming
to be known. He wonders how he should feel about
that. The draught of Rhenish gives him no answers.
As for Alleyn, the word is that Henslowe has him
marked out for his daughter, who has a pretty
penny and a face like a frog's.

The wine is strong, and even the cups seem subtly oversized, as if Henslowe wants you to be a little incapable, a little off-balance. He stalks benevolently among his company, occasionally rearranging them. The comparison with chess-pieces is almost too obvious: Will thinks, Am I a pawn? Here, undoubtedly. But how if you were a different sort of chess-piece, not pawn, or knight or rook or any of the recognised ranks? How would you move on the board?

Marlowe appears beside him. He has drunk hugely, but looks merely refreshed, as if he has been swimming. There is a man with him, a chalk-pale, hollow-cheeked young fellow with a grey stare. Definitely a pawn, Will thinks, as Marlowe lugs him forward. And then: 'Will, here's my good friend Kyd, Thomas Kyd, d'you know him?'

Liquor-loose, Will cries: 'Yes. My God, Kyd. I mean, no. But I've played in *Hieronimo* a dozen times. Your pardon—I should say *The Spanish Tragedy*, but we always think of it as *Hieronimo*.'

'I know.'

'To be sure. Only I was never more glad—*Hieronimo* is so fine, so mightily powerful, I've never known it fail.'

'Aye, ghosts and revenge, and poor crack-brained old Hieronimo going mad with grief,' says Marlowe, airily, 'and all washed down with a watery draught of Seneca.'

'And terror and pity,' Will says, thinking: He's jealous. It's as if gods should have corns. But no, from first meeting with Marlowe—and now add awkward, baleful-looking Kyd—he has never felt in godlike presence. On the page, in the words, in the

222

spaces between the words, that's different. 'And an audience held—perfectly held.'

'You are very good,' says Kyd, frozenly. 'I confess once the piece is writ I am little concerned for its fate.'

'Like a wise parent,' says Marlowe, 'send 'em out into the world with a blow and a sixpence, and give them welcome if they come back rich.'

Kyd has a hungry, unhappily attentive way of looking at Marlowe, as if waiting for some word that never comes. 'The theatre is a place for a man to try his talents,' he says, looking reluctantly back to Will. 'Not a place to stay in for ever.'

'But you'll write more for the stage?' says Will, glancing at Henslowe, thinking: Why here, else?

'Aye, what do you fear, Tom, that you won't *please* again?' Marlowe says, his gaze sliding mockingly to Will. 'He's being coy. Like a girl who's yielded up her maidenhead but still wants to play the sly virgin. What's become of your designing Dane, your Saxo-grammatical Hamlet? Must be ready by now. A very pretty tragedy, Will. He read me the first act and I stayed awake, oh, minutes at a time.' He grips Kyd's bony shoulder, bringing his face close. More wolf than Kit, Will thinks. 'Lord. Won't hit back, Tom? Won't tell me to go fuck myself?'

'I should be glad of a word with you on quite other matters than these,' Kyd says through tight lips, with a wishing-away look at Will. 'The matter of my lord Sussex?'

'Oh, that. I've told you, I'll try what I can do. There's no hurrying great ones, my friend. If it's money you need, sell your play.'

'The question is not so simple . . .'

223

Pawn he may be, but Will knows when to make himself scarce. He finds a window-seat untenanted and sits with the casement a little open, trying to quieten the drink inside him. Outside and separate, a cool, dull afternoon. He wonders whether he should be afraid of it. He thinks of Marlowe and Kyd, little wasp jealousies and fooleries. If I could write as they write, he thinks, I would rise and soar, fearing nothing. You would live in a state of recompense.

'A good spot,' Marlowe says, sitting down by him, and drawing out pipe and tobacco. ' "Not here," they'll cry, "don't drink smoke here," as if I'm frigging myself or something worse. I have a second pipe if you want—no? Tut, and you're scarce drunk neither. You need some vices, man.'

'What for?'

Marlowe laughs, then applies himself to the demanding business of getting the pipe going. Once it is, he smokes greedily: most men go puff-puff, pinched. 'You write, don't you, or try to? Nashe told me. Well, then. Get some vices for experience.'

'Why does writing have to be from experience? Are you Tamburlaine?'

Marlowe's smile fades to a clench of teeth around the pipe-stem. 'No. But I couldn't have written him without being me.'

Will feels small, slightly angry, intensely alive. He wants to marshal great arguments against this arrogance, but fears his army are all empty suits of armour and jerkins stuffed with straw. 'A man may write outside himself, surely.' Tentative, temperate it comes out, though he believes it with passion.

Marlowe looks him over critically, dubiously. 'I don't know about *a man*. I don't believe in *a man*, if it's your common man you mean, or what's the fellow in that fearful canting old play? Everyman. The common run, the many many. Ugh. What I only believe in is the exceptional man. Life is too brief to count the difference betwixt grains of wheat. I don't include you. There's something in you, though I can't tell what.' Marlowe lays a hand on Will's thigh. 'So, who is Will, what is he for? You came from the country, I know that. Is that where you're fixed? Is that where you belong? Do you intend going back after you've saved fifty pound from playing Second Knight in sundry indifferent plays, and fit out a new barn, and live content for the rest of your days?'

Will twitches his leg away. He is irritated and alarmed by his faint cock-stand, yet in a detached way fascinated too. Because up close he sees Marlowe is not as handsome as he looks, as it were—somehow coarser, fleshier, *Not to my taste*, begins the thought, before he catches it up with bemusement. What taste? Being with Marlowe force-feeds you such questions, until you feel sickened.

'I have my ambitions like everyone else,' Will says.

'If you have ambitions, then you are not like everyone else. Grain, chaff. They think to be born a human creature on this earth is a mere drawing of a mortal lot. And if there is anything more to it than that, then priest or holy writ will settle it for 'em, and they can thus go forth with eyes on the ground and never look up till the grave shuts on them, never look up to ask, to question, to demand. And so we are half what we might be. So what is it? The barn? Marriage to a rich alderman's daughter?'

225

'I'm married.' Said prompt and loud as if to proclaim it, as a man might say, 'I'm king.' Though why so loud if the throne is secure?

'Truly? Well, I dare say it happens. But you're free now. Ah, yes, now I see it.'

'You don't. You don't understand it at all.'

Marlowe blows a smoke-ring and admires it. 'Don't like me, do you?'

'Does it always have to be that way? Can't we go a-ramble about the broad country of the mind, without going back to that plain little road with *you* at the end of it?'

Marlowe grins: he looks delighted. 'But I do understand, Will. Ah, nothing I like better than being the subject of a hasty conclusion. What's your father? Man in an honest trade, I guess. You think I sneer: I recognise. Hie you to Canterbury, Will, home of mummery and priestcraft, and ask for Master Marlowe the shoemaker. A goodly godly person, well reputed, except when he takes a drop too much and challenges his prentice to a fist-fight in the yard. Stripped. With his hairy belly wagging like a pregnant sow's tits.' Marlowe's pipe will not draw: he resolves the problem by smashing it deftly against the wall. 'But holy blessed canting Cunterbury has at least a good school. And from there, my fortuitous scholarship took me to Cambridge, away from being the old man's prentice. Like a cat Kit landed, up tails and away. You hate men who talk about themselves in the third person as much as I do, I'm sure. Why do it? Why do I do most things? It's like trying a shoe on. See how it feels. I remember my father on his knees fitting a boot to the son of a lordling. God knows when the whelp had last shifted his stockings.

The honour, quotha, the honour. The honour of grovelling in stink.' He suddenly looks lost, like a schoolboy questioned out of his knowledge. 'What's the place you come from? Stratford? Is it like that?'

Will nods. 'Take away the cathedral.'

'Oh, I have in my mind, many a time,' Marlowe grates softly, drawing his legs up into the window-seat: his toes rest lightly on Will's leg. Will doesn't twitch away this time, partly because he doesn't want to give Marlowe anything to read into it. 'I watch it blaze, before the kindly flames spread to the rest of the town. One by one the houses go. Naturally you spare one or two places, yes? But in reality you have to leave it. Once you get free, you can make yourself anew.'

Will shifts under his look. 'If you want to.'

'No, there isn't a choice.' Marlowe speaks now with pleasant precision: either an angel or a devil would speak so, you feel. 'Shall I tell you what the one true duty of man is? To make himself. The job as done by the almighty is a botch. Got children back there too? Christ. Well, all the better in a way. You're absolved. You've made souls for God's kingdom, you've been fruitful and multiplied, that must satisfy your Bible-Puritan and your old Papist. A lot of those in Stratford I'll wager. They cling to it. These are our old ways and precious to our hearts. Never mind that a set of priests imposed it on your forefathers, swallow it or be burned else. Get some vices, Will, live.'

'Now you sound like a play-villain.'

'That's what I am. I have a friend, or had, he's lately buried—died of the French pox atop of a surfeit of liquor. He had been in Italy, Flanders, everywhere. Kept a tally of the beds he tumbled into—he had his principles, you see, made it a rule never to swyve against a wall. Seven hundred and one was the figure. Seven hundred and one fornications. That superfluous one gives it verisimilitude, no? I had no reason to doubt him. When his nose began to fall off and the blindness set in he even began to regret. When they put him in the casket his corpse was so twisted they had to bundle it up with straps to get the lid down. And do you know what? I envy him still.'

'But you don't,' Will finds himself saying. 'Something in you says you should feel that, because it makes a flourish of life, but you don't believe it really. You'd rather live like a comfortable snail for ever, and never see the shooting stars across the sky, and so everyone would, in the truth of their hearts.'

'Dost call me a liar, Master William?'

'No: I call you an inventor.' Odd: he can imagine fighting Marlowe, as he could never imagine fighting anyone. Excepting his father, of course.

'Why, then, that's different.' Marlowe smiles seraphically. 'We're all that, Will, the best of us. You speak of imagination, and there we have it in us to be princes in the head. Now employ the faculty, please you. Imagine you could go back, just the once, to see yourself at—what? Fifteen, sixteen? Not to hover and gaze phantom-wise upon your younger self, no—you can talk to him. Take him, you, down to the alehouse for a pot of beer and a good deep talk together. Just the two of you. Would you do it? And what would you say to that young Will?' Marlowe's eyes glitter. Will wrests himself away from them, looks through the lattice at the street and in discomfort tries to put himself out there: it usually works. A brawny woman in a French hood, great slung breasts like panniers, is yelling at a man with an unmuzzled dog, threatening law or her meaty fist. Some boys are laughing and shying mud. A beggar sits in a doorway, head against the jamb, face blinking and dead. The afternoon is unchanged and unpromising,

'Well, I'll tell you what I'd say to young Kit, shall I?' Marlowe says. 'Or what I'd do to him.' He rolls his eyes, laughs with a sound like stones in a pail. 'Well, I was a comely youth, and after all, who better to pleasure you, for you'd know exactly what worked? There, oh, just there.'

'It's curious. When you strive for these effects, I don't mind it, because I know something worthwhile will come along presently, after the bombast has blown itself out.'

Gently Marlowe says: 'Answer the fucking question, Will.'

'I don't have to.' Will shakes his head. 'If we were going to be friends, I might.'

Marlowe swings his legs down. 'I'm not going in a pet, Will. I need more drink, and it's not that I find you any more tedious than anyone else. You're right, in fact. What shall I write about next, think you? Great tragedy of high-aiming soul—or write about Will, perhaps? The tragedy of a man who could not make up his mind.'

Is that me? Will thinks, as he leaves the inn; well, revealing question. At the touch of the fresh air he is drunk all over again, staggers, and for the first time since his arrival in London, gets lost. Alleyways and stableyards entrap him. Vicious little winds get up in their corners, sending brittle

229

dry leaves upward. All the leaves in London, he observes, whatever the season, are like autumn leaves.

Her arms, a warm brown egg-colour. He knows where she is in the house at any time without looking or listening out. Imagination. He hears it again in Marlowe's odd harsh, husky voice. The most beautiful word. Suddenly the Thames flashes from the foot of a set of slimy steps, and he knows where he is. Cold colours coming and going in the sky. Evening waiting to be filled. He ought to go and see Gilbert. He thinks of it, firmly and brightly: he likes the thought of seeing his brother; when they meet the meeting is pleasant, yet always he is reluctant to go. In his mind Marlowe asks him why—or, rather, he smiles, and doesn't have to ask.

*   *   *

Coming home from the wars, Ben thought, ought to feel more—well, it ought to feel more like coming home from the wars.

Not triumph, necessarily. A little acclamation, perhaps, to be met with a weary shrug, an easing of the lame leg. Or joy in his heart at beholding this stretch of his native land, tempered with a wry glance at the littleness of a world at peace.

Instead, this half-slinking nothingness. I might as well, he thought, have committed a crime and gone to prison for it and been released. The turnkey draws back the rusty, screeching bolts, a wedge of light falls on stone, and out you step blinking, half ecstatic, half fearful.

At least you'd be feeling something.

He was put ashore at Deal, after a rough

230

crossing. Mariners glared and spat as he and his fellows straggled down the gangplank. Seamen from the ship-owner down hated carrying soldiers, who were quarrelsome, lousy, and riddled with disease. You could only secure a fairly comfortable passage through bribery, and Ben had no money. What the captain left him after creaming off his pay went on powder and shot, green pork, stinking blankets, more bribes.

At the castle a clerk with a pudding face wrote down his name, misspelling it.

'Jonson without the *h*,' Ben told him.

'Musket, flask, belt,' said the clerk, shrugging. 'Any shot?'

'No, I fired it all at the Spanish, the enemies of our queen, while you were making lists in comfort,' retorted Ben. 'Is that a charcoal foot-warmer I see down there?'

'In your own parish by Tuesday first light, else you'll be clapped in irons,' said the clerk, tapping the pass. 'And your *h* won't make any difference there.'

Ben laughed: not bad; and he didn't mean the military bombast, anyway. Who could blame the clerk for making the most of a good billet, after all? Not he. When his company had found that abandoned farmhouse, hadn't they made it a palace against the howling Dutch winter, fires banked high and cheeses dug out of the pit where the owners had thought they'd be safe? Ducks on the spit. And when the fires sank and there was no more wood, they'd used some Lutheran Bibles.

Which made a mockery of what they were fighting for, certain. But that was one of the first things you learned as a soldier—that you weren't fighting for anything. There had been triumphal arches and garlands when the first troops came to the aid of the Dutchman, in Sidney's day, but now the allies cordially loathed each other, and everyone loathed the war. And, besides, you needed a fire when there were wolves about. At night you could see their yellow eyes just beyond the camp. Wolves, in thriving, well-ordered Holland. But they made you feel as if you were the intruder. When you were gone they would take the land back.

Down in the fishy, slimy lanes of Deal, he looked among the chandlers and slop-shops for somewhere that would buy jewellery, specifically the ring he had taken from a ditch-laid corpse on the march to Flushing. He hadn't liked doing it, but he had known he would need money, and the corpse didn't seem to mind. The dead, he had found this past twenty months, were the most amenable of people. The living could learn a lot from them. In the end, after a lot of insults about drunken soldiery— which annoyed him, as he wasn't drunk, though he intended to be—he found a rope-maker who gave him a couple of shillings for it. The rope-maker was drunk. Dead or drunk, that was what brought out the best in people, Ben thought.

He ate a week's worth of bread and meat in a tavern, filled a wineskin, and set out to walk to London. He arrived two nights later, staggering, with blood in his boots: chastened, though still able to smile at himself for turning so soon into the braggadocio soldier. On campaign there had been a lot more squatting than marching.

'You're back,' his stepfather said.

It was late when Ben walked into the old house in Hartshorn Lane. A couple of candles were burning. The man was sitting with a pewter plate on his knee, looking into the fire. He might not have moved since Ben had sailed away. One difference only: a dog lay at his feet. It snarled at Ben, then stopped—perhaps sensing a man who had been among death. When you had seen the way brains leaked from a man's ears while he still looked at the sky, you were not much impressed by a grumbling cur's teeth.

His mother appeared. She gasped, but recovered herself quickly: only he could see the tears in her eyes as she embraced him. This, perhaps, was something like coming home from the wars. He didn't expect it to last. He held her.

'I missed you,' she said; and, dutifully: 'We missed you,'

'So I can see. So much you got a dog to replace me.'

His mother shook her head, stroking his shoulder. Never a light-hearted woman, she had grown stern as a carved saint. His stepfather shifted. 'The dog's a watchdog. We've need of such. Only the one man about the house.'

'A jest, a jest.' And plainly no place for them here. He would have to remember. Black scourging laughter had kept them alive among the midges and mud, the desultory bleeding and dying of the unloved wars across the sea. 'Can I stay here?' Thinking: I can't stay here.

'Such a question. You're my son. This is your home.'

Two different propositions, he thought. Living under canvas and hand to mouth, words had become even more like living things to him. At Bergen-op-Zoom he had recited a whole book of Virgil to take his mind off the sound of the ordnance. It was reassuring to find his memory intact. It was about then, however, that he had begun to wonder if he was a coward. Remembering Master Camden and his scholarly method, he had decided to put the question to proof.

'So I issued the challenge. A single combat, in full view of both camps, against the enemy champion.' Ben told his stepfather about it some days later, in the man's favourite tavern. Same polished tankard, but the chair had moved closer to the fire. Grandeur.

'With swords?'

No, warming-pans. They had gone without hating each other thus far. Just a few growls, like the dog. It couldn't last. 'Aye, swords. Like a duel. The victor to take the spoils from the vanquished, the armour and weapons, a true Homeric contest.' Not that he had had any armour.

His stepfather took a pull on his ale. He looked puzzled. 'Why?'

'Because . . .' He wished he were with someone who didn't have to ask. He wished half of mankind were not fools, and he wished it were not his destiny always to be in company with that half. 'Because it was all a confusion there, a struggle without faces, explosions in the dark. But I was real and he was real, and so it was real . . .' Strange, he couldn't remember the Spaniard's face now, though he had put his visor back, and at one point as they hacked at each other he came near enough to smell his breath. He remembered the cheering, the half-frozen ground at his feet crunching like biscuit, the ribbons on the Spaniard's breeches, but not his face. And he could remember not being afraid, which was the point.

'Did you win?'

'Well, I'm here, am I not?' He bought his stepfather another drink, in a spirit of no hard feelings, and changed the subject. But his stepfather's brain was still on it, like a dim winter sun creeping above the horizon.

'You killed him, then?'

'Such is war.'

He had, hadn't he? That was the vaguest part. The Spaniard had gone down, bleeding at the throat, and his seconds had come hurrying to stanch, to carry him back to their camp, and Ben had turned to receive the cheers of his comrades, and nearly collapsed himself with exhaustion and faintness, the blood pouring from his arm. After that there was the bandaging, the settling of bets—at least half of his troop had wagered against him, he discovered—then a drenching rainstorm, which made both camps up-sticks and move to higher ground. Somewhere there he remembered being sick and sick again. Somewhere also he remembered the feel of bone crunching under his sword-point staying in his arm, like a chronic thrill: something far beyond the little sneeze-like thrill of lust. He frowned. It was a story that wasn't clean enough in his memory, somehow. It would have to be trimmed.

'Well, that's all over now,' his stepfather said at last. He set down his empty tankard with a little refreshed noise. As he grew older, or perhaps Ben was just noticing it more, he was full of these drearily appropriate little tributes. To the fire he spread out his hands and said, 'Ah. A chill breeze, brrr, cold.' They seemed to satisfy him, where

235

before life had made him surly. Ben wasn't sure which he preferred. On second thoughts, he was.

'You gained no money by it, I suppose? Soldiering?'

'None. But saw a little of foreign lands, men and manners, the great wide world . . .' He gave up. 'No, no money.'

'Hm. Well, you know you broke your apprenticeship. But since you were pressed . . . I'll talk to the master of the Guild about it. I stand pretty well with him now, you know.' His modestly proud expression sharpened, slitted. 'And you'll not wish to be a burden on your mother.'

No: he didn't. So the next week he resumed bricklaying with his stepfather. It was sickening, terrifying, how quickly he picked up the old skills. His hated tools seemed to have been waiting for him.

He still intended to be the most learned man in England. He thought about it, and about the way life turned, its surprises, its inevitabilities. He thought about poor deaf Nicol. And he gave himself five years. He would see where he was then. If he was still laying bricks, then he would think about doing something Roman and final, as Nicol had said he would.

Not in any morbid spirit. In the spirit of a man who had looked at life and used his mind. A spirit not given to everyone. Most of mankind was like his stepfather. Hens from the coop, pecking up the same little pleasures day after day, knowing no better. He saw them at the theatres. He didn't mean to go at first. He thought, after that bloody pageant of folly, the play would be a trifling thing. But when he went to test the hypothesis, everything changed. Within minutes of entering the round of constructed wonders, he knew better.

Because here, and not out there, was shape. Here you could impose a sort of order. And it wasn't a lie, because the order was there behind the shambling mêlée of life, and the mind, the tutored mind, could find it, apprehend it, steep it in language, teach and learn. Given the right play, of course, and he was still an exacting critic of plays, after the first starved indiscriminate rapture was over. Each play was all very well, but each had to take its chance alongside the perfect play that he saw fitfully thrown, a teasing shadow, on the wall of his mind. Someone would have to write it, one day—else what an opportunity would be lost. Look at them cramming in, stretching their necks, straining to hear, if not to listen. Only a bear-baiting or a hanging drew a bigger crowd.

Three playhouses open—Theatre, Curtain, Rose—but no shortage of audiences. Nor, alas, of stupidity. He didn't just mean the aping, gaping groundlings: my lord in the balcony was often as dull to the quality of the fare. Which was to Ben still exasperatingly mixed: he adored and detested together. He had seen too much of sloppy imperfection abroad to tolerate it here on the stage, where man was in control, where an example could be made of balance, taste, order. Still the dullards of high and low clapped in the wrong places and would not use their minds. Even in Marlowe; and while Marlowe had been emperor when Ben left, he came back to find him only a king. The rich territory of the drama was being disputed. A good thing, Ben thought. But in time some arbiter of taste would be needed, to sort out these jostling pretenders. To lay down the rules, if you liked.

'Ah, but who is to do it? A man would have to wield a great deal of authority,' said Master Camden. Ben had taken courage, washed off the brick-dust, and called on him at Westminster School. He expected the sight of the hall, the smell of slate and stove and hot fresh learning, to hurt him with the knife of what might have been. No sharper knife . . . But he felt little. A pinprick. He was rapidly putting on flesh—in more than one way, it seemed. Well, a thick hide was good too.

'Authority, exactly so. Which is what learning gives you. That's why a pupil hearkens to a master. Besides, good sir, I remember you yourself saying our English was still too raw for a refined literature.'

'Did I say that? A little arrogant in me. I don't know, Benjamin: can we fence Parnassus? These plays grow as they list, I think: they thrive in the sunshine of general approbation. Would they thrive under glass? Again I don't know.' A smile. 'I grow less certain of things as I get older.'

Ben found quite the opposite—but he held his tongue. He venerated Master Camden still, even if he felt, a little treacherously, that he had lived too easy up here with his books, monastic. Also Master Camden was inherently modest and humble. Again Ben venerated it—but he felt it would not do for him, any more than a lowering diet and chastity. You had to live by what suited.

And the theatre—yes, give him a throne of judgement, and he would speak on it *ex cathedra*, tell the world what was wrong with it and how it could be better. Marlowe was magnificent. Marlowe had faults. And so did this new king, or

238

pretender perhaps, William Shakespeare.

'Who is he? A player. Just a player.' Nicol was gone but there were still a few familiar faces among the young sufferers of play-sickness who gathered in theatre-side alehouse and skittle-yard. 'With Lord Strange's Men now, I fancy. *Harry Six* is his, yes, and the *Shrew*, and *Crookback*. Those I know for certain. Others he may have had a hand in.'

'A player? Not a man of learning? How long a player?'

But his acquaintance—a thick-necked scrivener's apprentice with a half-broken donkey voice—had little more to tell him. Ben suspected he had never liked him since he had corrected his grammar once, in front of his peers. Well, a scrivener should know better. Resentment, alas, was the reformer's lot. He was only trying to improve him.

As for finding out more about Master Shakespeare, Ben found that no easy task. Things heard, from asking around: Shakespeare, yes, a player. You might have seen him in something. In his *Harry Six*, I think. No, I think not. Plays drolls. No, tragical parts. He's from the country, I hear. A butcher's son. No, a lawyer's clerk. No, usher in a school. Very young. Younger than Marlowe. No, thirty and more . . . Ben even came across one alehouse gibberer who twitched and winked, and for the price of a pint confided at last the mystical truth he knew: that Shakespeare was not really a play-maker at all, and the plays he put his name to were brought to the theatre by night in a silk-tied bundle, with a peer's coronet on the seal. Then he fell over sideways.

Oh, he was real enough, of course, but certainly elusive. Even after Ben saw him and admired him in a play, remembered indeed admiring him in other things, a natural presence, understated, still afterwards he found he couldn't quite bring back his face in his mind. Something indeterminate in its good looks. And when he waited about with the other play-sick outside the Curtain to watch the players leave, he still found that Shakespeare had walked past him before he realised who he was— and even then he had to look again at the slender, taut-shouldered figure making its solitary quick way down the street to be sure: yes, that was him. It was as if he were one of those little bubbles on the surface of the eye that you had to concentrate to make yourself aware of. Always there: part of you.

Ben nearly ran after him, that first time. Not sure what for, unless to say: 'Master Shakespeare, you have it. In you I hear the true note of poetry. And unlike Marlowe it is the poetry that might fall from the lips of mortals, all too mortal, and not heroes half made of brass. You have it, and if only'—well, probably it wouldn't have been apt just there, in the street, to add that he needed to trim the luxuriance of his language a little, put a muzzle on his roaming imagination lest it turn wild. No, chiefly he wanted to shake his hand and declare himself an admirer. Found in him an inspiration, even. Especially as one of the unassailable facts about this new play-maker and pleaser—yes, he held them, gaper and listener alike—was that he hadn't come from the university. Ben even silently raised a glass on the strength of that, later, alone, when certain memories of hope and loss visited him and crawled over his drink-mood like spiders in a dungeon. And perhaps there was a little of this: what he can do, can I not do? But shut that out, no room for it when he had to be up early to build a wall in Lad Lane.

I shall meet him, though, he promised himself. It was one of those things that life simply contained: it was going to come, put together Fate and will. Unlike his next move, which need not have been; it was simply the result of a set of decisions. He chose to get married.

8

The Bloody Brother (1591–2)

Damn Marlowe.

He disappears from his life again, but keeps occurring in Will's thoughts where, yes, he cannot make up his mind. He is alarming: attractive, probably not as much as he thinks he is, but that never stops a whirlwind like him. He is lofty, absolute, with the extreme disdain of the lately arrived. (Will at night, before dreaming, walks into that Canterbury shoemaker's house and knows where the clothes-chest is and the stair-turning and can see young Kit there, fair head over a book, can almost reach out and touch him.) Like Tamburlaine in his chariot, he whips past you, dull plodder in his dust. Yet you feel that it's himself he's whipping.

Will mistrusts him and wants to be like him: that power to thrill and persuade. But he ought not to think of it. He ought to get on with learning his lines and earning his bread. You know besides that Marlowe thinks you a fool, thinks it is a world of fools, and somehow that does not take you very far: it's a little closed alley with no river rippling beyond

241

it. Still Marlowe comes to mind—or, rather, occurs to him like a sensation, like eating with a knife and doing what always made his mother shake her head at him, licking it along the blade to get the sauce, and you could taste the edge like dangerous knowledge.

When he does see Marlowe next it is in an unexpected place: in the theatre, watching him. *The Battle of Alcazar*, a new piece. Will has been up all night learning his parts, steps on stage half faint and dizzy and overheated, a full crowd at the Theatre under a muggy sky, and his costume is the heavy jewelled cloak that marks him as a Moor, though Abdelmelec is, thank heaven, meant to be light-skinned: blacking-up always gives him a rash. He'll get through it, always does, and once the momentum begins, and each of them stops acting alone and begins to trade off each other—catch a good glare, tread on the heels of a fierce speech with another—then the dull headache will lift. Always does. Always he finds himself, knows he is in the right place, that this is the summation of his wants. And the day it doesn't—well, that will be another day. But for now there's a trailing part of him still in the tiring-house where the boy-actor is trying to cover his spots with white-lead and young Richard Burbage, amazing Burbage, is actually snoozing on the sultan's prop cushion until his hero's entrance. (His father is the theatre proprietor, yes, but the coolness still amazes.) And part of Will sniffs out to the audience, gauging numbers and size of the box, looking out for the troublesome, the big, chomping lubbers betting each other they can hit you with their cracked nutshells, the simple sort at the front who are liable to reach up and touch you to see if you're real. He hates being incidentally touched.

And there is Marlowe. In one of the balcony seats, where the gentry loll. Someone is with him: Will glimpses silky beard, laced ruff, though typically whoever it is seems half crowded out by Marlowe. One of his high connections, perhaps— even Walsingham? Though they say he cares nothing for the arts: if he had to see a play, he would surely attend a Court performance and have done with it. Unless here to assess this play, these players, for dangers to the state. The only danger he can see is that Marlowe will notice the hero seems to have stepped from *Tamburlaine*.

By the end of the play, Will has forgotten about Marlowe. Some good poetry in it, and he feels it still on his tongue, a stimulating aftertaste like ginger or mustard. The piece pleased: Richard Burbage, toppling back on to the cushion and biting cheerfully into an apple, says his father is pleased too. So the part-scrolls, the plot-sheets and the playbook will be put carefully away in the property-master's strongbox, and the piece will play again.

Will can't be like Burbage. After a performance he is high-strung, hoarse and irritable with reality. This is how Marlowe finds him, just as he is taking off his Moorish cap and shaking out his hair.

'Will, you played prettily. Burbage, mind, was the triumph. He has such a natural way. Wish I could write for him. Your hair thinning at front? I fancy mine's going that way. Goose-fat and sulphur helps, they say. But, then, it's the heat of the active brain that causes it, and I'd rather have that.'

'What do you want?'

Marlowe's lower lip comes out like a reproved

243

little boy's: like Hamnet's, exactly. 'Your company, heart. You did well to leave Master Henslowe's affair t'other week. Some fellows, the ones who fear he'll put 'em in debtors' prison, started making toasts and speeches. Oh, great protector of Melpomene and Thalia and so on, and the old brute looks blankly, so they say, "The muses of tragedy and comedy," and that's no better. He probably thought they meant some of his whores.' His breath is furred with liquor. 'Look, I want to escape yonder grand dullwit, and he won't lower himself by coming back here. Lord, one obligation leads on to another.'

They eat a meal together, at a rather grubby ordinary close to the Theatre. Will can afford better than this nowadays; some perverse spirit makes him want to inflict it on world-conquering Kit Marlowe. But the perversity is turned back on him. Marlowe loves it, from the greasy trenchers to the scrofulous barmaid. He has a refined taste for the seedy, is soon swapping watermen's obscenities with a wall-eyed mumbler who eats his cheese with a notched dagger. 'Don't provoke him,' whispers Will, realising too late that this is the worst thing to say: devilment enters Marlowe's eyes at once.

'We could manage him between us. A little bloodletting gives you an appetite, you know. Oh, forget I said that. What's in this pie, think you? Cat or dog?'

'Rat. The meat's more grainy, look.' But he can't quite catch Marlowe's tone. The trouble, perhaps.

'Look, Will, what I want to know is this. What did you mean when you said we're not going to be friends?'

Startled, Will says: 'I don't know. Does it

244

matter?'

'That's what I'm asking.' Schoolmaster-sharp; but there is sweat in his hairline. He draws something with his finger in a pool of spilled drink on the table-top, something like a gallows-tree. 'I need to know you didn't take me wrong. And with you it's hard to tell. Never know where to have you. I suspicion that you are, after all, a better actor than Alleyn or Burbage or any of 'em. But not on the stage.'

'Why do you need to know?' It dawns on Will, then. Marlowe's rumoured tastes: he even hints at them himself, after all. 'Oh.' Nearly says flatly: Oh, just that. 'By friends I meant friends. Plain friends, Canterbury or Stratford friends, if you like. Meaning you and I will always tend to disagree. Beyond that I—I hold no opinion.'

'You understand, then.' Flushed, Marlowe rubs out the gallows with his sleeve. 'Not that I care a damn, Master William, what you think of these matters. But, naturally, the laws being as they are, you could make things difficult for me, if you took me up wrong.'

'Do you truly think I would do that?' Will says, in mild disgust.

'No. But who knows what men will do, if they're caught between danger and conscience? Or between conscience and advantage. I know whereof I speak. We burn men for addressing God in the wrong way. And we burn them—or assure them they'll burn hereafter—for desiring the flesh in the wrong way.' Bravado, but no fool: he keeps his voice lowered now. 'It would be curious if they should both turn out to be equally unimportant. Oh, I say nothing against the love of women. I did women for a whole year.' He makes it sound like a soldier's campaign or an apprenticeship. 'It was very well in its way. But something, I don't know, bread-and-sops about it. It's the only carnality the Church allows us, after all, and the Church always restricts us to the tamest of pleasures.' Abruptly he laughs and signals for more drink. 'Noose-talk again. I'll stop. Let's talk of poetry.'

'Gladly,' Will says, though the gladness is a sick, blue-lipped thing, scarcely able to breathe for envy. 'Are you writing a new piece?'

'Toying. A Machiavel piece in mind. Magnificent and devilish scheming. Fascinates. Yet part of me doesn't believe it any more. Your Machiavel shapes his ends so precisely, and which of us can plan what becomes of us beyond the next morning?' He scowls at the wall-eyed man. 'You want a drinking-race? Why, then I'll fit you.'

Will gets him out of there, eventually. The wall-eyed man is retching in the back alley. 'Weakling,' Marlowe calls. He staggers and laughs as Will holds him up. 'I must have thy neck, Will. Pardon, pardon. We'll set a great talk going. Don't fear, I'll write thee a testament: Will Shakespeare did not accede to my nameless vice.'

'Tell me if you're going to be sick,' Will says grimly. 'And tell me this—you can't truly be in danger, surely? I mean because of your irregular life—'

'Oh, it's regular, trust me, every fucking night, and you can alter the order of that phrase with no harm to the meaning. Like Kyd's verse, in fact. I know what you mean, Will, I have friends among the great, isn't that it? Perhaps I do. But who says that puts you *out* of danger, hm?'

'Well. You like danger anyhow, don't you? That business at the alehouse.'

'I'll tell you what it is. I court danger because I'm afraid. All the damned time. If I didn't put myself to the test I'd simply hide in a hole.'

'Why?'

Marlowe stops and, still leaning heavily on Will's arm, makes an expansive looping gesture. 'Because of all this.' Will comprehends in it the town around them, the unrolling, unending land beyond, the sky of nothing. Marlowe urges him on. 'I've got to sleep. Can you get me home?'

Home, to Will's surprise, is in Norton Folgate, an enclave of rackety Shoreditch. He supposed Marlowe living somewhere more fashionable: another adjustment. At the foot of the wormy stairs Marlowe pauses, finger to lips.

'Kyd,' he whispers, or tries to: drink undoes stealth. 'We're sharing a lodging. No, no. Good God, no. The man's a dried mummy. Only I want to sleep before he begins plaguing me—'

'Marlowe, is that you? Who's with you?' Kyd's colourless face floats above the banister. His glance falls on Will without interest. 'Oh. You said you would see my lord's secretary today, you absolutely engaged for it. What happened?'

'I did, I did, for God's sake. And I undertook for you, and plied him thoroughly, and I was your entire advocate, and so you may be assured of your interest with my lord. Now I want sleep.' Marlowe lurches up; Will keeps a hand at his back.

'You're sure? This isn't the liquor talking?'

'You needn't be so profuse with your thanks.'

'No—I am, I'm grateful, but when am I to wait on my lord?'

247

'Tomorrow. There, Will—just there . . .' Marlowe sways and slumps so that Will has to half carry him past Kyd to his chamber. Professionally expert in such things, Will knows he is feigning. Once inside and the door closed, Marlowe straightens, yawns, picks his way through incredible mess—clothes, bottles, fruit-peelings, books—to an unmade bed. 'Tom Kyd looks to be a noble's secretary. He wants to be known as a gentleman, not a mere rascally play-maker.' He drags off his shoes, boylike, by digging his heels along the floor. 'I suspicion you are going to say, "Why can't a man be both?"'

Will is drawn to the table by the window, where there is an astrolabe, writing materials, papers. The light is fading: it crawls across the page like disturbed spiders as he cranes, quickly reads. His mind runs hands of apprehension round the blocks of sound and sense, picks out phrases to find them stuck in him like sharp jewels. Not sure how long he loiters there. Marlowe is in shirt when he glances up, and approaching the table. His throat looks like a hollow in tawny sand.

'What dost want, Will?' There's a jug of water on the table: careless, Marlowe swigs, though there's likely a flux in it.

Will blinks, shudders, trying to splice himself back into reality, the heartless now. 'I want to be thee, Kit,' he says quietly, pointing at the papers; and it seems the crudest, strongest thing he has ever said, like blaspheming in passion.

Marlowe chuckles softly, breathes deep. 'Be me then.' It is as if they have emerged at the exit of a maze: here, sudden clarity. 'Incorporate me. There's ample room in there, no?' He places his hand on Will's breast, tapping. 'I'm sure I wouldn't be lonely. But thou must decide first, Will. Must choose, heart.' Yawning, with ribbed catlike mouth, he turns back to the bed. 'Thou art here, but not here. That new barn still calls, hey? You must burn the barn.' Marlowe stretches himself out to sleep. He gives the curious impression that he can still see you through his smoky closed eyelids. 'Burn the barn, Will.'

*   *   *

It was better, this summer visit. Longer, for one. He wasn't touring. And for long moments Anne could even convince herself that it wasn't a visit at all.

Seated opposite him at dinner, with the children standing at their plates either side of him—and how patient he was with their splashes and messes and dainty refusals—she could think this presence of his was not an exception but ordinary: a page like a hundred others in the book. But, then, she didn't understand books: she set herself a nightly task alongside Edmund, but he still outpaced her. And she didn't understand her own conclusion, from Will's tender, loving way throughout that summer—her conclusion that he was changing. That she was losing him.

Losing him, or losing a fight for him? Fighting who, or what? Still she felt no alien kisses on his lips, saw no absent shape in his fire-dreaming. A morbid sensation, Bartholomew would have said. She said it herself when she started awake in the morning and looked on her husband's face beside her—convinced, utterly convinced, that his face would be different: fine, comely, lovable, perhaps, but not the one she knew. But no. Where, then?

249

In the space between words, between the lines he wrote in their bedchamber after supper, crouching curled, the trunk as his desk. In the distance that opened up once when they spent the evening with the Sadlers, and Will—replying to Hamnet Sadler's genial question about tobacco-smoking in London—answered and then went beyond answering.

'And your tobacco-shop is not merely a place to buy, you can take instruction in the art there also. The juniper-fire always burns, so you may take the tongs and light your pipe and stretch your legs and there cogitate, day-long perhaps. I have seen men come out in the evening quite dried and kippered.'

'Curious, for so many say it's foul,' Hamnet Sadler said, with his beaming curiosity. 'And does it make a man drunk like liquor?'

'I can't say myself, for the taste of the smoke doesn't like me, and my tongue turns to a cinder. But from what I hear and observe it has a moiety of all sorts of drunkenness in it, without ever attaining to any singleness or height: so, a man may be fumy and busy-brained as if he has drunk arrack. Then there is a little Malmsey-wine in it that makes a man deep and politic and lay his finger to his nose with twittle-twattle, I know what I know; then a little of the mellowness of sack that makes a man ruddy as a Michaelmas pippin and all inclined to love thee, thou noble heart, have I told thee how excellent a friend thou art, none better, I will run this sword, look you, through the guts of the first man who says thou art not the world's sweetest fellow. Aye, that's your cider-drunk, with a hot-spurred temper that leaps ahead to your next offence before the first is committed; and then a tincture of your metheglin that sews up your eyes singing and makes an oaken table-top as soft as the poppied couch of Morpheus . . .'

And at some point, Anne could see, Hamnet Sadler was no longer following him. She found it difficult herself, but since their courtship she had grown used to hurrying after the cart-tail of Will's thoughts and jumping up on it when she could. Sadler didn't look resentful: only as if a draught had come in, or a good fire lost its cheer.

Judith Sadler didn't seem to notice anything. But just the mention of London was enough for her: different, exciting, far removed from the business of child-bearing and child-losing that left her permanently weary.

'Well, but he won't live for ever,' she had said to Anne not long ago, when Father John was being especially awkward. 'Brute in me to say so, but true. You're in the right place, Anne Shakespeare. Your three beauties growing up strong around you. What would you more?'

True. She took the truth like communion bread: unrefusable, without relish or savour.

He was here, and yet not here. He entered into it all, being in Stratford, being neighbour and goodman, admiring the Smarts' new pigsty, shaking his head over the story of the poor serving-girl who took washing down to the river in winter flood and was drowned. He watched with her the blackbirds' nest, built in a crook of rambler just below their bedchamber window. The parent birds were raising their second brood. Anne had watched the first grow, fill the nest, fly. Will was with her the day the second brood took to the air—all but one. It squatted in the down-lined bowl, teetered up,

251

squatted again. From the outhouse roof the parent birds made little screeches, like chipping on slate.

'What will happen if he doesn't fly?' Anne said. 'Would they leave him?'

'They always fly in the end,' Will said.

'But if they didn't?' Anne pressed her cheek against the diamond panes.

'He'll fly,' Will said. 'Or she. No telling at that age.'

And at last the fledgling did. It made a desperate plunge, landed on a rambler twig a few feet down, and then after a twitching agony of hesitation launched itself at the outhouse. Rose petals scattered. Ungainly, puddingy, losing height, it got there.

'See?' He looked gratified. And she was pleased because, after all, if the bird didn't fly it would die. But she felt a change in his certainty. They always fly in the end . . . He never used to be so happy with the inevitable, which was her horror.

And Stratford, too, was adjusting to Will. It was standing back and screwing up one eye and nodding, yes: placing him as one of those men who went away to work, sending money home, planning for a slow, broad-wheeled future. Becoming one of a recognisable sort. Anne preferred him, them, unplaceable. She supposed she was being unrealistic. But, then, with Will she had always supposed that was allowed too.

There was a box, now, instead of the cairn of stones. A small strongbox with leathern clasps, brought from London. When he opened it, she could not help sniffing: absurd, but that was London air inside.

'I'm becoming known,' he said. 'I'm worth my

252

hire. I'm not rich by it, Anne, but I'm saving, and if I can rise to become a sharer in a company, then I—well, you take a share in the profits of every enterprise. And then if I can sell a play of my own—'

'Oh, I'm sure you can.' She didn't doubt him: not in that way.

The box was for the money he saved. The money was to get them a house of their own. He seemed to want her to be more excited by the box than she could find it in her heart to be. She ought, perhaps, to shake it delightedly, or run her hands through the coins. Like a miser in a play.

'I'm glad,' she said, as something more seemed to need saying.

Gilbert was doing well in London too. Will brought a full account of him from his master in St Bride's. His father listened devotedly, actually sitting still for it; a rarity now, when he was restlessly moving about for most of the day, leg twitching or foot tapping, making sudden dives to pick up threads or crumbs from the floor, going a long, muttering way to dispose of them.

'And you, Will?' Joan said. 'Now you are quite the London player, will you perform at Court next, do you think? The Queen loves her plays, they say. What a thought, our Will acting before the Queen! Or wait, is that only the Queen's Men who can do that?'

But his father did not stay for this. Could not. There were pointless things that needed doing.

'No, any company may be summoned to play at Court, if it pleases her,' Will said. Anne watched his face as his father grumbled out of the room. It did not exactly change: it was like seeing water with a passing reflection in it.

Joan was bright and merry and full of the questions that Anne, perhaps, should have asked. But later, in the kitchen, a mist came over her eyes and she put her hands on Anne's arm.

'Reprove my folly,' Joan said, with a sigh, eyes closed, 'but don't leave me, will you? Not yet.'

Anne smiled, without in the least feeling like smiling. 'Where would I go?'

'Oh, you and Will are aiming at your own household, aren't you? No, he hasn't said anything. I just supposed. You'd be mad else. Only don't do it yet. It will throw such attention on me, and they have too much room for attention already, those two. God bless them and I love them, but . . .' Joan took a cup of uncut wine from the tray they were preparing, drank it off, wiped it, all in one go. Anne suspected she did this quite often: not too often. Enough. 'They should have been a king and queen or something like, you see. Nothing short of being a king, all its great duties and grand doings, would give Father enough to occupy him. And being a queen would furnish Mother with the chance she needs to be good, good, good.' Joan took a breath-comfit from her girdle and popped it into her mouth. 'I can't make you stay, I know. But if you go I shall have to hurry and get married, and I've seen no man I care for yet.'

'You needn't hurry,' Anne said, unsure why she said it with such a bitter snap, like biting on a clove.

Four days before he was due to ride home, Susannah came tiptoeing to their bed at cockcrow, begged their pardon for disturbing them, and said she felt something queer before being sick and fainting.

'A tertian ague. A sickly season, I warrant you. The afflatus is not encouraging. But she sweats well, that's good.' The surgeon changed his mind every minute. Damn it, Will said, it was high time they had a better doctor in this benighted place . . .

'It was a good enough place to raise you,' his father said.

Anne thought, God, they're going to go at it while Susannah lies dying betwixt them. The thought rose like a boiling pan in her head, overflowed. Will heard her soft wail, saw, understood. He gripped her hand as they sat by Susannah's bedside and gave careful, respectful answers to his father, who would scarcely leave the sickroom. Joan was right: his officiousness needed a kingdom. But he was genuinely attached to his grandchildren, wanted to share the night watches, seemed indeed to do good with his big tenderness, his oak whispers: 'Buck up, my chick, wilt soon be skipping again.' For Anne there was no time or room for anything but the love and fear, keeping her at a perfect tip of wakeful concentration. Sleep was one of many irrelevancies beside this pallor, this sweat-sticky fringe, this little backward baby-cry with which Susannah woke herself up in ashamed surprise.

Then the fever broke. Susannah sat up and drank her cordial in her ladylike way, putting up a hand to catch the drips. Will hugged her, then Anne: then it was all three. Susannah looked very slightly uncomfortable.

'Sleep now, love,' Will said.

'No,' Anne said, because she didn't need to, and because nothing mattered now; but as things didn't matter she lay down on the floor by Susannah's

bed and fell into good darkness. When she woke
the light had changed, Susannah was just coming
hungry out of a doze, and her father-in-law was
sitting by the bed.

'Hungry, hey? Well, thou shalt have the best
white meat, my pretty, but only a little at first, for
thy stomach will be tender yet. Mammy's sleeping
by, heart, and thy father has just gone down to wash
his head at the pump, for he's been watching long
and long. Aye, he'll be back, heart. Never fear, he's
here—and he won't leave thee again.'

For Anne, relief was still too vast and
overwhelming for anything else to qualify as a
feeling. She merely thought, as she roused herself:
He's saying that as a thing to soothe a sick child.
That's all. He won't *make* anything of it.

Even when Will came back, wet-haired,
weary-eyed, unmistakably happy, and Father John
cocked his head at him with that flint-and-steel
catch in his eyes, Anne didn't believe he would go
on.

'I was just telling this little gillyflower of ours,'
her father-in-law said, 'that she needn't fear. Her
father's here, and here he will stay, hm?' He smiled
down at Susannah, twitched and smoothed the
coverlet. 'I was asking yon doctor, and he was of
my mind, that it does a little child no good to be
forever lacking a parent, wondering when she'll
see him more; that it injures the health, and makes
them liable to pining and sickliness.'

And Will did not rise. Will did not rise by even
so much as a sharp breath or a clenched fist, while
his father repeated it, rephrased it, went on using
his child's illness as a versatile weapon, now the
flat, now the blade, to beat him with. Perhaps he

256

was feeling like her, relief making him invulnerable. But she didn't think so, and that was why she continued to entertain the quiet belief—courteous unobtrusive guest it was—that she was losing him.

Much later, when Will was making up his pack for the ride back to London, she asked herself why, weighed conclusions.

Why? Because if he could endure this from his father—and his father, she knew, had the secret of hurting him with a deeper twisting than she could ever know or want to know—then he must cherish some great recompense within him. It was as if somewhere there was another box, in which he kept his contentment, unassailable and secure: contentment or joy, she couldn't tell. Something made up for it; or someone. Anne believed that all somethings began with a someone.

But, actually, she didn't know what to believe. In fact, if you had asked her what was the most likely thing, she would have said: that I am sleeping away a summer afternoon at Hewlands Farm, and any moment I will wake in my bedchamber to the sound of Bartholomew chopping wood—wake a maiden, wake seven years back into the real, before all this long crammed dream.

*　　　*　　　*

Settling back in London, Ben had easily leaped into his old venery—but had very soon felt himself drowning and wanting air, down in the mud and silt.

Perhaps it was the memory of that whore at Flushing, who had leaned against a stable wall and gnawed away at a ham knuckle while the men lined up for her, one shuffling and shuddering

257

after another. Perhaps it was because the first discontented wife he picked up at the theatre permitted him every freedom in the bedchamber except a kiss: *Jesu, none of that,* she complained when he tried. It was then, perhaps, that he decided: not to get married, but that if he were to do this, it would be properly, with tenderness and respect—he was not so unrealistic as to say with love—and with, in other words, a wife. And then it all happened very swiftly, which was good, because he didn't want to waste a lot of time on it.

He did meet her at the theatre, but she was a maid with a gorgon companion, no eye-rolling available goodwife or badwife. She was pretty, hale-looking—he could not abide a sickly woman— and for all she was virtuous, modestly clothed and chaperoned, her almost-black eyes gave off a crackle: like whipping your shirt over your head on a close day.

Ben was mannerly, careful, even after he found out the old companion was deafer than Nicol. No stealth of the predator, not with this straight-backed young woman who smelt of nothing but her own body, and who raised her eyebrows in amazement to hear a gross fellow in the next balcony swear oaths by Our Lady's virgin arse.

She had sense. 'Do I have it right?' she asked after one scene. 'The lady has fallen in love with the man, though he is the one who killed her husband? And she has done it in a few moments, because of his sweet words?'

'You have it right.' A poor scene, indeed: it would need a genius to make such a scene work.

'Well, he should be careful after he has wooed and wed her, that's all. If she can be swayed so easily, she'll soon be swayed from him too.'

Ben bowed low.

'What are you doing that for?'

'I am abasing myself before you, Mistress Lewis. I've never known beauty united so with wisdom.'

'Oh, pooh, that's just fine talk,' she said doubtfully—a little sharply: her voice was not a low one, perhaps from the deaf chaperon. Not a lover of high-flown nonsense. He thought all the better of her for it. But she had a smile for a jest. Once they were on terms, and she had allowed him to press her hand and, with misgivings, her knee, he told her the hoary joke about the citizen's wife at the playhouse. Before they went in, the citizen told her to beware of pickpockets. '"Have a care for thy purse", he insisted, "have a care for thy purse"— and then, when they left at the end of the play, what does Madam Citizeness cry but "Hullo, my purse is gone." "Didst not feel any fellow fumbling under thy skirts?" cries he. "Oh, to be sure", says she, "but I didn't suppose it was *that* he was after."'

She kept her eyes fixed on his throughout this time-worn narration—and at the climax gave such a rewarding shout of laughter, slapped his leg so hard, and alluded to that wicked merry tale so many times that day that he felt himself to be, if not in love, then comfortably placed within love's suburbs.

This was better than lechery, he thought, in all ways. A year's labour at the miserable craft of his stepfather had put a little money into his purse, enough for a new book, perhaps; and if he were to study again in earnest, he must give his mind to it, which he could not do when he was dancing attendance on idle-living mistresses. In Hartshorn Lane he looked thoughtfully at his mother and his stepfather over the supper-table. A dismal sort of marriage, but she always had shoes and stockings, meat on the table; he did not hit out as much nowadays, but nor did they lovebird-coo as they had once; they were used to each other, in essence.

His mother, he thought, would approve her: her trimness, her straight gaze, the neat needlework of her own that she wore at her high, ripe but modest breast. As for his stepfather, Ben didn't much care. Of course, if he were to marry before twenty-four, it would break his apprenticeship. He looked into himself for a while, wondering if this was a motive, but not for long. Self-examination, he thought, was futile. He knew himself anyway.

There was the question—once he had settled on marrying her, and Ben's decisions were as prompt and reliable as his digestion—of what they would live on. Well, if nothing else he could work at bricklaying as a day-man. If his stepfather wouldn't give him work, he knew one of his associates who would—he regularly winked at using unlicensed labour, and the touch of rebellion in it appealed. And Agnes had a little money.

'Some people have supposed me an heiress, and I'm not,' she said, in her cool, downright way. 'You're not one of those, I hope.'

'You have my leave to run me through with a sword, if I am.'

'A sword? Lord above, where would I get one of those?'

'You are ever practical.' He laughed.

'No: I know you're not of that sort. And you're hardly in a position to hunt fortunes neither. Oh, I don't mean anything by it. I like you very well, though a plain man. I think I shall like none better.'

Practical, yes, and nothing of the light-of-love about her. They walked together in St Paul's: her little arched feet nosed in and out of view; he allowed his mind to climb pleasantly upward from them. She was proud of her spruce, berry-eyed self, and harvested the glances of admiration, speculation, but he didn't mind that. It seemed right that a pretty woman should enjoy the consciousness of what she was. Different for men, of course. He was happy with the difference.

Her parents were dead, and she lived with an uncle as guardian and the old deaf woman who had been her nurse in St Magnus hard by London Bridge. The uncle had been a tanner and had, reputedly, made a heap of money. So it seemed from the look of the house, when Ben at last made his formal call: bars and shutters everywhere proclaimed the miser's hoard. Within, he passed through so many locked doors, and little passages and vestibules—like infant rooms imprisoned and stunted—that he thought he might come out at the back door, never having been properly inside the house at all. He was brought into the uncle's presence at last, in what he thought was a lumber room. A bundle of old clothes moved, and that was him.

The old man approved Ben. 'I can tell a good deal about a man by shaking his hand,' he quavered, forgetting to do so. Agnes yawned and tapped her distracting foot while her uncle showed Ben, with much whispery ceremony, his treasured collection. 'Such a collection, sir, is not to be found outside the royal palaces.' Nor in them, Ben hoped, for Her Majesty's sake: he had never seen such miserable trumpery. The old man fondled a moth-eaten

261

tapestry that might have been made by a set of blind, palsied nuns. The Venetian glasses, thick and misshapen, had never been near Venice. But the old man mumbled and caressed. Put it about that you were mighty strong, and people marvelled to see you lift a middling load. They believed in a cobwebbed fortune behind these doors. They would do anything for belief, the poxed whore, but not for knowledge, the virtuous beauty. It was strange. The old man kissed him and promised to do well by him. Once they were alone Ben wiped his mouth and shared his first proper or improper kiss with his affianced Agnes.

For the first time, also, he saw a little fear on her face. 'Wilt be a good husband?' she asked him.

He thought of his dead father, of his stepfather, who spoke softly only to his dog. 'Only try me,' he said.

*　　　*　　　*

London swallows Will up again. He goes gladly into its maw and ripe capacious guts. Here he can't think, which is to say he can replace thoughts with a thousand others if need be. He goes to Blackfriars to forage among the galley-proofs, and to pass on news from home to Richard. Not good: old Master Field is failing. Wanders in his wits, and in church has been known to start undressing, as if he thinks himself going to bed.

'Oh, God.' Richard speaks more in weariness than alarm. Upstairs his baby heir is squalling. Richard has crossed that line: the new generation is the locus of anxiety. 'Well, I can't go back, certainly not this quarter. Unless I want to throw the

262

whole business in the dust.' He has this continual apprehension of catastrophe too. If prices stay as they are, he may as well set light to the place, and so on. Meanwhile he looks quite comfortable. 'Jacqueline's been on a diet of vinegar since the baby. Trying to get her figure back. If you ask me, the vinegar's affected her temper beside.' He keeps his voice down for that. 'Seen the new Ariosto printing?'

'No, can I borrow?'

'If you don't mark it. Lord, what news. I dare say Mother can manage him, though, hey?'

It is not, of course, a question he wants an answer to.

On his way out Will passes Jacqueline talking with a French neighbour: the two women stand close, solicitous, lightly holding hands. Their voices sound like hautboy and flute twining together. The exoticism of it thrills and pains Will: he wants to linger, as the tongue lingers over the cut in the lip, poking and hurting.

Shoreditch hums with the news of a killing fight in the street: drawn swords, screamed oaths, blood spattering the causeway. Nothing so very out of the ordinary in that district—until he hears the name Marlowe.

'What? Nothing's happened to him,' says Nashe. Will finally finds him at the Mermaid, almost walled in with books and papers, and lingering out a tankard of small beer. 'Well, apart from committal to Newgate. But it's a formality, he'll get bail. He was quite an innocent party. Well, as near as friend Kit can *be* to an innocent party. Buy me a drink and I'll tell you the tale. To be sure I'll tell you without the drink, but it will be a mean, spiritless species of

263

narration . . .'

So, there were three men in it. One was named Bradley, and the son of an innkeeper. Bradley accosted Marlowe in the street—in Hog Lane, no less—over a debt. Swords out: general agreement that Bradley drew first. (But Marlowe wouldn't be slow to respond, Will thinks.) While they were hacking at each other, along came Thomas Watson, good friend of Marlowe's, fellow poet. Watson protested or intervened or drew his own sword—accounts apparently differ—and the next thing wild Master Bradley was attacking him in turn. Watson defended himself, so well that his sword went six inches into Bradley's breast and killed him. So, committal for the two of them.

'Kit, as I say, will get his bail, and almost certainly be cleared, for he landed no killing blow. Watson did, but it was plain self-defence, and he'll surely be extended a pardon if he can live past the gaol-fever.'

'And all over a debt?' Will says. 'It's prettily paid now. I suppose there is no enforcing laws about the wearing of sharp swords.' He calls for, needs, a drink.

'Nor on men's tempers.' Nashe tickles his own chin with his pen, regarding Will brightly, subtly. 'And you wonder with me, perhaps, what *is* Kit Marlowe fighting when he does this? Himself? God? He believes ardently in one—and hardly at all, you may have divined, inappropriate word, in the other. For my part I would have people keep mum perpetual about their bed-tastes alike with their religion, but it's as if Kit wants to throw them in the world's face.' Nashe shakes his head. 'Brawling and stabbing, blood and death in the middle of hoggish Hog Lane: what a picture it makes!'

Yes: Will sees it, crude and bold in afternoon sun. If he puts himself in it, it is in the shadowed sides. Moving along the margins of life, where you can't be pinned down. But come, out into the open with this, Will: the leap and lurch of your heart when you first heard the bare mention of killing alongside the name of Kit Marlowe. Stratford and London, his two impossible, irreconcilable poles, meet at least in this. In both he knows what it is like to wish a man dead.

But he is like neither of them. No grand doer of deeds. No strong swordsman of life. Instead he has this, and to win he must take it up, light, with a sharp, sure tip to balance the world on: his pen.

9

The Chances (1592)

'With the hunchback, do you suppose him weak in the legs likewise?' Burbage says. 'How if I limp—or will that make him too pitiable?'

'Go by me again,' Will says, watching. 'No, I think no limp. I fancy he would move fast. Strength in his motion, like a blind man's voice. Mind, we don't want him pitiable at all.'

'No? Not even in the scene of the ghosts? "I shall despair. There is no creature loves me."'

'Good, good, give it so. You've learned so far?'

'I've learned the entire thing, much as you've tried me.' Burbage goes to the keg and taps it.

They need many pints of small beer to see them through these rehearsals, starting at cockcrow so as to utilise the light. The yawning prompter holds out a mug. 'I never conned such an infernal long part. But I warrant you, it's easier to get by heart than a Marlowe character. Your Crookback is more— well, he is himself, and not just so many lengths of verse. By the by, you know your accent's not regular there.'

'And elsewhere. So I want it. In Marlowe there is too much—' He stops. Burbage, stocky, sandy, round doughy face, gives him a wry, surprised look. 'I don't want regularity. Not like a clock ticking. Bend it, as you did then. There's an extra beat at the end, on "me". The voice drops at it. In that is Richard's sad recognition. "Me" is almost naught.'

'Yet no pity? For this is what pricked me, Will, to take him: that he's not a mere Tamburlaine vaunter atop the heap o' corpses. Everything he does is villainous, yet he's not all villain.'

Will remembers long ago sitting by his mother's side protesting, *We are what we do, surely*. 'I think we may feel with him and for him, but not with that pity which places us above him. Not looking down. More—looking in the glass.'

Burbage wipes his beard. 'Hm. Heaven knows I have my faults, but . . .'

Will laughs. 'Look you, if we were to be villains, what manner of villains would we better prefer to be? Weak vacillant ones, or tremendous ones, tip-full and exuberating? And have we not all overreached at some time in our own lives, even if not to murder and kingly thrones?' He half fills a mug: his mood plunges. 'And haven't I done so, with this? Overreached?'

266

'Dost think so? I don't,' Burbage says. 'I'd not throw my reputation in after it, if I thought it would sink. What you put together with *Harry Six* was very well, but that crowded historical pageanting goes only so far. And rot me if I could remember which duke was which for half of it. No, this is what I look for. Someone to write me a man, who thinks and lies and bleeds, and you remember him when you lay the book down or leave the theatre, recall and judge and think around him like a man you've known long to drink with.'

'We should feel more for him the worse he gets,' Will says tentatively. 'Will it answer?'

'Aye, if we keep our eye fixed on him. Less of the pageanting.'

'I've tried to keep it down. In fact, I fear the historical facts have gone under the straw and out of the window—'

'Where they belong.'

Will grins. He is addicted to hunting through the chronicles and compendia he has accumulated from Field's shop and elsewhere, and sometimes vividly dreams of reading pages full of rich matter and could almost weep when waking scatters them; yet once he begins to write he wants to shrug them off, like whining, insistent beggars. He has to be left alone in that place.

Burbage adjusts the stuffing of his hump. 'This thing keeps slipping. Come costuming, it had best be sewn in. So, entrance, does he soliloquise on the winter of discontent, or is he confiding?'

'Confide, bring us in, we are all human alike. Prowl and invite us to your secrets, so. The measure is irregular again, I know, purposed so. Just follow it: the accent hands you the meaning. Falls heavy

267

on the first stroke of *glorious*, for he's mouthing it with mockery. Now skip light along *by this* and land plump on *sun*—aye, makes you smile, like a wedge of hard cheese.'

'I have you. A slippery pulse. Think you Alleyn could speak this?'

'Never.' Alleyn is Burbage's great acting rival, stately, magnificent legs. But for Will, Burbage has twice the gift because of his presence—or, rather, the absence of his presence. When Burbage steps on to the stage he gives up on his self, leaves it like a snake's shed skin. Not dissimilar to how Will has begun, at last, to write properly and alone for the stage. He finds he does best if he takes himself almost by surprise in writing: sidle to the desk and begin jotting while standing, not sit down solemn to the great task of composition. Irritably leave it, walk away, pounce back on it half hearkening to an argument downstairs or a broken song in the street. Become a part of that argument, a note of that song, thread yourself into its progress and no matter where it takes you, as long as it's away from yourself.

This is the great, matchless discovery: a place he can enter and not be.

No set times, for that, too, would inhibit (here I sit down to compose), but he works long and hard, is never far from his writing-sheets. His barber notices them.

'A pretty comedy, that's what you should give them. Not these tragical kings. Lift chin. Mind, he was a rare villain, your Richard, wasn't he? Or so they say. More of a mixture, like any of us, perhaps, if truth be told.'

'Ah, but which truth?'

'Strange, some men lose from the brow, some from the crown. Yours is thick as thacking at the back, look. Truth, well, that's a thing as lies fair or foul depending how you comb it. Will it please you perfume the beard? Heyo, you know best. Grey hair, now, when that comes you can cry welcome, for it don't shed.'

'Is there no happy way, then?' Will says. 'To keep the hair and the colour?'

'If there is it's not this side of the grave. The Queen, now, she's been bald as an egg for years. A crown won't save your crown, as you might say. But would I change places? In a trice I would.'

Burbage and Heminges frown over Brakenbury's speech.

'I can't make much of him,' Heminges says.

'"Princes have but their titles for their glories,
An outward honour for an inward toil;
And, for unfelt imaginations,
They often feel a world of restless cares:
So that, betwixt their titles and low names,
There's nothing differs but the outward fame."

'It's merely an obliging sentiment on behalf of royalties.'

'To be sure it is,' Will says. 'We want to perform at Court, don't we? And always be first there? So, I put in something that will please. Grant you, it's a pudding principle. But think you this—Brakenbury may in truth be like Richard: acting, all the time.' He remembers Jack Towne deep in ale, himself hanging young and aching on his words. 'Like all of us.'

He writes the wooing scene again, and again: it's

269

a disaster and they postpone rehearsal, filling out the later acts. But it has to be done.

A hard thing to carry, all agree: for the lady Anne to be wooed by a man who killed her loved ones, to go from hate to love. The boy-actor struggles.

'Stage-minutes,' Will says. 'The audience knows they are not as real minutes. We make them forget how time works. In truth the wooing would be over a stretch of time, it would be sewn in with other things, but in a play we must forgo. And in that there's a sort of truth. Have you been in love?' The boy shakes his head, awkward; but he is sixteen, he must have been. 'When you fell in love, there was no one moment when it happened. And that is true of the most poetical love that ever struck a man all of a heap. For there is no such thing as a moment. Call it a second, or an instant, if you like. Now cut it in half—for there is naught in creation so small it cannot be divided. So now the moment is two—so which was the moment of love? Both, part one, part t'other? It can't be. A moment exists only when we look back at it. All in the heart and mind is flux and process, so it hardly signifies which moment we show in how the lady changes, so long as it convinces.'

'And that's just it,' says Heminges, kind, tactful, right. 'It doesn't convince.'

'Anyone would suppose, Will,' says Burbage, not always tactful, 'that *you*'ve never loved—or else you've forgot it.'

'Give me half an hour.'

He works furiously in the next-door tavern. Comes back with the sheets still ink-wet.

'"Your beauty was the cause of that effect;
Your beauty: which did haunt me in my sleep
To undertake the death of all the world,
So might I live one hour in your sweet bosom."'

Better, better. Burbage makes it throb. Looks
quizzically at Will. 'A pretty question it raises—if
a man can speak so beautifully when feigning, how
may we tell a true lover?'

A pretty question, about what means the true,
the real. The things Will is trying to make, as he
thinks and works and writes, eating, going to stool,
giving his laundry to the washerwoman to take
down to Thames-side.

'What do you look at, sir?'

'Your pardon—your hands, they must pain you.'

'Nay, not now. The lee-soap does that, you see.'
She chuckles, stretching the red porcine fingers.
'Makes the clothes good but mars me.'

Nashe, looking over his shoulder in the
Mermaid. 'Why do you write so fast?'

'To stop myself feeling sick.'

'What you write turns you sick?'

'The fact of it.' His script is crabbed, the pen is
never easy in his hand.

'And when it's acted?'

'Oh, then it will be no longer mine. Thank God.'

The Lady Anne is wooed.

'"Those eyes of thine from mine have drawn salt
tears."'

The boy-actor responds to it well, melting,
torn. '"I would I knew thy heart." Now she is truly
feeling, yes?'

'Yes,' says Will. That is to say, she is acting what
she feels.

Create the real. The wood where he and Anne came together, that was real: yet also they created it. Where is that wood now? Existing in some moment or half-moment? Nothing that is made can ever cease to be.

Will goes to see Gilbert. Fond, dutiful, but bored. In the kitchen Gilbert spits into the fire and talks of prices. Upstairs an Italian merchant is calling on Gilbert's master and lamenting long and beautifully a shipment of rare cloths lost at sea. I see them, in my dreams I see them go down and down. Will thinks of his work, of his Richard, like a little secret thought of a lover: thinks of Clarence's dream. *Methought I saw a thousand fearful wracks; A thousand men that fishes gnaw'd upon.* 'Aye, I tell thee, Will, another poor harvest and we are done for.' *Some lay in dead men's skulls . . .*

Home, sleeping, drowning in dream, he wakes to the sound of the watch crying the hour—or is it someone crying murder, murder? Or a gallant in jest, rapping his sword on the floors of rooms built crutched over the street? Oh, to be a lively capering self, taking on all the world, a Richard uncurbed. He suddenly remembers Wilson, his enemy in the Queen's Men, muttering one day, 'Ah, the gentle-Shakespeare act.' If we only knew about each other. 'Leave the world for me to bustle in,' says Richard. And walking home from the theatre, with patterns in his mind echoing the patterns of lighted windows, Will lets himself think of everyone in the city, in the world, taking sick and dying. All dead. Now you could go in all these, rummage, know all of people's lives. And how many, in truth, would you manage to pity?

'He does these things,' Will says, looking over

272

Burbage's costume, 'because he can. He has a mind to imagine, and leaps after it. Such is humanity. What have we mortals ever thought of that we have refrained to try out? Torture engines. Never a one that man's mind has balked at and said, "I have thought of this, but dare not build, or put it to use." Put yourself in killing mood, my Rick. "Well, I'll go hide the body in some hole." '

'Regular, there, your murderers are eloquent in their verse.' Burbage turns over the crumpled pages of his part one last nervous time, fiddles with his wig. 'You know they will not applaud your parade of ghosts, Will.'

'Who?'

'The high critical sort. The sort to cry down your learning, to lament the profuse lines too gorgeous dressed, to cry balance, sir, decorum, think o' the ancients.'

'Then I'll take the applause of others. Won't you?'

Burbage booms a laugh, cuffing him. 'Your Richard is the very devil, and I love him.'

Is he, Will demands of himself, alive? That's all. In the first performance of *Richard III*, his own proud, shameful, desperate work, Will plays King Edward, one of his typical parts—noble, a little ineffectual, soon leaving the stage to the vitality of wicked Crookback. Alive, that's all that matters, alive as these people in the audience cracking nuts and peeping over shoulders, ugly, handsome, infinite. They don't gape as they do at a Marlowe play: they look as if they are at home, forgetting where they are, on the edge of the bed just woken, themselves.

Richard—his king, his play, his man—is a

triumph. They laugh and weep and shout: they palpitate with the story to its headlong conclusion. They do what the thing did to him when it went through him, and which is now only an odd dead echo of a sensation.

'Ha, we stormed them, Lord, we conquered, what think you?' cries Burbage afterwards, hump coming undone, clapping his great hands. Will is trembling and thinking . . . well, thinking of the next one. He pats Burbage's back—and indubitably solid and fleshy as Burbage is, still the man seems a little less real now: a little less of him. The first indication that magic thins out the world. That this has a cost.

*   *   *

It begins with the plague.

Where the plague begins no one knows, though there are plenty of opinions. It is a miasma that settles from the upper air, having its origin in malign stars. It is brewed up by the villainous poor, living filthily hugger-mugger like and with pigs. It comes as a righteous punishment for greed, sin, luxury. For being Protestant. For being insufficiently Protestant.

Sometimes it goes away for years. Then it rises up suddenly and starts lopping lives, like a boy swiping dandelion-heads. London worst, but anywhere. A town is going quietly along, then it is burying a tenth of its population.

Anne: she can remember clearly the outbreak in Stratford when she was a girl. Her father stayed away from the town, even though he needed to send goods to market. Better lose money than bring that here. He urged Anne to pray for the poor souls of Stratford. She did, but she was frightened too; and she prayed that the poor souls of Stratford keep away from her. Bartholomew, she remembers, did a horrible imitation of a plague victim, staring and drooling. He said it sent them mad as well as making their flesh rot, and they were likely to seize you and kiss your lips so you would take the contagion. Only much later does she realise that the year of the Stratford plague was the year Will was born. His survival was then against the odds, which must mean something.

Will home—sun, and plague, earlier this time— but then she has stopped counting the summers now. He managed to visit in Lent too, but it's not that. Counting suggests counting down, a tally to be struck across: some limit. But Will the London player, the part-husband, that is the reality.

There have been plenty of beautiful times. The arrival, that is always one, with the children cascading through the house at the first sound of his voice. Presents for them. Always presents. And then simpler moments like the first meal together. Even simpler, walking through the town with him, arm in arm, in the evening quiet, the sound of their footsteps on the bridge, honk and drabbling splash of waterfowl. Talking. Seeing him wash the travel off with pump and pail. You could still count his ribs.

It's just this—knowing that coming home is part of his working life. Like rehearsing. (Like the writing he does when he is here, the making of plays, this new refinement of his career that baffles her more than anything in its silence, its remoteness from her, for he won't talk of it except to say, 'Yes,

I turn my hand to it.' And yet, good God, how it is filling the money-box.) It's knowing that he's home early this time because there's plague in London; theatres closed because of it, and no tour ready yet. Not here because he just wanted to come home. Anne smiles; but behind it a feeling like a hailstorm, so hard grainy pelting it could brain you. Luckily hail never lasts above a minute or two, and melts as if it has never been.

*   *   *

It begins with plague; which begins with headache and chills and fever and, oh, God, the light, take that light away. Before the swellings in the armpits and groin, the suppuration, the bleeding from within. It begins with warning red crosses on house doors, the carrying of red wands in the streets: to say, it's here. Perhaps it will falter and sputter, kill half a parish-worth, fizzle out. But no. This is a strong, lusty outbreak, a charioted Tamburlaine of sickness. By June the playhouses are ordered to close, because they spread infection, though the city fathers would love to see them like this permanently.

Choices for the players and the theatre people, some more stark than others. 'They'll keep them shut till Michaelmas,' Richard Burbage says to Will. They are spending the afternoon at a bowling-green in Lincoln's Inn Fields. Probably these places will be closed too, soon. 'Early to mount a tour, and then we must hope the country won't turn sick of acting companies, as we're all like to be out there.'

'What will you do?'

'Bugger. That's a villainous shot, look at that rub. Oh, I'll see what Father says. We'll find something

276

to do—the Theatre needs repairing and cleaning. What about you? Well, you've your family in the country, I know. Look you, I shan't mind if you tour with Alleyn. If you can stand being on stage with the great bag o' wind then luck be with you, man, that's all.'

'Home it will be. I'm never quite easy with either Henslowe or his crown prince, and besides . . .' Will lets the thought go with the bowl, trundling away, to end where it will. 'You know, there's room in the theatres for you and Alleyn.'

'I prefer to think not. A little competition, a little whiff of the adversarial, makes a man a better actor. Come, what's amiss? Art afraid they'll forget thee?' Burbage claps his shoulder, making Will stagger. 'Love thee no more?'

'Who?'

'Why, the public, who else? It's poor luck to be sure, a closure just when your name on the bills is tickling the audiences. But the other poets will be silent perforce too, hirelings and grandees alike. The crowd will come back for you when the flag goes up again.'

'Oh, the public.' Will smiles, or feels his lips doing it. 'I don't fear them. They don't know me.'

'Write me another Richard,' Burbage says, with sudden urgency, squeezing Will's arm. 'Christ, man, what we made of your Crookback was something worth. Bating flattery, Will, there's your golden vein, you please all about, the men and the women and the high and the mere. No more of your *Titus*, please you—not that it won't go: it's the prettiest piece of bloody Seneca that was ever carved reeking off the joint, but I only get to speechify.'

'Another Richard? We've brought the Roses

down to the Tudors.'

'Nay, leave off the history now, if you will. Tap your vein of beauty. Tender and true, to make 'em weep. But it must be an actor's piece and a crowd piece likewise, look you. Have an eye to what Marlowe's about. Still waxing heroical? He turned his last piece after your example, I swear.'

'Now you do flatter,' says Will, grimly.

Where is Marlowe? Tom Nashe isn't sure. Earlier this year he was abroad. Flanders, they say: arrested and sent back, they say—or is that what they want you to think? Certainly he has been in London lately, because he was bound over by Shoreditch constables to keep the peace. As ever Will wants to gobble up news of Marlowe and to spit it out. When Nashe said Marlowe came to hear *Richard III*, Will refused to believe him. 'You are too sweet and gentle, William, or perhaps too happily secure in your triumph, to remark you proved me wrong.' For he and Nashe worked together on a first draft of *Henry VI*, but Nashe extricated himself after one act. He couldn't flourish, he said, shut in this historical paddock. It's a space, Will said: that was all he wanted. As for Marlowe now, he may have gone out to the country as so many are doing, because of the plague.

This is how it begins: the great houses of the nobles with the gated gardens down to the river shut up, the deer lifting their heads in St James's Park unmolested. Doctors stalk about in long gowns and conical masks filled with rue and bergamot, looking like great spectral birds: not many, though. They prescribe the treacle medicine made of viper's flesh, vinegar, wormwood, but people keep dying; small wonder if they turn instead to drinking their own urine, to prayer. Or to blaming the foreigners. Yes: that will begin soon.

Will prepares to go home too. He has money, and so a breathing space. Because his clutch of plays have worked. Emulation, imitation, exultation. Knowing what he was doing and not knowing what he was doing. Why not? A player not a sniffing scholar. He stopped worrying about sounding like others when he realised there is no such thing as originality, except the originality that comes from synthesis. It all went in.

But he is more troubled by the interruption than he gives away to Burbage or Nashe, because he has just found himself and found a way, and now the gates are closing, for how long . . . ? And he's afraid he can't go back to the person he was before his work became acceptable: the sheets pawed over, the nod, yes, it will serve, the heavy pouch in his hand, and then it was *your* words cutting and floating on the cool afternoon air before the ringing rockery of faces.

He hates it, hearing his words. He wants to run away and scream and hide. His fluency in writing is deceptive. Really he is running over the lines like a man running over a pit of coals. Only swiftness prevents the torture. Yet in words he is home and self and free as nowhere else, and sometimes getting up from the desk he cannot for a moment adjust to the world being physical and not made by him, and he wobbles, as if his legs are turning to phrases and his feet to metaphors. But hate or not he is caught. Essentially he would give plays under the sea or on the moon if there were a way, rather than not do this, be this Will any more. He is all made of steel about it. Yet loving too. Hot and fierce-handed for what he does, in London.

Home, then. He is accustomed to travel now—the long hours in the saddle, the impossibility of impatience on muddy or dusty roads, the fellow journeyers falling in with you, and how you spotted the ones who would be tolerable or a menace. At some point on the way he leaves behind the Will who exists in London, becomes the one who belongs to Stratford. Fancy a post by the road, a stone, this marks the spot. He shouldn't think this way. It suggests splitting, damage, and he won't believe that. Useful lesson in humility in it anyhow. Along this road he is just another mark for innkeepers, possibly highway robbers, especially now his clothes sing out a little his growing wealth. Where he comes from—meaning London—he is turning into a name: a public figure, in a small way. A person attracting dislike, envy, even hate.

How he recoiled from that. I shall never, he thought, get used to it. On first hearing the attack on him from a fellow poet, he felt himself inside leap back high in the air like a cat touched by surprise, fizzing, arched.

'Oh, it's not just you,' said Nashe, who told him. 'He has pitched into Marlowe too. And eke your humble servant who has ever accounted himself Robert Greene's friend, since we were at Cambridge. But, there, what would you have? We go before the public, my friend, you upon the stage, I in print.' (Nashe is fecund now in pamphlets and satires; anything odd, sharp-edged, provocative is likely his.) 'We all stand up to be hit.'

'I'm not happy about those either but, yes, I'm a son of Adam, my saltest tears are for my own woes, and it's what he says about me that I resent. Have I met him, that he can traduce me as if he knows me? I've read some of his love-tales, but I don't recall the man.'

'We may have been in company together. You'd remember the look of him. Pointed red beard and most curious pointed red hair, you might fix his head up either way. But you're not likely to have been in his company of late. Oh, Greene made a show of it at first, you know, like Marlowe multiplied—gambling, wenching, drinking. He found them a flavourful curiosity, these whores and rogues, and then at last it was as if they had fixed his taste, like a man dining every day on hot mustard and radish. And he has been writing every moment since university, in every mode and manner—writing for his bread. So he seldom speaks—shall I say?—*measured.*'

Players are a low, impudent set, was what he heard Robert Greene was giving out, and it was a shame when a gentleman had to lower himself to write for their capabilities, but at least it was done gentlemanly. Now you have a beggarly player like this Shakespeare taking the play-making out of their hands, copying their style, imitating their methods, garnering the applause for his second-hand glories. It was reported to Will thus from several sides. Bad things said about you never fall into abeyance: they are dropped letters that people are eager to pick up and pass on to the right place.

It stung; it stings him still in memory as he rides the Oxford road with half an ear for the garrulous old man at his side anecdotally reliving his youth, the scampish affair that old men's youth always is.

In essence, Greene has said: You shouldn't be

here, doing this. Thou art a wrong thing in a wrong place, doing wrong. It beat at his temples, thinking of it: drummed like a confirmation of something.

Nashe excused and temporised. Marlowe, if he knew of it, would surely either laugh or reach for his sword. As for Will, he went to see Robert Greene.

Why? His scalp prickles with shame or embarrassment to think of it, but he was sure he walked down that Dowgate alley, in wharf-side stink, telling himself: I will make him like me, love me. The greatest of all defeat.

He kept thinking of Jacqueline Vautrollier—as she was then—issuing her simple invitation, among the innocent flowering plants. Temptation: surely it didn't have to lead to this, to peeling, fish-head squalor. Greene had left his wife after he'd spent all her money, Nashe said, and set up with a mistress, Em Ball, sister of the notorious thief 'Cutting' Ball—rumoured to act as Greene's bodyguard against the fellow writers he offended. There is a son of the liaison, a little boy called Fortunatus—call him Unfortunatus, Nashe said. Nashe loves words more than anything.

It was all so unreal. Cutting Ball. The bleak chamber above a shoemaker's, where Greene received him reeking of wine and rotten guts, dressed in the remnants of a good set of clothes— except hose, showing, uncaring, bare, fleshless legs between breeches and shoes. And that wild red peak of hair and beard. Grief does not sit well on the redhead, or privation. Greene's pale eyes looked as if flesh had been rubbed away to reveal the holes in him, his life, soul. There was nothing in the room but a couple of stools, a bottle, and paper.

He was writing, writing crosswise on the back of bills and inventories. He did not appear surprised to see Will.

'I can't offer you anything. Nor would I, naturally.' A glance at Will's clothes. 'My need is greater, a grating need indeed.' Will flinched from his breath. 'My apologies for the noxious mephitis: dying, thou know'st.'

Will glanced around helplessly.

'Starving, no. I do eat. My landlady has a tenderness for me and brings soups and stews. But nothing stays in, and no flesh accumulates, hence my fair conviction that belling death is on my traces. But don't let that stop you, lay on, you're Shakespeare, after all, and have a good proper grudge. I've seen you play. We met once at Henslowe's, but you didn't take any notice of me, you were busy being flattered by someone. Sweet Master Shakespeare. You see, I'm piling it up so you can strike at me and get it over, for I've a lot of work to do. A play, 'midst other things, aye, I'm trying 'em too, though with what chance against you I misdoubt. Sir Crowd-pleaser. It can't be right, you come along, supply yourself with some plain roast and boiled blank verse, a dash of Marlowe spice, and serve it up—' Suddenly Greene was on his knees, retching into the fireplace. The stuff coming up was an unthinkable colour. 'Your pardon. My bile punished with bile.'

'I didn't come here to strike.'

Greene wiped his mouth with his sleeve. 'Why, then? To crow?'

'For God's sake, it's not a contest. To ask you why you defame me. When I haven't injured you. When I haven't—'

283

'Oh, it is a contest, as you well know.' Greene chuckled, phlegm-cackling, struggling to his feet. 'Why? Does it matter? I fucking envy you. Look at me, look at you. I've been writing for ten years, yards and yards of print, most indifferent, some indifferent good. I grind it out from the millstones of my brain for the printer, quick sale and forgot and then another. I've tried for the high style and the hand of a noble patron to lift me, one step, two, where it's not so easy to fall back into the mire, everything I've done to be heard. We want to be heard, yes? And you—you are heard. And it hasn't *cost* you anything. Sweet Master Shakespeare, he goes home to his loving family come Lent or summer in the sweet-smelling country where the sweet showers fall.' Greene laughed. 'Now that's enough to make me sick again.'

'You had a wife, they say. You were well married.'

'Aye, and deserted her, sent her into Lincolnshire while I whored. What then?'

Will shrugged. 'So does that make a man a poet? Throw everything in the dust to hold tight to one dark thing? One self? Is that how you see it?'

'Me, Shakespeare, I'm going to die,' Greene said, with sudden quiet weariness. 'I just wonder—when are you going to live?'

(But the youth of today, the old man riding at his side complains, are a standing shame, nothing but fighting and getting wenches with child and wronging the ancientry.)

'Soft.' Greene came after Will on his way to the door. 'Your hand, there. Would you believe, Shakespeare, I wish you well? For I do.' His drained eyes searched Will. 'But just this. Hark.

284

Luck is a debt. Luck has to be paid for.'

When Will left, the alley was bright with sunlight, and bright horror, he knows, is quite the worst, like the dead cat he saw in the gutter, with another cat, very alive, contentedly eating its insides. Superb sunlit sheen on everything: sleek fur, pearly intestines.

Drag hence her husband to some secret hole, And make his dead trunk pillow to our lust. His mind was all large white space as he wrote it, and as he wrote one-handed Titus cutting the brothers' throats, with tongueless, handless Lavinia holding a basin between her stumps to catch the blood: kind light bathed the page and somewhere in the next house a man and a woman were singing to the lute, so sweetly.

When you make a play strong, you make the world a little less so. Terrible suspicion, that power is the best thing there is.

He is crossing Clopton Bridge, leading the drooping horse; he is almost home. Next he will see Edmund, for wherever he is, his young brother is always the first to greet Will, seeming to possess the ears of a hound. Here he comes, running full pelt from the other end of Henley Street. Twelve now, and more well grown than any of them at that age, broad across the shoulders, boy's fairness darkening.

'Brother, my sweet brother Will, thank the kind heaven that has sent thee,' he says.

'Your best yet,' Will says, and they laugh. Every time, Edmund greets him with a poetical absurdity: their little joke ritual. As he goes on to gabble out a hundred things he has been doing, Will hears a reed in Edmund's voice as if it is close to

285

breaking: very early. Some boy-actors keep their unbroken voice until eighteen, thankfully. They play women better older, even if the stubble has to be masked . . . Very much a boy, though, the way he skips sideways beside Will. All this vitality. As if his parents had handed some final energy to this their last offspring. Father especially: the same fine looks, strong bones. Unfortunate that everything in Edmund's personality seems to grate on his father. Unfortunatus. Too much of Will in him, perhaps. Loves a tale or a verse, and hangs on his every word about the theatre. Though Will tries not to talk about it too much, here, on the other side of the border.

'Anne.'

She screws up her eyes as he steps, reminding himself to duck, from the dazzled street to woody indoors. They embrace, for a goodish time. This is always in a way the easy part. Missing each other, reaffirming love: an imperative as if they have just survived an accident, darted—as Will did once in London—from the sudden fall of a chimney. Later it may be difficult, the complex simple business of being husband and wife, but not now. Now there are the children. They come running. It occurs to him that they would do this for a favourite uncle. Quickly he presses the presents on them, trying again not to be surprised at their growth, their rampant life without him.

He is easiest with the girls. Susannah is getting on for ten with all her mother's fresh rare field-flower beauty lying ready for her. She is a lady and thinks her father, like most men, an agreeable blunderer. Of the seven-year-old twins Judith seems, as it were, the least twin-like—greedy, careless, taking for granted the indulgence of the littlest. But Hamnet: his great blue eyes seem to see so much, they seem even to ache as if they let too much light in. And Hamnet is not happy with dashed explanations, the things said to a child as you might grab an apple from the store and thrust it into their hand, here. But where is the Quineys' pig? Dead. How dead? They killed it. How killed it? But the details he wants disgust him. And last year there was the awful moment when he came in to find Will new arrived, still cloaked and grimed, beard untrimmed, hugging the others and then turning to open his arms, and Hamnet burst into tears, ran away, crying, 'Who's that man, I don't know that man . . .'

Suspicion—terrible, about your own child!—that Hamnet was feigning it a little, for effect, for—what? Well, it was his grandfather he ran to, his favourite. He was like him in his desire for certainties. Truth. What is duller than certainty, thinks Will, what dead thing is deader than truth? Will tries to overcome that look in Hamnet's eyes with a bigger present, with gentle listening attention. But probably just being here more would do it. Ah, yes, that. The question that jogged here all the way with him. How long would the plague last, how long would the theatres stay closed, what would he do if it went on? Who was he, as Hamnet said, shrinking into John Shakespeare's belly. Decide.

* * *

The plague begins it, and it ends for Anne with such a betrayal of Will as her heart has never known.

That's where it all happens—in the heart, not the world, but the heart is the great arena or theatre, for Anne. This in spite of a shift in her authority: for she tends now to be Mistress Shakespeare, rather than her mother-in-law, in Stratford. It's in the tone with which people address her at market in the street; or when the women busy themselves around a pregnancy, when one of their number takes her chamber to prepare. Like Judith Sadler, poor womb-harried Judith again. They gather about the bed, commending the double shutters keeping out the poisonous air, flushed and chattering; and to Anne they extend this little extra respect, not quite deference. Notice her gown, of London make, that Will brought after securing the measurements from Mistress Gray, the Stratford seamstress. A risk when it's only a fitting that can assure you, but it came perfect, needing no alteration. Not many husbands to take such care, Mistress Quiney says, as the lying-in cup is passed about. He thrives, they say: a fine thing when a man finds his fortune.

What he does in London is known about the town without quite sinking in. Hard to credit that players earn such money, stand so well; but that's London, all enterprises are greater there, and what with the Court . . . It's all golden, to be sure, and how proud she must be of what he's made of himself, and still keeping up with Stratford and home. Yes, all true. She is proud, without feeling proud. Can *is* be different from *feels*? He would know, perhaps. And surely it can't be envy of poor Judith Sadler, effaced by miscarrying and infant deaths, preparing to go into the fell grip of childbearing again. That was over for Anne—they lay together so seldom, and she never seemed like to quicken anyway, and the unspoken conclusion was, the family is completed.

This summer, however, not a birth but a dying. Old Master Field, after a general decline, not plague. Old, sir, old, the clawed hands and the brain like a shrivelled apple core. They go to pay a visit of last respects: she, Will, Father John, making one of his rare stirs abroad. Dying hard up there, they say, like her own father. Anne and Will sit with Mistress Field while his old friend goes upstairs to witness the struggle awhile.

'I don't know what to do with myself now,' Mistress Field says, as if her husband is already dead. She half laughs, picks at her black skirts. 'Fly, shall I fly?' From above comes the deep rumble of Father John's voice: peace, my good friend. My good old friend, God's peace be with thee. He is good at this, notes Anne: the moments of high crisis bring out the best in him. Daily life, on the other hand, is a baffle and snare.

He comes down. 'Well, I fancy he knew me in his way. But he keeps asking for Richard.' Sad head-shaking, calming hand on Mistress Field's shoulder. 'He thinks Richard is still here somehow.'

'No, alas, another deserter of the family hearth,' Will murmurs to Anne: then grimaces sorry.

'It would ease him, I'm sure, if he could see Richard again,' sighs Richard's sister. She drank straight from the tap of her parents' Puritanism: she looks just made for a death-bed.

'Aye, but not to be, my dear,' Father John says. 'Even if he could know him.'

Will says: 'I could go up. Talk to him. He might think I'm Richard. Well, after all, we're of an age, a colouring. I can—' He wants, Anne thinks, to say, *I*

289

can be him '—I can be like him.'

'It's a lie. Sinful,' cries Richard's sister.

'He doesn't mean it,' growls Father John.

'But if it eases him.' Will insists gently. Anne wonders if he would insist so much if his father weren't here.

'Yes. Yes,' says Mistress Field, at last. 'We haven't agreed for years, him and me. I can't do anything for him. I can't reach love through old hurts, it won't go through. He needs something to lift him before he goes to God, else . . .' She doesn't say what else: just looks expectantly, tearless and grey, at Will.

As Will gets to his feet his father looms at his side, bitterly hissing: 'But you're not Richard.'

Will glances him over: simply, colourlessly determined. 'What does it matter who I am?' he asks, and goes up.

It isn't then, though, the betrayal: for she's on Will's side. And another time, a week after old Master Field is buried. Summer has temporarily given up to grey and cold; they are all trapped indoors. Edmund, restless, asks Will about the plays he has written for London. 'I want to read them. Don't you have them with you?'

'I have some sheets of something I'm working on,' Will says, cautious, evasive. 'But the plays belong to the companies, once they're finished. They keep them.'

'But you should print them. Why not ask Richard Field?'

'He doesn't think highly of plays. And if they're printed, they become common property. The companies don't care for that. Besides . . . printing is a sort of last word. I never want to say the last

290

word. When there are no more words, then . . .' He falters.

'You must remember them, though,' Edmund says, with the relentlessness of youth. 'Give us a little. It's a dull day, and here we are an audience.'

Will is reluctant. Anne feels the reluctance to do with her somehow. From his father, a twitch, a gaze fixed away. He never talks of Will's profession except in terms of money earned, days worked. Otherwise he presents a subtle blankness like the Sadlers in church, saving their consciences, probable papists. Joan adds her voice: 'But naught dark,' she says. 'We live enough in the dark lately.' Meaning the weather, possibly. Will begins to tell his comedy. Then, haltingly, to speak the parts—to play the parts. To be it. Edmund thrusts back furniture to make room, gasping, glowing. The thing is a galloping madness of twins and mistakes—two sets of twins. Only one in the original, Will says. Why change it? For more madness. He darts about the swept house-place and becomes, astonishingly, four people, throwing his voice hither and yon, drawing up straight and big, bending small. No wonder he never puts on flesh, Anne thinks, wondering at the vitality of it. And yet not able to give herself to it because part of her looks always to Father John, the smoky horizon of him, the wind blowing from his temperamental quarter. He does not, of course, like it. But Joan and Susannah and even Will's mother are laughing and admiring.

And then: misfortune. Judith and Hamnet come in from feeding the hens with the maid. Not understanding, they blunder into the stage-space, and Edmund gently but impatiently shunts them

291

out of the way. While Will acts people outside a house and also inside the house, by shifting his body.

'"Go fetch me something; I'll break ope the gate. Break any breaking here, and I'll break your knave's pate. A man may break a word with you, sir; and words are but wind; Aye, and break it in your face, so he break it not behind."' He ventriloquises a rasping fart so real that Joan flinches away, flapping her apron: oh, fie. And the laughter disguises it at first, until it will not be hid: the thin hard cry of Hamnet. He doesn't like it. It's not real. It's stupid. Father's pretending. It's frightening. Looking stricken, Will throws off the actor, bends and stretches arms to his son. Yet still perhaps there is something in his gesture that is a little stylised, that shows he is accustomed to assuming a feeling: even perhaps real ones have to be tried on first. And then she sees, unmistakably, a little flicker of irritation, that his son should be so difficult, so inclined to spoil things, so—well. It's to his grandfather Hamnet goes again, to be embraced. And in doing so Father John turns him right around, holding him across the chest, so Hamnet's teary face looks out at them all, accusingly: looks at them indulging the lie.

But what begins with the plague ends at last with this: one of those dreadful three-sided quarrels. Three-sided in that Will and his father take up opposing positions, but there is another ground on which you can step, if you are foolhardy or loving enough. Summer is nearly over, but not the plague. The theatres are to stay closed at least till Michaelmas, he has said so himself, and now Greenaway the carrier brings news of London still death-stalked, plague-pits filling. So.

'You'll stay here, then, naturally.' Father John says it offhand, a thing settled.

'I have a play to prepare.'

'If it's that manner of work—writing work'—Father John won't say it without a smacking of distasteful lips—'that can surely be done here.'

'It's not only that.'

'No? What, then?' Knights clattering on to a bridge, thinks Anne, wondering where the image came from. Some story told by Will, probably: so many of her mental pictures are of his drawing. Mounted knights advancing on each other, upward sway of lances.

'If I am to make my living partly with my pen, I must look to other avenues when there are no plays.' As so often, Will pacing seems to look everywhere but at his father. 'Many a man in London writes in another vein. My friend Tom Nashe is one. A play is for the stage, but printers and booksellers—well, Richard Field will tell you, they are eager for verse and tale. And there are gentlemen of wealth and breeding who will reward a poet with patronage, if—'

'Oh, and a thousand other things while you think of them. What is this, man?' Father John is breezy. 'You ran off to be a player. You've settled to it, aye, I'll say yes, and profited by it while you can. But it's a half-and-half business at best, and now it's all at a stand, and no knowing if your city councilmen may not say at last, pull the theatres down, if it comes to it. Face this, Will, 'stead of setting up new cloud-castles.' He turns a smiling, sighing look on Anne. 'You know I'm in the right of it, daughter. Speak to him.'

'We have spoke, sir. I know Will sees his fortune lies in London, as before, and there I place my faith likewise, and content me.' It's true. They have spoken of it. Rather than talked of it, perhaps. But there again she can't contend, not on the bridge of words.

'You're loyal,' her father-in-law says; and, with a complete switch of tone: 'She's loyal, Will. A true wife. I hope you value that, for assuredly you take advantage of it.'

'Oh, God.' Will is halfway to the door, just to get away from this, from the possibility of his own reply, because as she knows he is full of fire and he doesn't want to turn it on his father. It will be too much.

And this is when Edmund steps in: seeing his adored brother perhaps as retreating, defeated, and that he can't bear. Will is where he lives and sleeps, like a lad with a den, where he can be himself. Anne sees in Edmund's lit face that he feels it is up to him, and he likes the responsibility; and in spite of all slights he still doesn't see how he is going to anger his father as he says, so reasonably: 'But Will has lived in London, Father. He knows it as you don't, and so he must know what's best to do in his profession, and I'm sure—'

The slap across the face stops him saying what he is sure about, though probably makes his thoughts sure, very sure. Edmund nurses his face in the shame of having it hit, and Anne reaches out and puts her arm about his shoulders because she must—and, yes, she has been drawn in thereby to take a side or be a side, very well. And Will looks murder and contempt and readies his tongue.

She thinks: Don't say it. You say too high for

294

him, and he will feel his lowness.

'Pretty in you,' Will says. 'And thus the once bailiff of Shit-on-the-wold conducts himself in his wisdom and dignity. But at least no stripped sow's belly while you ply your fists, Father. May as well be, however.' Anne loses him now. Will doesn't look lost, though, looks right in the centre of his country. 'But a drunken shoemaker boxing with his prentice is better than a man who pretends to be Lord Mayor presiding worshipful at the Guildhall and meanwhile he beats his youngest son, the one whose skin marks best, who's not of a size to reply in kind, hey? I'm going back to London, certes I am, because it makes sense—to anyone but you. It's naught to do with Edmund, and you're a poor thing if you turn the blow on him you mean for me. Too much like me—is that it? And not enough like you? But that's how it should be, sir.' Will is almost coughing with passion. 'Sons should not be like their fathers, and damned confusion on it if they are.'

And this is Anne's betrayal. Loving Will, caring deeply for Edmund and his hurt, and finding her father-in-law at his worst, still she thinks: Oh, Will, can't you change it, just for ease? For ease, let it go by. Agree, allow him to feel he has won.

In other words, she wishes Will were not brilliant and different, and had stayed in Stratford, growing more like Hamnet Sadler, or like his father.

Will looks blind with rage: still, she wonders if he sees the betrayal in her face. Reads it. You know him and reading.

Such a betrayal: she almost feels, when Will prepares to go back to London, that by it she has invited anything that may come. Meaning the things she has always secretly feared will proceed from his being in London and playing and writing and living all of life that lies beyond her. Meaning, she has flung wide the door and said to the devil: Enter, then.

10

A Woman Killed With Kindness (1592–4)

He is so young that coming into his presence occasions an awkwardness, as of intrusion. Like nudity or someone at stool: I should withdraw from this. Even on his second reception by the young Earl of Southampton, Will feels it.

Deceptive, though. Yes, he is not yet twenty, still a ward of Lord Burghley's, having decisions made for him. But then you remember that he is heir to a noble name, a fortune, multiple manors. This house in airy Bloomsbury Fields is only one of the parts of the earth his influence touches: apt to see his white hand stretching itself on the surface of a globe.

'It inspires a new appreciation of the almighty's creation,' the young man says. 'But also of man's handiwork.' A beautiful, lustrous thing of German crafting. 'The question of how the world is made becomes yet livelier when you contemplate this. Look you, Master Shakespeare, this superb sphere, it must be constructed first and then the map pasted over. I asked after the method—but it must be a specific projection, you know, not a flat one after Mercator.'

They are alone in the library, or as alone as it is

possible to be with a young aristocrat like this: over by the fire sits an old tutor or governor in nodding watchfulness, a liveried manservant holds the door, and occasionally another peeps in with a figure seeking audience, to be nay-said or encouraged to wait with a shake or nod of the earl's head. Will has been there. Even the ante-rooms to the earl's presence are an education: he heard several new lute songs, had a first-hand account of a shipboard storm off the Azores complete with rescue by Moorish prisoner, and learned to pun in Italian.

'You know why I had so great a desire for this?' the earl goes on, butting his hound's questing nose away. 'Because of its incompleteness. These doubtful areas where our mapmaker has resorted to curlicued monsters. I would love to make these places surer, con the world aright. See, discover. Oh, I've been over to France.' Dismissively, as you might say Westminster. He sets the globe spinning. 'Places *sans* names, look you, are your only destination. Ye gods, how tiny we must be on this earth. Like the spoor of flies or fleas, or smaller, would you say, on this scale?'

'Smaller, smaller. Imagine the smallest thing you can, then cut it in half. Then cut that in half, and on and on.'

'And, *ergo*, you never come to nothingness, how terrifying!' But nothing terrifies this young man, Will sees.

Like bees about a blossom, Nashe said of the young Earl of Southampton, the scribblers and the thinkers and the singers flock to him, or shall I rather say like flies to their proper attraction? Nashe has hopes of patronage from Southampton too. The young sprig is not just rich and powerful but educated, cultured, as devoted to his library as his stable. A beneficent sun around which men of the arts may dispose themselves like stars, reflecting a little of the greater effulgence . . . It helped, Will found, to accustom yourself to the language of the thing: patronage. Also, this is something new to him, beyond the directness of play-maker and crowd. At its crudest, if they don't like what you offer they throw it back at you, slap, like spoiled meat in the tavern-keeper's face. But to lay your writing before a patron, an aristocrat, is to speak in another voice, to appeal to a wider and narrower world. Writing his poem, preparing his dedication, he has mingled the lofty sex of Venus and Adonis with images of hopeless subservience, booming doors slamming in his face while mute stewards hurried by him with rent-rolls, even, in whiter mood, princely munificence: I am well pleased, bury him in gold. Conjured them all as he inscribed the dedication, sought out which of his houses the young earl was staying in.

Close to London, it turned out, in spite of the plague that lurked through the winter. And then the approach, writing turned ritual. Look favourably on my poor wit and dry fancy. All mighty strange. It didn't alter, though, the central feeling, the feeling of creation. Is this the best of me? he asked himself. Plays are made in the air, in the space between the actors and spectators, like a storm between fanning breeze and hot still air. You wouldn't inscribe a storm. But this, *Venus and Adonis*, was him set out on a page, the craft and learning, and the thing he rode when imagination hit and words passed through him.

'You are a good sailor, my lord?'

'Oh, sick as a cat from the first spread o' sail, but what man would stick at that before the Americas and El Dorado? And then the anthropophagi in Africa, men with heads beneath their shoulders— though assuredly I've seen *those* at court.' He does an imitation, with the geniality of a man who will never know mockery. 'I know, I shouldn't. But, really, the flattery they bestow on the Queen is enough to turn a man's stomach. Well, my globe was a pretty purchase, no?'

Will allows a smile inside, for Henry Wriothesley, 3rd Earl of Southampton, is as greedy for flattery as any ageing monarch shunning the mirror's shrewd eye.

He is certainly a young man of unusual beauty, beauty a little ambiguous, as all male beauty must be: only the plain can be themselves. He is gorgeously dressed, as befits a young noble with the world before him, but there you can see simply the eagerness of tailors and jewellers, making him in their profitable image. The hair is different: a rare true auburn, longer than most women's, tied and looped over his shoulder. Few men could carry that off: you need that hawklike delicate mixture of feature. The beauty is effortless now, but in time it will need cosseting to be maintained. Will thinks of Jack Towne: he last saw him in an indifferent production, looking both grim and flabby. Something like regret touched him.

'A beautiful sight,' Will says, of the globe. 'An image of all that could be yours. Not like Tamburlaine, subduing. Possessing in the mind.'

'Alexander weeping for worlds to conquer. Oft mistranslated from Plutarch. An imaging of the futility of desire.' Just when he seemed most a boy, preening, he came out with these things: fruits of university, of this library he says Will must treat as his own. 'Naturally, I want to do everything. Italy, now—Master Florio says I should have been an Italian, and when I sing in a madrigal I think—but then I yearn to be a poet. Do something like yours.'

There is the manuscript, on a stool near the globe: is this the moment for abasement? Last time Will just read him a little, and had permission to leave it. Instead Will says, serious: 'Truly? Because I doubt it.'

'You shouldn't. You will reach a multitude when you print, and not just because it is so warm and amorous. Because it finds room to be comical too. At least'—he smiles—'I hope that was your intention, else I have just dashed you.'

'That's what I sought, yes. Lust is ridiculous because we fear it. That's why we laugh. The deepest most helpless laughter I ever saw was at a burying.'

'You fear the act of flesh?' For the first time the earl looks lofty, perhaps because unsure.

'Well, everything else we know whence it comes, where it goes—hunger, ambition, love of our family, our dreams, our God. Nothing of this is comprehensible. In nothing else do we look back on ourselves and behold such a fearful stranger.'

'They want me to marry,' the earl says flatly, signalling for wine. 'My family. My lord Burghley has particular notions . . . I suppose everyone marries in the end. A matter of what's suitable. Do you have a wife?'

Will bows yes.

'It's different for me, you see. When I marry, they'll have to get the maps out. The lawyers will measure out the bride-ale. Can it be like this? "Her arms do lend his neck a sweet embrace; Incorporate then they seem; face grows to face."' The young man blushes a little as he summons the quotation.

Now Will does make sure to bow. 'You do me too much honour. My poor words . . .' In fact, though, he is quite pleased with those lines. 'It is a picture of the ideal. Still—there's no reason why love and policy may not live together.'

'You don't sound very convincing. Excitement and steadiness together. A great deal to ask of life. Oh, I mean to ask it. Likewise my intention of doing everything, or being everything.'

'A man would have to be nothing, for that,' Will says, and thinks: It sounds extremely desirable.

The earl pours wine and hands him a cup. Great significance in these things when a noble does them: the old winking tutor stirs, noting the favour. 'Come down to my place at Titchfield. Aye, too grand of me, I know, disposing of your time. Forgive it, say yes. I've got to go, estate matters, and I want more of your company.'

After a moment's space, Will goes back into character. 'I'm yours to command, my lord.'

Drinking, the earl is seized with one of his sudden thoughts. 'Mind, if that were really so, a man could be invincible.' He gestures at the globe. 'But we live in the gap between the show and the truth.' He laughs. 'They say I'm over-susceptible, Master Shakespeare. We shall start a great tale.'

Ah, will they? Will travels down to Titchfield Abbey with the household servants, which is perhaps revealing. There is a cook among them, fussing over a new-bought *batterie de cuisine*, looking down on Will with his drab books and papers. On the way he thinks: New year, surely the playhouses open again, I can be myself at last. But isn't this? Well, part of him. Alarming to discover how many parts there are; and the challenge, keeping them separate. No, he doesn't think this is the wrong course: turning himself into the poet of formal modes, writing for the refined tastes of Southamptons. (What Greene wanted, really. Greene now dead and pauper-buried.) Like the theatre, a matter of uncertainty, favour, suspense. Actually he loves it, but wonders if he loves it more because his father hated it and wanted to tear him from its embrace.

But if Anne should say no to it? Call him back from these wanderings in search of a role to say, 'You have one here,' the lines learned by heart long ago, by heart . . .

The life of a country estate is new to him. Tenants and stewards, orchards. A loyal welcoming dance of maids and children. The long gallery, so admirably designed for those in-between times of the day, like walking the deck of a ship, he imagines. He is not untouched by it all, its rite and fittingness. The mother arriving with the state of a prince, outriders, dogs and horns, the wallowing coach, the little figure large with clothes gliding into the hall where Will waits with the musicians and the man whose exact place he does not understand, who knows the earl and cries from time to time, 'A boon, my lord, a boon,' and always it is 'Presently, presently.'

He expects to be forgot likewise, especially with the mother's coming, the colloquies of family state. Will roams the grounds and, very soon, the library. In one hand Italian, in the other Spenser, morbidly beautiful (and touched by his hands: great Spenser he has been here). Oh, you could do this for ever, and consent to be forgot—or, perhaps, await the greater elevation that may come, especially when the earl reaches his majority. A secretaryship, perhaps, trusted servant in charge of his papers, correspondence, library, acquisitions, with time to write also, each new production inscribed with greater affection. Tempting indeed, and what Kyd is after surely when he haunts Marlowe with his monotone my-lord this and my-lord that. And Will? Fitting in has never been his difficulty. And yet still he can't see it. If this is his way and road, then he feels he has made the wrong beginning, in the shout of the theatre. Of course that may be so. All his beginnings are askew, after all.

The earl sends for him one morning early, before hunting. Will finds him half or a quarter dressed, the rich hair down ungathered. White breast, long rider's thighs. 'Will, hold this looking-glass, will you? Hold it just so, I want to see myself in true perspective . . .' This is where you know he is a great noble and you are a scribbling player. Do it, though; because they are friends also, as far as they can be. Tilt and upward flash of the heavy mirror in his hands. 'No,' sighs the earl, after a long look. 'The trouble with me is, my feet are a little too big.'

A merry, dark, challenging look thrown at Will in the mirror, where they live together, as they cannot in the world outside it. No, my lord, not me, thinks Will, lowering his eyes. I have a strange relation to the attainable.

*   *   *

'You know what you should be doing, don't you?' Bartholomew said, swiping sweat from his forehead; the drops spangled in the sun.

'No, but you're going to tell me,' Anne said.

They were walking the field path to Shottery. Whenever Bartholomew was in Stratford, which was more often lately, he came to Henley Street. Dealings with Father John, she suspected. Whom her brother still thought a papist—but such things never stood in the way of money. The children were walking with them, or at least Susannah was. Hamnet was racing Judith, cheeks bursting, as if it were the aim of his life to beat her to the riven oak.

'You should bring them over to the farm more often. It sets them up. Poor air in the town.'

'Very well. Is that the thing I should be doing?'

Bartholomew shook his head at her, his old habitual look: Oh, Anne. 'So, he's being entertained, or he's serving perhaps, at a noble estate. How long?'

'I don't know. He's a guest—but there are many of those, he says in his letter. It's a great household.'

'Think you he'll get a position from it? Money? Plainly he's expecting some advantage.'

'Something of that, yes. While the theatres are closed, he must turn his pen to other things.' So much she had gleaned from his letter. Not revealing, Will's letters, even now that she was beginning to read them without help. The effort of being himself seemed to overcome him.

'So is that the purposed design? He'll go back to the theatres when they reopen? Or what—be a poet outside the stage, print and sell?'

'I don't know.' Whatever it be, she thought, it

will be beyond me.

'What you need,' Bartholomew said, 'is a house of your own.'

Loyalty flared. 'And so Will is working and saving for it.'

'Sooner rather than later. I'm almost tempted to say anything will serve. Great God, Anne, look at what he's doing to you. Yon father-in-law.'

'I thought you and he got along.'

'We do, on the right ground, but I couldn't live with him above a sennight. And that's saying a good deal, when I lived with you for so long.'

She's happy with him like this, or at least she knows where she stands: the brutal frank brother. 'Father John—Master Shakespeare has done nothing but make me feel welcome, considered, cherished, since we married.'

'And that seems to you right and fit? Come, the man's an eternal politician.' As usual when drunk, Bartholomew was more perceptive. 'Doesn't attend the council any more, but he plays with power at home, with those he loves, wherever he can. I don't know what long grey war has gone on betwixt him and Will, but assuredly you are his best weapon.'

She knew that. There was a peculiar horror in Bartholomew knowing it.

'And those children too. Look at what he's doing to them.'

She turned on him. 'Don't dare. My children suffer nothing. I am—'

'You are a loving, kind mother and a very lioness to them, I know. But mark, you said, "my children". Look, they see more of their grandfather than their father, and grandfather thinks they're angels descended, which no children are, nor no children should think they are. You stop seeing it, perhaps, because it's before your eyes every day. But you have my meaning, don't you?'

'Yes,' she said, and the word was as full as an egg with meat.

'Well, then, when Will comes back, speak out. It's up to you. After all you caught him in the first place, didn't you? You wanted him. You got him. And in truth it was well done, for there are few Stratford men so thriving. You set up your life well, Anne, so why stop? Now he has success, and London is the heart of his success—'

'Exactly, and he has to be there, so all of this—'

'Exactly, he has to be there, so why not you?'

Anne stopped dead. Ahead her children were leaping in light.

'Oh, I dare say it seems a great undertaking. But Parliament-men take their families up, lawyers when the courts are sitting. That's only to speak of temporary lodging. If he is to be a London man, then why not family there too? But this, I suppose, rubs on the whole question.' Blind with sunlight, Anne remembered when, as children, he put her nose up to a cheese. *Go on, smell.* Making her face things. 'I gather that old John Shakespeare still sees what Will's doing as a temporary errantry. He'll be back, he'll give it over. But no, say I. And I'm not his father, nor does he tumble me in bed, so I think I see it all pretty clear. Leave Goodman John's notions out of the reckoning, Anne. The family is yours.'

'Very well,' she said, throat dry, almost croaking. 'But I do not want Will to do anything unless it is a thing he wants to do.' Like us, our love and marriage, everything: none of it was forced, it was all chosen; or else where is heaven? It's a rackety platform halfway up a painted sky.

Bartholomew chuckled. 'You're very sure that people *know* what it is they want to do.'

'Yes, because you always taught me it.'

'Me, how?'

'Well.' She shrugged. 'You've always known yourself.'

'God. Never mind me. We're not speaking of me. You, Anne, and yours, think of them, work for them. Me—I've got nothing to lose.' And he walked on with the dog-grin of the boozer, fathomlessly unhappy, burying his reasons in caves you could never reach.

*   *   *

When the burly young man accosts him on the threshold of Field's shop, Will's first thought is that this is a debt-collector of some kind; that he is going to march him off to gaol. He is not aware of any debts, but this does seem to happen to everyone in his profession, so he is not wholly surprised.

And even when the young man says, thrusting a big square hand into his, 'Master Shakespeare, I have so long wanted to meet you that there's no further help for it. I admire your work so, I must risk displeasing you in telling you it like this,' even then, Will feels he has been somehow taken into custody.

'Sir, there is no displeasure, you are very good.' Will sees that the young man has his *Venus and Adonis*, unbound, under his arm.

Emboldened—though he doesn't look as if he needs much emboldening—the young man goes

307

on: 'I swear to you before God that you have it in you to be the greatest poet of our time. This, sir, without purpose. I know the world. You suppose such praise seeks a reward. I speak purely as a scholar, a lover of the word; I speak as one who learned at the feet of William Camden and can still count him as a friend. I speak as one who knows the originals, the *Metamorphoses* and *Amores* and the *Georgics*, that have gone into this.' He pats the book. 'And I have read nothing in English to compare to it. Oh, to be sure, it has a hundred faults, and not a few absurdities.' This with a broad smile, as if it were the most complimentary thing said yet.

'So few as a hundred?'

'I've seen your plays. Then came this, and I marked the printer, and asked about, and they said you could often be found here. Now, you'll meet a deal of foolish critics who don't know what they're talking about, so it must be to your good to meet one with knowledge to add to taste.' Jacqueline Field passes through the shop, with a troubled glance as if afraid these two are about to square up to each other. The young man dips her a bow, then seems to come for the first time to self-consciousness. 'Master Shakespeare, all I ask is that you don't judge me'—a proud gesture at his plain dress—'by how I appear.'

Will smiles. 'Certainly: and don't you either.'

And after that there is nothing to do but either say thanks, goodbye; or propose adjourning somewhere for a drink. Doing the latter, Will makes the acquaintance of Ben Jonson.

He chooses the Mermaid, thinking he might fit in some business, for the Burbages and Henslowe are often there. Then he wonders if the place might be above Jonson's touch; and he wonders whether secretly he wants it to be, whether he wants to show off his eminence to a young acolyte . . . But doesn't this man have the air of a real Londoner, more at ease, more unimpressible than he can ever be? Already Ben Jonson is someone who makes Will ask questions of himself. Odd that he doesn't run a mile from him.

'So, tell: how did you do it?' It is soon apparent that Ben Jonson is not averse to talking about himself: by the second mug of ale he has given Will his good ancestry, Westminster School, William Camden, soldiering in the Low Countries, and what he modestly mentions is only a touch of his wide learning. But he is even more eager to pluck it out of Will: everything—his life, his mind, his theatre. Will is well schooled in not giving of himself, so doesn't fear. Besides, with this man he doesn't mind it so much. His curiosity is a refreshing blast, like the hand-pump which it looks as if he washes his rough curly head under.

'How did I do what?'

'All of it. Plain Warwickshire man, you tell me. Yet you've turned out plays that tickle the general, and you've written to standards of the most exacting taste likewise. All this and being a player. Does the player part help? They say Marlowe disdains the theatre.'

'He appears to. I don't know where appearance ends and the real begins.'

'In Marlowe? You mean he poses?'

'In anybody. As for playing—it's a craft. Play-making is a craft likewise. You learn it in the doing, what hangs together, what falls apart.'

Jonson looks sceptical, even a little suspicious, as if at an unworthy joke.

'As for the rest . . . Well, there you are with my book in your hands. You've been candid enough to tell me you are engaged in a trade that you don't care for—'

'Oh, you needn't be courtly gentle with me. My labour is loathsome, aye, but I get a little money by it, and that money I lay out on the richest food of all, the food of the mind.'

Will nods. 'Then you've answered your own question. Love will always do it. By love I mean choosing. I chose this, and everything that goes with it . . .' He feels the nascent pain in the forehead, which means, one out of three times, a long, crushing megrim. 'For what you need, you find a way. Now Richard Field luckily is my old friend, and his shop is the field, indeed, where I range and graze. If you would crop up a little French, a little Italian—'

'And this on top of a mere country grammar-school? You've done well, assuredly,' Jonson smiles, 'when what you have can with justice be called a smattering.'

'They were wrong, you know. Whoever said this arrogance was charming.' Though he knows where he stands with this man as he does not with Marlowe or even Nashe.

Jonson flushes—just a little. 'Arrogance is naught but strength of mind running ahead of itself. I assure you, Master Shakespeare, with you I am being humble, as humble as I have ever been. And in that spirit let me ask you, at what age do you think a man should marry?'

An unlikely clairvoyant. Will rubs his temples.

The headache is still making up its mind. 'You expect fine figures, a couplet? I can only answer dull. An age when he is able to support a wife.'

'So, so. But this answer is various. Feed her on bread, or clothe her in silks?'

'You—he must learn her ways first.'

Jonson considers. 'Well, that's not so hard. There are only a few types of people after all. Local variations of temper, of disposition, aye, but they're only the spots on the throstle's breast, and we still know it from a blackbird.'

'No,' says Will, jolted, 'there is a world in every feather. And a universe in the spaces between.'

'Hm. But you can't think like that, for you'd linger over the shape of every pebble and quibble over every word, and you'd end up mad. When'— Jonson asks this almost incidentally, wiping ale-froth from his lips—'when are you going to reform the drama?'

Will feels stiff and reluctant, like a strongbox lid eased open. 'A vast subject. I don't think beyond the plague ending and the theatres reopening.'

'You should.'

'I can hardly say how much I dislike being told *you should* in that way, Master Jonson.'

'Oh, but let's put that aside,' Jonson says, shrugging: you can tell that your feelings will never come in for a great deal of attention from him. 'Let's consider the essential question: why do you write for the stage, after all?'

Will says, promptly: 'Because it pays.'

They laugh. The kind of easy, parallel laugh that declares friendship. Though Will is not sure they are laughing about the same thing.

311

A late parting. God, they have ranged. A remarkable young fellow, Jonson, a brain he can use like a thumping arquebus or a lancing needle. Will only hopes—well, he doesn't know what he hopes. The headache fades as he climbs the narrow stairs of his lodging, the chandler's fat, yeasty-voiced wife calling after him, does he lack aught? Nothing. Just this. Open the door. The careful, artful space, clothes, the table devoted to paper and ink, part-scrolls, books, books. A mirror covered over. He greets the room with a lover's sigh: ah.

*   *   *

Ben would willingly have stayed talking all night. He didn't regret introducing himself, not that he ever regretted much. Shakespeare, player and play-maker and promising poet: well, it had not been a disappointment. There was a man for you—no doubleness. Remarkable humility. Having none himself, Ben knew how to admire it in others, though he still believed that, like wearing green, it did not suit everybody. As was his habit, he swallowed a last draught and heel of bread before bed, slept and sweated it out, and rose early to read.

To write a little also. He had resumed it for the first time since Master Camden had guided him through Latin verses. English now: you had to adjust yourself. Fewer rules, which perturbed him. It occurred to him as morning nosed over his page that he had not waited on his lady for a few days.

He found Agnes in, he thought, crabbed mood; but that was women, they held no sway over their own selves. Ignoring it, he told her of his purchase of *Venus and Adonis*, of approaching Shakespeare's narrow back at the door of Field's shop.

'We might read it a little together. It has already earned a reputation as a warm piece, you know, and some citizen-husbands are warning their wives against reading it, lest it—I wonder what? Excite appetites they cannot satisfy?'

She was not much inclined to laughter today. Oh, well: he did not founder into silence, for he could entertain himself with his own conversation while Madam sulked. At last she stirred and mantled, and out with it: 'Do you mean you laid out all the ready money you have on that book?'

Such an unaccountable question: all he could do was offer information. 'Books are not cheap, honey. Nor should they be.'

Agnes began marching about the room, skirts swinging, jaw set. He watched with curiosity. Women: all that energy, you could turn a spit or grind corn with it, and they used it for nothing. 'You said you would begin saving against a place for us to live,' she said at last. 'I shan't live at home, Ben, as a bride, nor with your people neither. And if you are to dispose of your money so . . .' Suddenly he found a peep-hole through the wall of incomprehension: she was reproaching him. A kind of light, giddy apprehension came over him: was she turning into a shrew, even before they were married? So he put it into words, those words: half laughing.

'Oh. Oh, you should take shame to yourself for speaking so,' she cried, stamping. Tears leaking too. Absurd, when she was as strong as a youth, this little-girl business. Time to be clear.

313

'Now,' he said, 'don't, I entreat, use me like some underfoot, downtrod husband-worm, my lady, for I won't abide it. I do, you see, as I please.'

She looked at him through her tears, and he noted the effectiveness of that—as, no doubt, she had. 'And not ever what would please me? What do you mean? Is this the way of it, Benjamin, for our marriage? What do you mean?'

'A fart for thee.' His liberated tongue was quick. 'Truly, sweetling, if art a shrew o' this kind, then I want thee no more. A fart for thee in parting, and a shitten pot on our marriage, the no-marriage, the no-marriage from which sweet heaven has preserved me.'

And he was off, with feelings like cool breezes of relief. If that was the way, then that was the way: Ben liked nothing better than an absence of alternatives.

And it was odd how when a heavy drunk burbling man got in his way at the corner of Thames Street, Ben knocked him down and yelled foulness, yelled as if he knew him and had been mortally offended by him and wanted to grind his blubbering face into the fishheads. Where had that come from? Well, never mind. Not everything had to have a reason, damn it. His mother was curiously irritating when he got home as well, tiptoeing round him as if he were his stepfather.

*   *   *

Violence. This charge in the air. It begins perhaps with the plague as the finishing touch; winter hasn't killed it and now with the muggy spring it's coming back in force. Add the new corpses, the new fear

314

to the toppling heap of distresses, the prices and shortages, soldiers returning from the dragging fighting that the Armada victory was supposed to finish, everything edgy and not right and—look. The strangers among us.

They've been coming for years, fleeing religious persecution, usually, Protestants from France and the Low Countries (ah, but are they always, how can you tell?), bringing their trades, thriving. How much they stand out varies. Often you don't notice them. But at times like this they are conspicuous, and damn it if there don't seem more of them, and thriving altogether too much. That is, where they don't thrive at all, where they pile ten into a room and because they don't mind living in filth they push up the rents for those who do. Too rich, too poor. So many of them. So few of them, and yet look how influential. It begins with changing minds. Now those Frenchies on the corner who you've always said are not so bad, you begin to wonder . . . It begins with glances at odd items of costume, broad breeches, deep hood—mind, if they don't wear odd costume it's even more troubling, for then they're trying to pass as English. And it continues with prentices gathering together on half-holidays, chanting dirty rhymes, making little resolutions. Libels. Printed sheets passed from hand to hand or, more daringly—for the authorities are on the watch against all these demonstrations—pasted prominently up. Printed words come to the aid of this swelling inchoate thing, giving it rule and shape. Rhythm. It continues with here and there a little manifestation. The dead animal left on the Huguenot family's doorstep, the Flemish weaver finding his window smashed. Prentices stamping

315

and clapping and linking arms to sweep down the street in the areas where they live, like Southwark, East Smithfield, St Martin-le-grand. Which is where it begins for Will.

He has been stalking books in St Paul's Churchyard, though a poor day's hunt, and is thinking besides of a new narrative poem now that *Venus* is out and the Earl of Southampton has accepted his dedication. He has sent Will also a gracious note and a promise, this is not all, come to Southampton House next quarter, so things in the offing but a feeling of not yet, and now *Venus* is seen through the press I should go home surely, for a space at least, but not yet. What's keeping me in London when pullulating plague places its heavy lock on the playhouse doors and lays its bar across my future? God knows where I should be.

Out of sorts also from supping last night with Richard and Jacqueline Field. Of course he must think of her by that name and not, which she hasn't been for ages, Madame Vautrollier. Yet so she is still in your memories and those irresponsible dreams you would pluck out if they were splinters in the flesh. But they occur as they please: the mind is not our own. The soul is borrowed of God, they say, but what then of the mind, when it moves in ways we don't control, who does that belong to, when it turns loose in dreams or drink, like the fairies turning the milk and plaiting manes? Madame Vautrollier, no, Jacqueline, has a way of leaving a great deal of space around him at table, after supper when they have the lute, or he reads aloud, making a physical detour as if he is a great fat man, a man obtruding into her life-space. He turns down another alley off St Martin-le-grand, frowns at the dense crowd. What Jacqueline seems to be saying: *noli me tangere*, touch me not, for Caesar's I am. But not of herself: of him. Is that me? Not to be touched?

It dawns on him that the crowd is not a fortuitous one but a gathering. Prentices again. Kicking a bladder, shoving and shouting. The young in a mass. Instinctively he hates it, though he plays on it, of course, when he acts and when he writes, get them all in a net, thinking and feeling as one. Terribly, wolfishly handsome, the young: their profuse hair, strong teeth, beautiful shallow eyes. Some men with them, though, old enough to know better. They have some broadsheets, he sees, and they are pressing them on people—one on him. Crudely copied, smeared, stale stuff about the foreigners among us: he barely glances, throws it down. But finds he is being assessed for that.

It begins like most of these things, in messy confusion. The prentices jostle and trip an old man—was it intended, an accident? Hard to tell, but they give him a good look over as he struggles up unaided among them, put their faces close to his (face grows to face). 'You ought to leave an honest Englishman be,' he cries, lusty-voiced and accusing. 'I'm one of the last hereabouts, it's naught but those fuckers in every house. I've watched them come and crowd us out one by one.' They like that. Victim to victor. Will was all ready to go to the old man's aid. He turns. 'And there's one for you.'

A woman, stepping out of a porched doorway, looking up at the overcast sky, putting hands to her hood, shaking out her skirts, doing all the little things we're allowed, that drive the prentices to fury. She does look somehow foreign, meaning she

317

draws a second glance.

Will moves with them. But not *with* them, never with any group; he feels uneasy if his stride happens to fall into step with another's, like with Southampton one day after hawking, when they went on a walk about the estate . . . They make a ring around her, leaving a space, roughly the space of another body. *Noli me tangere*. And she does what Will can see and sense is the very worst thing at this moment: she hardly notices them.

'Hoy!' One young brute edges into the space, seeming half afraid of himself. 'Madam French, are you?'

Occupied with fitting her gloves neatly to her fingers, she frowns up, shakes her head, wants to go past them. Youngish, rather than young, dark, slight. Will struggles through them, with a flash of memory: his hands burning. Afraid for her because again she is doing the worst thing, just being dismissive of them, of their surge and bristle. They start to chant—unison voices, the surrender of the human: 'Madam French, Madam French . . .'

'What? Yes, I came from France, what then?'

No accent at all that he can hear, unless a certain crispness of utterance, like Jacqueline. Now she is really looking at them and, dear God, they hate that too, for instead of glancing over a nuisance like a puddle in the street her turning eyes take them in, contemptuously. 'Yes, *messieurs*?'

Will is already pushing through, hand on sword-hilt. Brave of her, or mad. Or furious: he reads it in her look, *I thought men not rats . . .* They're not going to let her go. When she makes a brisk, exasperated stalk forward they don't touch her—they just rearrange their insensate selves, a

318

shuffling, staring dance, blocking her way.

As he does it—as he thrusts through them, drawing his sword—he is aware that this has a flavour of the stage about it, except on stage there would be parley or fencing, swift to a resolution; also he realises he is a little afraid and hopes, with a ridiculous strength of apprehension, that the Frenchwoman does not perceive it.

'Threaten a woman?' he cries, with a voice he knows how to pitch so that it carries over heads. 'Oh, brave crew, threatening a lone woman going about her business. Get home to your masters, and thank your stars if you're not brought before the magistrates, for they'll know you, lads, they'll assuredly know you . . .'

A mild disgust at himself, as he takes his ground, for this calculated rhetorical mixture: oh, not wholly brave, Will. Then, as he sees the prentices back slowly but steadily away, grumbling and sighing, he is struck with another realisation. He is older than them, near thirty, and looks it: looks, no doubt, the picture of drear, dispiriting, authoritative age. More cold water than hero.

Still, he does believe in what he has done, the essence behind it; and that's rare enough. The prentices straggle away, begin kicking the bladder again. He sheathes, turns and offers the Frenchwoman his left arm, sword-arm still free.

'May I go with you?'

She looks at his arm: briefly, all over him. She has a heart-shaped face and rather sallow skin and appears as gentle and neat as a cat. Just for a moment you can imagine the mouse thinking so. 'Where?'

'Wherever you were going. They'—he nods at

319

the lumpish figures funnelling themselves into the next alley—'will be about for a time yet.'

'I was going marketing, I thought.' The black crown of her head is just above his mouth. 'Not with any great need, I confess. But I had better go, when you have done such a great thing for me—had I not? But what do you say, sir? Whither should I go?'

Sweat shines on her long upper lip. She has an indoor smell, like burning pastilles and beeswax and sun on boards. A lump of mud is shied, half-heartedly, not reaching them.

'Well. This way, whatever you choose.'

'I choose this way. And now my thanks, for which you have waited long enough.' She studies his face. Will has an intense consciousness of what she sees there: fingers tracing the map of him. 'You're not French? Hollander? So. Disinterested goodness, then.' She sets her mouth as if taking medicine. 'I must try to believe in it.'

'Most Englishmen would do the same,' he says.

'Except those forty Englishmen. Shall I tell you what I wanted to say when you came along? "At last, a man with a cock." Well, it was in my mind. I would have had to have had a great deal of courage. Yes, hear me manage your terrible English tenses, though French-born.'

'Like a native. When did you come to England?'

'Oh, as a child.' She pronounces the word with distaste, as of some dishonourable past. 'You're doing that, are you? Working up an interest in me? Well, I can go along with it, if you like. My name, Isabelle Berger. Protestant French. Lodging at the sign of the Compasses, Hay Passage. Twenty-six years old. Widow. Will that do?'

Almost hostile. But he senses something that he recognises very well: dislike of being beholden.

'Madame Berger. Your servant.' Bland unction is one of his best selves, a cloak for all weathers. 'William Shakespeare, of this city.'

'Shakespeare.' She tries it over. '*Chaque-espère*. Every-hope. It nearly works. This way, if you please.'

Aldersgate. No gangs of prentices here: some shops and stalls, presumably her destination. The moment to make a leg and go, he supposes, and doesn't know why he doesn't. It was only her situation that aroused a feeling in him: nothing else, nothing.

But she stops at the entrance to a courtyard with an ornate gateway, shadowy tall house, porter hovering.

'Here. I have work to do here. I'm a seamstress, sir—though don't think you can ask me to mend your shirts. The lady of this house pays me well and kisses me when I go. What say you to that?'

He can't remember anyone being so awkward on so short an acquaintance. He bows. 'I'm happy for you.'

'I don't see why, it can't contribute to your happiness. You wonder why I lied. About where I was going.' He is about to say he is not wholly fascinated by everything about her, but she forestalls him by touching his arm and smiling sweetly, as if they are having a charming chat. 'Well, after all, what is life without lying and pretending? You should know that. I remember you now. A player, I've seen you act. Not as good as Alleyn.'

'Yes, I thought of using those words as my epitaph.' He bows again. But she detains him with

321

her grip on his arm: hurts, a little.

'I'll show you what I mean by pretending,' she says. 'Stay here, don't come near.'

A little past the gateway, in a swept stable-entrance, she wraps her hood and cloak about her and drops herself down. Lies there, motionless, face turned away. He finds his heart striking hard even though he has been warned. He waits. One man, stout and sober, glances and carries on by. And Will understands that: don't get involved, preserve thoughts and self. A lot of him, more than he cares to think, walks on with that man. The next is a plain young woman, servant perhaps or goodwife, hard to tell. She sees, draws closer. 'Mistress? Mistress, are you sick?' Not very loud, though, nor the touch on the Frenchwoman's shoulder very heavy. She glances round: Will keeps himself out of sight. The Frenchwoman's left hand (Isabelle, her name is Isabelle Berger, but this is nothing to him, like Jacqueline Vautrollier, an exotic name that stimulates his love of words, that's all) is outstretched, and two rings wink against the olive skin.

The young woman goes for them. So hurriedly that it's as if she wants to catch herself unawares as much as her victim. Grab, tug, do it quick, and then it won't have happened: Will is there with her too, alas. When the Frenchwoman leaps up, pouncing at her, she screams and runs. She pounds past Will, flashing her plain red face up at him, and he sees she is going to cry.

The Frenchwoman is brushing down her skirts and laughing quietly to herself. At least, he presumes it is to herself.

'I think,' he says, approaching her all glowing

322

like that, white of smile, harsh, perhaps mad, 'you hardly need protection.'

'No,' she says, with satisfaction, and curtsies him goodbye. 'But I think you do.'

*   *   *

'Isabelle Berger, to be sure, I know her,' says Jacqueline Field, untenderly wiping her son's bubbling nose. 'Her husband was a silk-weaver, from Lyon. Left her pretty well, but she does fancy-work for ladies besides. She is a good creature, an excellent creature.' But Jacqueline Field says that about almost everybody. Possibly even about him.

*   *   *

Just the once, then: so Will promises or threatens himself, as he picks a muddy way along St Martin-le-grand in search of Hay Passage and the sign of the Compasses. Rain is falling, the only sort of rain this plague season offers: fat, humid, seemingly dirty before it hits the ground.

Here it is, the doorway with the shell-hood porch. He is pointed to Madame Berger's staircase by a prentice—a seemly, gentle-mannered youth, impossible to imagine him rampaging through the streets and accosting foreigners. Though perhaps they are all like that, taken singly.

At her door he holds his fist-bunched hand suspended as notes of music spike the air. The virginal: as if a dandelion-clock of sound has been blown.

He listens, not recognising the piece, yet

feeling he has heard its acid melancholy before. On this threshold, something unreal. The narrow stair-turning with its warped casement looking out on rain-wet leads, that's real enough, and so is he standing here with uplifted hand and outrageous heart, but not their existence together. It is as if someone is dreaming him here, and he might vanish like wind-caught leaves when the dreamer stirs.

Suddenly the music is silent and the door swings open.

'Master Shakespeare,' Isabelle says, without surprise.

'Madame Berger. I came to assure myself all was well with you, after the trouble the other day . . .' This is what he told himself to say: the commonplace things. But in front of Isabelle he acts this part very badly—so her look seems to say.

'Well, come and look.' She walks ahead of him, into a room curiously close and overheated, though he sees no fire. A table with a green brocade cloth: on it sewing, a silver goblet. The virginal is of the spinet kind, inlaid with tortoiseshell: the lid bears the motto *Nil magnum nisi bonum*. Nothing is great unless good. A bird hops back and forth in a hanging cage, back and forth, with pendulum regularity. 'What do you think? Does all seem well, or ill?'

Through another door he glimpses hanging clothes, bed-curtains. That bird, he thinks, would send him mad. He shouldn't have come, but he knew that. 'Your pardon. I intrude.' Already bowing out. 'I only thought—those prentice gangs are still about—'

'I know, they were making a great noise in

Round Court last night. I stayed indoors, I couldn't rely on a gallant player to come to my rescue.' She laughs, picks up the goblet and drinks from it. Her voice has a peculiar monotone quality, as if one should play on only two keys of the virginal. 'Let them enjoy it while they can. They're all going to die, like you and me; and will the memory of splitting someone's head make up for it, when they lie and blink at the last light fading on their eyes? Ah, at least I did for that shitten Frenchie, now hey-ho for hell.'

'Some of them, yes, I fear that's how it will be.'

'Fie, misanthrope. Or are you just indulging my mood? I have wine here, but I would prefer to have it all for myself.'

'I would prefer that too. Madame Berger, it turns out we have a common acquaintance—Mistress Field, who used to be Madame Vautrollier.'

'Dear Jacqueline, she's a wonder, isn't she?' She doesn't say what kind of wonder. She goes over to the cage: the bird, blissfully for Will, freezes into stillness as she looks in. 'So, you will have been asking about me. Furnishing yourself with knowledge.'

'No. Why should you think that?' He should never have come, the woman is intolerable, and so he may as well deal in her own hostility before he goes.

'I don't know.' Her eyes mist: he wonders if she is drunk—now, habitually. Yet her movements are so contained. 'Perhaps because I'm not accustomed to people being kind to me.'

'It's a bitter shame that you cannot walk the streets without—'

'Oh, I don't mean that. Naught to do with being

325

a foreigner. Or an alien, as they say, which is a better word, I think, don't you? You have to make a grimace to say it. Well.' She sits down at the table abruptly, stretches out her feet, and gives a little pleasurable yawn, like a bite from a cake. 'We don't have to keep playing, do we? I dare say we both have things to do.' The bird resumes its clockwork hops as absently, with faint weariness, she begins unlacing her bodice. 'Naturally you want the reward of your gallantry.'

'You have the art of the insult,' he says, as temperately as he can, and gets out of there, thanking God, as he fumbles and stumbles down the stairs, or the lucky stars he doesn't deserve, that this was revealed to him so immediately; that something has ended and not begun.

*　　　*　　　*

But in those jammed hot streets what began with muttering and gathering is suddenly transformed. Suddenly hate speaks in the most exciting language of all: the language of the theatre.

It appears overnight, like a late frost or a crop of fungus. Pasted to the wall of the Dutch church in Broad-street, where the foreigners go to worship. Another of those inflammatory libels— but what an example. It's like a great speech from a play. In thirty lines of heroic measure it exhorts the suffering true-born Englishmen—read apprentices—of London to rise up against the alien presences who are draining their lifeblood. Rise up and strike, burn, kill. Allusions to Marlowe's work sow its fierce length; and it is signed TAMBURLAINE.

'Not a bad piece of work,' says Nashe judiciously.

326

'Lacks something in finish, no doubt, but then it was written to order, as 'twere, and there one always finds faults.'

'But it can't have been Marlowe,' says Will. Cold sweats have been sweeping over him ever since he heard. He keeps imagining not *Tamburlaine* at the foot of it but his own name.

'Oh to be sure. Still, it does a good job of evoking him, I think, which I dare say it's meant to do.'

'Why?'

'Who knows, when it comes to that? I don't understand half his dealings with the great. They say he's intimate with Raleigh now, and Raleigh is at odds with my lord Essex. Interpose in a Cornish-wrestle of giants, and you're like to get crushed even as you squeak to them for peace. Then there's this school-of-night name attaching to Raleigh's circle—'

Will can't help his bleak laughter. 'What do they do? Hold black masses?'

'Philosophy, I think. Than which there is nothing more dangerous, you will allow. God and not-God.'

'Where is Marlowe, do you know?'

'Staying with the Walsinghams is what I hear. I don't enter his confidence much lately.'

'He'll be safe then, surely, from any association with this.'

'You would think so. Yet somehow I can't put the word *safe* together with Kit. Like mingling Greek and Latin.'

The libel is torn down, but not before its phrases have established themselves on the lips of the angry delighted—the manipulated? Who knows, and who knows who is manipulating them? The streets seethe anew. Calling at Blackfriars, Will finds new

327

bars on the door. A friend of Jacqueline's was set upon in the dark, beaten—but it might have been normal London malice, not something special. Will sees the lustre of brown eyes in powdery shadow, the little covered yawn of scorn. Tastes something, like some forgotten treat of childhood, piercingly sweet.

The Privy Council stirs. Doubtless it would close the theatres if plague hadn't done so. The Dutch Church Libel, as it is soon called, manhandled the names of great lords in its muscular blank verse, suggesting in fact that they are in the foreigners' pockets or vice versa; only the Queen is innocent, really. A blow must fall, somewhere: the lifted arm of the state is too heavy.

'Kyd? Why arrest Kyd?'

'Ah, perhaps that's the idea. So we ask ourselves, why him, why not me, who next?' Nashe is enjoying himself.

Sedition: Kyd. Was he capable of that? Whenever Will saw him, which was seldom—he seemed to have left the theatre—he had the same pained detachment, as if trying to refine himself away: as if he wanted to change form altogether, as dragonflies did, leaving the nymph carapace, flying jewelled. Perhaps that was what being close to Marlowe did for you.

'Of course, everyone connected to the theatre must be careful,' says Richard Field. 'But your patron sits well at court, they say, and has my lord Burghley's interest, so that's a useful connection. And then as to seditious views . . .'

'Is there anyone less likely than me?' says Will, half laughing. But what's in the other half? A long corridor of darkness. A good place to hide,

328

perhaps. Safe, safe. He avoids St Martin-le-grand. He imagines himself in Stratford and feels the tick of his children's eyelashes against his cheek.

Burbage brings Will the news.

'Kyd's out. They let him go on Wednesday, I think. Henslowe saw him. Well, Kyd went to him to beg a loan, to pay his doctor's fees. Henslowe actually gave him the money, can you believe that? But apparently he looked so fearful it even shook old Brass-sides.' Burbage lowers his voice. 'He'd been before Star Chamber. Apparently they racked him. Racked him after he had talked, which seems a peculiar refinement of torture. Dear God. Let them take their eyes off the theatre, please, or just go back to calling us whoresbirds and vagabonds. Mind, you've half left us anyhow, haven't you? Sir Proper Poet. No, I jest, I understand. Needs must.'

Needs must, you do what you have to do. You survive. Do you survive at any cost? Questions in the tainted spring, warm as a haybox, as airless. Nashe finds out where Kyd is lodging. They go to see him, to see if—well, what? If he has said something about them, perhaps? And Will's quiet inner voice, Keep away, don't touch. Don't touch Will, keep him clean. *Noli me tangere.* Jacqueline makes way; Isabelle looks him up and down.

Kyd keeps his room dark. Still, you can see what's been done to him. The best torture is supposed to leave no marks, but you can't alter that twisted mouth: those eyes.

'They searched my papers. They found things, writings. Things that weren't mine. They were interleaved.' He makes it sound like an obscenity, a perversion. 'Dangerous sentiments. Atheistical sentiments. Well, in the name of dear Heaven,'

329

a moment's trembling appeal, 'you know me.' An admission in Kyd's lowered face that he has preferred not to be known. 'It was him. It was all Marlowe's writing. As I told them, we used to share chambers, and there was but one writing-desk, and so our papers were mixed up. He used to talk that kind of thing, you know, and I tried to stop him— though after a while it was best not to, because it would only make him go further. Merely for shock, I thought. The only true profane love was buggery and Our Lord Jesus Christ knew it and knew his disciple John in that way . . .' Kyd utters a hoarse laugh of outrage, at hearing himself say it, perhaps. 'Such things he would say, there were more of them, and so I told them. You see, don't you? I had to tell them. Any seditious writings, any trouble in the state, I fear you'll find Kit Marlowe behind them. It grieves me to say it but I'm thankful too. Thankful I'm free from his unholy spell, aye, I thank the God in whom I verily believe and who has preserved me—'

'But you don't believe Marlowe wrote the Dutch Church Libel,' says Will.

'Why should I not?' Kyd says, wiping and wiping his brow.

'Because—because it's not well writ enough. It's done by someone who wants to make you think broadly of Marlowe. As art—'

'It isn't a matter of art,' Kyd says helplessly.

'No. No, I know.' Oh, but it is. Everything is. Kyd weeps. Nashe sends out for a bottle. Will thinks of high green meadows, the fetching intricacy of woods.

*   *   *

330

They arrest Marlowe next, once they can find him. He is indeed staying with his patron Walsingham, the late tremendous Sir Francis's cousin. Not a bad connection, when you have to go before the Privy Council. Kit will land on his feet, Nashe says. Will digs away at his new poem, *Lucrece*. Sir Proper Poet. Whether it's the dark subject of his work, or the heat, he sleeps badly, interrupted by dreams that can't quite be called nightmares—full of horrible images, but a glass between him and them: can't touch.

*   *   *

At the Mermaid Will talks to Ben Jonson about it: seeking, perhaps, a sort of detachment. Compulsive follower of the theatre though he is, still he is a bricklayer, belonging to the other world, a daylight world. But if Will is hoping for comfort, he doesn't get it.

'Difficult for Kyd. Also for Marlowe. Difficult all round,' Jonson says briskly. 'So, the question is, what would you do in such a situation?'

Will takes a long drink: to think. 'I would never put myself in that situation in the first place.'

Jonson laughs and drinks in turn. 'You said that as if you meant it.'

'Did I? That's a habit I must rid myself of.'

Of course, as Jonson's bright, sceptical look says, it was no answer at all.

*   *   *

Marlowe: he bursts upon Will in Bishopsgate, as

suddenly as if he has come up from a trapdoor. Clamps a hand on his neck.

'What, Will? Don't want to be seen with me, the infamous blasphemer? Never fear, you're safe.' He steps away, grinning. 'Arm's length, Will, arm's length where you like to be.'

It's the smell that makes Will recoil. What must he have been drinking, to turn his breath like that?

'You're free? What happened?'

'Free, we're all free if we only hack the shackles from the mind. I like your *Venus*. I've been writing in that vein myself, on Hero and Leander. You must look it over and give me your opinion some time.' The thought hits Will like a low branch in the face: Yes, outdoing me, I'll wager. 'Oh, I'm freed for now, but I have to present myself daily to the Privy Council. Show Mamma thy clean hands. Such shite and cockcheese, of course, that I would write those contemptible bills. Oh, mark you, I'm all for a massacre here and there—we weed fields, why not people?—but in truth the foreigners are hated because they are cleverer than poor English Toby Trot. And name me an emotion stronger than envy, hey?'

'Jealousy.'

'Say why.'

'Jealousy has fear in it. Envy, compared, is just a kind of bunching of the muscles.'

'Oh, well. It's obvious you know whereof you speak.' Marlowe stops to peer inquisitively, smile in dazzling, alarming place, into the faces of several passers-by. 'God's blood, the dead dull nullity of this town lately. Never mind the plague, you'd need the frogs and the locusts before this set would even begin to know they were alive. Look you, as

I must make daily attendance on their lordships or worships or whoreships, I shall seize the opportunity to lay our case before them: when in pity's name are they going to allow the playhouses open again? It's a murderous intermission of the mind's life. Scarce anyone's heard my *Faustus*.'

'I have.'

'And what did you think?' For a moment Marlowe looks almost unsure, uncomfortable.

'What everyone must think. It's the most powerful thing yet written.'

'Ah, everyone *should* think it, but only you and I know it.' The detaining hand is back. 'Now, if you had a bargain with the devil, Will, what would be your wish? Long life, perhaps? Solid prosperity for you and yours, or a woman or a man of such surpassing quality you forget everything—'

'We're back here, are we? Trying to get your fingers into my head.'

'Where else?' Marlowe says, with his peculiar two-voiced laugh.

'Besides, how do you know I haven't made a devil's bargain already?'

'How do I know?' Marlowe releases him with a parting blast of that corrosive breath. 'Well, I'm still here, aren't I?'

*   *   *

Afterwards you feel something must have been forming in that fetid London air, that some inevitable result lay at the end, purposed, perhaps, like the shape of the fresh-coming play, as he turns over the pages of a stale and shapeless tale. Yet at the time it is life, middling mid-stream. The disturbances remain just that, in spite of the authorities' alarm: no full-fledged riot bursts out from the apprentice musterings, no slaughter of the aliens, blood running in the streets. Another time, possibly. Plague lingers on; the pits fill. Any remaining libels are plucked down, shredded, burned. Kyd goes to ground, plainly just wanting to keep the eyes of the courts off him, the instruments off his limbs. The theatres stay closed, and with them the bear-baiting yards, so word goes round of private baitings laid on in closes and cellars illegally: folk will always find a way to be entertained. Actors go on tour where they can. Grass sprouts in the ground of the Theatre, where Will walks with Burbage, talking of and trying to conjure up the future: this is where he is when the news comes.

'Well, the experiment of joining up the companies may after all be a prophecy,' Burbage says, listlessly gnawing an apple. He is always trying to lose flesh. 'Once the plague is over, we can't scatter ourselves so wide again. Not that there will be enough of us left for that, I fancy. We can come out of it stronger, though. A good close company of sharers, all seasoned actors, all committed to the hilt . . .'

Suddenly his brother Cuthbert is there, panting, giant belly wobbling: Burbage's terrible example. No actor, but manager, moneyer, fixer: and always the first with news. 'Did you hear? Marlowe's dead.'

Some kind of sound comes out of Will's mouth. Mostly gasp. But as for the word: is it *how* or is it *who*?

* * *

They piece it together, as much as they can. Will,

Nashe, a few others who knew Marlowe. He proves to have had, in the usual way of the dead, not that many friends.

And it seems like another of those typical Marlowe encounters, those violent eddies that follow him around. He was with a party of men at a house in Deptford. They were supplied by the dame of the house with food and drink, probably a lot of that. What men? Strangers, known to him? Known to him, presumably—but with Marlowe, who knows? A quarrel broke out. Nashe, who goes quietly down to Deptford to ask around, believes it was over the bill. Or it may have begun with that, and escalated. The trouble is, they have already buried him there, and now rumour is the only loud sound to be heard; and that is more hollow than ever, with Marlowe's reputation so dubious even before this happened. Someone saw a body taken away and thought it was a plague victim. A prostitute who knew the neighbourhood said it was a matter of buggers, and Deptford, with its dockyard and sailors, was known for buggers, and buggers often came to blows over other buggers. A dagger was drawn, somehow, and however it began it ended with the dagger piercing and so ending Christopher Marlowe's brain, and so ended other things, many other things.

*　　*　　*

The Earl of Southampton is being measured for a new suit of clothes. Will reads to him while the crouching tailors circumnavigate his body: the opening of his new poem *The Rape of Lucrece*.

'A more solemn strain, this. As befits, I dare

335

say.' Southampton extends his arms: tape measures record his symmetrical perfection. 'But you besides. Something's in you. What happened? You're not here.'

'There's no hiding anything from you, my lord.'

'Oh, come, you don't have to do that any more,' the earl says irritably. But he senses, perhaps, that Will is hiding behind it: the role, humble servant to patron. He dismisses the tailors. 'I would say someone died, if you were wearing black.'

'Someone did die.'

'My God, tell. What is it? Can you not say in what regard you knew this person? A friend, something more?'

'Friend? In a way. A rival. He was—he was the same age as me.' He sees interest wane a little in Southampton's eyes: oh, a mummy near thirty. 'And now—this is the curious thing I keep dwelling on—I shall always be older than him.'

Suddenly a twitch and flash: of course the earl knows his theatre. 'Oh, you don't mean—'

'I don't mean anything,' Will says, as respectfully as he can. 'Certainly not to be such dull company. May I read more?'

For what can he say? That more than once, struggling, aspiring, feeling the clogs of his aspiration, he has wished Marlowe dead? Because, after all, no flight of the imagination can make that his fault. It's just a thing inside. It's a thing to add to the hundred pounds that Southampton has ordered his steward to have made over to Will when this stay is over, a thing to add to the shadow of apprehension as he becomes more fabulously himself—that luck like this must be paid for.

Ben: when the burning sensation came on in his breeches, he thought about Providence.

His relationship with God was a complex one, underlined by a single simplicity: he felt that in the author of the universe he would find, for once, his intellectual superior. He was not inclined therefore to quarrel with whatever Providence pointed out to him, as long as it were bold enough. He liked complexity, as testing to the brain, but he disliked ambiguity: it was where falsehood could smuggle in. So when he resumed playgoing, along with eager audiences, in the long-awaited reopening of 94; and heard Juliet dying in beautiful ecstasy, that was him—split. Such poetry: hearing each line was like having a petal plucked from the stem of your soul; but was this right, to sink yourself into such beauty? To lose yourself, in fact? He didn't know: faced with this, he didn't know how he felt, and that was his quarrel with it. He was directed to too many feelings without being told which was the true way to go.

So, with this illness: Providence was rewarding or reproving him for the lechery, which, unthinkingly, he had lapsed into along with the plays. He did wish he had someone he might talk to about it: where to find a surgeon who could help, was the treatment as unpleasant as they said. There were friends, among the playgoers. There was Will Shakespeare with whom he could say he had a friendship born out of admiration, nurtured by a mutual love of words, belonging to the special arena where they met, the theatre edges, taverns, bookstalls. He flattered himself that Shakespeare, who was not reputed one of the debauchers of the theatre, always made an exception with him, staying late over drink and talk. Never over-indulgent, though: he had a peculiar look of costive pain when he had had enough. So far from the repute of Marlowe, whose passing Ben saluted with a short sigh. People died.

Couldn't talk to Shakespeare about this, though. Served him right, perhaps. If it were the worst sort of dose, he might end up with his nose falling off, or go to an early grave. He wondered about that: did not fancy it, in spite of his own resolution to kill himself if he could not escape bricklaying. He must have a greater appetite for life than he supposed. Life at any price? Perhaps not, but life, God, yes, life was a sweet donation, close on the pulses, streaming with the sun and sharp, like winter cold or the barber's trimming scissors laid intimately against the soft part of your neck. Sweet Jesus, let me live; and if it be the Lord's will, prevent my member turning black and my nose falling off.

He went to a doctor in Westminster, but the man talked such appalling dog-Latin that Ben gave him up. On impulse he tried instead an old woman who sold nostrums from a booth at the south end of London bridge. She got him to piss in a pail, sniffed, dipped. A disorder of the bladder, she said. She purged him, told him to live clean and sober for a fortnight. It worked. He went back to thank her, but her booth had gone, she had been moved on, arrested perhaps by Puritan city fathers. He drank to her and resolved to learn his lesson, and then— here he suspected the intervention of Providence— he saw Agnes.

It was at the theatre—and, again, miraculous or providential that he turned his eyes from

338

the stage to see her, for this was no run-of-the-mill performance. There were only two major companies left to attract the spectator of discernment: the Admiral's Men at Henslowe's Rose, with Alleyn at front, and this troupe, the Chamberlain's Men, newly constituted, Burbage in the chief roles, Will Kempe in clown parts and better, Jonson thought, than Tarlton ever was, with Will Shakespeare in secondary parts. And writing for them, writing pieces like this (*Romeo*—yes, in spite of everything, he was there again, for there had been nothing like it, and nothing like this grip and hush). This was the company to watch, with such a genius, untutored and undisciplined though he might be. *Night's candles are burnt out and jocund day stands tiptoe on the misty mountain-tops* . . . And Burbage was more natural than Alleyn, who almost sang instead of speaking his verse sometimes, and the Admiral's Men were still relying on their staple of Marlowe; and though *Faustus* and *The Jew* were still drawing there would be no more from that source. No, this was the place to be for—for what? The aspirant? Was that when it began? Years before, perhaps, the mind in long readiness, poised to leap. But first, yes, there was the heart to be dealt with: call it that.

Agnes: in one of the balconies, her old gorgon at her side. But, great heaven, changed. Thin, pale, the splendid buxomness almost gone. Green-sickness? Surely too old for that.

Ben-sickness. He found it out, bit by bit. He approached when the Nurse was on, doing one of her comic monologues; he would dispense with that if the piece were his—it spoiled the unity; a tragedy shouldn't have comedy in it. Art wasn't life, as he

339

was trying to explain to Will the other evening; art was rescue of order from the messy wreck of life . . . At first she would have nothing to do with him. Actually set her face away, refused to open her mouth. When he persisted she got up and left. The old dragon wagged a finger at him. 'You're the start of it all,' she whined. 'The way she's been. Oh, the way she's been.'

He was admitted at last to her house. The old uncle couldn't remember him, or couldn't remember forgetting him. My dear sir, let me show you my collections . . . Finally he managed to be alone with Agnes. The way she'd been: well, he was human, he couldn't help but be a little flattered in between being shocked, saddened, ashamed. When he broke with her, she had not picked herself briskly up and carried on, as he had supposed. She was wretched. She loathed herself, she thought she would never be happy again, she even took to drinking sweet wine in the mornings. And then a draper from St Mary Axe wanted to marry her and she said yes, though she didn't care for him, but she wanted to get her own back at Ben. Bastard, bastard. All this she told him in her direct, guttural way, in between crying into her apron and glaring hate at him through eyes made enmazing with soft tears on violet. He was already hers then, probably, even before she wailed, slapping out at him, that she had loved him consumedly, the draper had been nothing, worse than nothing, but at least he had not walked out on her.

'But after he had got some kisses,' she made a face at the memory of them, ha, not like mine Ben wagered to himself, 'he would fall asleep by the fire and snore, and wake up shivering and bid me

340

stir it for he was prone to chills. And I would do it, God help me, and he would say, "Prettily done, thou art a good child . . .".' She was not laughing, not quite able, not yet; and also it was serious, he could see that, and he was serious, too, at that moment. Serious with himself for making her so unhappy, and for throwing away something so valuable, someone who loved him so much. Though he thought well of himself, he had to be honest, it seemed unlikely he would inspire such love again. So he said: 'The man was a wretch. But where is he? He cannot have left you. That is reserved for fools like me.'

'No, it was me. I wanted no more to do with him because . . .' She looked her miserable loving fury: almost about to hit him.

'Stir the fire, says he? For you a man should be ready to thrust his hand in the fire, for a prize like you, idiot that I was to throw it away. Sweet Agnes, he should have been ready as I am, thus—' He did it. It didn't hurt as much as he had thought it might; at least, not just then.

'Oh, you great fool,' she cried, as he cradled his red trotter. 'Do you think that's what a woman wants?' She fetched butter, smoothed it on.

'Tell me, tell me what a woman wants,' he said, 'but no, not a woman, the woman, the only woman . . .' They had been at *Romeo and Juliet*, and the intense was in the air, perhaps. Also it was abominable for her to be thin and pale over him. The simple transactions of love could cure it, like the crone's purge, and they were not expensive. It made sense. And her kiss was as bewitching as ever, though he was a little light-headed from pain.

The old mad uncle would have let them live

there when they were married, but she wanted to be away from him and the mouldering tapestries. They began housekeeping in Westminster. Ben had found half a house to rent, not far from Hartshorn Lane. Bed was delightful, and he looked forward to having children to bring up in the right way. She started trying to change him within about a month. She didn't like his drinking, sleeping it off, and rising to study: how was she to fit into that? He shrugged: she wasn't meant to, really. She was impressed at first by the new strength of his theatrical connections, the way he could count on a reception from several of the actors, above all from Master Shakespeare, the poet of tender enchantment who had made *Romeo*—that was remarkable. Alas, ammunition too. Would the man who made *Romeo* snore so, leave his clothes about?

'You had better ask his wife, my love,' Ben said. 'She is in Warwickshire where he comes from, and she never sees him from one quarter-day to the next.' It quietened her for a while. Not for long. Sometimes if he was really tired of it he would stump over to his stepfather's house and sleep a night there. 'They're all shrews, more or less,' his stepfather said. Ben only grunted. He didn't like it coming from him, for it was an aspersion on his mother, whom he had long considered the womanly exception; but a sort of truth in it, he had to admit.

Still they had pleasant times. Walking out in their best dress to take the air and watch the archery in Finsbury Fields. Coming home one day, in content and harmony, he found the carpenter who lived in the other half of the house—a chucklehead, an idiot—had dumped cess on his doorstep. 'We don't know it's him,' said Agnes,

342

who was overly concerned with impressing the carpenter's fudge-faced wife. His stepfather's rows with his neighbours had always been ridiculous, but this was different. 'Let it be, Benjamin, we can't afford to—'

'What can't we afford to?' he roared, for this was the bottom of degradation for a proud man, to be told to *slink* in the world: he wouldn't have it, he wouldn't slink before some ignorant carpenter who couldn't write his own name . . . He wasn't sure how it went on after that. There was shouting, and he remembered the feel of the man's chin in his hand. One forgot these things, like a swift carouse after work. But he found his throat surprisingly sore after, as if he had been shouting, and a mysterious cut on his knuckles.

Agnes was quiet for a long time, making supper. When it was on the table she said informatively: 'If ever you strike me, I shall poison your food.'

He looked at the stew, wondering for a moment. Wondering about himself, chiefly. But he ate: it seemed a fair bargain. And the next day he apologised to the shrinking carpenter, and bought a new shawl for his wife. It didn't seem to matter when one considered how temporary this all felt—a thing like the weather, that affected you along the way, but didn't determine your life, not at all. His play was half done, and he had a question to ask of Will.

11

A Larum for London (1595–6)

Fires begin with hope.

'How did it happen?' Hamnet cried in sheer wonder, as they huddled together in the street. They got out when the wind seemed to be bearing the fire towards the Shakespeare house. Their neighbours did it too, piling their goods in the middle of the street. That was the part Father John hated, Anne noticed, his things in the public sight. He urged his remaining sons, Richard and Edmund, to throw cloths over the heap, hide them.

Beautifully horrible, the orange flames making their flourishing way from High Street, to Wood Street, at last to Henley Street, throwing out windows, sucking down roofbeams. Smoke darkened the sky, making misplaced evening, and the flames could be seen in her children's eyes. How they stared. And then when the pigeon flew out too late from the eaves where it was nesting, singed, falling . . . Susannah covered Judith's eyes and they moaned together, in the unity of girlhood. Hamnet could only turn his fire-primed eyes up to his mother, seeking.

How did it happen? Fires begin with hope, destruction begins with it, with a benign shutting of eyes to what may come. The blind side of hope.

It was an accident. A spark in the thatch somewhere, added to a favouring wind . . . But that would not do for Hamnet, whose mind moved on moral lines. Whose fault was it? It was no one's fault, Anne thought. There was an ordinance against thatched roofs in these streets, and people were careful with their houses, but then they added outbuildings, malt stores, sheds, and those they thatched because it was easier, and the outbuildings, after all, were different: they were not like inhabited houses. Though one or two people, she knew, in High Street and Wood Street, rented their outbuildings to strangers who came looking for work, and they shouldn't have been in the parish either, but again the blind eye, the feeling that if it was not shrieking out wrong, then it could not be wrong, or not very. Oh, Anne knew that way of thinking very well.

So, hope, that was what caused the fires. Hope that the worst would not happen. What could be more human and natural than that? But Hamnet's moral mind would not have it. Someone must be to blame. It was his grandfather who supplied the requisite: 'Someone kindled a fire where they should not have, or lit a taper and left it untended in a draught. Someone neglected their duties as a householder. Hence the result: a house lost.' Hamnet nodded solemnly.

They were lucky. The fire did not reach them. It wasn't the splashing of the futile leather buckets but a drop in the wind, a connecting wall battered down with hammers. Dust mixed with the smoke, and the terrible greedy crackling stopped. An end. The town mourned its defacement: Alderman Quiney prepared to petition London for assistance. Father John was glad to get his possessions back into the house. He gave out charity, but he took no one in who lacked a home from the fire. Not coldness, Anne thought: secrecy the precious habit. Also she suspected he still hoped to emerge from the tunnel of his decline some day, unfeared of the sun, and bask in all his old admiration as if these dusky years had never been.

When it happened again the next year—another swathe of fire, this time on the north side of town—Hamnet, three inches taller, was ready with his response: 'Someone has been careless again.' It made him sound cold, which he was not.

By the time of the second fire, however, things were different. Life was different. Anne had written her first letter. It said *Yes, we will come*.

Too short for a true letter, she knew that, but, oh, how much it took from her. All writing, even practising the alphabet, seemed to her an extraction of self. But this especially. She left it for Will to see, on the chest in their bedchamber, after their quarrel. It was a signal, writing it for him like that: a signal that she was joining his world, breathing his strange air.

And it was the only thing to do, short of a surrender she could not contemplate. The surrender of what she had believed when he had put a glove on her hand, then a ring on her finger.

The quarrel had begun perhaps with Hamnet, if you had to find a spark in the thatch. Children were dreadful for passing things on, and Hamnet had an indelible memory and he couldn't be diverted. 'Mother wants you at home,' he announced, when Will arrived for Lent. 'You need to stay, because Mother needs you. She said so.' Being the man of the family, as his grandfather was always telling him he was. He glowed with it: responsible householder. At ten he was within sight of a formidable handsomeness, while Judith his twin was all heron legs and tomboy grimaces. Anne tried to mime a modification over his head: she had said something like that in a burst of irritation one day when the children had been too much for her. 'If only your father was here,' she had snapped.

'Would that make things better?' Hamnet wanted to know.

'Certes it would. Why else be a husband and father? Does he just want the name?' It had been the time of her menses, which were getting more exhausting as she drew near forty. So, irritable, she had let fly.

Perhaps it was right that Will should hear of it; perhaps she should have said it herself. Well, the quarrel came about, or the approximation of a quarrel.

He said, with his iciest gentleness: 'Don't use the children to reproach me.'

'I don't. It was Hamnet's choice to say that. He heard me complaining one day, he took it to heart. He's like that. As you'd know if you were here.'

'I'm not here because my work isn't here. You know that.'

'Oh, yes, I know that.' So it went grimly, in stiff circular steps. But in the end they faced a proposal. A change.

He said: 'Listen. I've put down money on a good lodging in Bishopsgate.'

'What's that to me? I don't know your bishops and gates and all those London places.' This is what we do when we don't know each other any more: make weapons of odds and ends.

He persisted: 'It's in the city proper, not outside the walls like Shoreditch. The house is a good one, the position airy, fair and decent rooms and none built over privies. Worth more than I've put down, but it's someone I know.' Another notable, baffling thing—he had become this Will of dealings, who always knew someone.

'Well, I'm glad for you. London's a pestilential place, though you don't seem to mind—'

'I want you to come and live there. You and the children. There I'm— Anne, I can give you life. Here I can't, I'm . . .'

John Shakespeare's son. She filled in his silences so easily, though she didn't know if he realised it. Again, such a gulf. And not to be crossed, surely, so simply—and, besides, did she want to? She knew what her father-in-law would say: 'Don't do it, require him to settle properly, not drag you his way.'

'You don't truly want that,' she said. 'You can't.'

'Why?'

'It's a thing you've—you've just plucked out of the air because we were fighting.'

He gazed steadily. He made her feel that she was snatching, looking for excuses, rather than him. She wondered if he was right. She thought of Bartholomew, unlikely prophet.

'I want you and Susannah and Judith and Hamnet to come and live together as a family, a household, in the place where my work is.'

'Leave Stratford?'

A shade of a smile. 'People do. Richard Field. Gilbert. Me—'

'All men, making a man's way.'

'Richard is married, has two babes.'

'Married in London, to a London woman.'

'French,' he said, with an odd emphasis: as if it made any difference. 'Only let us try. Spend a season there. Wilt try one season? We can live well, Anne. I promise thee a good life.' He struggled. Will, struggling with words: it showed how desperate things had become. And then the words he chose: 'After all, what dost thou leave?'

And at that she walked off. She couldn't go away to another world as he did, but she walked away, down gutted High Street to sit and spin and talk with Judith Sadler, with purl on the hob. God-sibs, sighing over their men. Not what Anne liked, generally. Awareness still that her going off like this marked a certain something about their relation; he was not one to lock the doors against her, as many a man would do with a mutinous wife. Still, as she grumbled with Judith Sadler, I may have a husband who does not beat me but still there is this. What should I think of it—for after all I have perforce a life. 'I am a fish in this pond,' she said loudly, then laughed at herself: the purl was strong stuff.

'Beshrew me if it's not the old tale,' Judith said. 'It's always down to the woman pleasing the man.'

There were, though, weapons you were permitted to pick up, as Father John was always hinting to her. You could protest ill-usage, work the man round to a consciousness of himself as detestable, less than a man. You pitched your rights as a wife and his duties as a husband: you made, in essence, a council-chamber bye-law matter of it. Or, as Judith Sadler said with fierce set teeth, you nagged and wheedled, withheld, threatened. 'Make him rue.'

Anne could see the satisfaction in that. Especially after last time, when he had come home with his decision made: presenting to her the tightly bundled future, that was the insulting thing; like a present, when it was instead a puzzle. Undo this if you can.

'A sharer. A sharer in the Chamberlain's Men. That's what I have become.'

It helped him that she was dazzled—everyone was—by this distant patron who had handed him up. The earl of. Dear God, the earl.

'He's a very young man who is generous to poets and such poor cattle,' Will said—but that only made it more alarming, that smiling casualness. It was beyond her.

And in that beyond, Will had taken the money his patron gave him and converted it into his future.

A sharer. They talked of it a good deal, and John Shakespeare joined in, for this was a deep matter of men and money. Edmund, who considered himself part Londoner and part player, was briskest of all.

'It's the best and only notion, trust me. A player earns a fair wage. A play-maker gets more, when he writes a play and it's acted. But as a sharer, he has a stake in the company, so he stands to make money from everything it earns.'

'And to lose if it loses,' said his brother Richard, heavy and cautious. Nowadays he ran the shop for his father, and was happy with it.

'Aye, that too.' Edmund frowned in tousled impatience: he was young, what could possibly be wrong with risk? 'It's the best of all, for a player, it's putting your whole substance into it.' And to Anne, exultantly—with the exultation she should be feeling: 'He's climbing to the top of the tree.'

Yes: exactly. He's made his decision on his life. So, she ought to be paying him back for this new imposition.

But it was complicated, and she was glad of

that in a way, for she dreaded the day when it all became terribly simple. Now lately she had woken with the words in her mind, transferred from dream to murmuring lips: the words *Once I was loved*.

So what did she want? She ought to have wanted to pin him down. But what she wanted really was to be what she once was, wielder of magic, world-changer. Once I was loved, maybe. Once I was power, yes. Once I created.

So she wrote it. *Yes, we will come*. She found him poring over it, as if it were the deepest of works. He reached out for her hand. She decided, after a moment, to give it to him. She wondered if he could feel her cold, cold fear.

There was a last question: Edmund. Though Joan had once begged her not to leave, when it came to it she was resigned. 'It only means,' she sighed, 'that I had better start thinking about that husband before my bosoms point downward.' But Edmund: once he learned they were going to live in London, if only for a season, he looked like someone bleeding, bleeding at the eyes. It was Will he approached, in the end: not Anne, the sharer of small secrets, dancer to no music.

'Edmund wants to come with us,' Will said.

'I know that.' She studied him: the slightly worn complexion, the heavy eyes, the curved and speaking mouth. If she were meeting him for the first time she would probably fall in love with him, and part of her fear at the prospect of London was actual shyness of being so much with him. 'Have you said he can, then? Made another decision for me?'

'I see no reason why he shouldn't go.'

'No? Not the very reason why we are going, to be

our own household and family, you and me and the children?'

The trouble was, she could see the other reasons very well. There was practicality: he could help look after the children, who adored him. And then, Will and Gilbert had had the chance of London, why not the youngest? And, besides that, there was the question of leaving him with his father.

He would, Anne knew, come in for it all. Will had always borne the majority of it, and she and her children had shouldered some, but they had an elsewhere in heart and mind to live. Edmund left here would have nothing. Richard was his father's man, and as for her mother-in-law, she had decided early: my man matters most. Now there was nothing for her except to embrace the martyrdom of her church, at the shrine of the holy St John. Oh, forgive me for thinking it; and if He will still hear me, God forbid that I am like that, going with Will to London, to start a new life at near forty.

So to this: the road south, and the Shakespeare family starting on it, including Edmund, with London their destination. John Shakespeare came out to see them off: actually came out to the Swan yard to see them mount the horses. Change in the air. Certainly his face was set in disapproval. He mourned his daughter-in-law and his grandchildren going over that sun-bit chancy horizon. And yet here he was braving the ostler's stare, and murmuring advice about cast shoes and highway robbers. Change. Trace it to the conversation, the other night. A true conversation between him and Will, with no dog snarl.

Will had been telling the children again about the Queen. The Chamberlain's Men had played

352

before the Queen at Greenwich Palace, and so he had seen her. They never tired of it.

'When will you go again?' Judith cried. 'Has she asked you back?'

'Well, she summons one of the companies to perform for her each Christmastide. You may imagine how we contend for the honour.'

'You mean you fight for it?' Judith, assassin of spiders and worms, liked the sound of that.

'It's a professional matter, goose,' chuckled Edmund. He was lying on the floor, long legs up against the chimney-breast. 'They don't draw swords on one another.'

'Let's hope not,' his father said darkly, with a faint shudder. 'Remembering what you told us of that Marley fellow.' But he listened as Will presented it again for the children's ears. (Will had already told it to Anne, in bed-curtained night: the melancholy gaunt Queen moored in her billowing costume, head on hand; the courtiers exchanging continual nervous glances in the torchlight; the peering ambassadors struggling to comprehend the dual shows of stage and throne.) And then they began talking, father and son, around the matter of the Queen first.

'She has had need of loyal subjects, and they have been repaid with steadiness and protection,' Will said. 'Even those who find a—a difference in their souls would surely not see her turned from her throne, and the country over to civil war and bloodshed. To see her is to know she is the greatest of Englishwomen.'

His father inclined his head. 'Well, I am apt to believe you. It is a sentiment to do an Englishman honour.'

'And the Shakespeares—you know this better than any, Father—stand well in this regard; we can pride ourselves on being servants of the Crown, not just now but formerly.' The Shakespeares, Anne thought. When had he ever said that? 'It seems an opportune time to assert it. I thought, on my return to London, to make application again to the College of Heralds.'

'Application—again?' After a long stare into the fire, his father mouthed the words, tentative as Hamnet when he had a lingering loose milk-tooth.

'I mean the application you made,' Will said. 'For us. For the Shakespeares. Their gentlemanly estate.'

'Does that mean a coat of arms?' cried Hamnet. For once he looked, excitedly, from father to grandfather: usually they were too much for him together. 'And would I have the coat of arms then? I would, wouldn't I, because I'm the man?'

'Hush, hush,' his grandfather said. 'That would be so, yes, but—but I think your father is not in earnest.' His voice questioned sourly, yet he could not sit still, and the firelight caught his face in arrested flickers of wonder. And if Will was not in earnest, he was playing this part very earnestly: the son dutifully reconciling. Almost the prodigal making his own reformation, supplying fatted calf at his own expense.

'I am in earnest,' Will said, not quite looking into his father's eyes.

'Well, but thy father speaks of possible things only,' John Shakespeare said, drawing Hamnet into the big-sleeved crook of his arm. 'A grant of arms, that makes a man a gentleman, and all his issue after, and so thou see'st, it's no light matter. Thy

354

grandfather made application some years since—
with right, with every right—but it's a long and
ticklish business, trust me.'

Hamnet did; but now it was to Will he turned his
fidgeting eagerness. 'You will get it, all the same,
won't you, Father?'

'I want it,' said Will, considering. And then: 'I
do seem to get the things I want.' So quickly and
awkwardly he made it sound like a sickness.

*   *   *

Simply, she had never been so far from home once
they were ten miles past Clopton Bridge. From now
on every moment was new ground, in every sense.

She felt alone with it. The children, she
discovered, loved the new more than home.
Hamnet rode before Will, Judith before Anne: both
wriggled and shouted with unflagging pleasure.
Susannah rode her own mount, dainty and straight-
backed, like, Anne thought, some abbess from the
old time.

Looking at new places, the new places looked
at her, and revealed an Anne Shakespeare she
had not suspected. Along the road she was treated
with respect as a gentle dame—London-dressed,
husband plainly a man of the world: probably not
to be trifled with, suggested the lowered eyes of
inn-servants. But surely that isn't me. Inside I'm
young and a fool.

At the inns the children, excited beyond sleep,
frightened each other in the unaccustomed night:
hear that sound, what is it, it's someone digging
your grave. Hush now. At Thame there was no
room, or little, at the inn so they bundled together

355

in one bedchamber, Will and Anne and the children cramming into the bed, Edmund lying on the floor. And all caught giggles, couldn't stop. Hush, hush. Anne was a little afraid of the innkeeper.

'Why, we've paid,' Edmund said from the floor. His voice sounded odd and froglike from down there and set them off again.

'No, we haven't,' Will said. 'I shan't pay till the morning.' And that seemed so absurd they squealed and gasped, and Judith said she would wet herself as the bed shook with laughing.

And this was good, this worked. Anne thought: Let's do this for ever, never halt, keep endlessly travelling.

But London had to come. She had been picturing its immensity for so long that inevitably, when the city rose or lazily shouldered up on the horizon, it didn't seem so very large. And she found a moment to smile at Will's pride in pointing out the landmarks; the Abbey, St Paul's, look there. It was touching—men and things. Like Bartholomew with his new hay-cart, walking all round it, noting the painted wheels. And then suddenly fear stopped her chest and she couldn't feel her fingers as her mount wagged its steaming neck through streets and streets. When they were held up by a slipped girth she found herself staring at a house across the way, a single tall house and its smoking chimneys. No different from those of Stratford or, indeed, any of the other towns on the way here. And yet: she would never know the inhabitants of that house, or what they put on the fire that made that particular smoke—and that was certain. The world was bigger than she could ever understand. And now it was done, the drawbridge had been pulled up. Now I have to make myself.

'Here we are.' Will seemed fresh as they dismounted outside a house in a long, noisy street that seemed to be all inns and stables. Anne felt exhausted. She felt half rubbed out, like that chalk obscenity on the wall yonder. Why draw such a thing? 'Don't stare,' Will warned Edmund, who was doing so, vastly, rocking on his legs. 'They don't care for it hereabouts.' In confirmation, a groom leading a string of horses swore and spat. Edmund laughed. Wonderful. Like hearing a lion roar, she supposed: satisfyingly expected. Will slipped his arm around her waist. 'What do you think?'

I think I can never live here. But not to be said. 'Handsome.' Squeezed in with narrow windows, and hard to tell where it ended and the next house began. But she just wanted to get indoors, away from this strange outdoors where everyone seemed to be shouting, a little angry or exultant. No mellowness; like a world in which there was only ever blossom or thorn, never fruit.

And then it was better, it was like travelling again, the exciting feeling of trying to fit in, this is us in a foreign place. The children loving it, questing up and down the stairs, look here, see this. Water-work on the walls. The Quineys had it, but nothing like this. Highly coloured birds and mythical beasts twined amid impossible branches and pillars.

'There aren't any real birds like those,' said Hamnet, sturdily.

Will laughed. 'Thou art in the right,' he said, 'and why paint birds that never were?' He scooped his son up for a piggyback around the clattering house. And Anne thought: I should stop being selfish, thinking of me. If this brings Will closer to his son, then no complaining.

The first night in a new home was always difficult. Will's hand stroked hers, while he talked of what they would do, see. Impossible to cry denial, say, I don't want to do anything. At last he subsided, his breath buzzed. She got up to peep out of the slit of window. Dry stale air, no hint of season. Outside a scattering of lights burned. Footsteps clicked on mysterious errands. A watchman wailed the hour, sounding in pain. Somewhere a horse kicked and kicked at a stable door, like a wild thing out of place.

*   *   *

Engaging servants, that was one of the new things. Both maid and man. The latter for when she went out, as Will explained. The gentle dame with her manservant, my God. These new things, at first, reflected their newness on her and made her feel new likewise. In the bedchamber stood a looking-glass, clearer than she had ever known. I look, she thought, not so very bad. If I can just shake those old eyes with their foreboding, their expectation of no good.

The first time shopping for provisions, she was intimidated by the aggression of choice. Prices seemed high, and she wondered if they were swindling her. But there was no one to turn to you knew: that was grim. You took what you could see, untrusting. She would get used to it, perhaps. But the sights they saw intimidated her too: the Tower, the array of prisons south of the river, the spiked traitors' heads on London Bridge, even the Exchange with its thick-thronged merchants in furred robes, like commercial animals, and its parading ladies—or were they whores?—white-painted, frizzed, giant-shouldered. The things they *did* to people here, as if people were like food for a great cook, who stuffed larks within fowls, made ingenious transformations. But, then, perhaps she would get used to it.

They would need a tutor for Hamnet. From slow beginnings he was quickening in learning. Susannah could read and write after a fashion; Judith yawned and protested at the sight of a page. Not that learning was much use to women, but . . . Will scratched his head. 'I ought to have taken a hand in it,' he said.

'But you weren't there. You were here.'

'True. Now we're all here . . . and so things will be different. You don't regret coming, do you? Look how well they've settled. Look at Hamnet: he has so much more address.' Look, look at something else, look anywhere but here.

True about the children, though. They went abroad in those labyrinthine streets with far more confidence than their mother. Their talk became so quickly London-flavoured she could hardly follow it. What d'ye lack? they cried, in hoarse imitation of the shopkeepers and street-sellers, fresh cowcumbers and medlars: they talked of the fairest price for a wherry across to Southwark, of which grandee was staying at Durham House. They are going to belong to this, she thought, in a way I never can. I mustn't hold them back. In Hamnet she could even see a future sketching out in Will's eyes. He had made an appeal to the College of Heralds, as he had told his father: gentleman status might

359

await, and Hamnet, as a gentleman's son, could go much further than the moderate dreams of Stratford council-chamber. One evening Will was talking of an acquaintance who had been educated in a nobleman's household: Hamnet's head went up.

'He went when he was eleven?'

'Aye, though it can be any age. I mean, it needn't be so young.'

'It's not young,' Hamnet, eleven, said staunchly.

'Young to go away,' Anne said. But he was taken with the idea, she could tell. Of course, it was natural for your children to grow beyond you. But she thought: Leave me something of them. A stupid thought, and she was careful with it, like many of her London thoughts, keeping it deep within, far from her tongue, far from her expression.

Will needed to be from home a lot, and straight away. She could tell he was trying to stay while she settled in, not to leave her too much. But of course his work called him, and it was not like going across the yard to the workshop. One day she went past a glover's and the familiarity of the smell hit her with incredible force of longing. Which was ridiculous, for she had never liked it. It showed how the mind worked: it was treacherous, it would weep for anything gone. So she tried to be robust. If she got lost in the streets, what was the worst that could befall her? But she preferred not to answer that.

'Go, go,' she said to Will. 'You can't always be keeping your fireside, you have a deal of business to attend to.' Which he did, now that he was a sharer, even when he was not acting, or rehearsing, or writing. And that he did at night. She wouldn't hear him get up from the bed. Just suddenly be aware that his shape next to her had been replaced by coldness. And then, if she listened hard, she could just hear the quill, like a little creature furtive and determined.

'But you know, he's a wonder, your husband,' said Richard Burbage. He came to the house early on simply to pay his respects (others, she knew, to get a look at her). He brought a basket of flowers, sweetmeats for the children. He seemed decent and sincere: though all was seemings nowadays. 'Such fertile invention. Such succulent sweetness of wit. Yes, yes, I'm flattering him, because we want our new piece from him. He has no rivals, you know.'

'Don't talk nonsense,' Will said: the words decorous, his face oddly thunderous.

'Oh, others write, but they don't please like him. Well, what now, man? You do please.'

'Perhaps I could do more.'

Burbage shook his head at him, as if he were a stubborn child. 'Never blots a line, mistress. Well, that's our boast and jest. Lucky thing too, with his handwriting.'

Will's work: a man's world entire, she had forgotten how much, though she knew there were no women on stage. It struck home to her when she went with him to the Theatre during rehearsal. Burbage was courtly, but plainly they were not used to having a woman about them. Even Edmund forgot about her there. And watching the youth rehearsing a woman's part made her feel strange. He was good, natural—almost too natural. It seemed to make you unnecessary.

Edmund came back to himself gradually on the way home. His eyes lost their shining, blinded look. Oh, it was where he wanted to be, she could tell.

361

But could he do it? His voice had broken early, so he was no good for those roles. (She was pleased about that, for some reason.) And then what would John Shakespeare say? She must remember he was far off, in every sense. Here they were removed from his influence completely. And yet, curious thing, she wasn't. He came often into her mind. As for Will, if his father was mentioned he stiffened so slightly only she could see it.

Gilbert came to Bishopsgate to sup. In him the Shakespeare good looks, visible in adolescence, had altogether disappeared in a sallow adulthood. But he was out of his time, practically running his master's haberdashery business, and doing well: rings on the fingers with which he gave her a cursory handshake. 'Never fear, sister, you'll soon have the London squint, half down your nose and half on your purse. Then you'll never look straight at anyone again.' He certainly had it; and a cough like a donkey. But she always seemed to be hearing that in London, and for all the children revelled in the new life she did not think them in broad health: they sniffled and had no colour and sometimes their breath was not sweet.

All Gilbert's talk was of the city. At the Fields', Richard went out of his way to talk to Anne of Stratford, which she supposed was kind of him. (Though did it show so much that she was gasping and flexing on the bank?) Mistress Field she could not take to. Though it was interesting to meet a Frenchwoman, no doubt. Yet Anne wished she could just have these interesting experiences over, like the diseases of childhood. And Mistress Field had too good a figure for a woman who had borne children, and you could tell she thought so. And too many wise words about teething and the care of linen, as she smoothed her enviable flat belly. I never get along with the wise, Anne thought. A pity her husband was plainly frightened of her. No one could say that of Will. But perhaps she should be exercising a little fear over him. Be a little of the termagant wife. Was that what others did? She never used to care what others did, disdained it, even: felt that behind their closed door she and Will lived by their own rule.

She wondered a lot of things, and they jangled in her head so much that sometimes she followed Joan's prescription. Before coming to the Fields' she had had the maid bring her up a cup of wine, and now as Mistress Field offered her almond-milk or sack, she had no difficulty in choosing. It helped a little: the mind found one thing to fret about instead of several.

One thing it dismissed. As they rose to leave the Fields', another woman came in, a dark, frowning, half-pretty woman who looked, as so many did here, as if she ate and slept badly. 'Isabelle, my dear,' Mistress Field said.

And the woman looked up at Will and said: 'Master Shakespeare.' But gave his name a peculiar pronunciation, which made Anne conclude she was French likewise.

'Madame Berger, your servant,' Will said.

The Frenchwoman took no notice of Anne at all. 'You must come and see me again,' she said. And Will bowed, not looking much enthused. And Anne thought: Well, my God, if there were anything, it wouldn't be as fearfully obvious as that.

Still, she said as they walked home: 'Who's she?'

'A Frenchwoman. A silk-weaver's widow. I

helped her once, when there were disturbances against the foreigners.' He added: 'She's mad,' as easily as one might say, she lives up the hill. Nothing there, she thought: surely.

Naturally his work took him away. Away from the house—or just away. Once he said, 'I must go,' and soon afterwards she found him upstairs, writing. And his look seemed to say: Well, it's as I said.

She watched him with the theatre people, heard dimly their talk. Box-takings up. This latest broadsheet from the Puritans attacking the theatre, poorly writ but, Lord, what a siege-train of citations from the Bible. Trouble ahead from the lease of the land the Theatre was built on: well, we must shift somehow. Clowns improvising, man, that belongs with slashed doublets and rhymes, we want none of it, the words as writ on the page or else. Two lionskins and a bearskin and a tree of golden apples, all lost: well, someone's stealing properties, that's all there is to it . . . He was so much a part of them: but did any of them know him? she wondered.

This man, perhaps, more than any other: Ben Jonson. At first she was relieved when he came to Bishopsgate, square and stocky and shovelling up food and drink with his big work-cracked hands, and taking very little notice of her as he talked to Will: for a space she almost felt she was with Hamnet Sadler, moored in a quiet Stratford afternoon where nothing was expected of her. And she was glad—though she would not have said so, just then, under torture—that he was apparently nothing to do with the theatre. She heard him talk of his day's labour, of his wife's coming confinement, and thought: Finally, something that hasn't been crowded out by the theatre, the grand brute that pushes life with its elbows to the unregarded edges.

But soon Jonson's talk climbed winding into the high and learned, where she could not follow, and where even Will sometimes seemed hardly bothered to pursue him. And then Jonson offered to hear Hamnet's lesson.

'Who is this governor you've appointed to the whelp?' Jonson boomed. 'I've never heard his name.'

'Tutor only, not governor,' Will said, smiling, 'and allow me respectfully to suggest, Ben, that you haven't heard of everyone.'

'Everyone worth knowing. Well, come hither, boy, I shan't bite thee, saving thy Latin is villainous, and then I can't answer for myself.'

That was when Anne began to be in two minds about him. Plenty of people used 'thee' for children they didn't know, but she had never liked it. Nor did she entirely like the way he loudly challenged Will on things to do with learning, arts, poetry. Perhaps she didn't wholly understand: she could see it was a sort of fencing, and that Will seemed to enjoy the exercise, and he never ended up banging the table as Jonson did. Still, she felt curiously oppressed when Ben Jonson called, as if the room were suddenly overheated.

But that might have been something else at work. A sort of transferred fear. Because from what she could gather, Jonson was in the process of leaving real life and entering the theatre. And Will was— what? Helping, responsible, involved? (To blame?)

Another friend of Will's—a long, lank, inwardly

smiling man named Tom Nashe, whom she did not like at all—was there when they talked of it. Will, it seemed, had directed Jonson to Master Henslowe: and she had picked up the word about him: beside Burbage he was the other power in the London theatre. A little like the two big farmers about Shottery, always looking to buy up a morsel of land, and win out.

'And so you are employed, fruitfully, dutifully employed, by Henslowe?' Nashe said. 'And pray tell which of your bollocks did you have to hand over to his keeping to seal the contract?'

'Pah, the man's gentle as a sheep with me,' Jonson said, big bristled chin jutting. Anne sat by, knitting hose for the twins, though Will urged her simply to buy these things in London.

'It's journeyman work,' Will said. 'Henslowe has need, as we all do, of plays, and if not a whole play then a play-plot to be worked up, or an old play warmed over. With a little, I say only a little, recommendation from me, Ben is doing these things for Henslowe, here and there.'

'A little, a very little effort from me, you know—a mere thumb-nibbling insult compared to what I *could* do—and, lo, the piece is transformed, and I think Master Henslowe will soon be loving me above every other,' Jonson said.

'Here's Ben going through the manuscript,' Will said, putting on the barrel chest, the chin. '"This too long. This to be moved to the end, 'twill balance better. Add six lines heroic measure to bring out the rival, he's too faint. Tut, a laughable figure, out with it. Tut, polish, polish . . ."'

'Aye, a fair representation,' Jonson said, smiling and red, 'and in truth the piece was worse than that.

It was so artless and sprawling I thought *you* must have had a hand in it.'

And Will laughed—which she could not understand. 'So, if they'll have you, will you go?'

'Why should they not have me?'

'Well, I heard what Pembroke's Men thought of your acting, so—'

'Oh, I haven't,' Nashe cried. 'Pray tell.'

'They made me try out a most lamentable poor part. There was naught to be done with it,' Jonson scoffed.

'They said blustering is not acting,' said Will, temperately.

'This company is of a different mettle entirely,' Jonson said, 'and better able to appreciate a man's new-minted but solid ringing worth. And when they set out in June, they say, I may thoroughly count upon a place, all being well.'

'A travelling company is a very fair fit place to begin,' Will said, 'as I well know. But it does mean beginning, Ben: choosing that life, and everything that goes with it, and not turning back. It must be all or nothing.'

'Oh, I know that. She knows that. I'm ready.'

He never referred to his wife by name, Anne thought; and bit through the wool with her teeth.

*   *   *

At the top of the house there was a garret where the maid did the laundry, hanging it to dry on a pulleyed string across the street. Very London, Anne thought: you put out your shifts and drawers for all to see, yet of course no one looked up to see them, because that would be countrified. Would

367

they look up if someone were hanging there? Another of her wonderings. She wished she could stop them. This, she thought, when she went up to the garret, is my head. Full of flapping shapes and light, and the heat rising.

*   *   *

'Dance with me?' Edmund said. He had found her alone, and without her face ready: her London face, plucky and responsive.

'We haven't done that for a long time,' she said: meaning no.

'Too long.' He had hold of her hand. He hated seeing her unhappy—Edmund hated seeing anyone unhappy, indeed—but she knew that he particularly wanted her to stop being unhappy now, here, because he was so very happy. And her being unhappy probably spoiled, a little, his happiness. So he wanted her to dance him into reassurance.

She did it. Well, it was not much to do; and it was part of the old Stratford life, besides. Ah, and there you heard a chime of revelation. That Stratford life was what you wanted. With Will, without Will? Dance, hear the mind-music, don't hear the question.

*   *   *

'Edmund wants to do what you do,' she told Will. He was undressing for bed, hardly able to stand for weariness; she had been lying sleepless behind the curtains for hours. Different clocks. Different skies.

'I know. He's said so—or tried not to say so. I wish he could.'

368

'Do you? Why?'

She sensed him, in the half-dark, jerking back from the shin-barking directness of that question.

'I mean,' he said, sitting on the edge of the bed—the very edge, 'I wish it were more probable, since it's what he wants. But I doubt whether he has it. The ability to be a player. Well, call it something else, for it's a species of inability, in truth. Edmund's too much himself. If he were to try acting, I'm afraid he would always be Edmund.' A pause, in which something in Anne, a prentice yelling revolt in the street, cries out: *Good for him, so he should be.* 'You can see the difference in Matthew.'

Oh, yes. Him.

*   *   *

Richard Burbage brought him, though obviously Will had agreed to the fact of him earlier. She watched them from a first-floor window, standing in attitudes before the street-door: Burbage with his hand lightly on the boy's shoulder, Will with arms folded, the two grown heads in discussion—and the boy between, a blob of fairness atop slenderness, a dandelion-boy. He was looking at a waiting laden donkey as if he could look at that sight for a long time, hands folded before him: as if he could find plenty there to occupy him, for now.

If not for him . . . How wicked of her. She should have felt motherly, no doubt. But surely there was meant to be a limit to that, and that was why they had come here, to narrow family down, not spread it out.

Naturally, it was Will's work. Matthew

369

Hollingbery was a boy-actor, to be trained up by a seasoned actor. It was not a formal apprenticeship, but it was very like it. Will was master and tutor. Also landlord and, perhaps, a kind of father.

'It's how it works in the theatre,' Edmund said to her. Increasingly he made these explanations, or excuses: his brother's advocate. 'It's a professional matter.'

But Edmund believed what he wanted to believe, which gave, she thought cruelly, a slightly strained look to his muscular eagerness, like a man at the fair bending iron. Of course it couldn't be just professional, unless you were inhuman, which Will wasn't. There must be some warmth involved, some connection. All the more, in fact, as Matthew belonged to Will's work—for that was where she suspected Will's heart, elusive bird, settled most.

And impossible not to have the suspicion, when in the evening Will and Matthew withdrew to the garret for an hour to go over lines, try out voice and gesture, that he relished this. Even when she heard a nagging or weary edge to his voice—'Come, pat on your cue, Matt, hearken else all's lost, for God's sake—' Anne suspected he was enjoying himself more than with his own children, who were so very much themselves.

She hated herself all the more because Matthew was so unassuming. A schoolmaster's son, she learned, orphaned, then placed with a relative who had been vicious. A refined manner, but without affectation. He would sit in the window-seat and read, or gaze out. Blue eyes. An odd-looking peachy complexion—odd-looking to her, a mother, who saw all children as not quite coming up to hers in looks, and their hair strangely cut. His gaze at

370

her was humble yet not submissive. If anyone, he put her in mind of Will when she first knew him: when he could blanch his identity from the room, turn into a sun-drop, a breeze-touched cobweb.

Hamnet was eleven. Matthew was thirteen. They had nothing to say to each other. Hamnet watched his father. Came out with it.

'What you said about boys going into a nobleman's household . . . If I did that, what would you think, Father? Would you think more of me?'

Will gave a start. 'Great God, how could I think better of you than I do?' he said. He hugged his son.

Anne, divided, could have told him Hamnet didn't much like embraces now, even from her. Blacker thought: London has certainly done this, it has shown that we really don't mix well as a family, and it was silly and countrified to think we could. And perhaps none did: thinking of her father, her beautiful past, she realised she was a sport, a white blackbird. The common way was thus: father governed all, mother governed children; father and mother conducted themselves towards one another with proper esteem and respect. Love was there; but you all took your places at its table in due order.

And as for the sacred domestic hearth, here in London, here in the domain of the theatre . . .?

Well, perhaps again she was being unrealistic. Some players were married, certainly. Still, they were more with each other than with their wives. Sometimes, instead of an inn, the Chamberlain's Men adjourned to this house after rehearsals, occasionally performances. They made a great noise, drank and ate hugely. Sometimes she heard them harsh in hilarity. Bawdy talk too. Will tried to restrain it. Still she could not help wondering how much he joined in when she was not by. A cup of perry nerved her to ask him.

'Oh, it's mere fantastication, a game of words, not real.'

'That's not what I asked you.'

'I know, and I'm not going to answer. Women talk bawdy among themselves, that I know.'

'How do you know it, if it's only among themselves?'

'From listening at doors.'

They were so nearly playful with each other: so far from at ease, or happy.

'Is it not a pity that men and women must be so separate? How, if women were to act on stage, might that not change things?' she said: or the perry did. 'I know, it would shame their modesty to make a public exhibition. But at least they would be real. Not these invented women—a man writes them, a boy presents them. Not a touch of woman has gone into their making.'

'Unless the man who made them is part woman.'

Startled, she said: 'You mean the boys who play? But surely there's nothing of that about them—'

'No, no, I didn't mean that . . . You don't care for Matthew, I know.'

She felt herself impugned as mother and woman. 'He is a good young fellow, I wish him well. But I didn't expect him—that's all.' There was a sharp whistle from the yard below. Anne opened the window and waved. 'That's Betty. She's a cow-keeper. I buy milk of her. Fresh from the kine. And we have a rare talk. She's a real woman, not someone pretending.' She added that angrily, because he looked somehow surprised and disappointed—at what? Her making friends with a cow-keeper? Who else, then? she thought, as she went downstairs. Belly-smoothing Jacqueline Field, whose talk was all of narrow candlelit city doings? That other Frenchwoman who always seemed to be there, with a subdued stare and a cryptic greeting for Will? (And Will hardly spared her a glance. No, that wasn't what she had to fear.)

Betty: she was about Anne's age, comfortingly slow-moving as her cow, her voice softly burred: ready to stand about the yard and agree that the sun was hot today, mortal hot, but then the season, aye, without ever wanting to whip the conversation to some dazzling finish. Each day she came in to London from St Giles, which Anne thought at first must be another of those city parishes packed like boxes within boxes.

'Nay, it's country there. Not like this.' Betty jerked her thumb back—at London. Oh, thrilling dismissal. 'We live by the old spital wall, with an old oak for shade and a herb garden and a well of sweet water. Drink water here and you're bent in a bloody flux.' Spotting Will on his way out, she went on: 'That your man? They're pretty things in their way, aren't they? As long as you keep them in their place. My Dickon's a fair sort. Poulterer. A haynish item, but no harm in him. Married when I was fifteen. It was his eyes that did it. Handsome eyes, I thought. Now I know they all have handsome eyes when they're young. What's your man?'

'A player.'

Betty grunted, hefting her pail. 'Well, they're all that.'

His new play was coming on. Anne was going to see it. For the first time since they had arrived, she was going to step into a theatre.

Edmund had taken the children to see Will act in pieces written by other hands. Why had she waited? Loyalty, perhaps: reserving herself for a play of his own making.

Or, perhaps, until she could put it off no longer.

She had heard snatches of it. The boy Matthew was in it, and she had overheard him rehearsing; Edmund had read—overcoming grim reluctance— Will's own copy, and went around murmuring lines. *Sweep the dust behind the door.*

Anne looked too. Will left it on the chest in their bedchamber. A breeze fingered the pages, ahead of her reaching hand. Soft spring-laden scents should have come with that breeze: not here, though. She looked, read a little, but it was too difficult for her, *ill met by moonlight proud Titania*, to manage it for long. Will said they weren't for reading anyway. How came her eyes so bright? Not with salt tears. She left it, and went to help Susannah with the dressing of her hair. It had thickened amazingly of late: felt heavy as rope in the hand. She wondered if Susannah had started her menses yet. An attempt last winter to raise the subject had elicited one of Susannah's loftiest responses: 'Dear Mother, please, let's talk of pleasant things.' Susannah was happy behind her fences. She thought of the bird in the kitchen at Henley Street, and how she had once left the cage door open by mistake. A forlorn piping had alerted her. The bird could not be happy until the door was shut.

Betty would be here soon. Anne went downstairs to wait for her. She was growing quite addicted to milk from the cow. *I am sent with broom before, To sweep the dust behind the door.* And there was some, she saw. On impulse she wrote in it with her finger. She wrote: *somewhere it is spring.* She preferred that to pen and ink. You could just wipe it away.

*   *   *

And now here she was. Flag blaring and trumpet rippling on high, trample of feet, press of voices. Hawkers with neck-slung trays, beer from the back-borne keg. Prostitutes bare-necked and balancing their bosom-wares, looking at you as only they could: as if you'd intruded on them, but they'd let it be, this once. Mud underfoot as Anne and her family squeezed their way through the gate, money-taker knowing, bowing them in. Edmund thick-tongued, almost glazed with excitement: Hamnet nearly as bad.

'Father made this. Didn't he? Didn't he make all of it?'

'Well. Not this building.'

'I don't mean that. I don't mean the building,' Hamnet said, in his slightly laborious way, his grandfather's way. None of the quicksilver that went into Will and Edmund. She hugged him with the sudden fierce love of a child's flaws. 'I mean,' he said, gently pulling away, 'what we're going to see.'

Well, he was right. It was years since she had been to the play, and never in London, in these strange crammed circles made for the sole purpose; and she half expected more show, more appurtenances of illusion. Instead she faced a bare stage lit by clear sky, a few properties, the heavy bob and whisk of rich costumes: and the words.

And it was nothing horrible, as she believed the *Romeo* play was that everyone talked of. Edmund had read out some, and there was love and death and it was all like a dream of a black rose pressing velvety and smothering your breath and she feared it. No, this was beautiful and often gay, like dancing in words. It was in the wood and of the wood. It was about the madness of love and what madness leads men and women to. It made her remember a pair of gloves being slipped on to her hands; Bartholomew watching her across the threshing-floor as she danced; a wild bird eating from her hand; many things. Many things that belonged to her alone. Yet this play was no whisper but a participation. Everything belonged to everyone here. Will had them, somehow. As if he had the secret of all their lives and put his ear to their sleeping breathing lips. As the play went on the crowd warmed, cracked like logs on a well-laid fire. He was seducing them. She sensed the surrender, and certain stars shot madly from their spheres to hear the sea-maid's music, and it gave her as much unease as pride. Somewhere there is spring. But here is midsummer, and such a season created as makes the real unnecessary.

Then the laughter. The man with the ass's head made the children roar—but Anne could not join in properly, and it was to Edmund that they turned their laughing faces, his arms that went companionably round them. A man with the head of an ass, and a bewitched queen loved him. But this was too real. Love looks not with the eyes but with the mind, and therefore is winged Cupid painted blind. She looked with her mind and shuddered, for it did not seem right somehow that the inmost madness of life should be turned inside out to smiles in the sun. *Sweep the dust behind the door.*

The lovers were lost in the wood. They would never get out of the wood, perhaps: find their bones at last under a heap of stones, perhaps. Everyone was subject to enchantment, even the plain and countrified. I have had a dream, past the wit of man to say what dream it was. She knew, though. There came the countrified characters doing a play. A bad play: but she wondered if there were any bad plays. And it was only at this point that she realised if Will was a player in the piece she had not noticed him.

There was a happy resolution. *So shall all the couple three ever true in loving be. Sweep the dust behind the door.* The crowd sighed, trilled, bellowed, and applauded. Anne clapped, but soon needed her hands: to grip the splintery edge of her seat in fear.

Because this was where Will had gone. This was where he had taken his self. And this, she saw now, was where she could not follow him. Oh, she could offer him truth, perhaps, beauty, love—but nothing, nothing compared with what he could make.

*   *   *

It was crowded and stinking in the tiring-house: no place for them to linger, especially with men half undressed.

'Burbage is going to make a speech,' Will said, with a grimace, kissing her. Unreal: as if a figure had reached out of a painting. 'Then there'll be a supper at the Black Bull. I'll not stay long.'

'You never do,' cried Bottom the weaver— but, no, this was Will Kempe the comedian, big, golden-haired, like Bartholomew. *My brother thou art translated.* She felt sick. 'You should learn to exult, man. Cultivate a reckless side.'

'Then what would become of my other sides?' Will said. 'Matthew was fine, was he not?' His eyes went proudly to the boy, who was taking off his wings as if shedding his school satchel. And Hamnet saw that, Anne could tell. But his own pride did not diminish, not a whit. His face still shone with what his father had wrought.

Edmund was a little doleful, the heavy afterwards of intoxication. 'Let's go home,' he said, and went to find the manservant, their guardian through dubious Shoreditch to decent Bishopsgate. Anne hurried them on, not because of that, but because she had had a sudden thought: she might miss Betty. It seemed desperately important.

'The cow-keeper? Been and gone, mistress,' the maid said. Adding brightly: 'I bought a pint for you.'

No, no, this wouldn't do, she had to have a talk with Betty each day, a deep, warm, earthy draught of her; it mattered. Anne took up her cloak. Edmund looked his question: where? 'Out.' If she had missed Betty coming to her, then she would go to Betty. These things seem small and undistinguishable, like far-off mountains turned into clouds. She walked north-west, along by London Wall, judging by the setting sun, asking when she went astray: not shy, because this had killed shy, this feeling of importance to her alone. Who knew or cared for Betty, the cow-keeper of

St Giles? She did. Barns appeared, timber-ponds, vegetable rows, though still London did not seem quite to fall away. *I know a bank whereon the wild thyme blows, where oxlips and the nodding violet grows.* But where? New fine houses rose up, some still building in choice brick: habitations of the wealthy sort. But she was looking for something plainer, simpler: a cottage by the old spital wall, with an old oak and a sweet well. She found a church: St Giles, very well. Found remnants of old monastic wall among a scrubby rambling sort of village, but where . . . ?

At last, an old woman had heard of Betty the cow-keeper and Dickon the poulterer. She nodded Anne to a tumbledown hovel she had already passed twice. The oak was a dead stump. Still: to airy nothing give a habitation and a name. Love looks not with the eyes but with the mind, and Betty loved this spot of earth.

Above the open door hung a couple of skinny fowls: another, hardly more alive, scratched on the threshold. Anne's calf muscles burned from the walk. Getting soft from London: next she would be carried about in one of those new coaches. She would say this to Betty, and they would chuckle.

'Betty, art there?' She hadn't used *thou* with her before, but they were friends after all. She went forward in semi-darkness. Damp straw squelched underfoot.

'Don't come dunning here, mistress! You'll get naught, hear me, get naught!'

A man loomed at her, breathing drink. A strap dangled from his hand and spit from his lips.

'Master Dickon?' she quavered. She had expected someone like Peter Quince the carpenter,

379

solid and jovial. This man was like a rat nosing from an alley.

'Who'd know?' Behind him a small child grizzled on the floor, another stood nose-picking and staring. A sickly goose squatted in a sort of wicker pen directly adjoining the bare room.

'I'm a friend to Betty. She keeps a cow, has a milk-walk in Bishopsgate—'

'Oh, a friend, hey?' His crusted eyes ran over her clothes, adding up. 'Not a dun, then, hey? Your pardon, but a man must wonder, when a stranger comes asking of her.' He hit out at the crying child, with a blind fly-swatting motion, while his face rearranged itself into troubled friendliness. 'That's my Betty, yes, but she's still from home, mistress. Late. Always she's late, the bitch.' He belched sourly and grinned. 'Jesting. She's a good creature in the main. But what's goodness when there's a pest on your fowl, and sick children needing delicate food? Nothing, that's what.' She noticed the prompt way he stepped forward when she stepped back. A drunk, and a hitter. She brought to mind how Betty always kept her arms covered, even in warm weather. *What hempen homespuns . . . ?* 'Now you say you're a friend, but I don't say friend until I see money. Money's what's needed, you see.' Wheedling, sidling to block the door. 'And I see money about you, mistress.'

Not for long. She wrenched her purse from her waist and scattered the coins on the filthy floor and ran.

And ran.

In mud-spattered Bishopsgate Street, in grey dusk, she ran straight into Will, who was out looking for her. She screamed and fought him for

380

the few seconds it took her to understand this.

'Where have you been? Edmund's out seeking you, I've been everywhere—in God's name, what . . . ?'

She told him. Leaning on him, half staggering back to the house, she told it all: why not?

Indoors he dispensed quick explanations to the children, urging her upstairs. In their bedchamber, door shut, he gently took off her drenched cloak, then knelt and eased off her mud-stiff shoes.

'Why?' he asked, as he had to.

She considered. Her wet hair felt like weed clinging to her face. As if she had been dredged from the deeps of wild seas, and certain stars shot madly from their spheres to hear the sea-maid's music.

'I thought,' she said, 'that it would be like the wood.'

She heard him suck in breath, and in the room's unlit dimness saw his teeth. Was it exasperation she saw, was it a wry laugh? Don't ask me, I can barely read, let alone read Will Shakespeare.

'The wood,' he said, 'is no place.'

Inside her heart, deep in its silent sea-caves, sounded her answer: I know that now.

*   *   *

'As Her Majesty's former officer in chief of Stratford and Justice of the Peace, he should be entitled to bear arms.' Will had been to the College of Heralds again, and was explaining to Hamnet. 'And as property-holder, and as husband to Grandmother, who is of the Arden line. They take all these matters into account when they grant it.'

381

'What about you?' Hamnet said. 'You're an important man too. A Chamberlain's Man. A play-maker. They ought to give arms for that.'

Will laughed and slapped his son's shoulder. 'Not the same in their eyes, I fear. But thank you, Hamnet, you are gracious.'

A beautiful moment: beautiful, the glow on Hamnet's face. Here I come to sour and curdle, thought Anne.

'Will they grant it?'

'I don't see why not. There are men bearing arms who never gave such good service to Crown and country.'

'Lord. Now you're sounding like your father.'

They had this hesitation around jokes. After a moment Will put down his guard. 'Lord. Please, knock me on the head first.'

She opened the window to let out a fly, and let in warm air like the inside of a shoe. 'This is the sickly season in London, isn't it?'

'Yes. But we're well situated here. Why?' Suddenly he was close, looking into her eyes, anxiously conning her skin. Oh, that tenderness could make up for a lot: if you could just prise it out, give it a different setting. 'No, no, I'm not ill.' The fly returned and crawled on her hand. It was hideously soft and intimate. 'But is there plague about this year?'

'I've seen one red cross. But south of the river, Bankside.'

'Judith's been sick again. No, she shows nothing like that. It's this flux that keeps preying on her, and she can't shake it off.'

'Poor creature has been pale lately. Too young for green-sickness, think you? Where is she?'

'Lying down. Edmund's reading to her. He solemnly promised not to leave her even if she fell asleep.'

'Like Hamnet when he was small.' Hamnet had gone through a stage of irrepressible nightmares. Edmund swore to stay up all night and fight them off. And he did it: when Hamnet woke at first light there was Edmund sitting fresh and upright by the bed, saying: *I got them all*. Anne and Will shared a smile of memory: or, at least, both smiled, individually. 'I'll go see her before they come.'

'Who?'

'The sharers. We're meeting here.'

'I didn't know.' She clapped the window shut. 'There'll be eating and drinking, no doubt—'

'We'll be sending out for that, to the Black Bull.'

'I hope it won't turn into a carouse.'

'It won't. We have a quarter's accounts to divide and an inventory to revise.'

'I don't want Judith disturbed.'

'She won't be.'

'Now if it was Matthew who was poorly, clever exceptional Matthew, then it would be a different matter.'

He studied her in deep apparent puzzlement. 'Why are you like this?'

'Like what? A shrew-wife?'

He had an air of someone taking careful aim. 'Not yourself.'

'Who's that? You don't know who I am, Will. Certainly not here. You can't even see me here. I'm like a little dun sparrow in a great tree. Now you, you're showing what a significant man you've become. Was that the whole entire reach of the notion—so that I'd be duly impressed and humbly grateful? You're showing the wrong person, Will. Your father should be here.' She let that sink in. She let it sink in that she was actually saying these things. '*You* should be here, but you're not. Or, at least, you're not with me.' She sat down heavily, faint with heat and candour. 'Will, I want to go home.'

'So I thought. Did it need to be said in such a way?'

'Probably not. I want to go home and take the children. This is not a healthful place in summer. You've told me so.'

'But it's more than that,' he said dully.

'No, no.' *Mop up the blood, let not a spot remain.* 'Forget what I said. I'm sick with heat, and I can't face any more men having great talks, and I simply want to know that I can go home. Soon.'

'You know you can.' He knelt down by her: took her hand, with excessive gentleness, as if she had asked him to look at a wound. 'And you know I have to be here. Is it—would you live here again?'

She shook her head. It might have been the shake that says, *I don't know.* And she really didn't know. Except when she thought of the road, oh, God, that road leading away—she wanted to throw on her cloak and overshoes and start walking now.

'Well. As soon as it can be managed, then. And naturally, if the children will thrive better in the country . . . Anne, I have tried. No good, perhaps. But I have tried—' He stopped. As if refraining, temperate, Will-like, from adding *unlike you.*

*   *   *

Go home? Yes, yes, the children cried. Coming

384

away had been a novelty, now going home would be. Besides, they were missing Grandfather.

And beyond that, they were Anne's children and their loyalty was to her. Susannah, certainly, knew she was unhappy, and had perhaps said something to others. So, take advantage of this loyalty? Exploit it? Oh, yes. People did worse things. The beggar whipped through the streets, his shoulders intricately laced with bright blood. The screaming monkey tied to the bull's back and the dogs set loose on them. She hadn't seen that—Jonson had told her about it—but it was as if she'd seen it. No detail was lacking.

A procession of such memories accompanied her on the ride north. They would fade, no doubt. Will rode with them too, though business would take him straight back to London once they were safe returned. And Edmund, because he had to: though she knew he would willingly have lashed himself to London drawbridge to stay. Harvest-ripe fields shimmered, sky sang blue. The sun pointed out new lights in Judith's hair as she rode before Anne: new roses in her cheeks too, or was that Anne's wishful thinking? A goose-girl plodded, prodding with her stick, scowling up at Anne, and she saw again Betty's husband looming from dark filth. But that would fade, surely. And so, please, God, would her feeling of failure.

She had never guessed at failure's magnificent potency. She had never seen the sea, but on the Thames she had seen great ships bleached and weathered and scarred, with the marks of the sea on them; and when they had taken a boat to Greenwich to see the palace, she had felt the tidal tug under her feet, and had imagined it strengthening and broadening and becoming. Becoming sea: a perfection of horizon, an absolute breadth and depth and power: so much so, it could contain monsters.

That was how failure felt.

So it was surely wrong to feel happy as they came to the Stratford road, and to views that made sudden sense to the eye. Wrong, having failed so profoundly, to feel the spirit lifting like this.

But this was no slinking home: why think it so? The neighbours who came out waving and reaching up, as soon as they were over the bridge, plainly thought no such thing. If anything they seemed a little in awe of Mistress Shakespeare and her brood who had spent a season in London. And at Henley Street there was prodigality of welcome, John Shakespeare all heartiness, embracing, hoisting the children, smiling with glistening eyes—not laughing, for he never quite did—and congratulating.

'You did it, daughter,' he said to her, enfolding her hand. 'It was bravely done.'

And she liked it. Liked being told she was brave and that it was done, finished and achieved. And Judith did seem better at once, unlikely though that seemed: she thundered up and down the stairs as she had never done in London. Which had been, perhaps, after all, one of those long, long dreams that left you exhausted. I have had a dream, past the wit of man to say what dream it was.

It was Will who drew his father aside at last. A reversal: always before that had been John Shakespeare, a great drawer-aside and turner to grave matters. She knew what they were talking of. Well, let it work their peace, if peace there could ever be between them. She wanted to brush out her crumpled clothes, and hear of Joan's health and the price of flour, and devote herself to small things.

Will stayed another day, seeing them settled in, soothing his saddle-sores with goose-grease, and trying to cheer Edmund, who had gone from fire to ashes, gently smiling as he shambled about, hopeless. There were more grave talks apart with his father; once, for a moment, with the sun behind them in the yard-gate, they looked for the first time ever like each other; or, rather, if they were on stage, acting father and son, you would think them convincing. Will still had London in his face, she thought.

Before he left she told him: 'I thought your *Dream* play was beautiful.'

Surprised, he said, 'I'm glad,' and waited.

Surprising herself, she said: 'And I know it's foolish of me, but I don't think somehow such things should be. It's one thing to shine, another to set ourselves up against the sun.'

He inclined his head, respectfully. Alas, to be the victim of Will's respect.

In some buried sea-chamber of her heart she wanted him not to go, and him to know it without her saying, and abandon his travelling-cloak and London and eminence, and just stay.

He put on his travelling-cloak.

She said: 'I hope Matthew will do well.' The sun was strong, and squinting up she could hardly see him. When the kiss came, it was like a touch in the dark, making her jump. His beard was less soft, more wiry: older. Will was past thirty now. It seemed to her that they should have stopped time, somehow, between them: that they had had an opportunity and lost it. 'Have a care for thy purse, and drink no water.'

He laughed softly. 'My heart with thee.'

So, Will left again for London. And so, Will was not there two days later, when Hamnet said in the middle of dinner, 'Pray you, I feel faint,' tried to leave the table, and slithered down to the floor.

*   *   *

It begins with the plague: does it end so? The doctor is unsure at first. He doesn't find the swellings, the buboes, but it's hard to investigate when Hamnet is in such a high and frantic fever. A well-grown eleven-year-old is not easily restrained, even with Grandfather on one side and Edmund on the other. And Anne, on the other side of the round earth, reaching hopelessly for him and screaming inside, even as she puts the cold wet cloth to his fiery tossing head.

The plague: yes, when there is a short intermission of fever, the doctor finds the signs. There it is, alas. He has come a long way on a broken-winded nag, and has no magic. Where has the lad been lately? Where might he have taken the infection? Ah. Not that there is any telling whence, nor whither. We must pray to God. He's young and strong. There is always hope.

There is always hope, but not when your child is blind with agony and his skin is turning black.

Outraged, Anne holds him, holds him. At the crisis she lies down beside him, as best she can, to wrap herself around him, contain his whimpering heat. Vividly present to her is the birth of her twins, a long, painful peril crowned with triumph, the two sweetly raging faces brought to her breast.

But, of course, if that happened, if that birth was so momentously achieved, then it can't end with this: it makes no kind of sense. She clutches Hamnet to her, all along her body, and even though he doesn't know her, doesn't know anything, she holds on. It is her mother-in-law who tugs and coaxes her away at last, when there is no longer any hoping or denying or pretending.

*   *   *

It is impossible to say that London killed Hamnet. But Anne knows that it must be on her face when Will arrives, summoned by letter but still a week too late: so she may as well use words, too.

'We should never have gone. Before that, Hamnet was never ill. We should have stayed here.'

He seems to accept that, at least. He is stiff, ashen, and slow-moving. A footpad could despatch him in a moment, she thinks.

But, then, where is the fault to be found? It lies somewhere in that great space between them, as they stand by the fresh lively earth of Hamnet's grave. They touch fingers across the space, but distance renders them cold and inert. Such distance.

He wasn't here. Somehow that's what she cannot get over. He left her alone to face their son dying. Oh, not alone, not literally: Joan is kind and strong, Edmund tries, Father John masters his grief to attend to hers. Even Bartholomew comes over to place an awkward arm around her stiff shoulders. And Susannah and Judith are as good as children can be in such circumstances. But this is the bitter revelation: that with all this, still without Will, she considers herself alone. It's like some debt that can never be repaid, no matter how much money you have.

'You weren't here,' she says to him dully.

'No. Tell me all.'

She can't, but she tells some of it. He listens. Weeps. He speaks of their son, his life. Inevitably there are gaps. But he speaks beautifully. He speaks as only Will can.

However, that's no good. Anne has a new knowledge: that no amount of beauty can make up for this, ever; that no conceivable Heaven can atone for one pinch of Hell.

He wasn't here to see his son dying. He is here, perhaps, to see something else weaken, fail, begin to die, or cease to have a reason to live.

*   *   *

The letter arrives in October, when there has been no Hamnet for two months, and a dank spoiled harvest lies thin in the barns.

Never a quick reader, and growing dim-sighted, John Shakespeare hands it to his dutiful son Richard. It's from Will, of course. And at first Anne, listening fitfully to Richard's monotone growl through the wool of grief, can't quite understand it.

'"Faithful and approved service . . . Gold on a bend sable, a spear of the first, steeled argent, and for his crest or cognisance . . ."'

Her father-in-law has risen from his fireside seat as if to do something—one of those little fidgets or dustings that occupy so much of his day—but instead he stands quite still, hands extended, eyes open wide and lit as she has never seen them before.

' "Motto, *Non Sans Droict*, meaning Not Without Right. The arms to be borne by his children, issue, and posterity . . ." ' Richard glances awkwardly at Anne as he reads that part. She is taking it in now. The Shakespeare grant of arms, it seems, is made. No Hamnet to carry it on, of course. Yesterday a maimed beggar came through Stratford when she was marketing, and held up the stump of his arm beseechingly, and she looked at it thinking, Yes, what?

'Well, well. What think you?' Her father-in-law glances unsteadily around him, balancing and trembling a little, as if he stands atop a high pillar. 'What think you, hey?'

It's Edmund who speaks: given, at long last, the chance to say the right thing to his father. 'Sir, you are made a gentleman,' he says, bowing, 'and it is richly deserved.'

'Aye, aye. May it be so. Edmund, heart, go fetch thy mother, she must hear of this. Well, well.' His eye falls on Anne. 'You must be proud, daughter.'

She wants to ask: of whom? But she can't speak, or the effort of speaking is beyond her.

No matter: John Shakespeare is happy to repeat it, like a prayer, or an order. 'You must be proud.' At last he moves, stepping away from his perennial fire, going to the window that looks out on Henley Street. 'Fair weather for the season.' Outside, grey cloud lowers. 'Ought to take advantage of it. Go about a little. Aye, time to go about.'

So, Anne thinks, Will has won him. So he goes on winning everyone. I wonder how he will ever win me again.

12

The Broken Heart (1598–1601)

'How did you come here, my son?'

Ben shook off the intrusively gentle hand. He had been trying to float his mind on the placid, lucid waters of the ancients, to meditate on the stoicism of Epictetus. But this wretched priest would not leave him alone.

'I'm not your son. You're scarce older than me, for one thing.' That in itself gave away that the fellow was a priest—but he had besides a milk-fed look Ben associated with papists. 'As for how I came here, by the same gate as you. And I dare say I'm going to the same place.'

'There I differ,' was all the priest said, with a smile of peculiar sweetness.

The smile stayed with Ben when he rolled up in his bedding and tried again to steep his mind in philosophy. Such a smile seemed out of place not only in Newgate: it was, surely, out of place in the world. Or at least the world as he knew it.

The priest was back in irons, he noted, peering down the long dungeon room: incarceration here had given him the night-eyes of a cat. Doubtless he had run out of garnish money, or of friends outside to bring it. Ben was lucky in that regard. He had Agnes, and she made sure there was enough to keep him out of irons, fed and warm. Not that she liked coming near the prison, which he understood, what with the danger of gaol-fever, and little Ben, his son and heir, at home. Also she said she would never forgive him for putting himself here, and possibly on the gallows: but, there, that was women. They didn't use words to convey information, but to create an emotional effect.

He listened for a few moments to the noise of Newgate, which for most of the time he managed to block out of his consciousness, as he had at nights in Flanders when dying horses had bellowed long. Nothing edifying: drunken shouts from the tap-room, distracted rattling of chains, curses. Somewhere a woman repeatedly threw herself against a door and screeched: 'I'm with child, I'm with child.' The condemned cells? Hard to tell the direction with the echoes. Pleading her belly, obviously, but it didn't seem to be working. Perhaps she was pretending. She must have been ugly indeed if none of the gaolers would impregnate her.

In all the racket and stink the priest was the only one, apart from Ben, who seemed self-possessed.

The thought that the priest knew something he didn't was, to Ben, infuriating. Even here in Newgate, Ben Jonson maintained his pride, his sense of himself: he wore the inviolate crown of his mind. And, after all, why not? He had done nothing wrong.

To be sure, he had killed a man. But under such circumstances as made it forgivable, surely. Well, there was the question. On that—apt pun— everything was to hang.

He saw the priest doing it to another prisoner: the hand on the arm, the enquiring look. The prisoner was an incoherent bull-neck who had sold everything, even his shoes, for drink, and he flung the priest away to the length of his chain.

'Why do you keep it up?' Ben asked him, in

genuine curiosity. 'You know they'll hang you for it.'

'Probably. Or burn. But keep up what, my friend? You speak of the faith as if it were a trick or a habit. Burning: it's already a burning.' The priest shifted on his mouldy straw. 'Can you imagine waking each morning and thinking not, Oh, well, another day, but instead——' he gave a gasp of difficulty, smiling '——greeting the ineffable mystery: again, the ineffable, ever-renewed mystery of living with God and for God through his grace and his holy church?'

Ben scowled as the drunken brute lay down on his bunk with his hand groping in the front of his breeches. 'This faculty is not given to all men, I take it.'

The priest delicately inclined his head; the gesture seemed to include all sorts of possibilities, including amusement. These subtleties. Quite different from your slab-faced Puritan, at any rate.

'Perhaps. That is one of the many things that are hidden. We guess at the divine shadows as they flicker. But you recall my asking why you are here. It's because I have, I think, an answer. Mother Church has been waiting for you.'

'I need no mother,' Ben said quickly. 'I have one. I have the most excellent one.'

'And do you have a God?'

Ben shrugged irritably. 'You want to convert me to your faith, and it would be a deal less tedious if you just said so.'

'No, it wouldn't, because I can't do that. You can only come to it through your free will and the operation of grace.' The priest began to unwrap and tend his fetter-sores. 'I merely add: don't keep

394

God waiting.'

Oh, they had trained him well in Douai, or wherever it was. But it was lucky for the priest that Ben's curiosity overcame his disgust. And then there was the tremendous potency of that idea: of God waiting for him.

He thought about Agnes, a little; about his splendid son, a lot. He thought about lying here, a common felon, waiting for the trial where his greatest hope was to escape with his life. He hated the idea of being common and he hated the waiting, with its corollary of humble obedience. To be waited for, on the other hand, was impressive.

Also, he wanted to match this priest in lack of fear: measure himself against him, as he had the Spanish champion in the damp field.

Also, if they were going to kill the most brilliant man in England, he might as well *feel* his difference in every vein.

'I don't say anything of conversion.' He gave the priest a drink from his ale-jug and the heel of his bread. 'But if you were to hear my confession, what sort of step would that be?'

'A step.' The priest smiled wryly, as if to say he was the casuist here.

*   *   *

Very well. The confession of Ben Jonson. You should know first who I am. I am a poet of the theatre. I have been player, play-corrector, maker of play-plots, part-writer of plays with lesser men, and lately play-maker in my own right. And in that regard, I may as well say I am the best. There are one or two very choice spirits writing for the stage just now, but none who know what they are about as I do, none who comprehend the importance of classical models, of making a play exercise the intellect and not the jaws. And so I find it hard to believe that this is to be my end, unless there be some greater meaning overarching all.

I don't turn to you or your church out of fear. I'm no stranger to prison, to begin with. It's scarce above a year since they clapped me in irons for writing a play. Part-writing, that is. It was writ with Tom Nashe, an odd flighting fellow who can scarce pick up a pen without mischief. We made some glances at the Court, and Nashe may have spiced it with some slanders I didn't recognise. He escaped to Yarmouth when the Privy Council stirred, but me they took up and threw in the Marshalsea. Oh, the storm blew over, and I was let go; and the Crown must be protected from sedition, after all. You'll not convert me against my country, sir priest, I may as well say now.

When it happened—what put me here—I was at the top of the tree. My play was on, my first, if I may style it so, master-work. *Every Man In His Humour*. The first comedy to grace our stage that truly observes the model of the ancients and the requirement of comedy to *teach* and *reform* even as it delights. This purpose: this is what's lacking in my friend Will Shakespeare. Still, I love the man and his works, mark you—love them all the more for their frailties, which is how I imagine the love of God for humankind.

And it was Will Shakespeare who gave me my opportunity. Without him, I truly confess it, I might still have been patching broken plays for that titanic dullwit Henslowe. Or tramping the roads by the play-wagon. Not my taste. True, I was not the greatest of players. Oh, I had *presence*—perhaps too much of it. A player is only an imitating ape, after all. No, the writing for me, the handling of words, the shaping and constructing. And shaping to a moral purpose, to show humanity its true face in the glass. So my play, on these humours that men affect nowadays—one is forever jealous, another is forever melancholy. My fear was, in the writing, that I would write too far above the heads of our dear necessary Hydra, the audience. All those heads and no brain betwixt them. And Henslowe, the idiot I mentioned, shook his wooden poll over it. It was my good friend Shakespeare who saw its worth, and persuaded his company, the Chamberlain's Men, to put it on. Praise be! Come September, the piece was mounted at the Curtain—and I found myself the very ornament of the stage, the cynosure of the season, the North Star of the theatrical constellation. The booby groundlings clapped their paws; but the learned, I believe, smiled the truer approbation. I mean to have it printed, if God wills.

And from there—to here. The bills were still up for my play when I was placed under arrest. It all happened mighty fast. Yet the moment—the killing moment—seemed to endure an age. I fancy I still live in it yet, sometimes.

His name was Gabriel Spencer and he was a player. Not so long ago we were friends, of a sort. He was a good companion when the ale was good and his temper was good and no one set their voice against his. But there was a black side to him. I know that he once killed a young fellow in a fight, because he would make a brag of it, of how it was

397

deemed mischance and he was set free. Well, here is my fault, I think: being too high in my pride of spirits, from seeing my play triumph, and giving them free rein when Spencer was present and with the worst mood on him.

I was dining with a few acquaintance at a tavern in Hog's Lane, and Spencer joined us. The thunder on his brow should have cautioned me, but I was warm and over-easy. I spoke of the reform I meant to bring to the stage, and how I was particularly well equipped to do it. I learned of the great William Camden, no less. Well: it turned ugly. Spencer began casting doubt on my learning. Oh, this was easily crushed, I was able to quote him quite out of his senses. But then any sensible man would have conceded and drank about. Spencer must needs hang on like a dog with its teeth in the bear's hide. '*Malgré* all this parade of learning,' he cries, 'you're a mere player like the rest of us, and when your day is done, you will be glad enough to turn back to the honest trade you forsook to exhibit your abominable pride among us. And, my God, we shall be glad too. So to your tools, sir bricklayer, to your tools . . .' Forgive me, I have a capacious memory, and so I give it you verbatim.

A bricklayer, yes, that was the hateful craft I was bred to. A very good, honest craft, I dare say, for nature's bricklayers. Of whom I am not one. And so I said to Spencer—in so many words. But naturally there was no forgiving the insult he offered me. Nor would he withdraw it. So we came to a duel. A true fair duel with rapiers, none of this ragged drawing of weapons in the street.

We met in Hogsden Fields. It was a beautiful day: clear, warm, golden September. No day to be contemplating a killing or a dying. At the last, for all the foulness of his disposition, I fancy Spencer thought it so, and wondered about recanting. Me? No. Not for a moment. Never for a moment.

He wounded me in the arm—there, see. Thank God, it healed clean. He was a fierce fighter. I could see the fury in his eyes. What he saw in my eyes—well, the righteousness of a man traduced.

His reach was longer, but I made a stroke, a bold wild stroke, beneath his guard. And that was the one. It went deep into his side. It does not slice in, like carving meat. Even with the keenest point it feels more like thrusting your sword into something tough and jarring. Your whole neck and chest and shoulder ache at it.

It was the matter of the bricklayer, you see. And disdaining my learning. My stepfather is a bricklayer and I have striven, dear God, I have striven . . . Do I need to explain? I hope not.

Absolution? Well. I like the sound of it. The very word is like a cleaning blast of water. But we'll see.

Well, I was taken up. A man lay dying and mine was the red sword, and these things get about. A duel, but still a killing. Will the court find it murder? There's the question. Is murder an unclergyable offence? For if I plead benefit of clergy . . . Once I remember saying a man must be a coward to take advantage of this quaint old letter of the law, letting him 'scape hanging if he can read. Yet now it is my one hope.

In this world, I mean. As for the next, is that not your province? Repentance, aye, I understand there must be repentance. But tell me, where is the line drawn betwixt regretting your sins, and wishing you had never committed them?

Spencer had no wife or child, or none that I know of. But nothing could have made a difference. Nothing, after what he said.

Kneel?

Well. If you think it will help.

*   *   *

If anything saved him, he knew it would be learning. When the day of the gaol-delivery came, and he was marched across the incongruously pretty garden to the courtroom in Old Bailey, he knew he was going among enemies. The judge on high with the bunch of sweet herbs before his tender nose, the citizen jurymen blowing and staring: in the purest sense they did not care about him, and would willingly send him to be hanged, if nothing cried out against it. He was not Ben Jonson the most learned man in England here, but Benjamin Jonson the prisoner. The prisoner was taken up with the weapon still at his side. The prisoner stands accused . . . the prisoner admits . . . He wanted to cry out, *There is more to me than this*. But here, of course, there was not. And there was nothing he could say or do that would change their minds. The guard behind him yawned and shifted the weight of his halberd. Dust-motes rotated in a thin shaft of window-light. Ben tried to see God in it. Only learning could help.

'The aforesaid Benjamin Jonson feloniously and wilfully slew and killed the aforesaid Gabriel Spencer at Shoreditch.' The judge repeated it, though the juryman had a good strong voice, suitable for a theatre. 'Prisoner, how do you plead?'

'I plead benefit of clergy.' Now there was a voice for you. Fill your chest, expand your lungs. If the judge did not allow it—if books were consulted, precedents reviewed, heads shaken, then—then it would be very much like the dreams that had exhausted him the last few nights in his cell, dreams so brilliant and dramatic he had begun to mistrust the power of his own imagination. And so to Tyburn tree to dangle. They would need a strong rope. I am not afraid. But how did I get here? Sure never was so long a chain of mad mistakes . . .

The bishop's chaplain walked up to the dock. Ben took the psalter. It felt greasy in his hands, as if it had propped someone's dinner. It was salvation. Earthly, perhaps heavenly, but just now he had his mind only on the one.

'Choose your verse, prisoner.'

Verse? Let me give you the whole thing, first in Latin, then in Greek . . . He chose, and read with eloquent expression, fixing the chief juryman's eye. On impulse he kissed the book when he had finished.

'*Legit ut clericus*?' intoned the judge.

'*Legit*.' Read like a clerk. And so his plea was accepted. He tried to picture Agnes's face, or his little son's curly head, but all he could think of was great tall windows opening out. And the subtle smile of the old priest in his cell. Well, he thought: a bargain. The tears in his eyes surprised him intensely.

But then they did duty for what happened next, which was the branding. He had a little dealing with the hangman after all. And an ungentle brute he was, though Ben supposed that was part of the profession. Marched up to the brazier, which gave off a kindly Christmas sort of heat, he clenched his tongue between his teeth and resolved not to cry out. To his embarrassment, he did groan a little when the brand went sizzling into the base of his left thumb. Not just the pain but the nakedness of that letter T, marking him as a felon, marking him for Tyburn tree if he offended again. No benefit of clergy twice. He belonged to death, if he were not virtuous, and he hated belonging to anyone.

But he had survived. Marched back to the gaol, Ben wondered if there was anything he could not survive. That was the sin of pride, perhaps: he would have to find out from a priest of his new faith. Or perhaps consult his own understanding. The True Church had undoubtedly been waiting for him, but he intended being his own pope.

*　　　*　　　*

Ben held his son high, up to the rafters of their poky parlour: the lad crowed, he loved it, the higher the better. 'Oh, my chick, I love thee,' he said. He looked at Agnes, who had finished her relieved crying, and was sitting at the table, head in hands. 'And thee, sweetling.' The cloth was gone, he noted, and a few pieces of plate—pawned, doubtless, for the gaoler's fees had been heavy and they were short of money. He put little Ben down. Best get to work.

'Never,' his wife said, raising her stormy face, 'never put me through such a thing again.'

She actually looked fiercely accusing. He shrugged. Anyone would suppose, he thought, as he began looking for paper, that she was the one who had been in prison.

*　　　*　　　*

'The whole thing,' Will says, 'has seemed to me a terrible marvel. One moment I'm acting in your play; the next I hear you are marked for the gallows.'

'Why are we mortals so surprised when life takes a turn for the unexpected, when we cannot even tell what tomorrow's weather will be?'

'It will be cold, because it's January.'

Jonson laughs. 'Don't tell me you've never wanted to kill a man.'

'Oh, faith, that goes without saying.' They are coming out of the turreted lodge of the Marshalsea prison, where Jonson was thrown for a debt to another actor. Will has paid it off. Jonson looks pale but hearty. 'Will you promise me now to keep your head out of gaol for at least half a year?'

'Hm, that would be making an impious declaration against the will of God, which may be that I should suffer the martyrdom of the cell again. But no. For the love I bear thee, Will, I make thee a promise. Besides, there will be nothing worth presented on the stages so long as I'm out of commission.'

Freezing new year 1599. Harsh winters following lean harvests: full boneyards. But Will Shakespeare is still prosperous, if at something of a stand in his career just now. The Chamberlain's Men are without their usual home, the Theatre, the lease having run out on the land. In fact, the Burbages do have the substance of the Theatre, because they took down every timber and strut and tile of it in the winter dark and are ready to put it up again when they can find a site. In Southwark probably, where Will is living now, modestly. Giving up the large house in Bishopsgate has been a saving. (And, of course, it was imperative. He won't even

403

walk that way now.) Southwark, place of stews and actors, bear-gardens and prisons. A terrible marvel, Will called what happened to Ben Jonson, or rather what Ben Jonson inflicted: and he has hardly conveyed to his friend just how terrible he found it. It was Henslowe who first told him of it. 'Yon bricklayer has killed one of my best players,' he grumbled; and no one suitable to poach from the Chamberlain's.

At first Will suspected a theatrical exaggeration: not actual killing. When he heard about the brute scene in Hogsden Fields he had no trouble in imagining it—old imperishable memories of Knell and Towne rushed in there—but could not explain it. The waste, the waste: and Jonson just on the verge of great things with his play. There was a madness in men, one always knew that; but the madness of self-destruction was the most baffling.

And then, when Jonson was delivered from peril of his life by the fortunate accident of the neck-verse, he announced to his friends on his release that he had become a Catholic. Nashe was quietly scornful. 'Pray don't pay him too much attention on account of it,' he said, with vinegar smile, 'for that's all the reason of his conversion.' Will thought there was more to it. There must be, for a man to lay himself open to charges of recusancy, to lay up trouble for himself as a potential enemy of the state; and all for what? But he could hardly take up that question without exposing himself to Jonson's eager cross-questioning; and in himself he had dusky vacancies and gaps on which he wanted no searching light to fall.

When, three months after his escape from the

gallows, Jonson was taken up for debt, it seemed to Will almost a comforting piece of normality. And now he is free, and no doubt will want to rejoin his family in Westminster.

'Time enough for that. I worked on a new plot for Henslowe whiles I was detained, a neat piece of Terence brought up to date, and you might like to hear it through over a glass. Oh, Henslowe will forgive, man, because Henslowe, like most mortals, is made of self-interest, and I am useful to him.'

So, the Mermaid instead. Boat across the river, Jonson leaping the wharf-stairs three at a time. Such energy and appetite. Thrusting into the city streets, Jonson begins telling him at length of his plans for a sequel to *Every Man In His Humour*, in which he will set out his theories of the drama in a prologue or preface.

'And after the prologue or preface, will you have a trumpet-blast to let the audience know it's time to wake up?'

'A low hit. Unworthy,' Jonson says, seating himself at ease. The Mermaid features broad settles and stools, apt for his behind, which, unthinned by prison, is like a bag of laundry. 'You must buy me a drink to atone.'

They are joined by Thomas Dekker. Three parts ink and one part wine, a Londoner born and bred, with a sharp, dark, winking face and shoulders up to his ears, Dekker has lately begun pulling at the galley-oar of play-writing: a scene here, a rewriting there, wherever I am wanted. It is his boast that he was once woken by Henslowe at three in the morning with a mere play-plot, and he had the first two acts ready before noon. Will likes him, for his modesty and the earthy liveliness he brings to his writing; Jonson condescends to him. They make a sort of triangle.

Dekker shudders at the mention of the Marshalsea. 'Don't, I pray you. I've been in the rough belly of the debtors' prison. I don't care to be swallowed again.'

'Why, talking of it won't make it happen,' Jonson says.

'Won't it? As to that, I don't know. Observe how you come across a new word for the first time. Ten to one you will hear that word again within a few days.'

'What's your meaning? That mere superstition should govern our lives?'

'I'm content for anything to govern our lives, as long as it be kind,' Dekker says, with a placating shrug.

'Why, man, who would ever feel alive without adversity? Who feels the merry fire who's never starved in the cold?'

'Is this your priest's chop-logic?' says Will.

'You pale puerile Puritan. You have not opened yourself to the mystery of the faith.'

'A mystery that will land you with a fine,' says Dekker, 'or worse.'

'If you keep quiet about it you may still do pretty well,' Will says. 'The Queen said she wanted no windows into men's souls.'

'Quiet?' Jonson booms. 'Why should I be quiet?'

'Or how, indeed? It seems scarce a possibility,' Will says.

Dekker shakes his head. 'I don't understand a man's laying up trouble for himself.'

'Oh, you follow this fellow's lead, hey?' Jonson says, slapping Will's shoulder. 'Anything to be

406

liked.'

'Yes, I want to be liked,' Dekker says. 'For myself not so much, for my work certainly, I want to be popular. Who wouldn't?'

'But at what price, man?' Jonson says impatiently. 'If you write for apes you must write like an ape.'

'But bating all flattery, Will doesn't write like an ape, and he is popular,' Dekker says, with a look both innocent and shrewd. 'So how do you account for it, grave Master Jonson?'

Jonson twitches his shoulders in irritation. 'I need more drink if I'm to bear this nonsense. Besides, you're thinking of retiring from it, aren't you? The house in the country. Setting up a future, clovered, away from all this, isn't that in your mind?'

'No. I've never thought of that,' says Will, hastily: too hastily. 'The house is for my family. The money invested for their future. But I'm devoted whole-heart to the Chamberlain's Men. When they raise the new theatre I shall be with them. If the pale puerile Puritans allow.'

'Though at least they're zealous in what they believe,' Jonson says, eyeing him.

Will signals for more ale. 'Now why would Ben Jonson, a man of reason, a man who never prated of religion before, join the papists? Could it be he must have a stick to beat the world with, even when it is not at odds with him?'

Jonson does not answer until the jug is refilled, and then he speaks, quite temperately for him. 'You may be in the right of it, my friend. But it would be good to see you take up any sort of stick, for once.' And from the grave Will hears Robert

Greene enquiring, just as temperately, just as sharply: *When are you going to live?*

*   *   *

The years: when you were young, they were like great rooms. You entered each one with attentive solemnity, you looked all round it, accustomed yourself to its dimensions, its furnishings, the feeling in its air. You were going to spend some time here.

That was how it used to be, for Will. Now time has changed its manner of living: turned nomad. Now he's out in the open, and there are no thresholds, and he moves on without quite knowing how far he has gone. The years are invisible. Except when you look in the mirror and think, I've slept and woken and missed something; or find an old grief or joy, thin and reproachful, like a tethered beast you forgot to feed.

It is Matthew who reminds Will most forcefully of his ageing. A magical being, with his shooting growth, his transformations. Will watches in troubled admiration and tenderness, trying to locate his feeling. Fatherly? Ah, but that shouldn't be. Not after Hamnet. When he revisits that place in the heart, there is so much grey ash, he can hardly move, staggering and choked. Better to put yourself in this, this living world, this professional world where he works on bringing out Matthew's gift. The youth has all and more of the ability he once had to lose his self in playing. Even, above all, his sex.

'"Come, woo me, woo me; for now I am in a holiday humour, and like enough to consent." So?'

'Excellent,' Will says. 'All simplicity. As simple

408

as a woman disguised as a man pretending to be a woman can be.'

Matthew laughs and rubs at his corn-fair hair. 'Thank God for the disguise part. I swear the Rosalind wig is lousy.'

'Do you ever have trouble remembering the real you?'

'Remember? There's no past in it. I am whoever I am at that moment,' Matthew says. 'You must know that.'

'Must I?' Watching Matthew sit bonelessly, painlessly, on the boards, Will feels as old as the rocks.

'Yes. You taught me it.'

Sometimes there seems to Will something almost cruel about Matthew's luminous gentleness, like the sure-handed care of a good butcher. Sometimes he imagines Matthew has a twin, who is unteachable and awkward and dark.

'"Men have died from time to time, and worms have eaten them, but not for love."' Again that shining, cheerful simplicity, as if life is indeed a garden, with nothing at its edges but ivied kindly walls.

Will writes home, enquiring about wool prices.

*   *   *

New Place.

This is the house in Stratford that Will buys for his family to live in. The house that says to the town, Look at what Will Shakespeare's strange scheme has wrought; and says to his father, simply, Look: we are restored.

It is the second biggest house in the town, built

409

by the eminent Stratfordian Hugh Clopton who also took the south road to make his fortune in London, and ended up Lord Mayor. It stands on the corner of Chapel Street, three sides around a courtyard: as big, Anne thinks, as many a whole street in London. Needing a great deal of work when Will makes the purchase—but the work can be done, there is money for that too.

'Ten fireplaces,' murmurs Judith Sadler, when she and her husband make their first tour of it, when the builders are still hammering and sawing. 'Count them. Ten fireplaces, husband.'

'Aye, heart. So you can warm your backside wherever you find yourself,' says Hamnet Sadler, with his little apologetic, unhappy laugh.

New Place, being made new for Anne, for Susannah and Judith and, of course, for Will whenever he is home. Which will surely be, in time, more and more, else why fix himself in Stratford so grandly? And perhaps something else is embodied in these stripped panels, clear-glazed windows, barn and stable and buttery: something like a new start. New Place, and this new place they have come to in their marriage, their lives.

A place of ultimate division.

The absence of Hamnet is the absence between them, of understanding, of warmth. She cannot forgive Will for Hamnet's death. Cannot forgive him for living on, acting, making plays, making money, instead of being swallowed up by that death as she is. And she cannot forgive herself—for these things, and for looking at her husband, when he's home, and thinking: Why can't I have my son instead of you, when you're no good to me, and we can't love each other worth a farthing, love

410

each other in a way that changes things? Surely the only true love: spell-love. And if you had said to her, 'You want something from Will that will bring Hamnet back, or make up for his death, and that's impossible,' she would have said, 'Yes, that's what I want, exactly.'

The years, for Anne: she is not like Will, she has never moved neatly through them. She has always drunk time and dipped in and out of it, flowing, and sometimes she couldn't breathe for it, sometimes it exhausted her, but always she has been of its element. Now it pushes her, the years, the days, like a constant head wind. She wouldn't be surprised to hear herself talking and walking backwards. Often, quite coolly, she supposes she will go mad.

Once she approached the ultimate madness. She woke from a dream of Hamnet so real that it was unbearable, simply, to return to the life where he was not. It was before the move to New Place. She woke and went into Susannah and Judith's bedchamber. Sleeping, they were so beautiful, characterful, perfect. And yet. And yet it wasn't enough. So she realised a terrible thing: that there was a limit to happiness, but no limit to suffering. So she went downstairs. The household was asleep, though it was at least two hours before midnight she reckoned: early to bed in John Shakespeare's house. Quietly she unbarred the door and went out.

It was summer, you see. He died in the summer, among the heat and the green. And here was summer breathing its choicest. Brought up on a farm, Anne lived in as close relation to the sun as pears on a wall. Familiar, that sensation of lengthening days, the light of evening persisting so long and light of morning appearing so early they left only a sliver of night between them. Going out of Stratford she found the world brimming with light. Always before, summer had had the feeling of life announcing something. Now it was mute. Oh, she had never known till now what silence was; how silence, through the long waning of the afternoon, could seem in its accumulated weight and profundity to be on the verge of an utterance. The living summer was dead. The sky was still lit, there was a running sparkle on the river, trees washed their reflections. Movement in the branches, some spirit abroad, perhaps. *Give me that boy and I will go with thee . . . Not for thy fairy kingdom.* Anne stood on the bridge looking around, looking down. Beauty. She looked at it like a patient parent with a child's drawing. A long dry moan came from her. She already knew she would not climb up and leap. She was too afraid—afraid perhaps that what lay at the bottom of the river might be the same intolerable dream. No choice but to be.

So she returned, through a landscape still at eleven o'clock seething with rose-stained shadows; and for the first time she realised that today was the longest day of the year.

New places. After Hamnet's death, Will gave up the big London house, and took modest lodgings near the theatres. Unspoken, that there would be no more London household. Instead, this, with its ten fireplaces.

'The handsomest property in the town,' John Shakespeare said. 'He has done well, daughter. We— Certainly he has done well.'

He gives you this, Anne thinks, the first time she walks around her new home-to-be, in return for what he takes away.

'You expect too much of marriage,' Judith Sadler told her. She seemed to grow more snappily scornful of Hamnet as he grew gentler, more thoughtful, even handsomer with age. 'It's a matter of shaking down with the fellow, and then be sure of your family well placed, and all the rest is flummery.'

You didn't have to tell Anne that, though: she knew it perfectly, intimately, as you know your supreme folly.

'You'll not be minded to move in until the work's finished, I think,' Will said, as they stood in the courtyard, surrounded by New Place, and their usual dead, tingling air.

'Well. We could. It's habitable. The children want to move in now.'

'Hm. Children always think they know what they want.'

'And then they grow up, and cease knowing.'

Soon, she thought, we won't say *the children*. Instead we'll say *the girls*. And that will be Hamnet dead once more. Discovery: you never stop losing a child. Not worth trying to say, though, across this crippled air.

So she and the children, the girls, moved in while the house was still half repaired, and Will went back to London, leaving her in charge. Bartholomew expected her to be helplessly at the mercy of builders and tradesmen. 'I won't be imposed on,' she told him, noticing the broken veins on his nose. 'Once, I might have been.' But unhappiness of this kind, it seemed, was a great simplifier. Large areas of life now had no power against her. Anne directed the renovations, reckoned up day-wages and costs, and even tore up floorboards herself when it was going too slowly for her.

A new place, living apart for the first time—so it seems—from John Shakespeare. So, freedom, in all its complexity. No longer the ally at her side, fighting her cause. And yet that Father John, her champion against the giant trampling dreams of Will, is fading, almost gone. See him instead walking about New Place, measuring its capacious rooms with a bright, wondering eye: and then see him walk on down the street, slow and steady in the sunshine, lifting a hand in sober greeting here and there. Master Shakespeare. Good sir, your servant. On his way to the council chamber, where he has resumed his place, his so rightful place. New place: where he is not just John Shakespeare, alderman, but John Shakespeare, gentleman.

She can't begrudge him the happiness he carries so reverently. Especially when it's Will who has given it to him. Will has won his father's heart. She only glimpses how much that means to Will, though a glimpse can be revealing.

Did I ever have him? She does wonder. When he is so many-sided: when he can be the man who made that beauty, more tuneable than lark to shepherd's ear, when wheat is green, when hawthorn buds appear; and at the same time the man who bought New Place, at a good shrewd price, talks of malt and wool with his father. Suspicion that she had only one of his sides, as lover, wife, and it happened to be turned to her for an unusual length of time; and now, the infinite diamond of him has turned again.

Meanwhile, as it were incidentally, she is becoming the most significant woman in Stratford. Though when Joan tells her so, she shouts with laughter.

'Well, mirth apart, Mistress Quiney speaks of you with envy dripping from her chops. All the town ladies do, and I know 'em, trust me, for they forget to pretend before me.'

Joan is preparing to marry. At last, as the god-sibs doubtless say. William Hart is a hatter, plump, agreeable, eyebrows perpetually raised in admiration of everything Joan does and says. Flattering, Anne suggests.

'Oh, I dare say. Yes, he'll do very well. We laugh. We do laugh, which is a blessing. But, Lord, I don't want to put my whole life in his hands. And the bed matter, that's as rank and tedious as it sounds, is it?'

'I don't know what to say,' Anne says: matron, still thinking like a maiden.

'I hope it doesn't take you away from yourself. I said to my lord there——' a jerk of the thumb, as if Hart is always present '—I told him we must have two sides of the hearth. Me here, you there.'

'A relief,' Bartholomew says, 'for Master Shakespeare to get her off his hands at last.'

'Yes. And she didn't get with child first, unlike me.'

'Did you?' He looks blank for a moment. 'To be sure. Somehow I'd forgot that.'

Oh, dry, crackling woman. I shall cultivate this part of myself, perhaps: the sharp tongue, tart as capers. It gives a woman an occupation. Though in truth she has plenty to do. Reluctantly she accepts that Joan is right about her significance, as she settles into New Place, becomes its chatelaine. Many things to take charge of, and Will entrusts them all to her. Money apportioned, difficult letters construed: the rest I leave to you, heart. Perfect trust there, at any rate. She is good. Sets the new outhouses working, brings in willing young girls, so there are butter and eggs and yarn for the market. People are beginning to think of her as a solution: when a beggar comes into the parish with a doubtful pass, when a maid claims a pregnancy, they say, 'Let's send to Mistress Shakespeare, see what she thinks.'

So, a good thing, this New Place. And consider, after all the money and time he has put into it, surely New Place says, 'This is my place, our place, here I root myself. Here is my heart.'

Except, no. When his bones are too old to mount a stage, perhaps, his fingers too weak to hold a pen. In the meantime, it is a huge golden apology, a magnificent regret of stone.

He is home for Joan's marriage. He makes handsome bride-gifts, and seems preoccupied. Anne still understands him. It's Susannah, who is of marriageable age. The years. Susannah sees it, too, in his watchful, wistful look. 'Now, Father, be of good cheer, you'll not need to make me a dowry just yet.' He smiles as she cuffs him. This easy mocking affection, exclusive to them. Judith, since Hamnet's death, has been both quieter and more noisy. She seems to be trying to find a personality that fits her. Sometimes in the night she comes wet-faced and curls up in bed beside Anne.

'Our daughter is almost a woman,' Will says, as they make their way to the church.

Anne looks at Susannah, wand-like, serene: and Judith, her hair for once coiffed and presentable, trying to copy her walk. 'And our other daughter is almost a girl.'

416

They laugh, a little. Fond parental jesting can only go so far; and then it comes to the brink, the chasm of Hamnet.

'How does Matthew? A quick learner still?'

'He's gone beyond me, now. I learn from him.'

She is close enough still to feel a little irritated by this.

'The Chamberlain's Men will do well if they can keep him. We need our permanent theatre. Our Globe. That's how the Burbages think to call our new place, when it's finished.'

'Why?'

'Oh, it has a fine grand sound. And then, besides, all the world will be there.'

'For you, it will,' she says, deadening. Lack of love is a miraculous marvel: a loaf that never runs out.

Very well, she thinks, when he goes back to London, this is my new place: here I have been set loose to graze, and so I will. Peacefully, I hope. Not like a beast everyone thought tame, suddenly maddened by hornets, trampling and wild.

*   *   *

Ben: for him, the years were a steady progress towards his aim. Or perhaps a voyage to a new land reliably reported, with charts missing just a few details: sometimes a wrong course, sometimes a storm.

There was marriage, which, leaving aside the splendour of his son and the lesser but still notable splendour of a daughter squalling at the breast, was a dull business taken all in all. Agnes kept a good house on unreliable funds and always looked handsome, but she was shrewish and tongue-clacking, or perhaps all wives were. He was not much interested in the question, and spent as much time out as possible. Sometimes she wept and bewailed her lot; but other times she had her female neighbours in and, he guessed, dissected him over the griddle-cakes and cock-ale, and that made her feel better.

And then there was the playhouse-public: capricious and unreasonable as any woman born, as easy to please with the right chosen word, as implacably sullen once they had taken against you. Still he worked away: aiming for that shore of lasting fame, scholarly renown, the true reward of learning and art applied to the errant muddled stage. He was too clever, too truthful to appeal consistently to the mob—as his friend Shakespeare did, with his tender enchantments, rhapsodising lovers, kings winning battles across six feet of battlefield, and lopsided pillow-stuffed entertainments. So he had perforce to sell his talents at a cheap rate, providing plots and extra scenes for a purse from Henslowe, collaborating with the opportunistic journeyman likes of Tom Dekker. Hateful, necessary compromise.

Tribulations on his journey, but the end never lost sight of; and he was printing, he saw his work presented in all its irreproachable correctness on the page, and his lines were plucked and gathered in selections from the choice authors of the day. And men of taste and wit, men of good estate, had tendered him their compliments.

All the more galling that there had to be this war.

There had to be: that was a given. Left alone, Ben knew he was the most peaceable and retiring of men: his ideal was Cincinnatus, called from

418

the virtuous plough only when duty would not be denied. But, like Cincinnatus, he was a doughty warrior at need. Once insulted, he must be avenged.

'You don't understand,' he told Agnes, while young Ben, arm-girdled, practised his ABC in the margins of his script. The lad's hair smelt like spring. 'They have aimed another hit at me, on the public stage, and if I don't strike back—'

'Aye, what then? It will be forgot. Sooth, if I go to the play I want to be taken away with a story, not hark to a set of playhouse cats spitting at each other about who has first piss on the chimney-top.'

'And thus,' said Ben, thickly, 'you like to see your husband's reputation traduced.'

Agnes grimaced as she unwrapped little Mary's soiled clout. 'Does Will Shakespeare join in this fool contention? I thought not.'

Will Shakespeare join in? Of course not. It might make him an enemy. It might interrupt the devoted wooing of his fat, smirking mistress, the public. So Ben might have said, if he had been of a jealous disposition—which, thank heaven, he was full armoured against by reason.

Besides, Will was a romancer, his pieces played out in imaginary dukedoms and forests and never— as the true poet should in all conscience—holding up a mirror to the real world. That was his strength and his weakness. And that was the risk Ben took in his own work, where he stood up tall and addressed the matters of the age in his own ringing voice: the risk that the shabby and petty would seek to bring him down with cheap gibes and calumny.

They did it, naturally, when he tried to rise. He was looking for a better place to display his talents. The Chamberlain's Men made a great deal of their new theatre, the Globe, but still it was the same cacophonous arena where the most delicate flights of a man's wit were thrown in the dust with the nutshells. Ben's publisher stood near the Inns of Court, and there he had cultivated improving friendships with learned students who understood what he was trying to do. A restrained and chaste theatre, they told him, was what he needed: he would be heard where he could be heard. And then came the boys' theatre at Blackfriars, looking for plays. The child actors made it decorous, and the fact that it was indoors made it select.

The new freedom made him, perhaps, indulge a little; direct a few well-chosen blows at the more arrant pretenders of the theatre. And if they recognised themselves there, then that was revealing in itself, and one would have supposed they would take the lesson to heart. Instead they were foolish enough to turn on him.

Dekker was one. Poor patched, zany, sottish Dekker, the mere broom-seller and cress-crier of the stage: he could hardly have risen to such impudence, Ben thought, without being pricked to it by a craftier spirit—and there he was, John Marston, John Mar-all, Ben would call him, a slovenly half-clever, half-Italian smiler, who wrote by the yard for whoever paid him. Oh, how neatly he slapped them down when he presented them in his *Poetaster*, in all their pretentious folly, with the wise figure of the true poet Horace purging them at last . . . But then they were donkey-headed enough to reply, instead of taking their medicine, and the thing became mere coarse insult. The piece in which they gulled him—he would not dignify it with the name of play—was put on by the Chamberlain's

Men at the Globe.

Yes, Will acted in it. To do him justice, he played no great part, and plainly could not give himself to such a gimcrack gallimaufry. Still, it was low for the Chamberlain's Men to stoop. Ben saw it: he was not so thin-skinned as to stay away. But it was poorly done, he thought. They had put his character of Horace on the stage and tricked him out with— well, mere tricks to hit out at Ben. Horace had been a bricklayer, he had fought a duel, his skin was marked with the pox, and what-naught. And this they called satire! As for the vices they attributed to this poor puppet—the vanity and conceit, the way he puffed up his own compositions, the way he stored up his fawning letters to great men—well, they were so crude he could scarcely credit even the Globe audience with genuine laughter. They must have been soused to a man.

But it was no use trying to convince his wife. She lived for small things, it seemed, and could not appreciate the great, which was the besetting sin of most humankind. Unluckily, just as he was dipping his pen in its most brilliant scourging gall, ready to put his buzzing foes to flight for ever, it was snatched from him.

Authority poked its nose into the playhouse again, and did not like what it saw. Ben, in the fertility of his invention, had jousted at a few other targets in his *Poetaster*, including some that sat high; and there was to be no more of it. Ben felt the itching brand on his thumb, and acquiesced. One of his friends from the Inns of Court put in a word for him. He was free to write, but no more barbs.

Very well, he would write, and he would write in such a vein as no one had suspected in him before.

Dignified, aloof, he would retreat to contemplate it. Never mind if it appeared that his adversaries had won. The philosophic mind rose above such things.

'You vermin, you roguy, beggarly pimp, the day was cursed when you were gotten on a poxed whore by the wambling village fool atop a dung-cart.' So he greeted Dekker when he came across him supping with Will at the Mermaid.

'Well,' Dekker said, with a sheepish smile, and a glance down at Ben's fist gripping his bands, 'I'm glad you've taken none of it to heart.'

'Peace, for God's sake, no more of it,' said Will, pulling Ben down into a seat. Ben thought for a moment about being offended by this, accepted the offer of a drink, then returned to the attack. 'Your pardon, Will, for the intemperate language; and as for your own small part in these outrages, as a member of the Chamberlain's Men, I forgive it. But I must know, before I consent to drink with you, whose part you take. You sit in amity with this hedge-bird, and so I must assume it is his.'

Will stared at him. Drink, curiously, made Will pale rather than flushed. He was very pale. His eyes were the colour of the pewter mug by his hand: a full mug. 'Part, I take no part. Are we to draw daggers over a play that will be forgot in a year?'

'You mean mine, or his?'

'All. Drink about.'

'You take a poor view of posterity. And I would still know, my friend, to which side you incline. To take a side, after all, is to take responsibility. And we cannot decline that. An artist has a first duty, and that is to the truth.'

'Artist?' Dekker said, with his most infuriating blinking innocence. 'But we only make plays.'

'We? You can scarcely include yourself in the honourable company, man. You're a wandering tinker hammering bits of trash together—'

'You've given us epithets enough,' Will cried, rubbing his right temple. 'Soft, for pity's sake, and an end to contention.'

'Well, do you believe the artist, let's say the poet, has a first duty to truth, yes or no? What of you, Will Shakespeare, why do you do it?' He had almost said, *How do you do it?* which was an absurdity.

'To create is the greatest thing in the world,' Will said, after a moment, frowning: the mug at his hand was still brimming. His eyes roamed past Dekker, past Ben, but did not seem to find anything. 'And also it means nothing, absolutely nothing, and we can speak of monuments reared up in the ruins of time, as we surely do, and precious words outlasting perished silver and gold, and it means nothing, it means absolutely nothing: my art, his, yours, it's the shine on the gatepost where the cattle rub by.' He pushed his mug blindly towards Dekker. 'Now peace, it's a battle over the disposition of a straw.'

Well: Ben surmised, from these sad wild words, that something must have been amiss, because no man with Will's genius, for all its flaws, could think thus. And he was, as usual, right. To do Will honour, he shook Dekker's paw, and once the fellow had drunk his head away and staggered home to sleep, Ben fixed Will's eye with his own. They were always better like this.

'You sit long in the tavern tonight, my friend, yet you hardly drink. Do you have news?' As Will did not answer he went on hurriedly: 'Thy children, Will, they thrive, tell me, for Jesu's sake.'

'Yes, nothing of that.' Will seemed to assess him for a moment. Gentle and sober and unremarkable as his face was, still to have Will do that to you was not, Ben found, wholly comfortable. 'My father's dying.'

'Jesus. A luxury I never knew. A father, I mean. I talk about myself all the time, my friend, I'm sorry. It's to stop something else, but I don't know what.'

'But you always know everything,' Will said, grasping the proffered hand. 'Oh, God. They brought me the news late this afternoon. Greenaway the Stratford carrier brought it, to my brother Gilbert first, and he brought it me. Failing, they say. Not in great pain or distraction, but failing, and so . . . I must go. Gilbert has business— he can't get free till the day after tomorrow. I must go. So I sit here, when I might have made a start this evening, hm? What does that say?'

'A night ride? You'd be mad.'

'He made me, you see. Even in my turning against him, and in my heart I turned more than he ever knew, or did he? Still, he was all. Now I have to face the end of that.'

'Drink. Drink, by Our Lady, or I'll pour it down your throat. I knew a lad at Westminster, raised by his uncle. The uncle beat him all the time. The lad had a permanent stoop from ducking blows. When the uncle died the lad wept and wept, and tried to jump into the grave. Something like?'

'Translate it to the mind, the thoughts, the feelings.'

'Ah, those. You go tomorrow?'

'First light. Well, hence these tedious low spirits, forgive 'em. Likewise the self-talk, which is something musty.'

'Do you want a companion? I'm the world's worst rider, mind. My body was made for a tavern-chair, not a horse. It was divinely appointed so, and I am not one to quarrel with my maker.'

Will shook his head. 'I'll go alone,' he said. 'I always go alone.'

'Everywhere?' Ben would get nothing more, he knew from Will's expression—an expression like a pack being fastened, lights snuffed—but he pushed a little, in any case. 'Why apologise for talking of yourself? Most men do it at some time, even if they are not passionate self-admirers like me. What do you fear?'

'You can't talk of what isn't there,' Will said, with a faint smile: last candle being put out.

Or what can't be measured, thought Ben. And then: Is that how he does it? The thought made his mind reel a little, and he sat on long after Will had shaken his hand and gone, drinking, until he had dragooned his thoughts into place again, and denied chaos.

*   *   *

Going to your father's dying: what speed, Will thought, should you make? Your heart and limbs are laggard, for you don't want to see it, no man does. Yet you fear to be too late, to find the shutters up, the dead face already bound, soul in flight. *Festina lente*, then, hurry slowly, hurry as in the stickiness of a dream, ever renewing itself in unlikely shifts and turns. At Oxford he stops at the Crown, eats an excellent mutton pie, so excellent he calls for another, feels he could go on luxuriously eating for ever. And the bed, always good at the Crown, clean linen and no fleas, but exceptional sweet and soft this time. You could live at a good inn, he thinks, with money enough: just stay there for ever, eating and drinking well, retiring to your soft bed, and never going home: never requiring home, or required by it. Perhaps that is how some people manage in the world. He has no dreams in the sweet bed. When he wakes he feels no urgency. It's almost as if they are staging a play with a good fortnight's rehearsals: every minute accounted for.

A better harvest, he notes, on the last long stage of the ride to Stratford. The gleaners in the fields don't have that hard, frightened look. They don't know him. He wonders if it's time to buy land. The Globe is doing well, though he is careful to avoid complacency: you have to be aware of shifting tastes, sense where the audience is turning. He is working on a tragedy of revenge, which seems to be coming into fashion again, and using as a model an old piece of Kyd's. Poor Tom Kyd, who died penniless a year or so after they racked him; who never had a good word for Will. Death is the only thing they will have in common. He goes straight to Henley Street, not New Place. As he dismounts he has a dizzying, unbearable sense of a threshold. He feels like a hinge about to break. A figure moves at one of the windows and something about it makes him think: That's Father, he must be better. But it's Richard, grown thickset, who comes to the door and says: 'Will.' And, 'He's going.'

And in the dim bedchamber Will howls, and then howls again to hear himself. Because he didn't expect this. His father, and dying, yes, and the two together. But not this perfect picture of death coming. Not this spareness, bone, stare, flat hands made of veins. Not this happening to John Shakespeare, as if the universe has singled him out, closed quarters, and kicked him into a corner. Not those eyes.

As he weeps, he is aware somewhere of Anne: of her understanding, and its helplessness.

*   *   *

His father murmurs a good many prayers, while his strength lasts. He calls down blessings on Mary Shakespeare, the best wife in creation, soon to be widow: everything for thee, my dear. He is more than seventy years old by his own reckoning. He has made his will. He does not have a hard dying, as the phrase goes. He is himself to the quiet last.

But there is this. Those eyes, which you can almost hear grinding and turning in his shrunken face like pestle in mortar, wander over Will's face, in the grey light of the final morning. The tight skin puckers.

He says: 'I don't know you.'

'Why, John, it's Will,' croons his mother, hand at his brow. 'It's Will come home from London.'

The eyes harden a little: with recognition?

Will bends closer. 'Father.'

'I don't know you.' Very softly: 'Why don't you let people know you? Why?'

His breath smells of the tomb.

'Father. I love thee.'

Very slowly his father shakes his head. 'No. Never, quite. I knew it. Bless thee, mind, a father's blessing.' He puts him far off with the faintest twitch of his fingers. 'But never, quite. I knew.'

*   *   *

John Shakespeare is buried in Stratford church, on a day of long September light, reaching its gold out as if to point to something both delicate and important. Enough colours in the sky to suffice for ever. On such a day the earth could hardly be more beautiful if it had been designed so. A good death and a good funeral, solemnised by aldermen, reverend grey and bald pates. Stratford receiving its own into its earth, full of years and honour. John Shakespeare, gentleman.

Anne observes Will's look as the coffin dips out of sight in a haze of dust. The look of a man on a deserted strand, watching his ship go away. You've left me: you truly have done it.

His look doesn't take her in at all. This is what it's like to be a ghost—but a ghost unseen, moaning in deaf ears.

*   *   *

'So, is this your Dane, and is he finished?' Burbage says, peering over Will's writing-table. 'Or, should I say, will he ever be finished?' His pudgy hands fidget through the manuscript. His lips flicker as he reads. 'It's fine, it leaps, it sounds great depths. But it's too much. We'll have to cut, sooner rather than later. You understand me, Will? In a perfect world . . .'

'Ah, that. We have the words for it, yet no one can imagine it. Cut, certes, cut, it's a play, we have to make it play.'

'And pay. You can always print the whole later. Like bully Jonson, correcting his every comma.' He does a squinting, tongue-poking imitation, then shrugs at the cheapness: everyone can do Jonson.

'You think it will hold them?'

'Man, give me your Dane shorn, a good boy, a fair day, and we'll hold them and carry them further than ever Shylock or Romeo,' Burbage says, squeezing his shoulders and lifting him an inch off the ground: in him a mild, undemonstrative gesture. 'You still mean to take the Ghost?'

'Oh, yes. I'm born to play it.'

*　　　*　　　*

'I still think you might have thought of me for Ophelia,' Matthew says. Gently reproachful, not sulky: the smooth brow clear. The skin of the young, Will thinks, is miraculous: they hardly seem to have inhabited it at all.

'You're too sane for tragedy.' Matthew has a lodging of his own now, a respectable place with a tinsmith and his motherly wife. But Will can see the bottle thrust behind the bed-curtain: and sniffing detects tobacco. 'So, when you gather with your friends to read over the latest script, do you find a pipe aids your appreciation?'

Matthew blushes, but at being caught out rather than in shame: he has, thank God, none of that. Like a cat, he sees himself as a handsome and worthwhile part of nature, deserving of a little cream. 'In truth it does. Have you not tried it? It brings a stimulation to the mental parts, and potently primes the understanding.'

'And also spoils the voice, which is of most importance to a player.'

With a deep bow, 'Yes, Father,' Matthew says grinning; and then: 'What's wrong?'

In the tiring-house heat of jabbing elbows and pungent stockings Will works the chalk powder into his cheeks, alone, coolly jostled. His lines ring his mind like a coronet: fixed in place. Memory moves in the midst. Taking his morning draught at Jonson's house. Jonson is drumming up patrons now, has taken more commodious quarters, though still you feel he views his home merely as a different kind of tavern-room. He was nursing a metheglin headache, in spite of claiming he never drank the stuff. 'That was last week's never.' He has a child's appetites and easy denials, and gets on famously with the sturdy little boy and infant girl who dangle about him for his bearish hugs. Mistress Jonson looked on, sharp-eyed, affectionate: she could not smile, Will noticed, without a frown grooving her brow. He suspected there were mighty quarrels. Jonson has read the Dane in manuscript.

'You won't carry them. Not with this.'

'Revenge, ghost, blood—'

'Oh, they may expect a revenge tragedy, but look what you've done with it. There is no revenge, for one.'

'That's what they're not to see. One of the many.' For little Benjamin he did a trick with a coin that Jack Towne taught him years ago. (How many? God. He'd had a dream about Towne the other night, strange, clear, piercing dream. At thirty-seven.) 'There, Benjamin, didst see where the penny went? Yet you like the trick, hey?'

'And then in your fourth part you send your prince away to England, for how long? I know, he doesn't get there, the pirates take him,' Jonson rolled his eyes in exasperation at that, 'and why not bring them on the stage while you're about it, have 'em sing a song? But my point is we must fancy a good deal of time passing while he's at sea. Months. I know you will never care for the unities, but this—it's a violation of sense.'

Will did the coin trick again. Benjamin watched with craving eyes.

'By God, if I had your genius,' Jonson grumbled, 'I'd know how to employ it.'

'Peace, make peace,' said Mistress Jonson.

'It's only nine in the morning,' Jonson said. 'Too early for that.'

'Mark this, young Ben,' Will said, giving him the coin. 'It's never too early for a man to make his peace.'

Jonson looked at him quizzically. 'With God? With death?'

'With his birth.'

Will finishes his painting. Chalk doesn't make his skin flare like blacking. Burbage strides by in giant, genial, anxious mood, booming: 'Is everybody mad? Good people, is everyone stark *mad*?' And when they groan *yes*: 'Excellent, it bodes well.' Kempe, the clown, has left them: usually he would be soothing nerves now. Will, chalked up, meets Heminges's eye with a wry smile of recognition. Heminges, solid and shrewd, always turns sensationally white before a performance. They all have something of this fear, though what do they fear? They are the Chamberlain's Men, a bad performance will not ruin them. It's the fear of the play itself, perhaps. Once you set it going, there is no turning back: it lives of itself. What sound in the world is more awesome, terrible, than the

431

first cry of a new-born child? He sees tiny Hamnet fighting the air on the way to Anne's breast. The last trumpet sounds. What sort of a crowd? Fair, middling fair. A cold day. Not as cold as the conjured night on the battlements of the mind, as the cold inside, it is a nipping and an eager air. And I am sick at heart. 'And I am sick,' Burbage is saying, 'of having to prompt the pissing prompter.' They huddle to shake hands and laugh nervously before the beginning. Ophelia is painted but not yet wigged: almond eyes, hedgehog hair. Some last questions of Will—'Eyases, how in hell do you say it?'—but not many: he is the giver of the words and a player among others, no overseer.

And how he feels about it: it's still alive, or still a thing being born. Yes, if we overrun, cut the business with Osric and the hat. The face Will presents, or self, is smooth and lustred, and you can see yourself in it, but peer further and there is space rather than depths. Like the space between the lines. Burbage, in black, tosses down his apple core. *'Tis not alone my inky cloak, good mother.* The lad with the mirror passes among them, the mirror a great flashing, polished silver plate, for glass always got broken in the hugger-mugger of the tiring-house. He tilts it at Will, at the Ghost. Looking well, sir. Is this how I will look when I'm dead? If only we could know. Do we hover, looking on, hear the hypocrisies of the funeral?

Now to go on, now to be Ghost. It banishes the other ghosts from his side, for a time: being someone else. Leaving the world, he steps on stage. Now, the real turn into ghosts. Like a snail in reverse, he can only live away from the shell of himself.

Faces, faces, so many and expectant. You learn not to see them individually, to let them blot on your vision like dandelion-heads. But no. One face stands out, in the nearest gallery.

There she is, again. Without seeing her, he sees her. Like the future.

13

A Game at Chess (1603)

In the Mermaid Tavern, two men face each other over a chessboard.

Regular customers look askance, wondering if it will end like it did yesterday evening.

Dekker was here: saw it all. Not their usual way, these two. Big fellows in the world, you know, princes out of my star—though to speak truth Jonson and I have writ together since we had our falling-out. He held his nose, you know. Shakespeare I've never writ with, he usually works alone. Fact is, he's too fast for any of us. Oh, it is a quarrelsome trade, anyone will tell you that. You'll have marked the brand on Jonson's thumb. In and out of jail and favour. Never Shakespeare, though, which makes it all the more surprising. Always seems to rise above it. Has his Moor on the boards just now, magnificent piece. Oh, and a success, to be sure: he never has anything else. Could it be that was what the quarrel was about? It could be.

*　　　*　　　*

Black and white.

Will stares at the black squares. Lately wearing black for the Queen. Great Elizabeth has gone to her rest at last—a heavy, painful clawing down to death, he has heard; and so the Chamberlain's Men, her favoured troupe, don the inky cloak.

Last time he saw her, at Whitehall in the Great Chamber, he thought her sleeping: a-slumber in the great upright bed of her dress. Then the squirrel eyes would unlock, move in the white face, and fasten on you. She always knew him, remembering his name just when he thought she'd forgot: a good monarch's touch, of course. Think of all the people one knew by name: in Stratford, fifty perhaps; here perhaps twice as many. People you know, happening to live in the same slice of time as you: spade in earth, worms moving in the wet black wedge.

Dekker approaches their table cautiously. 'Chess,' he says, 'excellent, a much better way to settle your differences. What *was* it all about?'

'A contention between black and white,' Jonson says, with a half-smile.

'Ah, but who is which? And cannot a man be neither?' Will says.

Jonson gestures at the chessboard. 'Without black and white, no game to play.'

'Well, you might have a chessboard on which all the squares are grey. There I could play to my true content.'

Jonson shakes his head. 'Make your move, man.'

Will stares at the black and white. Black king, white queen. *If virtue no delighted beauty lack, your son-in-law is far more fair than black.* What was it all about? A play, of course—what else is there? And things like truth. And a dark woman.

*   *   *

'How do you call this piece?'

Firelight streaks her fingers as they delicately stab the keys of the virginal. Always she has a fire burning, like his father. He sits at a distance: a good yard today. Tomorrow it might be two yards; or he might sit beside her, at her feet, study the little blue vein under the ankle. It is up to her decree. The music has no form. It leads you down delicious paths, then leaves you there without bearings.

'A touch-piece,' she says. 'They are my favourite kind. I like nothing finished. That's why I never say goodbye.'

Her fingers lift, and she closes her eyes, and he realises he is dismissed.

*   *   *

'She is a curious creature,' Richard Field says. Isabelle Berger: for a time she continues to haunt the shop when Will is there. 'My saviour,' she calls him, but then will not speak to him. 'I wonder if she drinks.'

'She has had great griefs, I think,' Jacqueline says, sounding faintly jealous. How people long for those—though only in the past, not now. Things to build yourself on.

What griefs? No one knows. And then she is not there any more. Jacqueline thinks she has gone to the country for her health, but isn't sure. No one is very sure about anything when it comes to Isabelle Berger: as if her very existence is conditional.

Perhaps that's it. Will writes, acts, looks for himself in the great polished plate. Looks in vain for a hero or a king.

*   *   *

Jonson puts his fingers to his black king, changes his mind.

'Not to renew the quarrel,' he says temperately—though temperate in Jonson is as awkward and forced as a dog standing on its hind legs, 'but posterity will speak the last word.'

'We shan't hear it.'

'Our descendants will.' Realisation flashes on Jonson's face. 'Oh, damn it, damn it a hundred times,' he says, furious: his equivalent of sorry, a word he cannot pronounce. 'Curse me for a proud, stiff-necked, blabbering fool—'

'I did that yesterday. No more of it.'

Jonson shakes his head, moves his queen's bishop.

Everyone has quarrelled with Jonson at some time—or, rather, Jonson has quarrelled with everyone. Will is the exception. It is known around the theatres, and their concomitant alehouses and eating-houses, skittle-alleys, stews, fence-houses and knocking-shops, that Will Shakespeare won't be drawn.

And then comes Jonson's tragedy, *Sejanus*.

'You mean he's put this whole bloody lockjawed speech in, just because it's in his sources?' Burbage snarls.

'Tacitus,' Will says. 'And it will be his own fair translation, nothing inaccurate.'

'The public don't give a fiddler's fart for Tacitus.

And look—everything stirring happens off stage.'
Burbage sighs. 'Don't tell me: it's authentically
Senecan.'

'It has grandeur,' Will says. 'It is lofty, stately,
chaste . . .' He is struggling, and Burbage's
liverish eye says so. Ben Jonson's reputation in
the theatre is growing, and he has announced,
with characteristic boldness, that he is turning
to tragedy: and there is interest. But Will knows
that his was the deciding vote in persuading the
Chamberlain's Men to take on the result, *Sejanus*.
He did it for friendship.

'How do you say it?' Heminges asks, on their first
read-through. 'Ar-nus, or Ay-nus?'

'Tempt me not,' Burbage says, with an ashy grin.

But they go ahead. Burbage gets the vast static
speeches into his capacious head. Tries, really tries,
to make a living character out of—Will admits it
to himself—a set of marble attitudes. (Ben last
night, as they quarrelled over it: *I tell you, it will
outlast marble, it will last a thousand years.* Will: *No,
it only seems like that when you hear it.*) Perhaps he
should have said something, something clinching.
Burbage wants cuts from the beginning, but Jonson
refuses adamantly. As it is, or not at all. He means
it too. Time, declares Jonson, for the stage to bear
a correctly made tragedy, fashioned after classical
models, and inculcating virtue. No shrieking ghosts
or bloody swordfights. Time for people to be
serious, and learn.

And what the Roman people did to Sejanus
the man, the Globe audience do to Jonson's play.
Luckily a play can't bleed when torn limb from
limb.

Jonson is the first to acknowledge the failure.

He watches from the gallery with Sir Robert Townsend, his new patron. Yes, he accepts it; though, as he remarks, the Roman people were on the whole worthy of a great nation's name, whereas the English theatre mob are the dullest paddockful of braying asses that ever turned up their snouts at fine-chopped sweet hay to provender on pissed-on thistles.

What is Will to say? It was too cold, it was too stiff, it didn't move in any sense . . . Whatever he says will ally him with the idiot multitude who clap their paws for his Shylock, his Falstaff, his somehow-living impurities. How do I make them live? I give them life. And they give me a life in return.

When they all repair after the play to the Mermaid, Will hopes to avoid saying anything. Perhaps they can just be convivial, leave the subject untouched in the middle. But conviviality won't come. The wearying speeches, the goose-hissing of the crowd, lie heavily over everyone. 'Well,' says Burbage, half giving a toast, 'we gave it everything, friends; and everything we received in return, as due reward . . .' The speech falls apart. People find excuses to go home early. Will and Jonson, and a few others, stay on drinking. Unwise, after the event. But they are not drunk—or at least, neither of them loses coherence in liquor. Somehow the bare thoughts slip out. Somehow, instead of the usual fencing, there is the clash of verbal steel.

'But you can't lecture an audience into loving you.'

'There—love—you betray yourself. I don't want to be loved when I create, man, I want to inspire thought, reflection, moral improvement.'

438

'A great pill to swallow ungilded.'

'Let them choke on it, then.'

'You see, Ben, they can tell that that's what you think of them.'

'Aye, and why not? What is the mass of humanity but a parade of voice, vanity and folly?'

'Everything, and everything besides. Look in that mark left by the tapster's finger there, and you fall into an infinity of worlds.'

'It's a fingermark like any other, and he's a tapster like any other.'

'Nothing is like anything else.'

'Wrong. One fool is like another, one thief is like another, and if we do not march them in file in our mind, then chaos is come again. Aye, your words, Will. Your words spin a wondrous penumbra over the mind, in which it cosily blinks and can hardly see a good strong shape.'

'And they beguile the fools and thieves, no doubt.'

'Men of sense, too. I don't deny that. But it's the cheers and plaudits that lead you, is it not so, Will Shakespeare? You follow where Goodman Plain wants you to go, laughing comedy or shrieking revenge, and even when you touch brilliance you have a care for him, never take him out of his depth but keep his great flat feet ever on the ground. And you make him feel that he's a fine fellow, even as you grub up his money.' (Careful, thinks Will, with alarm, as Jonson says this, shaking: this is how disappointed and jealous Jonson is, beside himself, beyond himself.) 'In that, you are very like the best class of whore.'

Careful. 'You would know more about those than I.' Too late.

'Oh, I make no denial, I am no domestic mouse, and I suspect have a by-blow coming in a little yard off Hog's Lane, what then? I am no hypocrite.' Crimson now. 'Contrast sweet Master Shakespeare, modest darling of the stage whom everyone loves, dutifully sending home his loot to furnish his honest burgher's mansion and ray his country wife in silks, and all the time keeping his dirty little mistress in town.'

Heads are turning. Jonson looks a little frightened at himself: Will is half on his feet. And yet for the moment he is taken merely by sheer astonishment. Not that Jonson knows something—rumour would trickle out eventually—but at the way he says it.

Keeping a mistress. Is that—great God—is that how they call it?

*   *   *

Ironies: he first moved to the Cripplegate district because Jonson spoke of settling his family there. Also, it seemed a sensible shift for a man of his age and wealth, away from the theatre environs of Southwark and Shoreditch, rackety, quick-knifed. Instead the northern edge of the city, with the country heights visible from his upper window. A better air, as he wrote to Anne, not supposing she would much care. Also it was closer to Matthew's lodging, so he could keep an eye on him. (A fatherly eye? Well, why not, when the lad had no father?)

A better place, a new place, away from temptation. And it was Jacqueline Field who recommended the house in quiet Silver Street. It was kept by a respectable French Protestant family of her acquaintance, the Mountjoys. Tire-makers in a thriving line: head-dresses for noble ladies, even royalty, it was murmured. Sober, industrious people, a well-kept house, and there he had two good chambers, meals if he wanted them.

And Mistress Mountjoy, it turned out, knew Isabelle Berger.

That might not have meant anything. So, she was back in London: so, if she saw him no doubt it would be like at the Fields', wanting to draw some response from him that he didn't understand and didn't care to. Strange, capricious, sallow woman he knew once. A little hole in the road, a stumble, and on.

Except . . . something about the time. The years, dark years without form, without doors in or out, where he walked alone. Anne lay on the other side of the turning world—where he had placed her, or where she had placed herself, or where the great division had left them.

And on the page and in the theatre he was always occupied with character and exploring what made a person, where the self ended and began. And in Isabelle he discovered a self that he could not read or write. Once it was begun, he could not stop. Because of the mystery.

Will stares at the black and white squares and thinks: How explain that to Jonson? Would he sneer, say he knows exactly what sort of mystery that is? Will moves his queen's rook. His queen is peculiarly powerless in this game.

*   *   *

'Ah! I was just saying to Mistress Mountjoy,' Isabelle

said, the first time he came downstairs to see her there, warming herself at the fire, 'how quiet her lodger is. I said, "What can he be doing up there all alone?" But now I see it's you. And now I know. Master Shakespeare, our most excellent play-maker. What are you working on now?'

'A play of a man who kills a woman for love of her.'

'Oh.' She yawned. 'Another stale old tale.'

Pretty, birdlike Mistress Mountjoy looked a little shocked: she esteemed Will highly.

'Oh, never mind me, my dear,' Isabelle said, pressing her hand. 'I may say what I like to Master Shakespeare: he knows my true feeling for him.'

And then, a look in her eyes: a snap, a lick, God only knew, everything in a look, as he had never quite believed possible. He had tried to avoid the poet's convention of seeing stars and wonders in a pair of eyes. Eyes could only contain so much, he had thought: until then.

He blundered back upstairs, trembling as if he had stolen something, and it was under his shirt, precious and spiked.

*   *   *

So, he stood once more at the stair-turning with the warped window looking out on the leads, and the pastille-scent creeping up to him. And he thought: You knew, didn't you? You knew you would be here again.

'Let us talk,' she said. She led him into her overheated rooms by the hand. He stayed for three hours, and her hand was all he was permitted, or ordered, to touch. Near the end she put the tip of

442

his forefinger in her mouth, before sending him away with a look of mild contempt.

He would not go again. In his bedchamber at Silver Street he lay face down, as he had not done since he was a whipped boy, as if exhausted or flattened, blinking, and heart-raging.

*　　　*　　　*

'How did you know,' she asked him, licking wine from her hand, 'about Ophelia?'

As always, when called on to discuss his work, he felt a shield lift.

'The madness,' she went on. 'How did you know that's how madness is?'

'Not mad. Distracted.'

'The difference?'

'It's the end of a path. Our path, not a different path. We all fall short of madness, while we have luck, but it's just over there. How did you know? Or what did you recognise?'

Isabelle laughed. 'Great God in heaven, you won't catch me like that.'

'What?' Her laughter could sometimes hurt him like a punch in the chest.

'By asking. Because you cannot even conceive, believe me, the right question. How is your boy-girl?'

'Matthew. His name is Matthew.' He had told her all about his apprentice. Had told her, probably, everything: he couldn't be sure—strange memory lapses afflicted him after being with her, as in drunkenness. She drew it out of him, like the conjuror he saw at Bartholomew Fair, pulling the coin from his ear with a smiling wince. That was

Will, telling his life in the dark, scented, too-warm room: sitting at a distance, if she is in banishing mood. Or sometimes seated next her on the settle, and Isabelle throwing her leg over his, negligent, boyish, as he and Richard Field used to. The cock-stand was like a long bright headache that did not fade. She knew, saw, was scornfully amused.

'Do you lie with whores?'

'No.'

'You should. It's not fair on your wife to be your whore, not after childbearing.'

'Don't speak of my wife.'

'Oh, is that today's game, you pretend yours is the control? Diverting. Why, Monsieur Berger used whores all the time, and I was glad of it. I used to smell them on him and think, Ah, now he is full of guilt, so he will be kind.'

'Was he often not kind?'

'He used to beat me. And worse things—slow, clever, cruel things.' She turned her head away and wept. Or did she only seem to? He didn't know what to do. The floor seemed to ripple beneath him. Suddenly she was looking at him and laughing. 'There. Good, wasn't it? Really, we should allow women on the stage, should we not?'

Savagely he jerked back. 'Do you think I would laugh at that?'

'No. I don't want you to laugh with me, ever. When we laugh we go away to a distance and look on and I don't want you up there.' Her voice was rushed and harsh, a wind of October with leaves and spiders in it. 'I want you down here with me in the hell dark, sweet.' She leaned in and bit his lower lip gently. That would be today's.

*   *   *

Black, and white.

'Your move,' Jonson says. He makes it sound a dreadful prospect.

*   *   *

'Will you hear me read my part? Truly?' Matthew said. 'It will be dull work, for it's the dullest part ever writ.'

'It won't be dull,' Will said. And it was not, though the writing was so execrable. Just to sit here, in the tavern garden, and be near Matthew's cheer and lightness and sometime silliness. And when one of his friends turned up and they fell to drinking, boasting, mock-boxing, silliness indeed, still then Will was happy to sit by, and let a little of it lie across him, like the edge of a bright bar of sunlight.

*   *   *

'You are quite a stranger to me,' the Earl of Southampton said. 'In all ways.'

'Not in all ways, I hope.'

'I've seen your Dane every time. He transports me. They say I spend too much time at the theatres.' He sighed, a rich, careless sigh. 'You're better where you are, my friend, where you may walk unseen in the shade. So how do you call these sonnets?'

'Sonnets, my lord. Every poet has a tilt at this target. They make a shapely vessel to pour one's small beer in.'

Southampton looked at him critically. Matthew

did that sometimes, when he was talking wisdom: as if he could see someone behind him, prompting his lies. 'Not these. I see something of me, is that so? Marry and beget. Did my mother urge that on you?'

'Something of you?' Will said. 'Something of everything I have ever seen, done, also, and of everyone else. We breathe the air that Caesar expelled from his lungs.'

'Hiding again, Master Shakespeare.' The earl tosses down the manuscript and motions Will to follow him. The echo of their footsteps welcomes them like gentle applause to the long gallery. 'I think it is, in essence, a sort of drama or play. Everything turns into a play in your hands, does it not?'

Will made an equivocal motion with his head. 'They may be that. Or—you might, my lord, call them touch-pieces.'

The earl seemed dissatisfied, today, with being unable to pin Will down, where once he had been intrigued. 'What next for the stage, then? That's where we would have you. No doubt you may write as you will now, and name your price.'

'Not so, alas. One piece that does not please, and you are cast down with the general.'

The earl pursed his lips, as if Will were pleading poverty. Something you accepted as you grew older: some friendships decayed, liking spread thin, and there was no help for it. You tried to accept it, at any rate.

'Meaning you still need patrons?'

'No, in truth. But I still know how to value those who have extended the hand to me.'

'I served your purpose, in fact.'

'If I must answer that, my lord, I would ask, did I

serve yours?'

The earl stopped and glared at him, a professional kind of glare. Then it thawed. 'Forgive me. That's life at Court: makes a man see nothing but double-dealing and interest.'

'And forgive me if I have been insolent.'

'You have, but you consider you have cause.' The earl put a hand on his shoulder. His breath was on Will's face. 'So you see why it would never have done. Too much arrogance on both sides.' His eyes dropped and he altered the touch, steering Will to a new-varnished picture. 'Come see my birthday portrait. What do you think? I'm content enough, but my mother cried out against it and was for stinting the painter's money.'

It was a beautiful picture of a beautiful man, but somehow it failed of beauty. 'Highly finished.'

'A deadening thing at best, to have a portrait made. Have you been painted?'

Will shrugged. 'I've seen no reason.'

'More false modesty?'

'That depends if you believe there is any such thing as true modesty.'

The earl chuckled. 'You're as jaded as a courtier. Or are you hiding again?'

After a moment Will said: 'I can warrant you this, my lord: if you put my picture on this wall, and invited all the court and city and country to bear you company here, not one among them would stop to look at it.' He hesitated. 'Thank God.'

*　　　*　　　*

'You can't hide it any more, Matt. You've been talking false, and it's the most fearful squeaking. Your voice

447

is broke, isn't it?'

Matthew gazed bleak, mutinous, at Will, not seeing him. 'So that's it. But look you, I can still take the parts, surely. Henry Bright still plays women, and his voice is long broke.'

'His voice is naturally light in pitch. And still I think he strains it. Yours is low, and it will growl and hoot and be absurd if you try to throw it. Why fear? You are a player, a surpassing player. You'll take male roles now, that's all. You know you have me to speak for you. You'll never lack.'

'I suppose.' Matthew chewed his lip. Redness surged, blood on snow. 'The woman parts make you feel exceptional. You have to reach so far. I don't want to go on stage and—well, rest, let it go. I don't want to be myself.'

Will patted his shoulder. 'That, if you can do it, is the one thing to avoid.'

Suddenly Matthew's brow was clear. Emotions flexible as his joints. The secret, perhaps, if you could maintain it, of skimming the pond of life: whatever you felt, it would not be for long. 'Well. The voice broke surely means I am a man now, and can indulge a man's liberties—drink, smoke, wench, hey?'

'And ruin your health and bewray your credit,' Will said, the mock-severity nearly real.

'And matters will change betwixt us, surely,' Matthew said, lightly teasing. 'No more of the strict father.'

Will, achieving a smile, shook his head. 'A man never loses his father.'

*   *   *

Jonson moves his queen. 'Check. My words were hasty.' His eyes slide about, Will's face, the black and white pattern set out, the tapster. He is a good friend and generous heart, but the whole business of the emotions fatigues him. Also he wants to win the game: this, every game. 'I think I only dared say them because of the love I bear you. Only to those we love do we dare the worst. Not so?'

Will gazes: black, white, imprinting his eyes. He says: 'I don't understand love.'

*   *   *

Climbing the grunting stairs, passing the warped window, he saw his legs entangled by rods of shadow and light. The entanglement, he told himself, is plain enough, and it is temptation of the simplest kind; therefore stop and come no more.

No, it's not, it's something else. It's a play I'm in, one unwritten: the best kind. And, besides, when he tried to reject the dark, think of the good and belong to the good, dead Hamnet stirred and cried in his grave and Anne, with all the stone force of dead love, rose and smashed him. So, why stop? What do I preserve, if I withdraw? The best and future part of me is gone down into the dark. Plays, they don't last: they're like human lives, stretching out their finished time. And I have fears about the eternity of the soul: how is it durable, when I can no more fix my own than nail thistledown?

'Today we will speak nothing but French.'

'But my French is weak.'

She did not accept *but*. She killed it with a glance, a twitch of her shoulders. Which, bared, were like smooth brown apples. He acquiesced, because he always did, because her strange brown quiet movements and her hair and look made him, and struggled through a bleeding evening of thorny language. She laughed silently at him, but then most of the time she did; that was nothing to remark. Some words she used were, he guessed, obscene, and some he was sure she invented.

Suddenly in English, pouring him wine, she said: 'Do you love me?'

A short, neat reflection, like the tensing of muscles to jump muck in the street. 'No. If anything, I hate you.'

'That will suffice.' She nodded, eyes closed, drinking. She looked desperate and thirsty and shrunken, as if perilously rescued. 'Why do you come here, Will? Is it hope? Hope that you will get at last into my bed?'

'Your bed,' he said truthfully, 'is just another bed, after all.'

She seemed quite to like that. But then the wolf grew in her face. 'Are you making a dream of me, when I'm not by? Don't do that, Will. Don't dare turn me into one of your dreams.'

He faced the wolf: you couldn't, after all, outrun it. 'Why, what else are you but a dream of your own, Isabelle? And Monsieur Berger, did you dream him too? Last week you told me he died ten years ago. Yesterday it turned into five years. Now, you do not forget a thing like that.'

She burst out laughing, as if the conversation had taken a joyful, high-spirited turn. 'But you don't understand at all. That is precisely the sort of thing I would forget. Monsieur Berger? Why, even when his prick was in me I used to forget about him. It was the only way. Ever felt a man press you down,

450

indifferent, as the fishmonger does with the eel to chop off its head?'

He set down his wine. 'I didn't mean to doubt you. Isabelle—'

She slapped his cheek, not very hard: enough. 'Your pardon, Will, but that was meant to give you pain, therefore to stop you feeling sorry for me, which is intolerable to me. Now this.' She took his hand and slipped it inside her bodice, and he felt her nipple strong and dry against his palm. His face ached, his mouth was full of stone. 'Now,' she gave him back his hand, 'we part.'

'For ever?' Feeling hope and terror hellishly combined, a basilisk emotion.

'What? Never for ever. Sweet fool, don't you see this is how I ensure it?'

The walk away from the house in Hay Passage, into St Martin-le-grand, was blindingly familiar, every cobble and doorpost, in sun and shade (but it was always in shade). Every step of it was irradiated with his anguish, like the glow of decay he had seen on broken dead fish at Tower Wharf. And everything he saw, every footfall resounded with a thump in his brain of resolution: no more, no more. Go back no more.

It was, after all, such a simple thing not to do.

*   *   *

Will sacrifices a pawn.

'Is it generally known, Ben?'

'What?' Jonson pulls his mind from the chess problem. 'About you and the woman? No. Rumoured more than known. In truth I made a lucky hit. Come, every man in the theatre has

451

his *amours* talked of. And even if there are none, it takes very little wit-work to invent some, just to pass the time, you know—'

'If you walk backwards any faster you'll fall over.'

'Look now. I've heard you have a woman tucked away somewhere. What do you fear? It will be reported to your wife, a hundred miles off? And even in that unlikely event, what does she suppose? That you live an anchorite in London? Why, if my wife didn't suspect me of straying, she would think there was something wrong with me.'

Does he fear it getting to Anne? Perhaps. More truthfully, it's Anne thinking of him as faithless. Their love may have decamped, but there is still something precious on the grey field.

'What did I say? Last night, when you spoke of my—of this mistress?'

'When we quarrelled? Well: you said that you don't have to buy love. You said the difference between us is you don't even have to try.' Lips set, Jonson moves his queen or, rather, propels her in his meaty fist. 'Check. A pretty exchange of insults.'

'Yes . . . Let us forget it.'

'You won't, though. You never forget anything, do you?' Beaming now, Jonson gives a rough chuckle. 'You should learn the art, Will. As I've said before.'

*   *   *

Playing parts and shifting identities, they both moved easily there. It was where their shadows touched. Will remembered Anne's stepbrother, stamping in grim fun. Treading on your shadow. Play was no play, he knew that: Isabelle too. Common ground. And lust: which he could hardly recognise for what it was, because he did not think her beautiful or attractive. The lust was more like pain, or burning or freezing, or some unknown form of extremity, miserably first-discovered by him.

Will stares at the black, the white of the chessboard. Demanding a move. Insisting on choice. How he hates choice, and its burden.

Playing at the Globe one afternoon—was this real? Black Burbage was kneeling sorrowfully, looking into the poisoned well of innocence, and Will was watching from his noble Venetian role. So often he played nobles and dukes and kings, eminences pained and withdrawn and powerless: chess-kings. And then he saw her. Not in the galleries, her usual place, but at the rear of the pit where the whores congregated, where they could prop themselves against the bulks and watch the play while they received exploring hands, sometimes tongues. And that was what Isabelle was doing. An old man was pawing her, and Will saw his tongue like a little snake flicking at her smiling lips. Isabelle is looking at and for Will. Who, after his heart goes up on a pulley, carries on acting. So, he supposes, does she.

By the time of the jig she is no longer down with the bared breasts. She is in the gallery opposite him, seated, demure.

'You thought you saw that. But did you?' She met him afterwards at the back of the tiring-house. He wanted to pick her up and throw her. He wanted to see her tongue. 'I don't know why I laugh. You don't provoke laughter in me, Will. Your face is too sombre and beautiful, also your hands, and the space betwixt your shoulder-blades,

453

as I picture it. Touch it before I sleep. I'm ill, I'm bad. It's one of those days. I must go home now.'

*   *   *

Usually it was him going to her: attending on her, waiting on her. Treading a strange half-sideways path to her, like the knight erring across the chessboard. But sometimes he found her waiting for him outside the house in Silver Street, perhaps cold or wet: like a lover. And she would tell him how she had been thinking of him all day, and weep. Once she put her hands up to him, there in the street, and he wanted to swipe them away, but held them and kissed her ticking wrists. He moaned: 'An end, an end.'

'A thousand pities about us,' she said. 'You know, it isn't only that you have a wife.' And she glinted at him from behind a dark knowledge, an eclipse of him. And the knowledge pressed smothering over him when alone he put out the light, and then put out the light.

And then a young man came to see him at Silver Street. Mistress Mountjoy, instead of sending the servant, came up to his rooms herself and said in her anxious pretty head-tilting way: 'I'd not disturb you, Master Shakespeare. I don't know the lad. But he won't be told. He says over and over that you'll want to see him.'

Matt, he thought, heart jerking—he didn't know why, pleased surprise, perhaps, for Matt never came here. It was always Will seeking him out: natural, of course. (And sometimes Matt could not conceal a little teeth-grin of impatience at seeing Will again but that was natural too, *in loco parentis*.) So, let the lad come up.

And when the dark youth, smallish, black-clad, swept into his rooms he experienced a moment of peculiar fear. He didn't know him—or did he? For some reason he remembered the last time he had seen Marlowe on the street, hyena-mouthed, full of himself; and afterwards Marlowe dead in a crammed room, in the crammed room of Will's imagination, where he had seen the dagger go in a thousand times.

The youth presented a narrow back to him, warming small hands at the fire.

'What do you want?'

'Oh, sir, good Master Shakespeare—' husky, almost sobbing '—I am come to beg you, won't you make me one of your boy-girls? It is all I've lived for . . . I have talents, sir, I have uncommon talents, and that's what's wanted, is it not?'

The youth turned. Will looked into Isabelle's eyes. It was as if he had touched spring leaves and found them painted green and pinned to the tree.

It was she who looked away first, her laugh of triumph choking off.

'I thought it a pretty jest. Also I thought that this way—how else, then?—I might surprise you into love.'

'God knows what you mean by love,' he said, going breathless to fling open the window. Stifled, suddenly. She had never come up to his rooms before.

'I doubt God does, which is one of the reasons I have parted with him. Do you? Do you know all of love?' She sat down on the hearth, crossing and embracing her legs. 'Is it one rule for all? I wonder. Now when you see the grass, you call its colour green, and so do all, they learned it as babes, see, my chick, see the green grass. But perhaps what you see and call green, I see as blue or pink. Or black, black. Who can tell? Another mortal's mind is the one place we cannot go. The solitary sanctuary. I rattle on and can't you see I'm afraid? I don't do well in strange places. And this is strange to me.' She looked round with a shiver. 'Foreign, even.'

He gave her a cup of wine, uncut. She had a stronger head than any of his boozing acquaintance. Marlowe again. He realised something about Marlowe: he had had a weak head for liquor in truth. How young we were.

'I make a good boy, don't I? Perhaps good isn't the word. I throw it to you, see what you can do with it. Oh, man made of words.'

She made it sound like 'man of straw'. She didn't really make a good boy, yet there was something refreshing in the awkwardness the breeches and doublet gave her. She made her own gowns, beautifully, and he was always irritated by their elegant delicacy, their difference. Wanted to tear them, perhaps. But also she looked something other than a woman, even as she snatched off the close cap and let her wiry hair fall. Some half-glimpse, perhaps, of that true self he was always trying to grasp.

'Well, and now I see your lodging, at last.' Her amused, scornful look formed. 'But where are you in it? It might be any room in the world.'

True, perhaps, compared to her place, with the mad caged bird, the virginal that gave off soft, musical creaks even when untouched, the wooden-soled shoes kicked off so you could picture her in them, fill up her stance. But somehow he did not like leaving traces.

456

'A man's lodging, perhaps. Sufficient for me. I'm sorry I can give you no better chair.'

'I make you apologetic, Will. I turn you all to thinking naught of yourself.'

'No. It doesn't need you for that, mistress.'

'Good wine, good Rhenish. You're growing rich, I think.' She held the cup out to him, made him draw near to take it. Her breath was hot with the wine. 'Will, are we not insects? That's why I love you, you see. Because I suspect you know that is all we are, yet you carry on trying to climb the mountainous pebble.'

'You don't love me.'

She shrugged. 'Yet something lies or stirs betwixt us, else why would I come here? You have a guilty look, Will Shakespeare, and yet I can't conceive what you have done wrong. Ever.'

'Another man said that to me once.'

'Another?'

He allowed the smile. 'Kit Marlowe. He was not unlike you, perhaps.'

She stood and looked down at her legs, the shape of the calf in stockings. 'How odd this feels. You men go much more uncovered in the world than women. No hiding. Well, you do, certes, but that's in the lovely groves up there.' She reached up to touch his brow. Her fingers traced the megrim-groove that wouldn't go, now; then she turned abruptly to his writing-table. 'What are you working on?'

He snatched up the papers.

'Why not let me see? It will be spoke in front of hundreds of people, after all: many fools like me.'

'Then it's different.' He laid the papers in his trunk. 'It's a black piece. That's all I'll say.'

'The best kind. Do you think I could pass for my brother?'

'I could fancy your brother looking thus, perhaps.' Her stare surprised him. 'Is that wrong?'

She barely shook her head. 'Is that more wine there? Give me, please. I've had dreams lately. And I do not allow dreams, sir. I made an order against them, long ago, when I found they made me more tired in sleep than eased. So I stopped them. Anyone can, with enough will. And yet now they come again, defying me, and I blame you. Because you make me think and feel. Because you stop me being alone in the world as I want.'

She swallowed two cups of wine.

'Alone?' he said. 'No. There must be someone, somewhere. In a place, in a past, in a vision. They're all one. It's the only thing I believe. We live our course by a star. But no knowing when we saw the star or if we will recognise it when we see it again.'

'Can stars be black?' She tapped at her breast, like someone sounding for a weak place. 'You've heard, I know, of the massacre in France. St Bartholomew's Day, the year 'seventy-two.'

'Marlowe wrote a play on it.'

'This is not about a play. This is not a play matter. I was there. I was a girl. I was seven. Now you know my age.' She sank to her knees on the hearth. Her eyes looked blindly heavy, like a child's on the brink of sleep. 'Let me repeat, I was a girl. My family was from Bordeaux. Not Paris. Perhaps here, with your plays, you think of the matter, the massacre, as in Paris only. Well, we thought that way too at first. Paris was where the fighting and the trouble happened, and the nobles coming to blows over the faith that was ours, making it a

458

matter of power, but we—we were small, a simple Protestant family, small people pecking up their grain in the quiet farmyard.' She stirred. 'Tell me, what do you know of it? I would not weary you.'

'The papists in France turned on the Protestants and massacred them. Thousands of them. That's how I heard it as a boy. There were sermons on it. I remember Master Field, Richard's father, said it proved the Pope was Antichrist.'

'I didn't see the Pope there. I saw people, mind, and he's one, is he not? We all have that doubtful honour of humanity. It started in Paris. We heard of all this great contention on high about the Protestant question. I never thought of myself as a question. Nor my father, nor my mother, nor my brother. Huguenots, yes, that was a word, but I never thought it was a bad word. We didn't go to the same church, we didn't celebrate mass. Things we didn't do—along with all the other common things we did, like eating and drinking and sending the laundry down to the stream. We were a different kind of flower in the meadow, I thought. Some red, some blue. They blow, they nod their hour in the sun. To be sure, we heard—being Huguenot—of burnings, of what the popish wanted to do to us. And there was the Queen Mother at the top, they said, the Medici witch, wanting flames, wanting an end. But still there was the harvest, and the wine, and the murrain on the sheep, and so many things in the world that saying mass was just one of many. Lost in the multitude. And it wouldn't change because Monsieur François, who was papist, owed money to Monsieur Tourreil the butcher, who was Protestant, and Monsieur Carette, the Protestant weaver, did work for

459

Monsieur Pellerin, the papist merchant. It was all so tangled, how could you unpick it? Tangled, that was good, I thought. I was not a very thinking girl, I believe. I liked sweetmeats and dressing my baby and listening to Grandmama's stories. I liked being in life, I found it a good place.

'But there were many who said that the Huguenots had too much wealth, too much power, being so few. My family was from Bordeaux, but we had moved to a village outside the city because my father had prospered as a mercer, and bought an old farmhouse and a little land and some pear-trees, and it was sweet. The high walls. The light used to sink behind them and make light-juice, I fancied, that tasted like bright pears. I made a mistake. I always thought my father loved me. He was not a man to prate of his feelings. I imagined clouds round him, like a peak. But kind, and I believed loving his daughter, though naturally his son was more important—when was it ever not so? He was the heir. In him the future lay curled. It matters so much to men, I know, the fruit of their loins, the line.' Lifting her head she looked at him, or through him: perhaps both. 'So we were outside the city, separate and quiet, when the news came that there were killings. Killings in Paris, well, there was always tumult there; the provinces were different. But, no, it was spreading. It wasn't rumour. My father had friends everywhere, educated, they could write, the news was soon going round like a poison in the body. The papist French were rising up, in Paris, in Rouen, in Orléans, and they were murdering the Protestants, and it was not being stopped. It was being directed from on high, they said. Was it?' She shrugged. 'Well, soldiers did the killing sometimes. And priests preached sermons exhorting good papists to do the Lord's work. But all that needed to happen, you see, was to let it happen.' She rose and walked past him, wine-scented, stealthy, to the window overlooking Silver Street. 'It could happen out there. A little like the time you saved me from those prentices. But with the authorities saying, instead of "Stop", smiling, shrugging, saying, "Do as you will, good people, do as you will."' The window turned her voice flat and muffled. 'Perhaps you heard the stories about the Seine being choked with the dead bodies and such. I think it was true. I think the corpses were piled about France, in those days, as the madness, or the letting go of sanity, spread. I hear they mutilated the corpses very often—though I don't see that that matters. Death is the only mutilation.'

Will wanted wine, but his hand was too unsteady to pour from the jug.

'We, or my parents, didn't think it would happen in Bordeaux. We knew too many people there, it was too sensible a place. Perhaps that's all it needs, the belief that it will not happen in this little part of the world because we are different. Which of us, after all, truly believes he will die? And my brother Robert was in Bordeaux. He was living at the house of my mother's cousin, a silk-weaver, learning the trade. He was eleven years old, very clever, very handy. He would be a great heir to my father. He had the longest fingers I have ever seen—he could untangle anything, undo any knot. He was kind to me when we were together. I think he thought it pretty and amusing having a little sister, he who belonged so early to the man's world. I loved him,

461

for what that's worth. I was a little girl, naturally I loved.

'It was smoke that first told us. Smoke above the city. They were burning houses—perhaps, from the smell, people. It was all so sudden. And my father had his horse saddled. He was going to see . . . he was going to see if all was well with the Clairets, where Robert was lodging—just that, can you believe?—and bring him home if not. Such was the way he clung to innocence, but I suppose innocence is never taken gradually. It is always cut off, with blood. And then a servant came running to our house. The Clairets' manservant. We couldn't recognise him at first. His face was all blubbered from weeping. He looked like a great baby. Dirt too, streaks of filth. He had been hiding in the cesspit. Yes, in it. Because it was better than being found: he was Protestant too. Do you want this part? But, never mind, you must have it. It's a long time ago. And everyone who matters in it is dead except me, possibly.

'They were killing in Bordeaux. A priest set it off, it seems. I don't know. I fancy it more like birds when they begin to fly south, drawing together, knowing what to do. Flocking. They dragged the Clairets out from their house and killed them in the square. A mob. A mob of their neighbours, that is. They killed them in the hot sun, it was hot, dry August, ripping them with swords and daggers. I don't suppose it took long to do. And, yes, they ripped up my brother too. Eleven years old. He was not the youngest to die, no, there were babes at the breast, which I conceive are as easy to kill as worms or snails. Surely. Think you so?'

'Don't.'

Her teeth gleamed: her eyes too. 'A question for another time perhaps. But a boy, my brother, strong, that would take a little longer. The servant heard that Robert tried to shield Madame Clairet before he was cut down, but who knows? The man was hiding at the time. Perhaps Robert wasn't brave, perhaps he whimpered and wept as they killed him, there in the sun. There must have been a great deal of blood on the cobbles. Well, they said the rivers ran red, you know, but again one cannot be sure. You haven't reached out to touch me, Will, and I'm glad of that, it's so very cheap. Almost as cheap as life. I saw my father weep, for a little time. Then stop. My mother's grief was longer, louder. She could give herself to it, perhaps. My father had to be thinking. And I—I cried too, and I wanted a little more attention for crying, for my grief, than I was getting. Because I knew exactly what I was crying for, I knew they had killed my brother. Children know a great deal. I remember a girl when I first came to London, when we shared a cramped house: she took sick with plague and said over and over, "I'm going to die," and shook her head sadly at her mother when she said, "No, no, you're not." She was eight, perhaps. She died.

'Well, we had to flee, certainly. They would soon come for us. We had to plan how to live on, while Robert's corpse was on the heap in the town down the valley there. Someone climbed on top of the heap and sang God's praises, I heard, but that might not be true also. The dead, though, they are real, the only reality. Robert used to embrace me sometimes, from behind, hands over my eyes, and say, "Who?" And I would say absurdities. Rodelinde de Piquemonsieur. He liked, as I said,

463

having a sister. My father, having me, not so much. Yet still I thought . . . I thought I had my portion of love. So: with my mother still wailing like a rooftop cat we gathered what we could. We knew where to go. To old La Farge's house. He was a fat, rich old merchant, who lived on the coast in a house with great gates, and he had a boat in a cove. Smuggling, they said—but La Farge had always believed this day would come and that the Protestants would have to flee France. Be ready, he always said.

'On to the cart, then. The risk that they had got to the old man first, or that they would stop us on the road, well, it was that or wait for them to come. The servant drove. We lay under sacks. The servant kept the dirt on his face to make him look less like himself: see how life turns like a play, after all. I can remember, through my sadness and fear, feeling a little excited at bumping along the steep road hidden under sacks, and I wished Robert had been there to share it, which made me sad again. My mother moaned and moaned. I put my arms round her but it was like embracing a stone or— something dead, say. My father was quiet. So quiet. Now I'm mindful that all of us at that time were, in essence, mad with what had happened. Yes? So perhaps none of it can be said to signify. Certainly when old man La Farge saw us, his face—well, he looked a little afeared. At what he saw. But then all was quickness, urgent, doing. He had the boat ready, but there was a wait yet for a favourable tide, and so where should we wait? He said we would be safe in his house but my mother wailed that we were safe nowhere. "In France, now, no," old man La Farge said. "I've seen it coming. We'll not be the only ones fleeing." He had friends who had already gone over to England. Where Protestants were free. The time had come, he said. And my father still said nothing. He looked like a man of chalk, as if dust would puff out from his skin. I think it was the first time I ever heard of England—yet how so? People of our faith always talked of it in those days, when there were troubles. Perhaps the word had never stood out till then, that night. They put goods on donkeys, and we went down to the cove and waited there, in the dark. I say *our faith*. I allude to something I never believed, myself, in my memory. It has always been empty, it seems. Perhaps once there was a fullness there. Here.' Her hand hovered over her breast, stomach. 'And then when the light came, and the tide was fair, my father spoke. He stood up, towards the shoreline, where there was still a little smoke. The donkeys were being unloaded, things thrown into a little rowboat, and the sail on the coaster was flapping and there we were, preparing to leave and flee France. Our world. It had broken that quickly. And my father picked up a bag and let it fall. Then he saw me. And he picked me up and held me up to the line of shore where the smoke was and said: "Why couldn't you take her? Take her instead. Not my boy, not my son. I could better have spared her." His fingers were tight and hard as they gripped me. My mother didn't say anything. She was still weeping. Perhaps she agreed, I don't know. After that he put me down quite softly on the sand. And then we sailed, and we were lucky, we escaped, and others followed, as you know, coming to England, and settled. Made welcome, except when hated. What a moral story. We settled at Canterbury first. That was where I first sat down, and looked at what life had shown me.'

Canterbury: Marlowe flashed upon Will's mind again. He imagined Marlowe hearing this story: his savage grin. It helped to keep it at a distance, to quiet the screams of the boy dragged out and slashed. Had he looked like Isabelle? Not in the picture in his head, no. More familiar. He felt tears somewhere in his throat or deeper. They weren't much use, now: words likewise. But he tried to find some.

'You do well to speak of madness, Isabelle. The madness was inflicted by those who did the killing. Not only the dead were victims. Living minds too. Your father—'

'Oh, for God's sake, don't you think I've been everywhere, down every path? He said it, Will. He meant it. And if we had been caught, I believe he would have said: "Take her, leave me him." And, in a curious way, I wish that had happened. We never spoke of it again. And as soon as we came to London, and my father began to prosper, I looked out for a husband. So I could go. I was sixteen, Monsieur Berger forty. It counted for nothing. What was my body anyway? What is anyone's, but a piece of flesh, to be desired perhaps for a time, in youth and a little later, now and then—but mostly it is a corpse waiting to be completed, like those piles in the squares and rivers on St Bartholomew's Day. When my father died I didn't go to his burying. Just another body.' She was weeping now. The tears came thick and slow, oozing, like blood. 'And yet you want mine, I know you do—and you might after all have had my body, Will, if you had not been so covetous of my mind, for this is what you've wanted, isn't it? To know, know about me. The true

466

possession. There's the pity: as mere bodies we might have done very well, you and I.' She came to the table, swallowed the last of the Rhenish. 'Good wine. But all wine is good. Don't come near me, now.' Shadow-fast, she was at the door. 'You've seen too much. Goodbye.'

*　　　*　　　*

'Check,' says Jonson. 'You know, you can't win with what's left on the board. Have you writ nothing for the new king? An ode, verses, something? You should, everyone has. Even clodpoll Dekker.'

Will searches the squares for a way out. 'And you?'

'Can you doubt it? His majesty must have the best as well as the dross.'

Will tries to picture the new king, James, who separately from his queen is making a slow progress down from Scotland to take up his new throne. None of the feared disturbances, after all, a smooth transition. Thank heaven. No heaped corpses, choked rivers. 'No. I've writ nothing. I can't quite— he seems not real to me, not like the late Queen.' For now I see a king with a round base and no legs, making his way across the white bloodless squares of towns, the chequered fields. 'We have hopes of favour, naturally, in the Chamberlain's. We hear from my lord Hunsdon that the King is much affected to the theatre.'

'There you have it, man. Yours is the best company. Make him know it. Get in the loyal verses while you can. It's not policy. It's a poet's true part to honour his sovereign. Ours are the public voices, the trumpets of the state, handmaids of the national

467

muse. I have a commission in the bud, you know, for the Queen's entertainment, when she comes to Althorp. Sir John Spencer entreated me. A masque, in the grounds. An enchanting thought: I see the prettiest little sport in my eye, chaste, classical, beyond the groundlings' brute ken . . .'

'I was right. Being popish hasn't hurt you.'

'Nothing ever hurts me. How else live?'

'The other way. Where all hurts.'

'Now you're seeing in black and white,' Jonson says approvingly. 'Checkmate. We're friends once more, yes? Out of that, then, I ask: what are you going to do about the woman?'

'Do?'

'Aye, do. Because knowing you, seeing your face last night, today, you will have to do something. You can't simply go on.'

With a flick Will knocks his king over. It rolls a little and lies still.

14

Revenger's Tragedy (1603)

'He's no Alleyn,' Henslowe grunted.

They were watching Matthew run through a second-man comedy part for the Admiral's Men. Matt, Will saw, was trying to broaden his gestures. Containment was one of the first things you learned when playing women. Now, hoping to get work as a man, he had to unlearn it.

'Well, there's only one Alleyn,' Will said: not meaning flattery, though Henslowe plainly took it so. He generally viewed his son-in-law as a sort of Christ to his own deity. 'But Matthew has spirit, wit, boldness—'

'And not much of a voice yet. How long broke? A pretty fellow, mind. Oh, they'll take him, as hired-man, for now. Your word would have been enough.' Henslowe sniffed, disliking the admission.

'How goes it here?' They stood in the pit of the Fortune, the newest of theatres, Henslowe's latest venture. 'You don't think there are too many theatres in London now?'

'You sound like a Cheapside Puritan.'

'No, a man of business.'

'What—is the Globe suffering, then?' Henslowe asked, suddenly hungry.

'No. And the Chamberlain's Men have hopes of becoming the King's. Sorry.'

Henslowe shrugged. 'Nay, trust me, we have not seen the end of play-fever yet. Why, we can fill this place to the rafters with cold drizzle falling and a mere indifferent comedy.'

'Which reminds me,' Will said, 'who wrote this?'

'Let's see, at least half is Dekker's, the rest a sharp, sour young fellow called Middleton. Know him? You should. Says he wants to excel Master Shakespeare.'

'Good for him.' Will watched Matthew take an inexpert fall: another consequence of woman-playing. 'You know it won't last for ever. This. We'll tire, or the public will, or something will. Well? Why else do you and Alleyn keep hold of your bear-baiting yards?'

Henslowe did not quite smile. He looked as if he had spotted a coin on the ground and was trying not to pick it up. 'Aye, sounder than gold, my friend.

When is spilled blood ever out of fashion?'

The sun shone brilliantly on a square, a white square; and a boy was taken, ripped, sacrificed, and the pooled blood looked black in the dazzle.

'Never.' The player with Matthew had his hand on his shoulder and was nodding: he was in. Matthew turned to flash a smile at Will, from across the stage, from across a score of years. 'I'm going home tomorrow. A short visit only. I must be here, with the coronation coming.' The only reason? No, I am flying thither, probably to fly back at once. An uncaged bird. 'Will you keep a watch on Matthew, where you can?'

'Needs watching, hey?'

Will shook his head. 'A good lad, an excellent lad. But everything excites. He has to see the bottom of the tankard before he believes it empty.'

'I'll watch,' Henslowe said. Not benign. Why should he be? These were his investments, his ships and vineyards.

As Will went to leave, he found Henslowe's manservant, the size and build of a bull, his arm against the jamb of the tiring-house door, denying someone access.

'No, sir,' he was saying, in a sorrowful growl, 'no, sir, I think not.'

'But look you, I come to tell him I *can* pay him. Not pay him *now*, but soon, very soon . . .'

A lightly frantic voice. The bull-man glanced back at Will, shifted enough to let him through. 'Your pardon, sir.'

Will edged past, and found himself chest to chest, eyes meeting, with Jack Towne.

Jack—surely not?—looking somehow as of old. Yet he must be, like Will, approaching forty. The flabbiness was gone, the long bones back (hunger?) and the fairness too. Ah, yes. He must have been on the tramp by the play-wagon a long season to be sunstruck so fair. Prominent cheekbones and brows. 'Jack.' Like turning a corner and bumping into your old self, that most unreachable of lost things. Marlowe spoke, grinning again, old ghost.

'Will.' Jack Towne looked at him as if he had asked him a bleak fateful question: as if they met on a dire heath. 'You thrive. Glad of it. Always glad.'

Will nudged the manservant. It was like nudging a wall. 'Let this man by. Master Henslowe will see him. Yes, yes, I will answer for it.'

Towne edged in. His shirt was worn away at the neck: you could see the clean straight line of his collarbone. His eyes made wild, unavailing stabs at Will's face.

'Here.' Will pressed his purse into Towne's hand. He looked grubby. He smelt like yesterday. 'And Jack, if you—if you need—'

Towne stopped him with a touch, eyes averted. 'Thanks, heart. But don't make it worse, hey?'

He went in, head low. He was abashed. Will was too grand for him now. The time ever out of joint.

Damn time, and we might open heaven.

*   *   *

Anne knew: as much as she had ever known anything.

Admittedly, that in itself made it incomplete. She was not great in knowledge. All she had to work on was this, her feeling, her sense: her conviction.

And she hated it. Because it put her in Judith Sadler's world of winking gloomy wisdom (not that she said anything to her—great God, no). It was knowing what they would say, in that world. With acid resignation. Aye, a woman can always tell. Lips pursed at the fireside, pursed at the drear old tale of men and perfidy.

'You've had a lot of your megrims.' She touched his forehead. He slightly withdrew.

'No. About the same.' He smelt different or, rather, had no scent, as if scrubbed.

Oh, you can tell. And once she thought perhaps she wouldn't have cared. Or cared less, cared without this ache and challenge. Because something was awake in Anne. A sense of herself, partly. 'You do know,' Bartholomew had said, 'that when he's away, you are head of the Shakespeare family?' Nonsense. But then it wouldn't be denied. Once you made that affrighting leap, outside yourself to the place others stood in, looking at you. Mistress of New Place. In her way, a woman of the world.

Ask yourself: am I worthy of Will Shakespeare's love? I verily believe I am, and so I must ask whether he is worthy of mine. Yes, something was awake: even if it was only suspicion that he had followed the path of otherness all the way. I know he has always pursued that path, the snaking words, the art of dream, the thickets of thought, where sometimes I can hardly see him. But how if he has followed it and found instead someone else there, amid the dapple—to be loved? For if it is so, I cannot have it so. I am not resigned. Who could live to be resigned, even at a hundred?

Head of the family—how so, when she was a woman and there were men? But Anne didn't feel fenced by womanhood, as even lively Joan seemed to now that she was wed. And even

472

though William Hart gazed moonstruck still and did everything she told him, quickly. Still Joan seemed somehow rather less herself, rather more generalised woman. Anne didn't feel so: she felt an independent creature, with her own borders and laws. Forty-seven years old. What does it mean? How you look, how you feel? Some people didn't know how old they were: even Will was unsure of his birthday.

Imagine, as Anne did when she dared the mirror, growing old in content. The warm side of resignation, if you liked: glowing and rounded and buttery. She knew that was how she could go— it was in her looks: she was still fair, soft-skinned, dew-fed, in that reflection in the mirror—except when you fell into those eyes. But it was a choice, a possible future, to be that woman: mother to her tall flowerlike daughters, aunt and relative to all, and as for her husband . . . Well, the buttery matron would chuckle drily: 'Oh, him, a good provider. He'll retire to the country at last, and then we'll see enough and more of each other, Lord knows.'

And the men of the family? Gilbert had settled back in Stratford, haberdasher, dealer, they said, in other things. An uneasy, secretive man who liked to catch people out. 'I caught him finely,' he would say of a good bargain, 'like a tickled fish.' She suspected him of an unhappiness too big for his narrow personality. Richard had taken his father's place in the shop, but with none of his father's assertion. And then there was her mother-in-law, who had taken age to her heart like a long desire. She was islanded in it: silver-haired, shadowy. 'Just a little,' she would say to the cold beef: 'just a little,' if the fire needed stirring. 'Less and less, my wants.'

473

But Anne, no, more and more my wants. Something was awake.

Will's was a short visit home, no time to do some things, to visit all old acquaintances. And when he packed his bag for the morrow journey, he was suddenly stricken.

'I haven't been to Hamnet's grave.'

'Neither have I. He's not there, now. For a time, he was, but no more.' And that's as it should be, isn't it? Something in her wanted to say that, and for a moment she wondered if she had. The unspoken was so much a part of their conversation, it was hard to tell if it had slipped into the garment of speech.

She should have followed this with something. She was trying to say—what? That her heart moved and changed, without loss of love? That they did not stand as they had in the black aftermath of Hamnet's dying, when white was gone from the world? But how say it? They would have to lay the naked sword of their marriage on the table between them, instead of Susannah's dowry and the repairs to the outhouse roof. Easy things to take your attention.

Besides, her breath was stopped, her tongue pinched by suspicion. Freezing, binding suspicion.

How did he appear? Will at New Place, bony, dark-browed, abstracted. Soft words for Judith, who was in sulking mood. Yet you knew that voice could fill a theatre. He had it under control. Never gave much away. His expression at the fireside did not belong here. Like a fox in a kennel.

One notable night of his stay he did something he never did; and she wasn't sure if she had prompted him. He spoke of his work, what he was writing. Haltingly, in dry fragments, as if he feared to put life into it. But as they lay in the unsleeping awkwardness that nothing could fill or hasten, he talked of a tragedy in mind.

'Are you done with comedies?'

'Of a sort. I can't see my way quite to laughter. It's up aloft but no roads run all the way. Tragedy is lit. I can move there.'

'Isn't it more popular also?'

'Perhaps.' His smile was a faint dark movement on the pillow. 'Jonson would damn me for following the crowd. Yet I don't have to think in that way somehow: what people want. It merely happens. There's the old play of *Leir* I acted in years past. I see it in different colours.'

And he talked of an old proud king, dividing his kingdom between two daughters with flattering tongues. For the daughter who spoke truth, nothing but banishment. Anne couldn't recall seeing the play, but thought she had heard a tale like that told when she was a girl. She saw the fire and smelt wood and felt herself blinking and imagining being the truthful girl, whom she pictured with pale cheeks and straight hair. And then, wasn't there an enchanter, magic . . . ? But no: Will in his light, clear voice, which came through the bedstead as a vibration to the blood, spoke tentative horrors. He conjured a lord of this court, similarly mistook in the virtues of his sons, who comes to grief as the old king does. His eyes are put out, and he is turned out to wander blind—though less blind than he has been. And the old king is turned out on the blasted heath, ragged and friendless . . .

'And the other daughter,' Anne said, sitting upright, 'the good daughter, she returns, and

475

restores him, yes?'

'That's the old play. Not this one. I see her killed, and the old king bearing her body, mad with grief. Yes, that's how it must be: only can be.'

Anne pushed back the bed-curtains, wishing for a light. Light in darkness. 'I think it will not work, Will.'

'Why?'

'Because such horrors will not be believed.'

'Oh, you don't know, my dear,' he said; and turned from her.

Turned into stillness and silence. Not sleeping: somewhere else. *My dear*. Never that before. It seemed to say everything but *wife*.

On the roof was the vivid percussive sound of night-rain.

Her smarting eyes measured the space between their bodies. You could fit someone in it.

You don't know. Oh, I do know, now.

*   *   *

So, she did a thing that was bad: because she had to know.

Bad, in that it was double, hollow, not straight and true—she could hardly find an image for its equivocal quality. Bartholomew would probably have scoffed at the notion of its being bad at all. But Anne wore her decision like a hair-shirt. She would never have done it if she had not been driven, urged, lashed by the thing that was awake and would not sleep now. Not until there was knowledge, one way or another.

*   *   *

'Edmund,' she said, 'I will speak to him.'

Edmund was chopping wood in the yard at Henley Street. As she spoke his scalp lifted, the hatchet dropped from his hands: his eyes shone at her. He could not disguise his happiness and hope. He could never disguise anything. So unlike his brother in that, she thought.

So, to do it. The prickly, queasy, wrong feeling came also from the fact that she did not doubt she would succeed. Edmund's one aim and joy was to follow Will and be a player. More than once he had come straight out with it, and more than once Will had temporised, saying the times were not propitious for players, they must think on it . . . Edmund went on desperately hoping. But hoping on nothing. She knew Will didn't think him cut out for the player's life, and that he would go on setting his face against it for ever. And Edmund loved Will too much to press, demand, make a drag of himself on his brother's mind.

Only one thing could change it.

Very hesitantly, Edmund had asked Anne before if she might put in a word for him—just a word. But he blushed in asking—not wanting, she thought, to come between them, and not wanting Anne to think any the worse of him, because he adored her. Such knots they tied themselves in. Yet how easy to cut through, once she had decided.

'Will, Edmund is sorely grieved.'

He was mending a pen. He came out from wherever he went. 'Why?'

'Oh, you must know. He has not spoke of it this time—but in that silence you can surely read. I can read it. How he longs for you to say yes.'

'Oh, that. Well, yes, he hasn't asked, so I supposed he had let it fall.'

'No, you didn't.' She put a hand on his arm, and he jumped as if at a bailiff's arrest. 'You've set yourself against it. Because—well, there I wonder, what? You think he will not thrive as you did?'

Will shrugged. 'I fear he has not the temper.'

'As Matthew does?'

'We are not there again, I hope.'

'No,' she said, pressing against the stony look, 'but you tell me Matthew, for all his talents, has a young man's unsteadiness. Edmund is three-and-twenty, dost think he is in worse case? When it's what he longs for above everything beneath the sun?'

'Matt was raised to it from a boy. Edmund has lived so different . . . I fear me he will not bear the knocks, and be hurt.'

'Thou wert not raised to it, Will.'

'Edmund isn't me,' he said, with pale finality.

'And thou art not thy father. And wouldst not, surely, play the part he played thee so long, blocking the way, nay-saying—surely.'

A risky, or daring stroke. For a moment something seemed to mask his eyes, like the side-lids of a bird.

'He's asked you to do this.'

'No. I ask, because I don't want to see such unhappiness go on, when it might be mended. And if there is hurt, then, Will, it must be: wasn't that the risk you took, and took gladly, when you went away with the players? Don't we all have to live with it, or not live at all?'

And she won. Because he would not refuse both her and Edmund. And also, terribly, his giving in was another sign. If his heart had been with her, he might have contended more, spoken more: given this matter its due weight of significance between husband and wife. A thing so close trod on the skirts of love. But Will gave in, she thought, because it was easier, and it kept her sweet, and his mind was still far, fixed over there.

So it was all impure, on both sides: you couldn't drink cleanly of it. But the waking thing drove her, the need. Jealousy? Too simple, too answerable.

She went to Henley Street while Will was going over the household accounts. A long, painstaking process. He was not particularly slow in reckoning, but he checked the numbers as if they were words, and might dance about in meaning. She asked Edmund to go a walk with her, down to the river. He came, in luminous silence. By the bridge she pressed his arm, smiled. Felt his breathlessness.

'You've spoken.' He still didn't dare: too far to fall.

'It's done. You are to go back with him to London, and he will find you work as a player.'

Edmund took her hand and kissed it. She let it lie in his for a moment, looking down at the river, smelling the coolness of wet stone, weed, sweetly decaying bulrushes. Stickleback darted and teemed, like blown drifts of smoke under the water.

'But you must do something for me,' she said; and as the words came out she wondered if this was how actors felt, for they seemed to have been made somewhere other than her own brain. 'I want you to find out if Will has a woman in London.'

Edmund caught his breath. She could not look at him, could only bury her sight in the draggled water, but she knew what his expression would be.

479

'And—and then?' Horror for him, who loved them both so, horror and poison. But he would taste the dish. Will's fearful tragedy of Titus, she had read it in part, shuddering—the one where the woman's children were baked in a pie, and she ate of the pie before the heads were revealed . . . But taste it. When desire drives, you taste. Edmund squeezed her hand, painfully. 'I don't want to, Anne.'

'But?'

'Yes. And then?'

'Then come and tell me.'

And then the great cliff to face, to scale—or fall from. Then the final knowledge of self and him, and if they could ever meet more.

*   *   *

Well, Will had known this must come. Edmund had been angling for it ever since their father died. In a way it was a relief to be forced to it.

'I shall not disgrace you,' Edmund kept saying, on the ride to London. 'Trust me.' He was wholly obedient, even subservient. Will suspected that Edmund did not sleep at all during their two inn-halts on the way: that he just lay there, eyes shining in the dark at what was happening to him. It was faintly irritating.

But only faintly. Why, after all, had he resisted this so long? Because he feared his brother would be a trouble to him, an inconvenience? Or was Anne closer to the truth, when she suggested he was walking in his father's shoes?

And it was, after all, not so bad. Edmund was too old for a true prentice, but Will found him a lodging with John Heminges. He had a decent house and was married to a pleasant, sensible woman who, Will had learned to his shock, was none other than the widow of William Knell, whose death at Jack Towne's hands had opened his world. Some sort of circle completed, perhaps. Heminges undertook to train him up as far as he could—he was much occupied with the company finances— and they could probably get him regular work with Worcester's Men. When he watched Edmund try out Will found him just as he had feared—stiff, over-eager, shrill—but he passed, and Will's name alone was warrant enough.

And perhaps that was it. He said as much to Ben Jonson, over a farewell supper at the Mermaid: Jonson was setting forth for Northamptonshire, to present his masque to the new Queen.

'I question me whether I am a fraud. I love him dearly, but I misdoubt whether his talents could advance him saving my influence. So, am I not watering down the strength of our theatre, lowering its quality?'

'You're too particular, man. The lad is green, but will learn from good masters. And it is besides a proper part of your position to advance your family and friends: how else does the world wag, from the Court to the stage? What—would you rather he stay slumbering by the Avon?'

'Shrewd in you. For I look within and see something of that. Perhaps I wanted to discover whether it was possible, after all: to stay, to stay as I did not, and be yet happy.'

'No one can live life for you,' Jonson said.

'No? Dear God, how I wish it.'

But all in all it was not so bad. Edmund set himself devoutly to learning his lines and his trade, listened respectfully to everyone involved, called on Will infrequently. He did not seem drawn to the taverns and gaming-dens, as Matthew was: Heminges reported him sober and domestic. It was as if he woke each morning to the miracle of his achieved wish, and resolved to do nothing to endanger it, ever.

To be sure, that might not last. Will considered his brother every bit as susceptible as—well, as himself? But for now there was health in it: straightforward affection between brothers, doing the expected thing. Not that sickness which he saw, now, was in his other, dark and incidental, life. Isabelle.

He could pity her, though he knew she would turn and rend at the first sign of any such thing: pity her for that naked pulsing past, for what it had made of her spirit. But he could see, also—was it the short visit home that did it, the light blue touch of eyes that would not reach him?—that there was no good for either of them in their continued game of fascination. Only pain could result. Destruction. It grew round them, like mould growing round the surface of a fruit.

Yet it went on. It flowed on, turbulently, casting up vivid fragments of memory when he lay down at night.

The first visit to her on his return to London, the visit meant to be the end. He meant absolutely to break it. But her bird had died. It had died the day before, and still lay on the bottom of the cage. Will found he missed that infuriating ticking.

'I am not a delicate woman, Will. As you well know. Why then can I not move it? Because once you do that, it's dead, dead—isn't it?'

She wouldn't let him see her weep. Still he felt it, the weeping inside her, as one felt rather than heard bees in a hive.

He found a patch of soil in the yard behind the house, and dug a hole for the bird with a piece of wood. It seemed incredibly laborious: sweat fell from his eyebrows. He remembered blood dripping into Stratford earth: was suddenly appalled by age, its very existence. Stop time, stop it.

He stayed with her an hour, after.

For how could he break with her now? And, after all, what if, in her strange way, she did love him?

But then that meant nothing. He was married, although his wife was dead to him—or, rather, love was dead to him, that was all. All and everything. Still, he did not want to see Isabelle hurt. Previously he would have thought it impossible, but since her confession to him—so he figured it—he had revised all his thoughts of her.

But those thoughts must be crushed. Because of Anne. Not what they were to each other now, but what they had been, and might have been. In Stratford he had felt the presence of that other Will, whose shape had indented the mattress, whose hands when small had grasped the banister of his father's staircase that shone from its thousands of touchings. He was there, like the dead, like dead Marlowe (whom he would not have been surprised to see hailing him from across the inn-yard). He was there like the imagined, like old Lear, whose proud breaking accents were beginning to intrude on his mind. He was real, like the people you avoided being.

Yes, he was a hypocrite. He could not be the

true gentle Master Shakespeare, just as Jonson had hinted. But I do not have to be this man, he told himself, caught up in a species of attraction that was like lust turned cold and slow. As if a man without appetite found himself compelled to eat until he was sick, and then to eat to make that emptiness better . . .

The next time, he would tell her. And if this turned out to be another lie to himself, then self-hate must come to a new and killing pitch. Already he woke up couched in his skin with mistrust: oh, it's you, me, is it? His own mind a cutpurse, smiling, stealing away from him.

*   *   *

'I tell you, I'm not in the vein for talk this even.' Isabelle picked at chords on the virginal like someone picking at a scab. She threw him a look, fiercely weighted. 'Mark me well.'

'None of your prohibitions,' he said. 'No more of that, Isabelle. I speak as I would speak to anyone, as I should have spoken long before. No play, no game. I'm here to say farewell. Declare an end.' He fixed his eyes on her stilled hands: saw the lifted defensive posture of a caught crab. 'I do wrong to see you. You do wrong to continue our—our mutual trouble.'

'Wrong.' She turned, with an odd, skewed briskness. 'Wrong? Is that the best word to be found, by the man of words? Dreary, mouse-crumb word, wrong, meaning nothing to anyone in their secret truth. Where wrong—here?' She darted to him and placed her hand on his heart, for the space of a beat. 'Or here?' Her hand found his groin, met it swelling. 'Not wrong, they say, not wrong—'

He stepped backward, but there seemed nowhere to go. As if the room was surrounding him, a determined crowd. Her face loomed.

'Don't leave me. Leave me, and I'll die. I swear. I have no fear of it, Will, I have it ready for the coming time, in my trunk; a sure certain dose mixed, my quietus, as your Dane called it. But not now, the time. Could you do it? Not you. You don't kill, do you, Will? You make life. Make my life. Leave me another day. Will, leave me another day, yes?' She sucked his lips and breath. One high hand reverent, tremblingly touching his neck: the other low and worldly firm on his cock. 'Time will atone. Don't kill me. None of your hurt, Will—instead, here. Here.'

So, at last, it was his move that turned the game.

He had never meant it—or had he? Or was this her best stroke of play ever?

Her clothes went off, as if she had longed all her life to be rid of them.

All such conquests, he thought, somewhere along the grim delirious evening, are also defeats. Her bed was warm: unnaturally so, as if someone had just left it—or as if it were a living thing, breathing beneath them. He was amazed at her strength: one moment he seemed to feel himself nailed to the board of her sex. Then, it all seemed to go and she was kittenish-weak. Her eyes kept seeking his throughout. She allowed no closing. As if resolved that this must be witnessed: this, the completion.

'And now, try to leave me.' She spoke with easy, murmurous security. She had on only his shirt, and sat on the bed with a crook of dull-gold thigh and calf turned to him, and hair heavily down. 'Though

485

yes, to be sure, you will try.'

'Is that what you suppose?' Stripped he sat on the harsh boards, cooling hands clasped around his thinness. 'Just this, and then an end to appetite?'

'What—are you so different from other men?' She chuckled, was briefly thoughtful, then raised crystal new-amused eyes to him. 'Let me tell you, Will, you are not.'

'Give me my shirt, Isabelle.'

'Take it.'

'Hm. If I refuse, if I go without it, what then? Will you die, again?'

She yawned, stretching back. 'Any of us may die at any moment, don't you know that? There's plague creeping in at Southwark, so I hear, ready to jump across the river. You're too foolish fond about a mere thing like life, Will.' She sat up and folded her hands deep in her lap, the taut arrowing triangle of his shirt pointing down. 'You'll come back.'

'Will I? What's left in the box?'

'You're bold now because your cock's soft. Just like a man getting up from a banquet who says he'll never fancy eating again.'

'You're no banquet, Isabelle.'

'I know,' she said, yawning. 'I'm poison. How you moaned when I bit your teats, and how hard and high you were. Jesu.' She smiled hazily to herself, then clawed off his shirt and tossed it to him. 'Here, take. You'll look foolish without.'

*　　　*　　　*

Outside he breathed in puffs of sharp, painful air, as if woken from bad dreaming. For a few moments he could hardly stir, had to lean against the wall; as if the hatred of self that occupied the centre of his being had, literally, unbalanced him. He got moving. Saw people ahead: a beggar with a crutch, an alewife, two gallants pretty-legged, earringed, fox-faced. Somehow he couldn't bear for them to see him. He ducked back into the alleyway, and collided with a cloaked figure.

Edmund.

'Dear God. What are you doing here?'

Edmund equipped himself with a smile, ahead of words. 'I hardly know, brother. I'm all out of knowledge in London still. I was seeking . . . How's it called—Aldersgate?' He licked his lips.

Will pointed. There was a fungal taste in his mouth. At his feet the refuse of the kennel seemed to call to him, speak with muddy moving tongues.

'Ah, there. Do you go that way, no? Very well.' Edmund clapped a hand to his arm. He looked young and fresh and somehow exposed, needing some carapace against the world. 'I love thee, Will, and naught on earth can ever change that.'

An echo of their old joke whenever he came home. Yes, try to think of it as a joke. If any subject of thinking could be bearable now, like home, love, truth. Suddenly they were lopped ruins; pick your way among them, look for something, something left.

*   *   *

The letter: it comes with Greenaway on a day when they are entertaining at New Place a new arrival.

Stratford has a much-needed physician: Dr John Hall, young, well trained, sober and industrious.

487

Beautifully pale, square face, intense black hair and beard—a face as arresting and finished as superior portrait. A fine catch for the town in all ways, as the matrons of Stratford must be thinking. And Susannah, plainly, is much taken with him.

He with her? Difficult to tell: he is so grave, no lover's simper. They say purges and glysters are all his love. Anne watches her daughter pouring his beer, seating herself modestly at a distance. That upward flash of her eyes in admiration, especially when he drops into Latin. Anne thinks: Have a care. Not that she would say it. Even now she does not think of herself as entitled to give advice in that way. Doesn't feel, somehow, old enough. At the Quineys' there has been a deal of gossip about a widow from Drayton who has married again at the age of forty-five. Fancy, thinks Anne, but there, she must know what she's about at that age—figuring the widow as much older than her. Somehow she lacks the confidence to feel forty-seven: if she did, she would be conscious of a fraud. Perhaps that is the great separation in the world, between those who know they are frauds, and those who happily go on pretending not to be.

But, please, Susannah, have a care. Make the right choice. Or, rather, recognise a choice when it comes along. That's what we miss, so often. That road? I saw only one road.

The letter crackles in the pocket of her gown while Dr Hall makes his grave farewells. Though she is not good at discerning between hands, she is sure the writing on the direction is not Will's but Edmund's.

If so, she hopes to God there are no testing words in it, for this—she is sure—is not a letter that can be shown. Whichever way it falls.

But why a letter? She exacted Edmund's promise, in a last red-faced whisper before his departure, that he would come home, when he could, and tell her face to face. Perhaps he can't: work, money. Perhaps he has found the whole suggestion so absurd that a scribble is all that's needed: sister, you're a fool, be easy. Perhaps she should open the letter.

'His smell mislikes me, it is thorough distasteful,' Judith is saying. Judith, eighteen, still pimpled and gangling, her menses a torment. Passing through the gates of growing is grim for her. Hamnet would have been eighteen too: how would it have been for him? But then how can one imagine troubles for the dead?

'Why do you say that?' Susannah yawningly asks.

'He savours of deathbeds and poultices. I should be sick to have him much about me.'

'Well, *you* need not fear that, sister.'

'What do you mean?'

'Peace, peace,' Anne cries. 'My head aches with it.'

'Best fetch Sir Doctor back then.' Judith stamps out, pleased with herself.

Susannah draws close. 'What's amiss, Mother?'

'Nothing, heart. Say, are there wasps in at the north chamber window again? I swear there must be a nest somewhere in the eaves.'

At last, alone, by candlelight, Anne opens the letter.

Dearest sister, accept my word that there is
naught, naught of what you suspected. No one. I
wish you had not put this upon me, for the love I

bear you both. Let us forget, in love, and be to one another as we were. Edmund.

A short, quivering declaration, meandering down the middle of the page. Oh, Edmund, she thinks, as her legs buckle and take her clumsily down to the solitary bed. Oh, Will is right: you are really not a good actor. You might as well have written her name.

*   *   *

'What ails you, man? You're long in the tooth for green-sickness.' Ben spoke briskly, but his heart misgave him, seeing Will so pale and lean, so heavy-eyed. He had marked several plague-crosses since coming back to London from Northamptonshire. Sometimes the sickness worked slow . . .

'I'm at work on a tragedy,' Will said. 'Didst ever see a man in such case skip at the heels?'

A light of a sort appeared in Will's face, and Ben allowed himself to be reassured. 'Why, it needn't be so. See friend Dekker, he looks the same vacant dolt whatever he's writing.'

'Why do you let him do it?' That was the young dark fellow, Middleton, lately taken on to write for Henslowe. All great solemn watchful eyes. Mordant tongue. Something in him, Ben thought warily.

'What—make myself an easy target?' Dekker said readily. 'Why, with Jonson's poor loose aim, what other kind can he hit?'

'Well, let's have more drinks, and be easy,' said Will, ever the peacemaker. He couldn't get out of it now, Ben thought: these fellows began actually to act themselves, at last. 'And tell us of your triumph in the country.'

He told; though he doubted even Will, the choicest spirit there, could truly take it in. The genial splendour of Althorp and its proprietor, Sir John Spencer, stout and plain and true as his avenue of oaks: loyal to the memory of his wife; all that a country gentleman should be. And then the Queen being entertained there—a true queen to Ben, lovely fair and gracious star of the north, Anne of Denmark, and her enchanting son, the young Prince Henry, already with all the spirit and address of a true Prince of Wales. Ben thanked his God that he had never esteemed a lord merely for being a lord: no, what impressed him here was true grace and elegance mixed with the good salt of domestic virtue. Cultured, too; the entertainment he devised for her called on all the resources of his fancy, learning and wit. They had set it in the wooded grounds, where fairies and satyrs danced in the dapple and hailed the delighted Queen in rhyme. Perfection of artifice married to the natural . . . And then such a crowd of nobility on the day of her departure, when Ben's farewell address was read on the terrace to the sound of trumpets, a piece so full of sweet turns and charming conceits that diverse among them were moved to ask who was this poet raising Helicon by slow Nene-side?

'How,' Dekker put in, 'did any of them hear it, what with the crowd and the trumpeting?'

'Those that have ears will always hear, no matter how loud the donkeys bray,' Ben snapped. In his mind he was feeling Sir John's hand on his shoulder as they walked in the park and talked companionably of planting and prospects, timber and taste, as man and man. And gone was his

491

stepfather, the bricklayers' tools, the narrow lanes and yards of Westminster, the boy who strove and burned for the university and fell with charred wings: gone, under the benevolent sun and among those generous acres, where Ben Jonson the poet was an honoured guest, where he brought verses for a queen, scrupulous and perfect in their learning. This was, if anything sublunary could be, content. He turned to Will.

'You should take up such a commission. There will be many such with the coronation, you know. The new Queen has a great taste for shows and masking, and an open purse. The old Court grew stiff in the joints. A new age comes.'

'Perhaps,' Will said, his eyes everywhere. 'I am a play-maker first, and the Globe has first claim on me.'

'Your first love?' Middleton asked: seriously, and wanting to know.

Will smiled, a little shielding smile. 'Ah, who can remember that?'

'Something must have drawn you to the business of play-making.'

Will inclined his head. 'As you also, good sir.'

'Yes: you, in part,' Middleton said, still fixing Will with his eyes, as if suspecting an illusion. 'Kyd, Marlowe also, but your pieces were ever my especial study. You'll find, as you know me better, that I don't incline to flattery. I speak truth only. I learned from you, sir; and I would learn more.' Middleton gave a smile that was like dry pickles. 'I mean to write everything that will advance me as a poet, be it play or pamphlet, or jigging masque for an idle court.'

Will faintly pursed his lips. 'This is good,

admirable.'

'Yet I mean to write well for all that. I have,' Middleton said, drink untouched, 'perfection of art in my eye.'

'Pray you, cut it out,' Will said. 'It will blind you.'

Middleton would not be put off. 'Whence your inspiration, Master Shakespeare?' He was black and avid. 'A muse?'

'Do you need inspiration to dress of a morning?' Will said.

Middleton seemed to put that away, stow it in his skull, but went on. 'This is pretty—but it is not an answer, or not a full answer. Do you mean—'

'Learning,' put in Ben, for the younker was far too fond of his own voice, 'learning and long study, that's what you need, young sir, look no further. Now, did I tell you of the little princess-in-arms?'

Another glance at Will as he talked: fellow still looked haunted. Was it that mistress of his? They could be rapacious creatures, especially when there was wealth like Will Shakespeare's to batten on. Ben thought: Advice? But, no, Will never took it. Listened, but followed his own path.

When Ben left the tavern Middleton was still examining Will's every word. Looking for the measure of that self.

But what if there were none? No depth, no width to assess? The thought hit him and winded him in the street. Those sonnets he had seen. Strange, tortured stuff, not a success, he thought: the reader didn't know how to take them. Who are these people shimmering in and out of the verse? Ben stood looking back at the windows of the Mermaid, shapes moving against the lemon light. Who are you there?

'But when I try to be myself,' Will had said once, when Ben took him to task for hiding in his work, 'I can only create a self. I have to see it standing there, like someone on the stage, before I can believe in it. The real does not convince. Come, whoever looked in the mirror and believed that picture was truly him? We all discern the fraud.'

'I never look in the mirror,' Ben had said. 'I know myself without.'

But now, in the middle of the straining muddy street, he stood against the jostling and let his thoughts free to terrify him, just for a moment. Shapes in the window, indeterminate. How if indeterminacy is Will's essence? But it can't be— because if he is nothing, how can he be what he so magnificently is?

The sun was sinking behind the roofs with a palpable withdrawal of warmth, like the shutting of a stove. Ben shook himself and plunged on. If it made no sense, he could not let it in. He refreshed himself with a memory of avenued oaks, park walls, limits and borders.

*　　　*　　　*

Under summer heat, under hot self-hate like packed straw in an overhead loft, about to catch and smoulder, Will enacted it.

All that was wrong in the earth was in it, and in him. But still he rose and took his morning draught at the sign of the Ram across the way, and wrote, and then sat awhile with Mistress Mountjoy to commiserate her troubles in getting her daughter happily married, and met Burbage and Heminges to talk business, share prices and the cost of candles,

494

and what the Admiral's Men were planning for the Fortune and the new proclamation against plays from the city, and took supper at the Ram or at the Mermaid with backbiting Dekker and Jonson, and often Middleton now with his burnished attention. And then he went to Isabelle and flung himself on the stones of passion.

And neither of these things drove the other out or brought it down. He had never expected evil to be so accommodating.

No doubting that it was evil, and that it came from him. You could call up images of spider and web and fly, and they came all too readily; but they meant nothing.

'Oh, it's a wicked world, Will,' she said to him once, pinning him down, laughing.

No, it isn't, he thought. It's the people in it.

Once she cut herself in the forearm with a knife, moderate deep, after he had put her away from him saying, no more, an end.

Once she lay under him absolutely unmoving, staring past his shoulder.

'What is it?'

'Nothing. I was just thinking what's in your brain.'

The next night she screamed and blasphemed and said she wanted to bathe in him.

Will thought of killing her or himself, both perhaps. But it didn't seem to solve the problem, or even approach it.

And meanwhile the city filled for the forthcoming coronation, swarming hot about the coming of a king. London lawyers and country gentlemen sniffed the air in city gardens and bowling-greens, outstaring each other: plague slashed red on doors, plague-bodies were trestled away in the humid afterglow when clothes felt like a rind. Food prices shot up. Loyal addresses and banners barely stirred in the no-air. Citizens grew used to the sound of Scots accents, and looked thoughtfully at the spare room, wondering how many mattresses it would take. (A Scots play, Middleton urged Will, that's what a man should think of in these times.) And in Hay Passage Will returned to the sudden persecutions of Isabelle's passion, in the room where no bird moved now: only the ticking ghost of its madness in the cage.

*   *   *

At New Place the wasps' nest in the eaves had become an insistent presence. It bulged out the plaster in the corner of the north bedchamber, the guest room where sometimes on market-day Bartholomew slept off his unhappy booze-fill.

Warm to the touch, this neighbouring nest: Susannah shrieked the first time she laid her hand against it, though Judith went back in fascination to that concentrated, intimate humming: full of subtle movement like a pregnant woman's belly.

'I'll send Hamnet to look at it,' Judith Sadler said. 'He'll know what to do. He contrived to rid my mother's outhouse of a nest, God knows how. Doesn't feel the stings, I vow. No sense, no feeling.' This was relatively warm for her. She made a home with hatred: every day wrapped in the familiar. Reassuring. After all, with love, how do you know where you are?

Hamnet came after the day's business was over at the bakery: the time of shutters, cook-fires being lit, water scattered to lay the dust before the householder's door, and the sun held like a bleeding ball by the roofs and chimneys of the town. He came broad and a little bowed, with his skin like a fair youth's against cropped silvery hair. He looked, as he was, a good, conscientious, slightly beaten man. The Sadlers had lost money to the great fires; and then there was the spirit, or heart . . . His upper lip dipped in the centre. All fourteen babies, living and dead, had that mouth. You could imagine him, Anne thought, suddenly striking out on a road, choosing to be alone with his neglected self, going off to ports and star-chased seas.

'Aye, you must needs do something. Sizeable. It might fall through in the end, with the weight of it.' He laid big tender hands against the waspy roof-belly. 'Then the swarm's in your house, maddened. Boiling water or tar will do it, late at night when they're still. I'll come help tomorrow night, if you will: have your Andrew keep a big fire all day.'

'Thank you. Do you think such small creatures feel when they die?'

'Perhaps they do.' He smiled sadly. 'But you'd go mad to keep thinking of it.'

'Oh, I shall think of some other foolish thing soon enough.' She laughed. 'Have you supped? Then stay, we have good roast ham. And Susannah has made quince tartlets.'

'Not to be refused. My thanks.'

'Shall I have Andrew go tell Judith you're staying?'

He shrugged. 'If you like. I'll not be looked for.'

At supper, and after, they talked easily and without intermission. With so much common ground between them, you could always light on something that brought a smile, a nod: a quickening. And so they stayed, talking, after the girls had taken their candles and gone upstairs.

'You'll be marrying them soon,' Hamnet said. 'The Quineys will take an interest, I'll wager.'

'Your own children marrying: Lord, what a thought.'

'Not a good one?'

She trimmed a smoking candle, proffered the ale-jug. 'Drink about. A good thought? Yes, if they are happy. But no. Because it means you must know yourself old.'

Hamnet laughed low. 'Old? Look in your glass, Anne.'

Afterwards she wondered whether she would have done it without that remark. Was it the hinge on which decision turned? Yet something had already prompted her to ask him to supper: that waking something, perhaps, or its malign shadow. She stood to trim the candle again, and her skirts brushed his leg, and she left it so instead of twitching away. The candle-flame glared at her like a merciless sun. What was Hamnet seeing? An old friend grown odd and whimsical? A discontented wife daring an intrigue?

'It's not a looking matter, Hamnet.' She drained her cup. 'It's feeling.'

She had called him Hamnet, simply, unthinkingly; but it was an acknowledgement that Hamnet Sadler was the only living one, the name had reverted to his sole use. Lost was the other Hamnet, and the loss had brought her to this precipice. My good went then, she thought, leaving an old nest of heart for scavengers to move into.

Scavengers and suspicions, hates and revenges. Hamnet, of all names to murmur in adultery: but no, very well, for everything now had a dark, freakish aptness.

'How does Judith?'

He grimaced. 'You know well.'

'She's happy, in truth. Not content. But happy.'

'Is she?'

'If not, she should be.' She spoke firmly, but into the dark. Her motives were blind formless things like new-born kittens. No good examining them for features. She sat down closer to him. She wondered what his bare legs were like, his weight, how harsh his beard. She had only the one experience of a man, and that was all broken on rocks. That man was elsewhere, love-embedded and separate: in her mind at least, probably in reality. Anne hid a sob and made her face cool. 'Let's not talk of her. Or any others, let them go. We should be ourselves alone, shouldn't we, and do only as our selves prompt?'

He gazed at her, looking quite young, and almost helpless with indirection: where would this go? 'Life,' he said heavily, 'life so seldom allows.'

'Life, the old jade, must learn to do better.' Was this real? Or was the room a painting, Hamnet a scarecrow set moving, her slow approaching body a dream of her self?

They began, so tentatively, with holding hands. Glances in the suffocating candlelight.

'I'm so alone.'

'Aye, so. I know what it is to be alone, Anne.'

'And folk would not believe it of either of us.'

'Aye, so.' Hamnet not quite listening. 'Thou art a beauty, dost know?'

499

Hands mapping, laboriously invading new places. Anne was not without pleasure, but she wished she could jump forward to when they would lie cooling apart in bed. To when she would be a woman who had achieved it, and claimed the far shore of revenge for her own.

Hamnet, gentle, sincere—but still not without opportunism, she realised. Kissing her, he mumbled about respect for Will and not changing things, but it was words. Everyone, she thought, as his hand kneaded her breast, was essentially furtive: walking in the daylit street, they stalked behind themselves.

'Art sure, heart? To go on?' As he spoke he lifted her skirts. 'It will be sweet. Promise thee.'

Yes, sure. No, not sure. His tongue and teeth claimed her world; they were too strong, there was too much of them. Breeches open, he put her hand to his standing cock: she touched and it seemed a strange hard fat clammy thing, not something that should be out in the air.

He drew his face back. Briefly scanned her. 'Are you afraid of Will?'

'No. Not afraid—'

'He doesn't beat you?'

She shrugged, and it was a shrugging him off, and he must have seen that.

'You know, Anne, he won't get to hear of it.'

Ah, true: and that was just it. Why else go through with it? To satisfy something in her? But it wasn't in her, she touched only vacancy, an echo. No thrilling note of vindication rang out.

She put down her skirts.

'You are too good a man, Hamnet, for this.'

He gave her a long regard, and let out a long sigh. Hitching up his breeches, he seemed to review acres of reflection, expectation, debate. 'I see it. Well, if I'm too good, I wish I might be otherwise. I wish I might be a bad man.' His glance flashed cold a moment, and she knew his was the power: whatever happened. 'I still might.'

'You won't, though.'

'No.' He shook his head, wry, caught out in his unavoidable humanity.

'You're free to hate me, Hamnet.'

His look was kind and grey. 'No. It doesn't go that deep, my dear.'

And that finished it. He put on his doublet, drained the last of the beer, took his leave, with no haste: why haste, after all? Meanwhile she stared at the small orbit of her burning world, the candle, her lap, a moth, a dribble of spilled beer on the board, her shame.

When he was gone, and she was alone, and she had finished silently weeping and digging her fingernails into her scalp until blood seeped, she sat in subsiding shudders and thought about things. She thought of Will. Chiefly with hatred, for his betrayal. Also, for making her helpless—or, rather, for his success where she failed. Look at him: he could play every part in life, and she could not even play the cheap adulteress for one night.

*　　*　　*

Susannah stood in the bedchamber doorway. Unlike Judith, who would have gasped or shouted, she thought for a moment before speaking, even though she must have been startled.

'What are you doing?'

'Packing.' Anne's eyes felt gritty from the

sleepless night, and the light of morning was in them like bright sand. 'For London.'

'Are we all to go?'

She shook her head. The white shift folded itself in her hands, submissive ghost. 'Your father writes me. It's an exceptional season. The new King, the coronation, favours to be granted. So all public men are fetching their wives to London, for we mustn't miss it.'

'But you hate London.' Susannah said it, then let it hang while she thought about it. She was subtle, and at ease in the presence of the unsaid. 'Wives, and not daughters.' She smiled.

'The house needs a mistress. You're a woman now. Andrew will ride with me. If you have need of anything, go to Uncle Richard.'

'How if I have need of you?' Susannah said; but she looked as if she did not expect an answer, or need one.

*   *   *

They were all deedily about it, writing for the King— Jonson, Dekker, Middleton, the others—all deep in loyal addresses and odes and pageants. And Will tried, seriously, because he believed that a poet must write upon any occasion, and build with what clay came to his hands.

But he couldn't. He was all shrunk to the pinhead of the personal, and he hated it, perching there. It was one of the many things, indeed, that he hated about his inclination to Isabelle: the way it turned him into an artist of the mirror, colouring everything with the hue of inescapable self. He longed to write outside. But the new King didn't do

502

it.

And then came hope. She was abstracted one evening, and even the dance of cruelty seemed to bore her.

'Come to sup with me tomorrow, Will, and we'll make an end.' She frowned at his look, which must have been high disbelief. 'No, I am in earnest, and I'll tell you why. My funds are low, and when I went marketing I couldn't get credit today, which frightened me. I can't live frugal—so I think I must marry again: and I can't do that while you and I are swyving. So, best end it. Hey?'

Looking at her, he could see no layers: just the top, the impatience. It seemed real. 'Very well. I will believe you are in earnest.'

'I've never been anything else,' she said, dead-voiced, taking up her sewing.

He wasn't sure, but he thought it possible she might drop him as easily as she had picked him up. She wouldn't want him, he thought, to draw any meaning from their association: that would be her worst failure.

'Be damned to the King, God save him,' Burbage said, when he asked what Will was working on. 'Come, he'll not lack addresses. A play, man. Something to catch his Scots fancy. If we can but become the King's Men, why, then, we're fitted. By the by, seen Henslowe of late? He's after your young Hollingbery's blood. He advanced him money, seemingly, on condition the sprig would be ready to play at the Rose on Monday. First leading part. But he hasn't been to rehearsals, and his landlord says he didn't come home last night. Drink, doxies, I don't know. But he'll fail, Will, in short order.'

'A pity,' Heminges said. 'He has the talent, if he could master the temper. He could learn from your brother there. My wife says she never knew a soberer man.'

'Aye, he applies himself, does Master Edmund,' Burbage said, 'even though he hasn't—well—'

'Hasn't a quarter of the talent,' Will said.

'Yes. Well, you did ask,' Burbage said. 'Oh, no, you didn't, did you?'

'The theatre needs its Edmund Shakespeares,' Heminges said. 'Earth, iron, jewels. It has to contain all.'

Damn Matthew. Was this how he repaid all the work they had put into his training? What was he about? Idling away his time? Dancing attendance on a mistress, perhaps. Self-hatred compounded Will's urgency. He roamed Matthew's haunts, from the south bank of the river to Shoreditch. He darted into the back rooms and upper rooms of theatre taverns, flung back curtains, received oaths and stares from numerous young men who were not Matthew. All the time, bits of his past and present jutted and tripped him. Tarlton fetching him in from the street and saving him from starvation. Nashe comfortably ensconced in the Mermaid, walled in with books. Greene lurking in his pride and poverty with the grave on his breath. Jonson accosting him at Field's shop. So much that was familiar; but in the course of the long, frustrating day he felt difference too, the way time, beyond a certain age, was a backward wave that left you in the shallows. The young he saw were cooler somehow, more knowing: they possessed life and the world as he possessed money, reach, doubt.

'Very well. Have him here Monday morning,

504

perfect in his part,' Henslowe had said, when Will went to see him, 'and we'll go on. Otherwise, he's done.'

Now the afternoon was late, still hot, a little thundery, sunlight suddenly spilling from the clouds on to the street with as physical an effect as the unrolling of great bolts of shining fabric. Will's legs ached, and his head throbbed, and he thought: Leave him to it. What is he to you? Not as if you're his father.

He went on.

*   *   *

'How did it happen?'

He had found Matthew at last, hiding out at a friend's lodging in a Westminster courtyard. He threw open the shutters. Matthew cringed on the bed.

'I told you, a fall.'

'A fall? You're young for your dotage. Show.'

Scowling, Matthew sat up and turned his face to the light. The black eye twitched. 'I laid a beefsteak to it to draw it out. But it still looks hideous, doesn't it?'

'Yes. But it will fade. It's a small thing, to set beside your life as a player. You're not indispensable, they can easily dismiss you. And then the word will go round; Matt Hollingbery is not to be relied on. Swift consequences. Also your landlady is troubled at missing you.'

'She's a good creature.' A reminiscent smile. Oho, Will thought, possibly. Or it might be just in Matthew's mind. 'I didn't want to go back there— be seen thus.'

'After your fall, naturally. So, what was the fight about?'

'God knows,' Matthew said, holding his head. 'There was drink in it, and drink is a great maker, a builder of towers from scraps . . . You've surely been drunk when young. Even you.'

Even me. Dear heaven. Will felt himself scatter like a dropped pack of cards. There, somewhere, was the true one.

'I'm not here to read you a lecture. Only to say opportunity is no deep well: it runs soon dry. So if you must carouse, then—then be like Master Jonson. He drinks himself to blankness, sleeps in a great sweat, and then rises early to study. Mix your debauches, if you can't mix your wine. You are too good to lose. For the theatre to lose, I mean.' He was rewarded with a half-smile. How different our rewards, our gratifications. Truly we are divided creatures. 'Come. Action. To your landlady, and make your bows and apologise for her distresses, and then your part.'

'I don't have it. I've hardly looked at it.'

'Where's the copy? Your lodging? Excellent, there we shall learn it, and make you perfect in it. I'll send a message to the Rose that you'll be there tomorrow for rehearsal.'

Matthew shook his head. 'And this face?'

'More beefsteak. Then, if it comes to it, paint with white lead. What's your part? Lucius the honest knight, very well. Is he esteemed for his beauty throughout the piece? Are there long speeches about the fairness of his eyes? Why, then, it won't be marked. Above all, remember what you do. You make the audience see what you want them to see. How else does Burbage make you see a tall, martial man, mighty-limbed?'

Matthew's smile faded. 'But I can't get the part by tomorrow.'

'Not alone, no. Come.' He gave Matthew his hand and hauled him up.

It's so easy to do the right thing, he thought, that we hesitate to do it: we suspect a trick. Children see no tricks. Be as a child.

'I feel so melancholy sometimes,' Matthew said, as they walked. 'Why is that, think you, when feeling happy is so much better?'

'We inherit tears. And then they dry, and we foot it across the world. And all the while the music plays, grave or gay. Have you dined? You'll need food in the belly, then something to keep you fresh as we work. Valerian has good properties, they say. Burbage swears by an infusion of ginger for late study.'

So, all night at Matthew's lodging, lighting candle after candle, repeating, coaching, bullying. There were a few tears.

'I can't do it. I don't want to do it. I don't give a hang for playing.'

'Plain enough, but I do. "And yet, methinks my lover has forgot . . ." Go on.'

'Can I not sleep a few minutes?'

'No. If you sleep you won't stir till morning.'

> ' "And yet, methinks my lover has forgot
> Our fixed bond, and all my comfort's lost
> . . ." '

'Good. Nearly there.'

'No, you're good, too good to me,' Matthew said impulsively, touching his hand. 'I'm not worth it.

You know, I called you an old woman to my friends the other day.'

'No, you didn't, you called me something much worse. Now, cue, "Farewell, and blessings attend thee".'

'I wish I could be like you.'

'That is not the line. Nor is it true. Or a part of me only.' He suddenly found himself imagining what Anne would think if she could see him now. It always took him by stealth, this thought: the only way, perhaps, like visioning your own death.

He left Matthew's lodging when first light was brushing the sky. Matt would manage a couple of hours' sleep before going to the Rose. His landlady, for the price of a little purse, had engaged to wake him in time and march him up there if need be. All that could be done. Will's weariness took the form of incredible clumsy stiffness, like a wooden leg taking over the body. At Silver Street he filled a pail at the pump and doused his head deliciously and shook it till the water-drops were like a rain-shower. And in each of them he saw a face.

And then he remembered where she should have been, last night.

*   *   *

The supper still stood on the table. It looked untouched—except that at some point she had dug into the wheel of cheese with a knife and made eyeholes and a grin, like a skull. A sated fly drowsed on a capon breast.

Having let him in, Isabelle drooped to the hearth and knelt down there, away from him. The bare soles of her feet were pink and delicately ridged.

508

'There's wine, if you want it,' she said, in a metallic voice. 'It's not poisoned.'

He took up the cup. 'Well, in a way it is.'

'Why do you come now? What does it serve, to come now?'

'To explain what happened. But after all, Isabelle—'

'After all it was to be our last supper, yes, and I meant it so and it would have been so. But instead you choose to end it with insult.' Her eyes flared, soft violet, lost in rage. 'You made me feel worthless as I sat here, Master William, you made me feel that I did not deserve to exist and that you wanted me to know it.'

'I meant none of that. For God's sake, what do you think I am? I was helping a friend.'

She laughed briefly, rocking back. 'All night? Oh, you sad fool. Helping a friend, quotha, and all night too.'

'Matthew.' He told it briefly.

She stared, and her teeth began to part and gleam as if she were about to bite these bare bones of narration, suck their marrow. 'And this,' she said at last, rising, 'this lessens the insult, is that what you suppose? Instead of magnifying it a hundredfold? Do you know nothing, Will, of me or of yourself? Matthew. Matthew.' She spat the name smiling. 'Don't you know that you'll tire of him too, once you've finally fucked the whelp's arse?'

He turned and groped for the door-handle, but it seemed to have disappeared in a black mist, along with everything solid, everything with dimensions. 'An end, then. You've said enough.'

'No. Just the truth. Once you've had what you want, you don't want it more: common enough for a man led by his tarse, but with you, Will, it goes further, it's like a sickness. You might love the dead enduringly, or a dream, or an angel, but we poor mortals standing on the earth don't have a chance at you. I wonder, should I tell your boy-girl about it—how you've been doing to me what you secretly want to do to him? It would be amusing. Revealing. But, no, I've no interest in your mumbled crumbs. Get gone.'

'Oh, I will. Your play's all finished, is it not? That I know. True, I don't know myself. I only know I have had more good fortune in my life than I have known what to do with.' He found the handle, got the door open: it felt giant, heavy, as if made of bronze. 'As for you, I don't know how you can bring back your brother, Isabelle. But not this way. Not with me, and I pray God with no other. That's the quick and essence of evil, it takes away.' His last sight of her was grey and crisp and unequivocal with morning. 'Only takes away.'

*　　　*　　　*

All the world was going with Anne to London, it seemed. Travellers were everywhere on the roads south, in groups and strings, on horseback and on mules and donkeys, laden with packs and panniers, cloaked, grimed, with here and there a new travelling-coach shuddering and straining and getting itself stuck, tilted, beetle-like, in the chalky ruts.

It was because of the coronation of the new King, of course, and what could be sought and solicited, grabbed and got: favour, office, influence. And so her excuse for leaving Stratford, conveyed also to brother-in-law Richard and to her wise-nodding lizard-lidded mother-in-law at Henley Street, made perfect sense. As for her determination to travel only with Andrew, the long-nosed, imperturbable manservant, she could press that home because of who she was: Mistress Shakespeare, wife of a substantial man who played before the Court. She could carry these decisions high.

And yet she knew herself a lie, fraud and exception as she rode with the others south under humid skies. She was doing this for the smallest, most limited, most personal reasons, which would make no sense to anyone else and were hardly lucid even to herself. The aim of her fellow travellers was large with significance, moated and acred and mortgaged, spreading to the horizon of a family future. Hers was a daisy in a meadow. She wanted to keep the daisy intact and the daisy was her feeling for her husband, and what it meant to her and to him and to them: how it must have that golden centre, those white rays. She was thinking not of knighthoods but of a gift of gloves, a green tunnel, a cradle of intimate days, a laughing look across butter-coloured stone, summer indoors, a staggering babe hand-guided from bemused mother to bemused father, lips turned and offered in sleep, the stretched fear of other sickness and wanting to take it on yourself: of the late-learned, never-learned truth of love.

Luckily, no one took notice of her. She didn't fancy scrutiny. So, mistress, whither are you going and why? To assess my life. To see if it's worth the living.

And all the time as she rode the dusty, jolting way, with the flies maddening the horse's ears as if horse and fly had been at creation proclaimed enemies, all the time, she had a strange feeling or conviction that Will knew she was coming. At the end of that cresting road, where the sky purpled, he was: and somehow he was sending out something of himself.

The people, on her way, at the inns. He must have made them. The world as Will's invention—well, that seemed enticingly likely, yes. How else this burly, sausage-armed, bragging captain complaining of the ale? 'Mine host, if you would catch a bird like me, you must lime your twig with stronger stuff, else I shall fly to your brother innkeeper along the road, I a man of large and generous spirit that must be floated on a tide of dark and potent ale, look you, not confined within a thimbleful of the mincing dribble wrung from an ailing baby's clouts . . .' Good-natured, though: he saluted her across the inn-parlour, laughing at himself, laughing at the sheer brazen impossibility of his existence. Will must have made him, and made what made him; likewise the pair with whom she had to share a supper-table, brother and sister to judge by their chiming beautiful faces, she cool, luminous, he twitching, callow. Some contention between them. If you loved me a little better—Do you conceive I could love you more? If so, you know nothing.—Better, better is of a different quality than more. To love me better would be to try to comprehend my feeling, not to pity it.—I never said I pity you, Edward. Not for something of your own making. It's her I pity in the case, not you.—And this is your love, is it?—Aye, so: there is love, and there is indulgence, and they may touch sometimes but they're not the same.

It explained a lot, these people, these creations.

But once she was attuned to it, she found it oppressive: all these stories going around her, these endless planets turning on the centre of endless selves. A vast drama of infinite acts and numberless parts, and there was no exiting from it.

And she, what was she but a queen? Head of the family, Bartholomew said. Queen of griefs and foolish private pains that flitted on her face just as when she was a girl. Queen of jealousy, she lay drowning in wonderment in the bug-rid inn bed, imagining Will in someone's arms, and the someone almost took shape when she dreamed, and woke with a start putting out her hand, purposefully. Doing what? She seemed to feel or see, with the melded senses of sleep, a dagger. Was she putting it away, or taking it to her? Was this—she lurched up—blood? She flung back the bed-curtains, consulted her hand in the undercooked light of foredawn. No: sweat. Hot. Was this the change of life that Judith Sadler groaned about and yet longed for? Change of life. That was always, surely: every morning. Besides, she had had her bleeding last week. Never troubled her overmuch. A thing of life.

She couldn't sleep again. Before everyone she was ready, impatient for the last stage of the ride to London.

The crowded yard glared and stank. A duck in a basket honked fiercely.

Anne stood to the mounting-block. Did you invent me, too, Will? Is that why I feel so insubstantial—as if the mare will hardly notice me in the saddle? Did you make me—and, perhaps, leave me unfinished?

Complete me, then, or unmake me for ever.

I have tears, but do not know how they are to be used, yet.

*   *   *

'Are we not to go with you?' Agnes said: or, rather, demanded.

It was unlike her to be so stubborn and insistent, Ben thought. In truth, though, it was very like her. He just had to armour himself with patience.

'It would scarcely be an entertainment for you, my love, nor the little ones. Master Cotton is a scholar: that is his whole life. He has brought together a library that is, they say, in a way to be the greatest in the kingdom. So, he invites me to his house as a scholar also.' Difficult to keep down the swell of pride at that; and, after all, why should he? Modesty was for the modestly endowed. 'The talk there will all be of the ancients, of text and line, of philosophical disquisition. The breadth and feather of poetry's wings. You would yawn.'

'Papa.' Little Benjamin, with his courtly firmness, plucking at him. 'Papa, may I say? I should like to see that great library. I'm a good scholar and bookman, aren't I?'

'You are, and some day you shall see it, that's my promise,' Ben said, kneeling, enfolding his son's hand in his. Softening, whitening now, surely: bearing no trace of the bricklayer's rough redness. 'Truly, Agnes, it would be too dull. It will be a man's occasion.'

'If you say so. I only wish we might go out of the city before the hot weather. There's plague about.'

'Oh, it hasn't crossed the river. It will flare and die down.' Already in his mind he was settled

514

at Connington, Robert Cotton's country house in Huntingdonshire, combing the books and deep in disquisition. Cotton had invited William Camden too: fine company for a long symposium, a heavenly vacation of thinking . . . And Ben would be an honoured guest alongside his old master, poet and play-maker of renown, invited for himself. Mellow-sweet the taste of it, suffusing the honeycomb mind.

'As long as you intend coming back,' Agnes said.

He took her hand and kissed it. They had lived apart for a while, when he grew tired of her nagging—or she had thrown him out, interpret it as you pleased. The point was, she had begged him to come back at last: she had stood pale and longing on his mother's doorstep. She knew how easy he found it to be a bachelor again. Too easy.

'You,' he said, 'and these sweet ones,' Benjamin's fond pushing head at his hand, 'you know you have all my heart.'

'I know,' his wife said, and with a faint smile: 'Such as it is.'

*   *   *

Anne found a room at the Bell Inn on Carter Lane. It was full, but became less so when she gave over a shocking amount of money. The innkeeper was unabashed. In London just now everyone, it seemed, had the hardness of money-making on their faces.

For a time she sat on the bed, holding herself. Keeping herself together. Like an overpacked trunk bound with tight clasps, leather thinning and fraying. London. Dense overripe smell, light defeated and sullen from the battle with smoke

515

and the ranks of high-shouldered roofs, an extra half-mad sharpness in the sound of dogs barking. She had never expected to come back here, never expected to allow this city into her mind and senses again, after it had taken Hamnet from her.

But, of course, it hadn't, and neither had Will, nor Will's choices and her choices. She saw it now, as she sat alone and alien. The death of her son was no purposeful unfolding of a play-plot. It was just death, final and unequivocal. You died, too, or lived on.

She had brought bread and cheese wrapped in linen, and she made herself eat, feeding herself like a reluctant child. He's in this city and he doesn't know I am. What if he bumps into me in the street? Why, Will, how dost . . . Anne let out a crumbled laugh. He would think he'd imagined me, perhaps. And perhaps he did. I can't quite remember the time before him, before the lightning-tree and the unborn calf, before his eyes stilling mine. Like one of those dreams you're not sure you had, a night-spot on your mind in daylight, a memory of a memory, infinitely disappearing.

Edmund was lodging at the house of John Heminges, Will's friend and partner. If she applied there it might get back to Will. She would have to send Andrew to fetch him. How find it? Ask, she told him, just ask. Remembering her own first fear of London made her snappish. They won't eat you . . . Ah, but won't they? She still half expected this place to start closing its city teeth around her, chewing. My meal, says Fate, at last.

*　　　*　　　*

516

Edmund arrived, full of brightness and wonder. 'But I didn't know, I had no notion you were coming! Will said naught. Where is he?'

'Will doesn't know I'm here.' They faced each other. Edmund looked away first. 'Edmund, it was your letter that brought me here.'

'Alone? You shouldn't have done it.'

'I have Andrew.'

Edmund shook his head. He had, she thought, that London sallowness, as if he were best seen by candlelight. 'I mean you shouldn't have come like this.'

'Why? Is it best not to know?'

'I told you, I wrote you, there is nothing to know.' He jumped violently when she took his hand, as if she burned him.

'You lied. You lie now. I know why, I think: it's to do with love, for Will and for me, and how you imagine us. And I know I should stay at home and count my blessings, live content in ignorance, as many a woman would. Think of your purse and your luck, and cultivate peace . . . But I have no peace, brother, and it's my own fault, doubtless, but there it is. That's the way I'm made. The way you're made. It brought you here, did it not?'

He still would not or could not look at her, but he nodded, fingers quiescent in hers.

'Well, then. Show me, Edmund. Take me to her. Do me the kindness.'

*   *   *

'All I know is he comes here. That's known. He visits here. But what's that, after all? Naught. There is a woman lives here, a Frenchwoman, but what's that?'

517

The words were jerked out of Edmund, as if he were hiccuping or sobbing, though his face was dry and composed, faintly annoyed. But, then, he was an actor now.

She stood in the shadowy passage looking about her, as if something familiar might leap out from the stones. There was a door with a shell-hood porch. There was a window up there, slightly ajar. A trickle of damp. A pigeon roosting.

'How often?'

'I don't know. It's—say, now and then. I've followed him here, seen him go in. Only because you told me to. I hated it.' His voice now had the hidden bray of a boy sadly blustering. 'They are not seen about together, never in my belief, so it's not a matter of—'

'Being flagrant about his mistress.'

'I don't know. What goes on. I don't want to. Can you understand that?'

She tried to soften it with a half-smile. 'Edmund, I don't have to.'

'He's my brother.'

'My husband.'

'Love—love bears all—'

'In silence?'

He swallowed, scrubbed his face with his hands. 'What do you mean to do?'

Ah, the great question. She didn't know. This seemed as great a brink, verge, and entry into darkness as death itself. She stepped under the porch and lifted her hand. 'See.'

*　　　*　　　*

'No.' The Frenchwoman shook her head. There

518

seemed a perpetual suppressed yawn about her, as of a person staying up too late and almost past going to bed. 'No, I still can't quite comprehend it. Why you should come.'

'Better to see you than imagine you, perhaps,' Anne said. 'May I sit?'

The Frenchwoman shrugged. She took up some sewing and held it to the light, or such light as there was in here. Somehow, though the shutters were back, the room, with its hangings and tapestries and crowded lustrous furniture, seemed to shut out the day. Outside it was noon, but in here it was any time.

'Does he know you've come?'

'No.'

'Resourceful in you.'

'Not what you expected of Will's wife?'

The Frenchwoman sat back and seemed to think, almost neutrally, about the question. 'I don't know that I ever expected anything, in truth. You were just—the distant wife.' Her dark eyes swept over Anne. In spite of the light, you felt she saw incredibly keenly, that the eyes struck like an eagle's on a furred movement. 'How old are you?'

'Turned forty-seven.'

'You look younger.'

A million times more strange and dreamlike than she could have imagined, this meeting: sitting with the woman with whom Will had betrayed her and being, if you liked, complimented by her and feeling—God, her head was going to explode—feeling a little awkward that she could not return the compliment because she thought the Frenchwoman a brown, harsh-featured creature for all her trim figure . . .

'Does he beat you?' the woman said abruptly.

'Why would he do that?'

'Oh, there must be something behind that look. You surely can't tell me you're a loving wife.'

'Why? What would that do to you?'

The Frenchwoman stood up and went to a table with silver wine-jug and goblets. The cloth on the table was fringed and embroidered in a way Anne had never seen and the silver was chased and unusual too. Everything about her had this elaborated quality, even to her hair, her expression: as if she had to go about life as a work of art. Somehow it irritated Anne; and the irritation managed to exist alongside the wild, mad anger and pain and disbelief.

'Faith, I don't know what you expect, mistress, coming here. Where's the need of it, since you've made sure of your suspicions? Aye, I've had your man in my bed, for what that's worth. What, then? Are we to rage and tear at each other like a pair of goodwives in a citizen comedy?' She drank thirstily. 'Or are you come to proclaim your wifely rights, and warn me off? If so, it's folly, you have no need. Do you think I'm a species of enchanter, is that your notion? Snares and lures and toils and coils?' She chuckled stonily. 'My dear, I began it, true enough, because I had a fancy for him. But I soon saw I was mistook about my power. I was naught but a convenience for him. He's an oddity, isn't he?' The bright look the Frenchwoman gave her then terrified Anne, somehow: she could almost have begged to be given some of that wine. She imagined its taste, complex, exotic, beyond her. 'What he wants. What he doesn't want. Perhaps you don't quite understand it. Lord, I was a fool to spend

520

so much time on him. He had me, and then when he'd had me he'd had enough of me. You know his boy-girl? The sainted Matthew?'

Anne wanted to say no—perhaps because, for the first time, in the Frenchwoman's lifted lip of contempt, she recognised something of herself. But she couldn't speak; and somehow the woman seemed to know her, the truth of her, agelessly, like a mother or God.

'Certes you know Matthew. Never ceases to talk of him, does he? You must know how affected your man is to that boy-girl.' The woman clattered the goblet down: either a little drunk, or not so nerveless as she seemed. 'You're in the wrong place, mistress. I'm not your rival.' She lifted her eyes to Anne's, and Anne seemed to catch a sharp sound from their blackness, like flint chipping. 'Matthew boy-girl and his high prime young arse, that's where your man fixes his desire now. And that's where you should be looking for him. God be with you, if you have one.' Tears—from that flint? Surely not. 'And leave me alone for aye.'

*   *   *

At Connington, country seat of Robert Cotton, Ben walks arm in arm with Master William Camden about the knot-garden. Gravel paths entice and soothe the feet; healthful herb-primed airs blow on the gentle lowland wind.

Ben, having spent the day among his gentle host's collections, is still marvelling. 'That Nennius. But then the *Historia Ecclesiastica* of Bede, did you see it? And the *Homilies* of Aelfric, those, those I must beg him to lay my hands on again tomorrow.

521

And the painted gospels. It sets a man to thinking, if this is what has survived, what more may have been lost?'

'A great deal, assuredly. We nibble the mere orts of a great banquet.'

'It minds us of our own responsibilities to posterity, that the flowers of our literature be not lost likewise. I shall take the greatest of care in supervising the printing of all my works.'

'Ah, and shall they be shelved next to Bede, or Nennius?' Camden says, with a delicate smile.

'I wouldn't blush to see 'em there,' Ben says robustly. 'But no, next to Spenser, Marlowe, Shakespeare. Or, let us say, just above them. And they must be safe guarded. Is the King a friend to such a collection, would you say?'

'I believe such is Master Cotton's hope. The late Queen had a fear of antiquaries being too inclined to hunt out precedents and meddle with policy. But His Scots Majesty is a scholar, and you know Master Cotton comes of the illustrious line of the Bruce, hm?'

'He has not mentioned it above a dozen times.' Ben chuckles. 'And I honour him not a whit the less. He ought to have all his library in one place, mind, not divided betwixt here and his London house.'

'Where would you fix?'

'London. This is beautiful, admirable, as fine in its way as Althorp. But the country is the place for reflection. The town is the place for acting on reflection. I could never be long from it.'

No, he is a citizen at heart, and he knows it. This is balm and delight, but so will be the return, a few weeks hence, to rackety, plaguey London, with all its plays and shows, in theatre and out. This, perhaps, is the height of felicity, to enjoy the now and to look forward no less to what is to come, with no division of the self, no clawing dark guilt or futile regrets. It was the moral sanity of the ancients; and in the verdant landscape surrounding the symmetrical house, where a civilised host served honest fare washed down with deep draughts of instruction, he sees a decent likeness to a scene from classical antiquity. It helps that he is in it too.

Master Cotton keeps an excellent cellar, and Ben does as full a justice to it as to the library with its busts of Caesars crowning each case. He does not remember going to bed but, then, he scarcely ever does—the retiring hour is to him as occult and mysterious as being born. You know it must have happened, because here you are. Here he is, waking in a strange bed with a strident need to pee, and no certainty of where he can do it.

Country house. Huntingdonshire. Library. His mind puts it clumsily together while he hops in his nightshirt, desperate. A pot placed? Where? He ought to mark these things before falling asleep. A rectangle of glimmer signals a window. He fumbles it open, hoists himself on tiptoes and pounds relief into the country night.

Relief, yet not relief: something besides his bladder woke him and tugs uncomfortably at him still. Something he did. He sinks down on the bed and interrogates the thinning darkness. *Go away from me.* That was it. Little Benjamin at his side, while he worked at his desk. Little hand plucking at his sleeve while he struggled with the recalcitrant demons of composition. Father, Father. And he shook him off and growled, *Go away from me*, and off the poor little fellow slunk. Didn't mean it, the irritation, the growl: it is just that writing, art, is such a serious business, even when comedy it is very serious, and he takes it with the proper degree of solemnity, and his concentration is so easily broke . . . Shame on him, though. He will make it up to the lad. And now the last illusions of sleep lift from him and he realises or remembers: that was a dream.

Yes, sweating here and no doubt snoring, he had a dream of shrugging his son off in just that way. So vivid—as, of course, so many dreams are. And with no element of reality, surely. Smacking dry lips, he consults memory, quickly cons its index. No, he loves the boy this side of idolatry, and while he always gives proper discipline, he has never lost temper with his Benjamin in that pettish way. Surely . . . Let it then be a remembrance, never to do so.

He sleeps again.

Sleeps again, and wakes to another day worth the savouring, and with the intention of looking up the inconsistencies in Alfred's translation of Orosius's *Historia Universalis*. Another walk with Master Camden in the morning cool: talk of their host's collections, of setting up a library for the nation, an academy. Oh, yes, an academy, there Ben is fiercely eager: an academy to tame the unruly English tongue, give its wayward mongrel habits a standard and a purpose.

And then the return to the house, and the manservant looking out, waiting: a letter.

From Agnes: he recognises the script at once. Competent penwoman, if haphazard in her spelling, as too many are, even the learned: Will

524

Shakespeare is one, making words fit his hand according to his mood. An academy, that's what's needed. Fix and purify. Why are his hands shaking? Perhaps because of last night, too much good wine, and also because he and Agnes do not often write each other letters; theirs is not that kind of marriage. It would have to be exceptional, for this. An exceptional event.

There is food set out on the table in the great hall. Master Cotton's generous and sensible habit— take a bite when you fancy it, in between study. Master Camden, after a glance at Ben's face, goes in and carves a slice or two of meat on a platter. Sets it down, and returns, seagull slow of step, face enquiring and kind as when Ben sat before him at Westminster School and longed to know more, more.

But this—this must be the end of knowledge. Ben grips the crackling letter and summons philosophy, ranges swiftly across his world of learning, and he finds nothing. Nothing of use. Great God.

Him, most of all.

'My friend.' Master Camden touches his arm. 'My friend, what is it?'

What is it? A terrible injustice, a flagrant injustice meted out to him—how could it be?—just when he has begun to garner the rewards of talent and industry, and is in a way to become the most learned man in England . . . Ben gasps. Masters himself. 'My son.' The words scald the tongue, now that he has no son. 'He took the plague . . .' Master Camden grips his arm: was he about to fall? Perhaps.

What Agnes has written: she wrote, first, *his*

sufferings were not great and then crossed out *great* and replaced it with *long*. *His sufferings were not long I thank God*. Oh, revealing emendation. This is a text beyond exegesis. Ben hears himself moan. Master Camden urges him to a chair.

'Sit. sit. My good friend, I have no words. Is it—'

'He has gone. He died on Tuesday night. It was swift, there was no time to summon me.' Ben finds himself lifting up his hands. 'What more?'

'God have mercy on his soul. Drink this. You need it, the shock. You can have had no suspicion—'

'No.' He sees Agnes's rueful, hopeless expression, damp with summer: if we might just leave the city . . . 'No. A shock, yet not wholly . . . I had a vision last night. I saw him. My Benjamin. Not little as he is, but grown, as he will appear at Judgment-seat, and on his forehead there was a scarlet cross.' Did he dream this? Surely he did, for it appears so vividly to him now, and it makes more sense than the other dream; this one comes surely from deeper springs of prophetic imagination, and it is more bearable, somehow, to think of . . . 'What could it signify? God marked out my boy to punish me? To remind me of him? What?'

'Such things are beyond us. The vision, if vision it was. Sometimes the mind sports without our will, devises its own devices. Providence will not be questioned, Ben. We shall have our answer in the end, in fullness. Be comforted, my friend. I know it is grievous sore . . .'

Master Camden is kind, and Master Cotton too, when he joins them. Ben will not wish to stay, Ben will want to go home at once, naturally . . . But Ben is not sure: he can hardly face the prospect of going into that house and no Benjamin there. No, no, it is beyond bearing. And retreating to his room he is, for a long time, not comforted, not philosophical. Not even, in the worst of his grief, Christian. (And to go into that house will mean looking into Agnes's face. No, no.) The supernal vision haunts him, growing stronger, until it almost overlays the reality: little Benjamin dying of plague, in pain and fear. The vision is masterly and reproving as the glance of the Redeemer himself. Look to your crime, Ben Jonson.

At last, panting, half blind, he sits down with pen and ink and prepares to write back to Agnes. There's no sense in rushing home to that aching vacant house. Just some words, some words from the heart to soothe a little their mutual wound of grief. But nothing will come. Nothing that does not seem to invite terrible pelting answers from a sky of retribution. At last his pen moves. Rhyme hums a quiet note, reason puts on the firm armour of metre. His breath ceases to be ragged and whistling. Shape from storm.

> *Farewell, thou child of my right hand, and joy;*
> *My sin was too much hope of thee, loved boy.*

He sits back. It will be a long process, for composition does not come smoothly to him. It will be a long process, to find his way back to life; but the bricklayer's boy did not come this far for nothing, surely, and is not to be defeated even by such a loss as this. *Rest in quiet peace.* No, the verse ripples too much. *Rest in soft peace*, better. Soft is a word blotted by a tear, as this one is. From somewhere in his heart Ben puts forth thankfulness, for this: oh, experience, the great true father of art.

*   *   *

'I told you it were best not done,' Edmund said, hurrying at her side through St Mary Aldermanbury. 'Now will you be satisfied?'

Anne stopped, for a moment. Fixed him with a look, for a moment. 'Satisfied? Brother, how satisfied, please tell?'

'You've seen her. Well, have you? Spoke with her?'

'Aye, so. I have spoke with her, and then—'

'And then it profits nothing, surely.'

'You know very little, Edmund. Even about your own brother.' A little incidental cruelty didn't seem to matter, in this world in which it is king and law.

'I know he never meant to wrong you.'

She hurried on. No feeling of hurry, though; she seemed to forge, glide through the toiling streets. 'How do you know?'

'Because he could not, not if he were in his right mind.'

'This is wishing, not thinking.' And too close to her own habit of mind: she put its friendly hand away from her.

'Where are you going?'

'To Will's lodging. Silver Street, that is northward of Cheapside, yes?' Strange, for now the fear of London had dropped away from her. New eyes saw the infinite glitter of diamond panes, forest of hanging signs, sky-lattice of washing, lumbering carts, barrels and ladders and tottering towers of baskets. She felt she owned it as these people did, pattened, loud-swearing, shoving for the wall, faces fixed on far deeds.

Edmund said: 'I'll come with you.'

It seemed an indifferent matter, unless he were to be disabused as she was: it surely wouldn't break him as it would her.

'I don't know what the woman said,' Edmund went on, 'but I wish you might consider it—nothing. If she spoke saucy, impudent, remember she is really naught to you and I verily believe to Will also—'

'She?' Anne dragged her mind back. 'Oh, God, yes. She's naught. It isn't that, now.'

What it must be to have this energy all the time, this strength. She felt as if she had been a long time convalescent, supping at a light diet of life, peeping over the covers at the shut-out day. Ahead of her two unmuzzled dogs savaged each other in circles. A blackamoor balanced a hod of tiles on a huge shoulder.

'What do you mean? It isn't that, what, then? Anne, stop.'

'Why? If I stop, then what do I do, brother? Consider? I am done considering.'

'I only ask—what can come of it? A great quarrel, then—what? Live apart?'

She said nothing. We have been doing that; but there are different ways of being apart. The air was cooling under thundery cloud, but the heat of the Frenchwoman's rooms seemed to cling to her, like cobweb twirled round a broom. 'Which way now?'

He showed her. The place, when she came to it, was surprisingly plain and respectable, away from the theatre districts: citizens' houses filing one orderly after another, no low taverns or stews. Another one of Will's many sides, perhaps. *I had him in my bed*. Did you, or did you only have a shadow of him? She might ask me the same. Oh, if he can fall for that self-creating spider with her tossed hair and needlework, then he is merely like any other man, and that can be lived with.

But I cannot live with what she said, if that is what I must face. Not because it is much more gross and bawdy: because there must be behind it such a long, deep lie.

At the house in Silver Street a pretty obliging little woman greeted Edmund, looked with shy interest at Anne. She murmured a good-day back. Let us be all courtesy. A snug parlour, a narrow staircase. Yes, Master Shakespeare is home, but has company, I think—

Up the stairs ahead of Edmund, well-oiled door, not squeaking as it swung into Will's rooms, revealing him sitting on a stool by a narrow bed: occupied, a fair male head on the pillow. Will looked up from thought, deep thought, as Anne stepped in, and saw, turned, ran.

*   *   *

How Will found him: it was that fairness.

The tavern was out of his usual way, but since breaking free of Isabelle he had sought to change all his ways, seeing the habit of her as a blight touching everything. Walk different ways, eat different meats. The tavern was a tight, glum little place in Southwark, penetrated by the smell of the bear-baiting yards. But it was not belonging to his time with her, and so he went in, and there he saw a fair head, and a certain set of the shoulders that called, Jack Towne again, and while he was putting these things together and waiting for his drink, the fair head plunged suddenly out of sight.

There was a commotion. Will elbowed his way into the tap-room where the fairness had gone down. The innkeeper was cuffing and slapping where Jack Towne lay long and knee-bony on the floor, apologising. He had slid to the ground from his stool, it appeared, whilst saying he could not pay for his dinner; and the innkeeper looked ready to slap the money from him, or slap out satisfaction at least. 'Nay, soft,' someone said, 'the man's sick, he's yellow as a buttercup.'

'And if he's sick as well as a thief, why should I trouble?' shouted the innkeeper. And that was when Will waded in, opened his purse, and said he would look to the man.

He put his arms round Jack Towne's shoulders and lifted him. Jack blinked up at him in annoyance, then astonishment. He was all bones, all broken beauty, bits and flashes of what he might have been: human, in other words.

The man who had spoken up for Jack spoke again. 'He ate a platter of meat. Then he turned faint. There's plague, sir, a deal of plague. Consider if it's plague.'

And if it is? thought Will. He got Jack up.

They tried, but Jack was lurching too much, too weak. Will persuaded a carter to carry them to Silver Street. No, it's not plague, for all the sweat, the muttering. The Mountjoys were not there: a prayer-meeting, perhaps. He half carried Jack upstairs. His arms and hands, swinging, were long and slender as he remembered.

He got Jack Towne into the bed, yanking off his shoes and doublet, merely purposeful. Jack stank.

531

His throat as he toppled flat looked like stripped birch. There must always be a Jack Towne, Will thought. It's in the weave of life. It is not always given for this to happen, that's all: for Jack to reappear. The visitation, the long, backward glance. He couldn't express it to himself, but he thought Marlowe would understand.

He even dared to think that Anne would too. Anne who knew what life was like. Who knew that life was not ponds, but rivers. That today was a weight swinging from the chain of all other days.

Jack slept, woke to drink madly, slept and went into a fever that made Will bring the physician. Then it was the long bedside again. Plague? No, they thought not. But if so, so. It was important to stay here. He thought Anne would say so, notwithstanding everything; and what Anne thought was important.

In fever, Jack floundered up: half out of fever, he sat on the edge of the bed with his white sad feet long-boned on the boards, beseeching comfort, so Will sat beside holding.

'Is this true, Will?' Jack Towne's voice rasped, its tone gone. 'Is this—at last?'

'No. But it was true once, somewhere. Or will be, somewhere, in mind or dream. Or flesh, perhaps.'

'Aye, perhaps. That's the random chance.' Jack held Will's hand. Their legs inclined quiescent together. 'There we missed, and perhaps it was meant so.'

'Still it's true, in that all that is loving is true.'

'I loved thee better than thou know'st,' Jack said, drawing away, lying down. 'Because I didn't seek to love thee. Thou wert set aside for something else, heart.'

'Someone?' Will said. 'Or something?'

Throaty, Jack laughed on the doorstep of sleep. 'Ah, it's you, old word-lover.'

Will saw him through the crisis. Not plague: a fever drawn out by hunger and hardship. The player's life, he thought, the other side. He hoped Edmund wouldn't call, and see.

Waking, deep-breathed, the sweat dried from his face, Jack reached and gripped Will's shoulder where he sat at the bedside half aware. 'You've saved me. Am I worth it, Will? Tell.'

'Saving, saving is all, heart. I've done enough of throwing away.' Will thrust himself into saying it— past the hesitation, the mistrust. Trust needed no firm grounds, trust had no provisos. It was a leap into darkness. It was necessary like breath, to be renewed every moment, else no life.

Then the door opened, and he looked up to see her, as if he had created her from wanting—saw her momentary, gone.

*　　　*　　　*

Anne found that Edmund caught her easily enough. So much for the heroic strength. She had only run a couple of streets, blindly running and weeping, before her breath shrank and her burning footsteps slowed and Edmund's hand brought her swinging and fighting to a stop.

'Anne, for God's sake, are you mad? What are you running from?' People swore, ducking round them, for rain was slanting down on a wind of mild thunder. 'The man in Will's room, is that it?'

'You call him a man, you players, is that how you call him? Or a boy-girl?' She shook his hand off.

'It's Matthew.'

Edmund's face hung dull with incomprehension. 'You mean Matthew Hollingbery?' he said at last, frowning. 'No, it's not him. Why on earth— Matthew's deep in work, he's playing at the Rose. I saw him go to rehearsal this morning. What in God's name did you think . . . ?'

Anne allowed it to curl round her. The snake of realisation. 'Nothing.' She blinked, moved aside for a beruffed old dame carrying a dog in her arms— no lap-dog, a great thing with lolling legs. Life kept kicking you with surprises, at the back of your knees. That was the feel of life. 'I thought nothing. I shall never think anything again. Well, you were in the right, after all, Edmund.' She searched a way through the crowd. 'I should never have come here.'

'No. I think it was meant, perhaps. Come.'

'Where?'

'Your husband.'

She tugged against him. 'No husband.'

'No? Change it, then. Define it. Something. We shall, Anne. Else I need not have lived.'

*   *   *

'Mistress Shakespeare. You may not remember me. We met long ago in dear Stafford. Damn it, Stratford.' The fair man had shrugged some clothes around him, and was sitting on the edge of Will's bed. A dull, plain lodging, Anne thought, clean enough, but still. A place for work. 'Where the Queen's Men came to play, years since, and we stayed to take your husband away to his—his beautiful destiny. His second beautiful destiny.' The fair man, Jack Towne,

534

bowed as he sat: he could do that easily. His nose was too short, his cheekbones too broad; but there was something about him. Anne couldn't recall him, and yet she felt she knew him. 'And he has flourished mightily since, praise be. I, less so. We loved each other well in those days.' Towne threw a blue glance at Will, standing reserved, wrapped, curiously tall by the door. 'And you know, mistress, that true love of whatever sort always endures. I speak not of perfect love, for that don't exist.' Towne smiled crookedly. 'I have been living somewhat reduced of late, and Will has been good enough to tender me the hand that Fate has been loath to extend for so long.' He coughed round a smile. 'Never fear this sound, mistress, it's the last whimper of the departing devil. An ague that bade fair to finish me, had Will not brought me home, given me his bed, brought in the doctor, and stayed by to hear me—no doubt— cursing like an alewife on fair-day, hey?'

Will smiled. 'Something like, but not so bad, Jack.'

Not that beautiful voice of his. I am proof against his look, but not that voice—the voice that lies, that he has employed with her in the little hot room of art. Storm shook itself wetly at the window.

'Thank God, I am in a way now to recover,' Towne said, 'and to repay, my friend, your kindness. Oh, yes. Once set up, once given a fair part to play, you may be sure every penny, every lost moment will be recompensed . . .' His voice trailed: trying to convince himself, Anne thought.

She spoke. 'Did you fear plague?' She addressed Towne, looking at least at the lower half of his face; but it was Will, for the first time, she was talking to.

'I felt low enough,' Towne said, 'to welcome its

535

deliverance, if it was.'

'But if it had been plague.' Anne's eyes moved everywhere in the room, except for the space of Will. 'What, then, if it had been plague?'

Distinctly, Will said: 'As Jack says.'

She risked a glance at her husband. His eyes hit her like a piece of sky; but, then, she loved him, or had loved him, and such things were to be expected.

Jack Towne stood, revealing his slender height. 'Mistress Shakespeare, do you know—though I hope you don't—the feeling that all, all is lost, and you cannot stir a finger to put it right?'

Her throat closed, but she overcame that. 'Do you?'

'Yes. Oh, yes. And then—then when hope begins faintly to come in—oh, such a feeling.' He drew a great half-smiling breath. Will remained a shade at the door. 'Who can describe it?'

And so, who is to answer?

*　　　*　　　*

Though he protests, they leave Jack Towne in possession of the bedchamber in Silver Street, to sleep off the remnant of his fever. Edmund takes charge of them, as neither seems to have any more volition than sheep at market.

He takes them to the Mermaid, bespeaks a supper-room, orders fowls and ale, saying they both need food in them. Food, aye, and what then? They both stare at him, like mutinous children.

'Why, then, to you,' Edmund says. 'I cannot make any more than this.'

Anne feels sorry for him: sorry across the world. 'Edmund. Forgive me. Forgive me that I tangled you in the matter. It was not well done.'

Edmund, arms crossed, studies her. 'Yes, it was. I'm not sorry.'

'Why?' Bitterly she is thankful for an opportunity, to rage and assert. 'You think we can be happy now? What is it? An enchanter from above descending at the end of the piece to make all well? I see none.' She gestures about the little brown-panelled room. A big creaking coffin all round, set about with a few pewter plates and candlesticks. 'Who can change this? I see none, I see none . . .' She finds herself croaking it over and over, doing herself no good. Will is a streak of silence near at hand. She sees the hairs on his wrist, the sunken green twig of blood pressed in the arm's white book.

'Because of truth,' Will says. 'Truth is best.'

Oh, now you give me room, and I shall use it. She lashes at him. 'The truth you were not going to tell me?'

And now they look at each other.

'You've seen her,' he says, quiet and ready. 'Isabelle? And that's why you came to London?'

'What else would you suppose?'

'Why, naught. The moment you stepped in, I knew.'

'Don't bewray your brother,' she says, wanting to protect Edmund: wanting to avert some violence that fails to come, like the childish tumbles of thunder, the jerky peppering rain at the window. 'I cozened him to spy upon you. It was all my doing. Set no blame on him.'

'There is no blame.'

'In you?'

'In me, there's much to blame.'

537

Edmund speaks: 'I need not have done it. I'm no one's tool, I have a mind and heart, and everything they are I owe to your example. Yes, you two. In you I've always seen what love can mean, and what things it can conjure from the coarse stuff of life. And so I still believe, even if it's gone awry, for now or aye, I hope for now only, but still I'll never forget the knowing of you two, the sweetness there was, the showing how a life can be when truly lived, each in the other on this one earth.' He is weeping, hating it, with doglike coughs. 'Your supper's cooking. Eat of it, and speak with one another, in pity's name. I'll go. Look for me in an hour.' Wiping his face with the back of his hand, he scowls at them. 'You both have my love, whatever way. Split it, split me, I can divide. I can do it.'

Edmund is gone, and there is just the creaking room with them in it, and the evidence of life beyond this moment, perhaps, like a wasp's warm nest beyond the plaster.

Will says: 'Was she foul to you?'

'Why? Is that what you would expect of her?'

'In a subtle way.'

'She told me a great lie about you. And I believed it.'

'There are no big lies about me. Only small grubby ones.'

'So I believe now. I don't know if that can change aught. I've been there, Will. That room, where you have been, with her. She tells me it's finished now.'

'So it is.'

'But it can never be, surely. Not inside. Not in that great hollow we share between us.'

The maid comes in, lays a cloth, returns bringing steaming laden plates. A bob, anxious, as she goes:

is all well, will she be reproved? Anne and Will interrupt each other's looks, reassuring her.

'I betrayed you with Isabelle.' Will speaks harshly, with a sort of grim flourish, as if preparing to cut the throat of possibility. 'That is the place we stand. Can it lead anywhere?'

'If you betrayed me, then you should know that we are quits, as far as that goes.' Anne says it first; then wonders about its quantity of truth; then realises it was right to say it, in any case; then looks for his response. 'What say you?'

He's an actor, used to adapting to the moment, he never flounders. Still: taste those salt eyes. 'It hurts.' Ah. She wishes this felt better, like worlds of pleasure, instead of a sour sip. 'It hurts, but I won't—I won't say no to the pain.'

Anne smiles, or grins: she can't tell the difference just now, hurting. 'How much pain can you bear?'

'I don't know. But I'm willing to try what you may give.'

'Me?' Anne groans drily. 'What am I, Will? Look you, I come here, I am full of rage and jealousy and I want to—to do something, shake the world about me, and I cannot, I cannot even hate as I would wish, and that's because you made me, Will.' She bats away his reaching hands. 'I can forgive almost everything but that, for once you made me I was yours, belonging to you, and that I cannot break.' Batting again, as if wasps surround her, or frightening fruitful bees.

'But you made me.' He's pressing home. Either he means it, or you are deceived. Take hence those hands I want upon me, that scent of self, that looming of hair and head and voice. 'From the day we met at Shottery, that was the beginning of my creation. You made Will Shakespeare, Anne. And without you there wouldn't be a life, but the unformed shape of one, never to be.'

Pretty, yes. But she lives in the world, where pretty won't do. She wishes otherwise. She draws on the grey, cool, straight. 'There's such a thing, Will, as too late,' she says, and risks his eyes. She is aware of a single tear rapidly crossing her cheek, like some busy little creature.

'I can only beg you not to believe that,' he says. 'But if you do, I'll abide.' As he steps away, she feels a turmoil in his stillness: the turmoil of a decisive man living with his decision. 'I crave your pardon for failing you. It was done in selfish darkness and I convinced myself you could not care. You never had less than all my love.'

'Ah, what does that come to?'

He nods. 'You know.'

All at once it is on her lips to say that they have failed each other. But to say that is to take the exchange on to entirely new ground, one on which reconciliation is a possibility. And she can't tread there, surely. The ground is sulphurous, unsteady; the light changes like a hundred days in one; you'd have to be mad or courageous or in love to enter it. She sees that fear has been a larger part of herself than she even suspected.

Suddenly he says: 'If we are quits—'

'Don't speak of it.'

'If we are quits, then may we not begin a new game?'

'Game, or play, which? What play is this, Will? Old marriage made new? Has a good sound, I'd say a good name for a play. And will it make me laugh, or weep?'

Will sits down, wearily rubbing his cheeks. He looks right doing so: he never looks exceptional, doing anything. 'You know me,' he says, slightly smiling. 'Laugh or weep, I must ever mix them. How did you come here, all alone?'

'With Andrew. I just did it. Courage came.'

'I want to take heart from that courage. That it meant—you had not given me quite over.'

'You can, if you like. You don't understand fear.'

'Me? Pray you.' He shakes his head. 'I am deep in it, none deeper.'

'What fear?'

'Losing. Losing what I have and losing what I make. One comes from another, perhaps.'

'What you make? You don't even print them.'

He shrugs. 'Let them take their chance.'

'And is it so with our marriage? Betray it, be damned to it, let it take its chance?' Now she is softly raging, beating at his chest, a fumbling sharp kick to his shins. Over to the other side of the room.

Not leaving the room, though. Because of what she believes, even now, in the roots of her. Because of what she saw and heard in Jack Towne, poor broken-down once-fair creature that she can see, in her mind's eye, as he was once, in Will's mind's eye back then, and what he opened up. Something he opened up, but not all. More opened up when the lightning struck the tree and her life struck Will's, when she made Will Shakespeare, believe that? Yes, somehow. Never doubted, really. And what she believes is the neverness of ending, the falsehood of finality. Yes, she would never print, too, if she wrote. She believes in the continuous, the river not the pond. She doesn't, in fact, believe there is such a thing as too late: that is death to her

541

creed. She believes in second chances. And third, and fourth. Because we're frail, not made of iron with lumps of stone at heart. No perfect love, as Towne said. But true love, that endures.

He comes to her across the room, she comes motionless to him, waiting to enclose him, as lovers do, as people do, just that. They hold, kiss, thrust low despairing happy heads against each other's shoulders and ringing arms.

At the window the wind stops its violence, and gives way to a clear stillness, and the threatened storm reveals itself a fraud. Just as with passion, the truest thing about it is the peace that follows it.